Inseparable Humanity

Inseparable Humanity

An Anthology of Reflections of Shridath Ramphal

[handwritten inscription]

Introduced and Edited by Ron Sanders
Foreword by Alister McIntyre

First Published in 1988 by Hansib Publishing
Tower House, 139/149 Fonthill Road,
London N4 3HF, England.
Tel: 01-281-1191. Fax: 01-263-9656.

Design, Typesetting and production by
Hansib Publishing Limited.

Printed in Britain by
Hansib Printing Limited
Unit 8, Caxton Hill Induatrial Estate,
Herts, Hertfordshire
England.

British Library Cataloguing in Publication Data.
Ramphal, Shridath S. (Shridath Surendranath), *1928* –
Inseparable Humanity: an anthology of reflections
of Shridath Ramphal.
1.Economic conditions-International
political conditions.
330. 9' 04
I. Title II. Sanders, Ron
909'. 0971241082

ISBN 1-870518-14-4

Note

The persons who have contributed to this book have done so in furtherance of the commemoration of the 150th anniversary of the abolition of slavery and the beginning of Indian indentured labour in the West Indies. No part of the proceeds of the book accrue to them.

The book contains material from selected speeches, statements and writings of Shridath Ramphal from 1971 to 1987. The texts have been revised in some cases for presentation in a more permanent form in this publication. Statistics have been revised where more accurate figures have become available.

R.S.

To mark the 150th Anniversary of:
The Abolition of Slavery
and
The Beginning of Indian Indenture
in
The West Indies

For my wife Susan who has given me thirteen deeply appreciated years of love and support

R.S.

Acknowledgements

This book would not have been produced had it not been for Arif Ali who cajoled me into doing it. I thank him for doing so for, in the end, it was a labour of great satisfaction. Barbara Cohen, who typed the manuscript with patience and good humour, died while this book was with the publishers. She is remembered with great fondness. Clive Jordan read some of the early drafts and offered advice for which I am very grateful. A particular debt of gratitude is owed to Dr. Amrit Sarup for researching the many notes and references in the texts – hers was a difficult task undertaken with amazing grace. Finally, I thank Shridath Ramphal without whose concern for the future of mankind and his willingness to traverse the world as many times as it takes to summon us to our "inseparable humanity", this book and its all important message would not have been possible.

R.S.

Contents

Introduction by Ron Sanders   15

Foreword by Alister McIntyre   31

Abbreviations   41

1. Beginnings   **43**

Perspective I   44

The Berbice Connection   48
Hull, 1983

Indenture: Another Slavery   59
New Delhi, 1986

2. West Indian Nationhood   **77**

Perspective II   78

Why Federation Failed   82
Lagos, 1976

Nationhood: Myth, Mirage or Mandate?   93
Port-of-Spain, 1971

The Case for Political Unity   102
Port-of-Spain, 1971

3. A Wider Unity   **111**

Perspective III   112

Building ACP Unity   116
Georgetown, 1975

A New Relationship with Europe
Brussels, 1973   122

The Challenge of Unity   131
Dar es Salaam, 1973

Lomé: A Promise to be Fulfilled   135
Lomé, 1975

4. The New Latin America   **139**

Perspective IV   140

The Realities of Inequality   144
Tlatelolco, 1974

The New Latin America   150
New York, 1974

A Caribbean Basin Initiative   156
New York, 1974

5. Caribbean Options   **161**

Perspective V   162

To Care for CARICOM   167
Montego Bay, 1975

The Lure of 'Realpolitik'   177
Port-of-Spain, 1985

6. Ending Apartheid   **193**

Perspective VI   194

Apartheid: Slavery's Modern Face   199
Hull, 1983

Apartheid's Ayacucho   207
Caracas, 1983

The End of the Beginning   216
London, 1985

Sanctions: The Path to Peaceful Change   225
Paris, 1986

Why the EPG is Right   231
Swaziland, 1987

The Cost of Political Default in Southern Africa   239
Washington, 1987

7. Redressing Poverty   **249**

Perspective VII   250

A Feudal World   254
Hull, 1983

The Other World in This One   262
London, 1976

Shadows in the Cave   278
London, 1981

The Trampling of the Grass   293
Addis Ababa, 1985

For the South, A Time to Think   313
Kuala Lumpur, 1986

8 Tomorrow's World   **323**

Perspective VIII   324

The West Indies in the Year 2000   328
Port-of-Spain, 1978

Democracy in the Global State   334
London, 1985

The World Is One   346
New Delhi, 1987

Making Human Society a Civilised State   365
London, 1987

Appendices:

A Grenada Declaration   387

B Gleneagles Agreement   391

C Commonwealth Expert Group Reports   394

Index   397

Introduction

The 150th anniversary of the abolition of slavery and the arrival of Indian workers under the system of indentured labour in the West Indies, provides a timely occasion to present this anthology of reflections and urgings of Shridath Ramphal. For he is one of the world's leading thinkers and activists about today's global problems and the nature of tomorrow's world, and his ideas and perceptions were first fashioned in the West Indies. Over the last 20 years, first as Guyana's Foreign Minister, then as Commonwealth Secretary-General, Shridath Ramphal ('Sonny' Ramphal to most who know him) has addressed many themes, from many platforms, in many lands. Few contemporary figures have matched the range and depth of issues which he has tackled.

The book covers the period 1971-87. Assembling it was a difficult task, for over the last 12 years Shridath Ramphal has made an average of some 40 presentations each year: addresses, articles, statements and interviews. The selection, therefore, concentrates on identifying and illustrating the world issues to which he has given greatest attention. The reflections are arranged under separate Chapters showing not only the evolution of regional and global issues whose resolution demand wholly new approaches by the international community, but also the development of Ramphal's ideas on the elements which such a resolution should contain. Throughout each Chapter, binding the book into a cohesive whole, runs the common

theme of Shridath Ramphal's profound concern for the
establishment of a world society based on principles of
justice and equity. As he put it himself, he wants to see:

> a more universal acknowledgement of the entitlement of all
> men to the functional enjoyment of a life of dignity and well
> being – an entitlement derving from their humanity, that
> aims at the satisfaction of the basic needs, material and non-
> material, individual and collective, of all men and women...a
> world that has begun to usher in a new economic order
> creating global structures more propitious to the realisation
> of those rights in the economic, social and cultural no less
> than in the civil and political fields.[1]

Progressively, the anthology details the trials of Shridath
Ramphal's forebears from India; his own beginnings in
Guyana with reminders of its twin historical experience of
slavery and indentured labour; his insistent advocacy of
regional unity for the West Indies; his early perception of
the need for a new closer relationship with an enlarged Latin
America; his out-reach beyond his own region to the Third
World in efforts to forge developing countries into a more
effective unity in their international bargaining with the rich;
his passionate crusade against apartheid and the denial of
freedom in Southern Africa and, finally, his prescriptions for
what every nation, but essentially the major powers, can do
to make tomorrow's world – the world of the twenty-first
century – better than today's.

Shridath Ramphal's deep concern for the universal
application of justice and equity developed in his native
Guyana (then British Guiana). When he was born there on 3
October 1928, it was a British colony whose economy, for
the greater part, was contracted to metropolitan companies.
Guyana's people – the descendants of indigenous
Amerindians, European settlers, African slaves, Indian
indentured labourers, Portuguese and Chinese immigrants –
were to a great extent still trapped in the environment which
slavery and indenture bequeathed and colonialism
sanctioned. One commentator wrote of Guyana in 1953 that
it was:

a small and largely forgotten country...run by a closed oligarchy under pressure from its master at home who tended to take the short-term and narrow view of any situation...even in 1953 the long coastal strip where most of the wealth and the population lay was nothing more than a tropical Gorbals, an enormous slum from which the underprivileged – whether Indian, Negro, Chinese or Portuguese – could look across at the seemingly impregnable positions of the British and a carefully selected few Guyanese.[2]

In the late 1920s, and throughout the 1930s, the situation was far worse.

Universal adult suffrage was withheld from Guyana until 1953. In 1928, out of a total population of 297,691, little more than 6,000 persons satisfied the combined literacy and property qualifications required to vote;[3] far fewer possessed the qualifications to stand for the minority 14 elected places in the Legislative Council. These limitations today seem absurd; then, they were the established order reflective of the views of the British proprietor class, essentially non-resident, one of whom, Sir Edward Davson, asserted in 1907:

I do not believe that in any colony of the Empire the white element should be subject to the coloured, whether it be black, brown or yellow – African, East Indian or Mongolian.[4].

Throughout the years of Shridath Ramphal's childhood, the country's natural resources and its production went abroad with minimal benefit for the labouring Guyanese. The British Guiana Labour Union, formed in 1919 by Hubert Nathaniel Critchlow, became, in 1921, the first legally recognised trade union in the overseas British Empire;[5] but it declined with the economic depression, and trade unionism did not effectively emerge again until 1937.[6] The interests of the Indian indentured workers were theoretically supervised by an official Immigration Agent-General; but the post was abolished in 1932 for it was an annoyance to both the colonial Government and the British sugar interests which owned the estates where over 50 per cent of the Indians lived and worked.[7].

The first ten years of Shridath Ramphal's life were overshadowed by the economic malaise of the 1930s. Dependent on only one or two export commodities, the West Indies as a whole suffered badly. Unemployment, reduced wages, hunger and desperation led to strikes throughout the region. In Guyana, over half the population was, directly and indirectly, dependent on the production of sugar and its by-products;[8] as sugar prices slumped, production was reduced, workers laid off and wages cut. Between 1931 and 1932 the Indians on the Guyana sugar estates were the first workers in the West Indies to protest against poor pay and deplorable conditions. But their discontent was shared by other workers throughout the region and riots spread across the West Indies. In 1938, the British Government sent out a Commission under Lord Moyne to investigate the troubles. After a year of enquiry, they concluded that the upheaval was due to 'a question of undoubted stark poverty'.[9]

The colonial system of Shridath Ramphal's childhood abused the people of Guyana; but, if the system deserved condemnation for the awful economic conditions in which it kept them subject, it was even more culpable for its clear intent to keep them enslaved as illiterate labourers. In 1917, 60 per cent of Guyana's population was illiterate: a figure surpassed in the Caribbean only by Haiti. And while the poor of every race suffered from unequal access to education, it was the Indians in Guyana and Trinidad and Tobago who fared the worst. Although the Education Ordinance, for example, required children up to the age of 14 to attend school, the same law only prohibited their employment if they were under the age of nine.[10] Hence, sugar estates freely employed children once they became nine years old – so much so that of 20,000 children of school age in 1917, only 6,000 were at school.[11] One Immigration Agent-General actually justified the labouring of Indian children by saying that to do so was "a source of pleasure" for them.[12]

In the event, it was education that liberated Guyanese such as Shridath Ramphal from the trap of colonial exploitation and gave them the opportunity to contribute intellect and ideas to the service of their country and the world. From 1885 a number of religious denominations, principally Presbyterians from Canada, established schools specifically for the education of Indians.[13] But, to a great extent, it was small private schools, set up by Guyanese themselves, that made secondary education available to the masses. One of the early pioneers of secondary education in Guyana was J.I. 'Jimmy' Ramphal, Shridath Ramphal's father, himself a product of that Canadian Presbyterian service to education in the country. He started the first of his schools in Georgetown in 1928 and strongly encouraged Indians to educate their children.[14] By 1937, the number of Indian children at primary school had increased by 50 per cent over the figure just four years before in 1933.[15] With his father the Principal of the country's leading private secondary school, Shridath Ramphal had the great good fortune of assured education. It was, perhaps, the key factor in the later evolution of his roles on the national, regional, Commonwealth and world stages.

For Shridath Ramphal, the final lesson of the experience of slavery and indenture – and the message which he leaves in the first Chapter of this book – is for mankind, as a whole, 'to ensure that relations with our fellow men reflect our oneness rather than a sense of otherness'.[16] He recognises – and wants the world to recognise – that African slavery and Indian indentured labour, though cruel and unjustifiable, were only brief moments in a long history of man's inhumanity to man; an inhumanity that was not only inflicted by one race upon another but by groups within their own race, white and black alike.

For him, these episodes should not be used to fuel passions for national chauvinism and racial separateness;

they should be employed to acknowledge that mankind as a whole was the poorer for the experience of bondage whose cruelties dehumanised the perpetrators as much as the victims. The challenge which Shridath Ramphal throws down to the world is to use the past experience of inhumanity to enrich all men and all nations by enlarging our perception that we have one world which we must learn to share more equitably than we have done in the past.

Nonetheless, the experience of African slavery and Indian indentured labour in the Caribbean left a residue of bitterness in the minds of successive generations of West Indians. The West Indian struggle for political rights and economic justice, the movement to end colonialism and establish independent states were natural outgrowths from the anger aroused by these two brutal systems. But the anger also turned inwards, particularly in Guyana and Trinidad and Tobago whose populations today consist largely of the descendants of African slaves and Indian indentured labourers. The Africans regarded the arrival of the Indians as a fatal blow to their power to bargain for higher wages on the sugar estates. Their feeling was that 'the Indian takes bread from the Negro labourer and lowers the price of labour'[17] and, curiously, they blamed the Indians and not the planters for this perceived injury. In the years which followed, this perception of injury assumed the status of historical fact in the minds of Africans. Professor Gordon Lewis has summed up the relationship between Indians and Africans in the West Indies in this way:

> The differences between the groups, concededly, were at bottom economic, for the Africans, in the main, were an urban mass hating the land and its slave memory and identifying itself with its middle-class brethren who had become the white collar proconsuls of the colonial structure, while the Indians were a rural mass trapped in the sugar estate prison. But the differences came to express themselves in racial terms.[18]

To a not insignificant degree, despite the "creolisation" of an increasing number of young Indians, these differences still plague the politics and consequently the economic and social development of both countries. Writing of the independence of Trinidad and Tobago in 1962, the late Prime Minister of that country, Eric Williams, said: "two races have been freed, but a society has not been formed".[19] Similar sentiments could have been expressed about Guyana where an examination in 1964 indicated that, in relation to co-operation between Guyanese of Indian and African extraction, while Government officials of African descent;

> stressed that there was growing racial co-operation in politics, they did not notice a complementary cultural integration. Indeed, they did not welcome such a move and their arguments against racial integration betrayed an appalling ignorance of the customs and attitudes of fellow Guyanese.[20]

Correspondingly, a study of Trinidad and Tobago society in 1960 revealed that to the majority of Indians "the idea of the East Indian group losing its ethnic identity and disappearing in the West Indian population is not acceptable".[21] The same study concluded that "the East Indian might like his circumstances to be better, but he has no desire to be anything else and least of all a West Indian".[22] Yet, when Indians in Guyana and Trinidad and Tobago were offered Indian citizenship 'by descent' under India's Citizenship Act of 1955, very few applied for it.[23] According to the novelist, Sam Selvon, the number in Trinidad "that showed interest in the venture came mostly from the country districts where the majority were still adhering, or trying to adhere, to the traditions and customs brought from India".[24]

The descendants of slaves and indentured labourers in Guyana and Trinidad and Tobago are yet to resolve the issue raised by Eric Williams of whether they are "two races" or "one society". But it is not an issue that can be resolved until Indians acknowledge their West Indian identity and join meaningfully in the work of proclaiming it which, so far, only a few such as Shridath Ramphal have been proud to do. By the same token, the African community has to accept and acknowledge that a shared history of transplantation, exploitation and colonialism binds them inseparably to the Indian community and, therefore, there must be room for both in national life, including the governance of their countries.

Unquestionably, Shridath Ramphal stands above this debate; not only because, as the late Dr. A. Z. Preston, Vice-Chancellor of the University of the West Indies, put it: "the single element which comprehensively identifies him is his West Indian origin";[25] but also by virtue of the fact that across the West Indies his work for, and commitment to, West Indian unity is fully acknowledged and widely respected. It is worth noting that no less a person than Jawaharlal Nehru had made it clear that, in his view, people of Indian origin settled overseas should give their loyalties to the countries they had adopted. This has been Indian Government policy consistently over the years.[26] In identifying himself so fully as being West Indian, Ramphal, while acting on the basis of personal conviction, was giving practical effect to Nehru's far-sighted exhortation.

Chapters 2 and 5 are a chronicle of Shridath Ramphal's work in the Caribbean in pursuit of a nationhood which sometimes seemed within reach but always proved elusive; they also represent an accurate historical record of the period as seen through the eyes of one of the principal actors on the West Indian stage.

This period of West Indian development and Ramphal's activist role in it are described in Alister McIntyre's Foreword to this book. As Secretary-General of the Caribbean Community and Common Market (CARICOM) Secretariat and, before that, as Director of the Institute for Social and Economic Research at the University of the West Indies (UWI), McIntyre collaborated with Ramphal in the late 1960s and early 1970s in the efforts to build a structure

of economic integration on the ruins of the dissolved West
Indies Federation.

McIntyre was also with Ramphal in 1973 and 1974 as he
sought both to redress some of the wrongs of colonialism
and to weld into a working unity the former colonies of
Britain and France in Africa, the Caribbean and the Pacific
as they negotiated a new relationship with the enlarged
Community of Europe. In his Foreword, McIntyre provides
the setting for this hitherto unprecedented attempt to forge a
community of interests and a common purpose among the
widely separated and vastly different countries; an attempt,
what is more, that came not from the big countries of Africa,
but from the small countries of the Caribbean. Ramphal's
speeches in Chapter 3 are important for the clarity with
which they enunciate the problems of small countries in the
international economic system and the obligations which
devolve upon richer and more powerful states. But they are
also significant because they contain elements that were
later to contribute to the concept of 'The New International
Economic Order'.

Bolstered by the success of welding the African,
Caribbean and Pacific (ACP) countries into a single
negotiating group with the European Economic Community
(EEC), Shridath Ramphal set out, in 1974, to bridge the
divide which had traditionally existed between Latin
America and the Caribbean. This division was a legacy of
competition and rivalry between imperial Britain and
imperial Spain; in Ramphal's view it weakened Third World
unity. He was also deeply conscious that both Latin America
and the Caribbean lived in the shadow of their large and
powerful neighbour, the United States of America. US
adventurism in the region in the past testified to its readiness
to be unmindful of the national aspirations of sovereign
states if those aspirations did not coincide with its own. In
proposing a deepening of the relationship between Latin
America and the Caribbean, Ramphal was attempting to
strengthen the independence of the region.

Chapter 4 relates Ramphal's efforts to promote co-operation between the countries of Latin America and the Caribbean. They were efforts that produced little result, principally because the late Eric Williams, then Prime Minister of Trinidad and Tobago, harboured deep misgivings about Venezuela's intentions in the Caribbean. In fact, in 1975, Williams addressed a public meeting in Trinidad at which he lambasted Venezuela, declaring that "the recolonisation of the Caribbean is in full swing today".[27] And Ramphal's departure from the region one month later to take up his post as Commonwealth Secretary-General left the Caribbean without a strong advocate for closer relations with Latin America; at least not one to whom Williams would give a hearing.

A word needs to be said here about a dimension of Shridath Ramphal's work that is not represented in any of the Chapters of this book – the Non-Aligned Movement. No speeches have been reproduced of this period for the simple reason that Ramphal's relationship with the Non-Aligned Movement occurred at a time when the Movement was greatly dislocated. His work took place behind the closed doors of meetings and his urgings were spontaneous proposals for taking the Movement out of the doldrums and advancing its causes.

It was the 1972 Conference of Non-Aligned Foreign Ministers in Guyana that brought Ramphal's negotiating skills and diplomatic capabilities to the attention of the majority of the world's governments. For it was this Conference, under his Chairmanship, that rejuvenated Non-Alignment after "a six year period of inactivity had left the Movement in a state of disarray".[28]

The Non-Aligned Movement had been inaugurated in 1961 and had its Second Summit Meeting in 1964, but six years elapsed until the Third Summit in 1970. By this time, the Movement was deeply divided particularly on the issues of according the Provisional Revolutionary Government of Vietnam the status of a full member and recognising the

Government of the National Union as the legitimate representative of Cambodia.

At the Foreign Ministers Meeting in Guyana in 1972 Ramphal, with the deftness of a consummate diplomat and the skill of an experienced lawyer, succeeded in persuading the Conference to entrust him with the responsibility of determining their decision on Cambodia and Vietnam on the basis of their debate. In a celebrated pronouncement, Ramphal concluded "that consensus – while signifying substantial agreement at group level on any particular occasion did not require or imply unanimity".[29] He seated the Provisional Government of Vietnam as a member and invited the Government of the National Union to occupy Cambodia's seat. Not all the member states were happy, but each acknowledged that he had extricated the Non-Aligned Movement from the disarray which had characterised its previous six years and opened the way for its advance including a summit meeting in Algiers the next year.

The Guyana meeting also helped to broaden the Non-Aligned Movement from an organisation concerned mainly with political matters into one which dealt seriously with economic issues; it added an Action Programme for Economic Co-operation among Developing Countries to the agenda of the Movement and that document has since formed the basis for all documents on South-South co-operation.[30]

When Shridath Ramphal went to the Commonwealth as Secretary-General in 1975 – spokesman for one-quarter of the world's people, most of them in developing countries – the cry for a New International Economic Order had become a persistent wail from the South. It was a wail to which the North turned a deaf ear, unwilling to admit the truth before their eyes – that centuries of exploitation, of uneven patterns of distribution, of economic and political injustice imposed by the rich had left the poor dispossesed and desperate. Chapter 7 sets out the way in which Shridath Ramphal took on the mantle of the South's messenger;

stalking the capitals of the North and storming the sanctums of the International Monetary Fund and the World Bank to warn that the world would not long survive in peace and in prosperity unless the North took account of the South in addressing the imbalances in the existing economic order.

And this Chapter also shows that, with the sense of balance for which he has come to be known, he did not fail to tell the South that they too were not without blemish; that their economic policies were sometimes flawed; that their increased spending on arms deprived their people of much needed social services; that through their disunity and backbiting they robbed themselves of a credible voice in negotiations with the North.

Shridath Ramphal is a sensible and mature radical; his judgements are born of deep and sober reflection on his first-hand experience of the unequal relations of states and their peoples. Not many others have had the benefit of his intimate knowledge of the world's current condition: few would have had the opportunity, as he has had in the last thirteen years as Commonwealth Secretary-General, to travel hundreds of thousands of miles, back and forth, between developed and developing countries to witness the growing disparities between the rich and poor; even fewer would have been invited, as he has been, to hear the anger of the young and feel the despair of the old who want a better deal in the South, anger and despair which have resonances among the young and the old of the North who, every day, grow more concerned at the prospect of a nuclear accident or worse a nuclear war.

But it is in Southern Africa that Shridath Ramphal confronts the spectre that disturbs him most emotionally. For, in its naked exploitation, dehumanisation and debasement of human beings, apartheid is the mirror image of slavery and indenture in the West Indies. In the nineteenth century the planters received strong backing from the British Government in their determination to maintain slave labour as a means of reaping high profits for sugar. The arguments then were not dissimilar to the arguments heard now in support of the British Government's refusal to apply sanctions against South Africa which uses apartheid, in Shridath Ramphal's words, "to provide a permanent subject labour force kept rigidly separate from the ruling class".[31] Today, the British Government justifies its position by saying that British jobs would be lost and British industry hurt from the imposition of economic sanctions against South Africa; a century and a half ago, against the background of 120 refineries in Britain providing thousands of jobs and a lucrative re-export trade in sugar to the European continent, the British Government also found excuses for its decision not to end African slavery in the West Indies. Chapter 6 focusses on Ramphal's tireless efforts to expose the wrongs in South Africa particularly to audiences in the West whose governments maintain economic links with that country. In the process, he provides a compelling analysis not only of the actions necessary to end apartheid but also of the dire consequences of a failure to take those actions.

Shridath Ramphal's crusade against apartheid has continued unabated, though it has meant putting himself at odds with the British Prime Minister whose influence in the world is not inconsiderable. But Ramphal does not put self before principle: had he been able to sacrifice principle for personal advancement he might have been elected to the post of United Nations Secretary-General in 1982. In his book *A Life in Peace and War,* Brian Urquhart, who served for forty years at the United Nations ending his career as Under-Secretary-General, said:

> Shridath Ramphal, the Secretary-General of the Commonwealth, had the qualities of intellect, ability, and experience to recommend him for the job, but he came from Guyana, a "radical" Third World country, thus ensuring a US veto, while his association with the British Commonwealth invited a Soviet veto... (He) would have been (an) independent internationalist in the Hammarskjold

tradition – a prospect certainly not welcome to the Soviet Union, and possibly not to other great powers either.[32]

This is the nature of Shridath Ramphal who more and more in recent years has been speaking to a world audience, with a heightened sense of urgency, on the vital concern of human survival – survival which he sees endangered by inequitable patterns of global production and distribution, by the arms race and super-power rivalry in general, by racial bigotry, by an endangered environment, by a weakening of the humanitarian ethic and the decline of internationalism.

But he not only summons world attention to the perilous state of the human relationship, he also actively proposes the means to change course, to put mankind back on track towards a secure and peaceful world structured on principles of justice and equity. For, as he asks in the concluding Chapter of this volume, if "we recognise that a national society cannot be at peace if power, privilege and prosperity are the prerogatives of only a few with deprivation, degradation and despair the lot of the many, why do we think our world society can be at peace when such disparities prevail within it?".[33]

It is his capacity for identifying the root causes of international problems and contributing ideas to their solution that, in part, led to his prominent membership of the Independent International Commissions on 'Development', 'Disarmament', 'Environment' and 'Humanitarian Issues' and of the 'South Commission'. These Commissions have made a unique and invaluable contribution to the process of global re-examination that has characterised the 1980s. Shridath Ramphal is the only person to have been a member of all five Commissions; he is better placed than most to feel the pulse of the world, to measure the capacity of all states, North and South, East and West, to rise above narrow instincts of national separateness and to recognise and respond to what he calls our 'inseparable humanity'.

Ron Sanders

Queen Elizabeth House
Oxford University
August 1988

Notes and References

1. *Infra*, Chapter 8, p. 329.

2. Peter Simms, *Trouble in Guyana* (Allen and Unwin Ltd., London 1966), p. 64.

3. George Mannington, *The West Indies* (Leonard Parsons, London, 1925), p. 160.

4. Cited in Eric Williams, *From Columbus to Castro: The History of the Caribbean 1492-1969* (Andre Deutsch, London, 1970), p. 471.

5. William Claypole and John Robottom, *Caribbean Story Book Two: The Inheritors* (Longman Caribbean Ltd., Trinidad and Jamaica, 1981), p. 94.

6. Arthur Lewis, *Labour in the West Indies* (New Beacon Books, London, 1977), p. 25.

7. Ibid.

8. *British Guiana: British Empire Exhibition, Wembley, 1924* (Sanders Phillips and Co. Ltd., Baynard Press, London), p.59.

9. Claypole and Robottom, op. cit., p. 101.

10. No. 14 of 1876, cited by Dwarka Nath, *A History of Indians in Guiana* (published by the Author, London, 1950), p. 188.

11. Cited by Cheddi Jagan, *The West on Trial* (Seven Seas Books, Berlin, 1972), p. 293.

12. *Administration Report for 1880*, cited in Dwarka Nath, op. cit., p. 188.

13. David Dabydeen and Brinsley Samaroo, (eds), *India in the Caribbean* (Hansib Publishing Ltd., London, 1987), p. 48.

14. *British Guiana in War Time:* A Bi-Monthly Wartime Series, Vol I, No. 3, 15 August, 1941.

15. Dwarka Nath, op. cit., p. 188.

16. *Infra,* Chapter 1, p.71.

17. James Rodway, 'Labour and Emigration', *Timehri,* Vol. VI, September 1919, p. 36.

18. Gordon K. Lewis, *The Growth of the Modern West Indies* (MacGibbon and Kee, London, 1968), p. 276.

19. Eric Williams, *History of the People of Trinidad and Tobago* (Andre Deutsch, London, 1964), p. 278.

20. Brian Irving (ed), *Guyana: A Composite Monograph* (Inter-American University Press, Puerto Rico, 1972), pp. 35-36.

21. Lambros Comitas and David Lowenthal (eds), *Slaves, Free Men, Citizens: West Indian Perspectives* (Anchor Books, New York, 1973), p. 296.

22. Ibid., p. 294.

23. Hugh Tinker, *Separate and Unequal: India and the Indians in the British Commonwealth 1920-1950* (C. Hurst & Co., London, 1976), p. 392.

24. Cited in Dabydeen and Samaroo (eds.), op. cit., p. 16.

25. Introduction of Shridath Ramphal in the Distinguished Lecturer Series of the Institute of International Relations, University of the West Indies, St. Augustine Campus, 13 May 1985.

26. See the statements by Jawaharlal Nehru, Prime Minister of India, in the Lok Sabha, 2 September and 17 December, 1957.

27. *Trinidad Guardian,* 27 April 1975.

28. Lloyd Searwar, 'An Architect of Non-Alignment', *Kaie* (No. 18, November 1985), Department of Culture, Guyana.

29. *Non-Aligned Special Issue, Guyana Journal,* (July 1973, Vol. I, No. 6), Ministry of Foreign Affairs, Georgetown, Guyana.

30. Searwar, op. cit.

31. *Infra,* Chapter 6, p. 202.

32. Brian Urquhart, *A Life in Peace and War* (Weidenfeld and Nicolson, London, 1987), p. 332.

33. *Infra,* Chapter 8, p. 353.

Foreword

This remarkable collection of addresses and statements portray the dimensions of thought and action that characterise the unique contribution of 'Sonny' Ramphal to the causes of decolonisation, Third World development and world peace. He has, for a decade at least, been in the front rank of contemporary spokesmen on international issues. The Introduction to this book and the text itself show that his career has been marked by single-minded dedication and prodigious work in applying his intellectual and diplomatic skills to the problems of his own region and of the Third World at large. His contributions deserve no mere commendation; they warrant exceptional praise.

The papers in the volume are not essays in nostalgia. They invoke a view of the world and of a common humanity which remains valid, notwithstanding the profound economic and political changes that have occurred in the years over which Ramphal has been speaking and writing. At the core of these essays is a vision of the world that sees the international system as a group of interdependent states which, while of varying economic and social systems, are committed to certain common objectives: decent living standards for all; safeguarding human rights through, *inter alia,* the effective participation of people in decision-making at both the national and international levels; protecting the ecology so that the earth's resources are judiciously used and preserved for future generations; and preventing tensions and conflicts both within and between communities and nations.

Ramphal is an international humanist in the finest sense of these words, seeing always the larger picture and taking a holistic view of the inter-relationships between national identity, Third World unity, human rights and peace. It is this perspective which underpins his concept of Caribbean identity as a blending of many cultures held together by a common historical and political experience. It is also reflected in his constant reminder to the Third World that it must view itself in outward rather than inward looking terms. This broad philosophical approach has also guided the linkages that he has made between poverty, under-development and the denial of human rights, exemplified in the abominable system of apartheid in South Africa. It requires only a further step to see that these problems are inexplicably bound up with the wider causes of disarmament and world peace. Taken together, they constitute a perception of a single global community working in harmony to create the conditions for progress, stability, and justice.

What strikes one most about the work of 'Sonny' Ramphal is the thorough professionalism with which he approaches every problem. His speeches and writings bear the stamp of careful preparation, both by way of substance and style. It is common for him to labour well into the night, going through successive drafts, and then to reappear a few hours later, fresh for battle, and ready to put to work his formidable skills of exposition and negotiation. Many of us, who have worked through long hours with him, have come away from these experiences exhilarated by the quality of leadership that he brought to the tasks at hand.

It would go far beyond the compass of a Foreword to make a full assessment of 'Sonny' Ramphal's contribution to development co-operation and to international relations. For present purposes, one can illustrate the magnitude of his contribution by references to two causes for which he has been a relentless fighter. The first is Caribbean integration, the second North/South relations.

As far as the Caribbean is concerned, Chapter 2 of the

book shows that his commitment to the regional movement has been long and deep. My own personal acquaintance with his efforts date back to the Heads of Government Conference which was held in Barbados in October 1967, when the original CARIFTA Agreement with three signatories was widened into an agreement among twelve. At that meeting, Ramphal played no small part in launching the larger CARIFTA, and in setting in process a number of studies designed to deepen it beyond merely a free trade area. His own stature and rapport with the region's leadership was also a factor favouring the decision to locate the regional Secretariat in Georgetown. Ramphal responded to the latter decision with enthusiasm, and in his capacity as Foreign Minister of Guyana, spared no effort to get the Secretariat established – finding appropriate office space, helping to put together an initial staff, negotiating a Headquarters agreement. He participated personally in the initial meetings of the CARIFTA Council of Ministers in Georgetown, making sure that the spirit of Barbados 1967 was sustained, as details of the trade agreement came up for negotiation and implementation.

In the period following the adoption of the CARIFTA Agreement, William Demas and his band of dedicated staff at the CARIFTA Secretariat began developing the conceptual framework for progressing from a free trade area to a Common Market and Community. These efforts bore fruit at the historic Port-of-Spain Heads of Government Conference in 1972 when the decision was taken to move from CARIFTA to CARICOM. This was a momentous occasion, marked by the brilliant and persuasive chairmanship of the Conference by Dr. Eric Williams, who utilised all of his skills of persuasion, cajolery, and humour, to pacify the doubters and to bring the Conference to a consensus on the establishment of CARICOM. However, the ink was hardly dry on that decision before doubts began to re-surface.

The principal area of concern had to do with the situation of the Less Developed Countries (LDCs) which are today more commonly referred to as the OECS countries and Belize. The OECS, in particular, were very reluctant to enter into more binding arrangements for free trade and for setting up a common external tariff and protective policy, unless they could be assured of commensurate benefits by way of secure markets for their agricultural exports, the allocation of specific industrial activities to them, combined with financial and technical assistance. For their part, the More Developed Countries (MDCs) while acknowledging that the LDCs warranted some preferential treatment (e.g., longer transitional periods for freeing trade and introducing the common external tariff), felt that as developing countries themselves they had only a very limited capacity to support agricultural and industrial development in the LDCs.

After the Port-of-Spain decision, the Attorneys-General of the region, assisted by a group of officials, laboured long to hammer out a draft treaty for establishing the Community and Common Market; but it proved impossible for them to bridge the differences between the MDCs and the LDCs about the programme of special measures for the LDCs. Accordingly, it fell to the CARIFTA Council of Ministers to attempt to work out a consensus on the outstanding issues, so that an agreed text could be submitted to the Heads of Government who were scheduled to meet in Georgetown in April 1973.

The CARIFTA Council met in early April to deal with the matter. The session was extremely stormy. Delegations were entrenched in their positions indicating that their instructions were so strict as to leave virtually no room for manoeuvre. After two days of very protracted discussions with hardly any progress on the outstanding issues, it was decided to prolong the meeting into the weekend. Prophecies of doom that CARICOM would be stillborn filled the air. Ramphal took up the cudgel and through passionate advocacy and persuasion brought the Council in sight of common ground. It was agreed that Lee Moore, the then Attorney-General of St. Kitts-Nevis and one of the leading spokesmen for the LDCs, should work with him on a draft of possible points of agreement. The Ramphal/Lee Moore accord, which followed ultimately, provided the basis for the Georgetown Accord, adopted by the Heads of Government on 12 April 1973, and formally gave birth to the Treaty establishing the Common Market and the Community. Because of his critical interventions, and his contributions to dialogue, rapport, and confidence-building among the regions' political leadership, Ramphal stands out as one of the main architects of CARICOM.

In the field of North/South relations, Ramphal's tenure of the post of Foreign Minister of Guyana, followed by that of Commonwealth Secretary-General, has been marked by an intense involvement with development issues. Throughout the 1970s, and now in the 1980s, no appeal to him to assist with development issues has gone unheeded. Sometimes he has been a lonely voice in calling for greater responsiveness by the developed countries to the particular needs of the developing. His stirring advocacy and exposition are always underpinned by facts, and even-handed formulations. His search is always for the common ground that could bring the international community to a workable consensus.

His first major undertaking was the initial EEC/ACP negotiations of the Lomé Convention. In the Caribbean we had for some time been studying the implications of Britain's entry into the EEC. By the time the matter was brought to Ministers, it was appreciated that the Caribbean's best chance of safeguarding and advancing its interests lay in forging a common position with the other developing countries concerned. Accordingly, as Chapter 3 shows, starting with an informal meeting of Ministers in Georgetown in 1972, the Caribbean took a series of initiatives to align itself with the rest of the ACP, and to promote the formation of the ACP Group itself. As far as the negotiation of the Lomé Convention was concerned, Ramphal was the principal ACP spokesman on trade, which in both conceptual and political terms, constituted an area of great difficulty.

Conceptually, the EEC had to be won over to the notion of a contractual relationship negotiated among equals, but providing for differential rights and obligations. This was reflected in the idea of non-reciprocal free trade in favour of the ACP countries. Although the principle of non-reciprocity had been accepted in the UNCTAD Generalised System of Preferences, this had been on the basis of a unilateral concession rather than a treaty obligation. Community spokesmen had difficulty in accepting the idea of being called upon to discriminate in favour of the ACP, while the latter would accord them in return no more than MFN treatment. They were also reluctant to accept that ACP states could give more favourable treatment to non-ACP developing countries with which they have entered into trade co-operation and integration arrangements, than they were according to the member states of the Community.

The trade issue came to dominate the negotiations, as it symbolised the new unity and approach of the ACP countries, which viewed the Convention as a test of the will of Europe to establish a new North/South relationship. Ramphal and his collaborators stood their ground even at the risk of failing to secure a settlement with respect to the products of special interest to the Caribbean – sugar, rum and bananas – which came only in the very last moments of the negotiations. In the end, Lomé I emerged as a solid testimony to ACP unity and determination, and to European enlightenment and accommodation. Despite its shortcomings, the Lomé Convention in its successive versions, has stood the test of time as a serious effort to put North/South relations on a durable footing.

The goals which have engaged 'Sonny' Ramphal's efforts in the Caribbean and in the wider world are still to be fully accomplished. CARICOM has lurched from one crisis to another. Inter-regional trade has contracted in the light of economic difficulties; a full common external tariff has not yet been achieved; the multilateral clearing facility has broken down; the Regional Food Plan has not yet recorded many successes; regional industrial programming remains more of an aspiration than a reality. Yet, the flame of Caribbean regionalism continues to burn, even if at times reduced to a flicker. Despite all the problems, the regional idea survives. Modest advances in functional co-operation are taking place, and the inter-governmental dialogue has been systematised. As the Caribbean countries turn towards the contemporary realities surrounding them, and to the forces that are emerging into the next century, they will no doubt once again look towards regional integration and unity as a guiding point in responding to the challenges that lie ahead. The region can count itself fortunate that it has available to it for any future efforts, West Indians of the commitment, experience, and sagacity of 'Sonny' Ramphal.

One can make a similar point about the Third World as a whole. The 1980s have witnessed a severe setback to development. In all but a few countries, it has been a question of day-to-day survival rather than growth. The principal contributory factors are well-known: recession and slow growth in developed countries, heavy debt burdens, weak commodity prices, protectionism, and policy inertia in both developed and developing countries.

Some efforts are being made to change the climate for growth and development, but they still fall far short of requirements. Accordingly, developing countries are at a critical juncture where they have to re-examine their assumptions concerning the external environment. One is the extent to which the North will continue to serve as a locomotive for their growth if present rates of slow growth persist in the future. Another is the willingness or ability of some of the traditional sources of finance for development to provide the needed support. Yet another is technological change, which is profoundly altering the structures of production and competitive position of individual nations, as well as the demand for particular products, notably the primary commodities on which many countries in the South depend for their export earnings.

All of these changes are contributing to the emergence of

a more differentiated and multi-polar world which, among
other things, will complicate the task of managing an interdependent global economy and of sustaining stable patterns
of development co-operation. At the same time, they could
open up new options for the South, and enlarge the room for
manoeuvre. This calls for a re-thinking of basic strategies
and tactics.

The South too is changing, raising several questions about
its continuing relevance as a concept. Do the export
successes of newly industrialising countries set against the
protracted crisis in Africa mirror a South that is becoming
more heterogeneous and, therefore, less suited to a common
platform? Should a new framework be envisaged for co-
operation and solidarity among developing countries
involving new alignments that might sometimes cut across
the North/South divide, requiring in certain cases, co-
ordination and concerted action along regional and sectoral
lines? Can the complementarity of goals and mutual support
replace the identity of interests as the core of Southern
unity?

The need to review both North/South and South/South
relationships was the basic consideration that prompted the
establishment of the Interdependent Commission of the
South on Development Issues. Working under the
distinguished Chairmanship of Julius Nyerere, the
membership of the Commission -- which includes Ramphal –
constitutes an outstanding group of thinkers and
practitioners in the development field. 'Sonny' Ramphal will
no doubt, as he has done on similar occasions in the past,
make his own distinctive contribution to the work of the
Commission.

Finding ways forward in North/South and South/South
relations is not easy. Yet, as the title and contents of this
book remind us, the imperative of a single humanity impels
us to spare no effort in making progress in these areas. So
long as poverty and under-development stalk the countries
of Africa, Asia and Latin America, so long as democratic

rights and processes are being denied to people, there will be a need for spokesmen and leaders to champion the causes of the poor, the weak, the disenfranchised, and the exploited. Several years ago, 'Sonny' Ramphal nailed his flag to that mast. His service to humanity is already acknowledged. I am certain that acknowledgement will continue to grow.

*Alister McIntyre**
New York
August 1988*

* It goes without saying that the contents of this Foreword represent my personal views, and should not be attributed to the United Nations Secretariat of which I am a staff member.

ABBREVIATIONS

ACP	Developing countries from Africa, the Caribbean and the Pacific, parties to the economic co-operation arrangement with the EEC under the Lomé Convention
ANC	African National Congress
ASEAN	Association of South East Asian Nations
CARICOM	Caribbean Community
CARIFTA	Caribbean Free Trade Association
CBI	Caribbean Basin Initiative
DAC	Development Assistance Committee of the OECD
ECDC	Economic Co-operation among Developing Countries
ECOWAS	Economic Community of West African States
EEC	European Economic Community
EPG	Commonwealth Group of Eminent Persons on South Africa
G 77	Group of 77, the grouping of developing countries which though not formally constituted meets periodically particularly at international economic negotiations to work out common positions. Name derives from number of member countries at inception; membership has risen to 117
GATT	General Agreement on Tariffs and Trade. GATT rules cover international trade and GATT provides a forum for negotiations to reduce trade barriers. In operation since 1948
GDP	Gross Domestic Product
GNP	Gross National Product
GSP	Generalised System of Preferences

IDA	International Development Association; an affiliate of the World Bank providing loans on easier terms than the Bank
IFAD	International Fund for Agricultural Development
ILO	International Labour Organisation
IMF	International Monetary Fund
LDCs	Less Developed Countries
NATO	North Atlantic Treaty Organisation
NIEO	New International Economic Order
OAS	Organisation of American States
OAU	Organisation of African Unity
ODA	Official Development Assistance
OECD	Organisation for Economic Co-operation and Development – grouping of 24 countries which includes all the Western industrialised nations.
OECS	Organisation of Eastern Caribbean States
OPEC	Organisation of Petroleum Exporting Countries
PAC	Pan African Congress
SADCC	Southern African Development Co-ordination Conference.
SDRs	Special Drawing Rights. The SDR is an international reserve asset created by the International Monetary Fund
SPEC	South Pacific Bureau for Economic Co-operation
SWAPO	South West Africa People's Organisation
UDF	United Democratic Front, South Africa
UNCTAD	United Nations Conference on Trade and Development
UNDP	United Nations Development Programme
UNIDO	United Nations Industrial Development Organisation

Let us acknowledge that a rather special obligation devolves upon us as children of slavery, of indenture, of colonialism. It is an obligation to ensure that no trace of servitude lingers or re-emerges in our societies under whatever guise. The legacy of servitude is a continuing one; one which only a vigilant humanity can eradicate. Wherever racism, oppression, intolerance, authoritarianism, dominion of whatever kind, encroaches on human freedom, it stalks in the shadow of slavery. We must never allow ourselves the complacency of believing that the long shadow has been lifted for all time.

*Shridath Ramphal**

Chapter 1

Beginnings

Perspective I   44

The Berbice Connection
(Hull, 1983)   48

Indenture: Another Slavery
(New Delhi, 1986)   59

* *Some in Light and Some in Darkness: The Long Shadow of Slavery,* University of Hull, 24 May 1983 (Third World Foundation, Monograph 12, London, 1983), p. 8.

Perspective I

The economic, social and political conditions into which Shridath Ramphal was born had their own beginnings in African slavery and Indian indentured labour – the foundations upon which the lucrative sugar plantations were built.

Slavery was abolished in the English-speaking Caribbean in 1834 by an Act of the British Parliament passed the year before. The Act of Abolition created what has been described as "a unique and unprecedented status for former slaves – it made them half-slave and half-free"[1]. For the Act provided for a seven-year period of apprenticeship during which the former slave would work a compulsory 40½ hour week for his old master, *unpaid.* In the words of Viscount Howick, Parliamentary Under-Secretary for the Colonies, the Act "gave with one hand and took back with the other".[2]

In the first few days following the abolition of slavery, the response of the former slaves to the enforced period of apprenticeship was predictably unhappy. In St. Kitts, Montserrat, Trinidad and the Essequibo region of Guyana, the 'apprentices' refused to accept the new system and they demonstrated in the streets. In St. Kitts and Trinidad, the militia had to be called out and the protests were brutally put down. During the apprenticeship period, the planters took advantage of their control of local legislatures to revive oppressive laws which had become obsolete and to devise new ones to govern, *inter alia,* the confining of apprentices to one area, the setting of low wages and compulsory apprenticeship for children.

The disquiet of the former slaves over the apprenticeship system continued; their old masters matched the increasing level of dissent with a rising scale of brutality. During the short space of two years in Jamaica, 60,000 apprentices received an aggregate of 250,000 lashes and 50,000 other punishments.[3] And, Jamaica was by no means the worst example; for the apprenticeship code in British Guiana appears "to have been the harshest in the Caribbean, and their experience of it hardly disposed the ex-slaves to a life of wage labour on the plantations".[4]

In the face of bitter apprenticeship strikes and unrest, the scheme of forced labour had to be terminated in 1838, three years earlier than scheduled. With its end came a crisis of labour for the owners of sugar plantations particularly in Guyana and Trinidad where the land available to the former slaves for purchase or squatting was plentiful. The freed slaves had no intention of staying on the estates unless they received better compensation, and when the planters refused to meet their demands they left in droves.

The planters scrambled around in every direction looking for new labour. Their efforts to recruit former slaves from other parts of the West Indies attracted only 2,900 mainly from Barbados, and they quickly left the plantations to join the villages being rapidly established by the former Guyana slaves.[5] Portuguese were imported in large numbers from Madeira, 599 of them landing in Guyana in 1835. But their numbers were decimated by disease. Many more died because they plunged into plantation labour taxing their bodies beyond endurance and depriving themselves of adequate food in order to lay away savings.[6] Reportedly, the planters became reluctant to employ 'these headstrong immigrants in arduous cane work; they simply died too easily'.[7] Meanwhile, the plantations still needed new labour or the owners would have to meet the wage demands of the former slaves.

Thus it was that Indians were brought to the West Indies, in the words of John Gladstone, the father of William Ewart (later Prime Minister of Britain) and one of the larger slave and estate owners in British Guiana, to make the sugar plantations "independent of our negro population".[8] The Guyana plantations got the majority of the Indians who went to the West Indies; approximately 238,216 landed between 1838 and 1917.[9] The first batch of 396 arrived on 5 May 1838 aboard the *Hesperus* and the *Whitby* which had set sail from India on 5 and 29 January respectively.[10] For the next seventy-nine years, the Indian indentured labourer was to experience the brutal and dehumanising process which had characterised African slavery.

In 1871, a former English Chief Justice of British Guiana wrote of the colony's 'some 150 sugar plantations':

> Upon these estates, containing in the whole some 100,000 acres of swamp land, 100,000 Indian and Chinese immigrants, 'introduced' for that purpose by the Government, have been, and about 40,000 of their number are now, confined and there 'bound' to labour in agricultural service...It is not a little remarkable to find that upwards of one million and a half sterling...(one-fifteenth of its total amount) accrues to the Customs revenue of Great Britain from the imported produce of British Guiana; and that considerably more than one-half of the first class sugar imported by us is the produce of that colony.[11]

But his indictment went beyond social conditions and economic gain. He said:

> the system of government is not only that of a complete and highly organised oligarchy; but a complete oligarchy, an irresponsible oligarchy founded on the traditions of slavery.[12]

It is these beginnings which form the first Chapter of this book as Ramphal describes the exploitation of Africans and Indians held in bondage and the inequities which were its consequences.

R.S.

Notes and References

1. Trevor G. Marshall, 'The Fraudulent Freedom – 1834', *Caribbean Contact* (August 1984), p.6.

2. Ibid.

3. George Mannington, *The West Indies* (Leonard Parsons, London, 1925), p. 224.

4. Alan H. Adamson, *Sugar Without Slaves* (Yale University Press, 1972), p. 31.

5. Ibid., p. 35.

6. William Green, *British Slave Emancipation: The Sugar Colonies and the great experiment* (Clarendon Press, Oxford, 1970), p. 286.

7. Ibid.

8. Basdeo Mangru, *Benevolent Neutrality: Indian Government Policy and Labour Migration to British Guiana 1854-1884* (Hansib Publishing Ltd., London, 1987), p. 13.

9. Dwarka Nath, *A History of Indians in Guiana* (published by the Author, London, 1950), pp. 10-11.

10. Ibid., p. 10.

11. Joseph Beaumont, *The New Slavery: An Account of the Indian and Chinese Immigrants in British Guiana* (Ridgeway, London, 1871), pp. 7-9.

12. Ibid.

The Berbice Connection

In 1983 the University of Hull commemorated the 150th Anniversary of the Abolition of Slavery Act 1833 and the death of William Wilberforce who, born in Hull, had led the abolitionist movement in Britain. As part of that commemoration, Shridath Ramphal was invited to deliver a public lecture at the University. He called it 'Some in Light and Some in Darkness: the Long Shadow of Slavery'. The extracts below highlight the special connection of Berbice, Ramphal's birthplace in Guyana, with the anti-slavery struggle.

Berbice is today a county of Guyana – the county of my birth. Initially a separate colony of the Dutch, it fell finally to Britain in 1803. Sugar estates in Berbice which were the property of the Dutch Government became the property of the British Crown – along with the slaves attached to them. Managed at first by the new colonial administration,[1] the estates and the condition of the slaves appear to have "sustained a progressive deterioration in all respects".[2] A proposal to lease the estates to a private individual fell through when he refused to accept conditions affecting the welfare of the slaves attached to the lease by the abolitionist, James Stephen, acting on behalf of the Crown.[3]

Convinced of "the impossibility of disposing of the Estates in any way so as to prevent the destruction of the Slaves, without retaining them in the possession of The Crown", the

Chancellor of the Exchequer concurred in a plan for ensuring in relation to the estates "such improvements as the Government itself... had recommended to the colonial assemblies to adopt and enforce upon private masters": arrangements which "could not, it was thought, be safely left to the colonial Government, or to individual agents on the spot, without the intimate superintendence and control of some authority in England".[4]

It should occasion no surprise that the 'authority in England' turned out to be Wilberforce[5] and five others (including James Stephen) duly appointed as Commissioners for the Management of the Crown's Estates in Berbice, "and for the preservation, protection and improvement of the negro and other slaves belonging thereto".[6]

Wilberforce must have seen the 'Berbice Commission' as a heaven-sent opportunity to demonstrate the practicality of the humanitarian approach – to refute the constant argument that the ideas of the abolitionists spelt ruin for the estates, their owners and the trade in their produce. Certainly he welcomed the Commission and, with kindred spirits as fellow Commissioners, was well set to carry the campaign to the plantations, and to some of the worst plantations anywhere – as that pioneer of modern West Indian writing, Edgar Mittleholzer, a fellow Berbician, so well dramatised in his Kaywana Trilogy.[7]

Wilberforce's zeal was in sharp contrast to the disfavour with which the intervention of the Commissioners was viewed in the colony. Even after the Commission had been appointed, the Governor was urging the Crown to lease or sell the estates "on almost any terms". "I see not the least prospect", he wrote (on 3 May 1811) "of benefit to The Crown by holding these properties".[8]

The attitude of the planters was open hostility. Wilberforce and his friends, after all, had carried the Slave Trade Abolition Bill through the British Parliament only a few years earlier over the fierce objections of the West India lobby and the sugar planters in the West Indies in particular. What is more, the approaches to that Abolition Act of 1807 had been skilfully prepared by Wilberforce and his friends through the 'Guiana Order' of 1805 abolishing the slave trade to the captured Dutch colonies in Guyana by an executive order[9] (authorised as a war measure) and then building on it the Foreign Slave Trade Act of 1806, confirming the Guiana Order, and deftly attaching to it all the prohibitions of previous and defeated Foreign Slave Bills.[10] The Guyana planters nurtured a special hatred for Wilberforce.

But abolition of the trade did not render slavery itself illegal. Despite the nuisance of exhortations from Whitehall, life could go on much as usual – for master and for slave. In Berbice, most of the planters were still Dutch, among the most brutal and tyrannical anywhere, and the prospect of Wilberforce and his band of 'saints' running the Crown's plantations in Berbice excited predictable consternation.

The confrontation was given a sharper edge by the circumstance that among the estates was Dageraad – a name that has passed into the history of Guyana and of slavery generally as a symbol of the bestiality of slavery and the courage of its victims in resisting it. Dageraad was part of the scene of one of the earliest slave uprisings, a rebellion starting at Magdalenenberg in Berbice in 1763, that came close to succeeding. Today, Cuffy, the rebellion's leader, is commemorated as Guyana's first national hero. But the rebellion failed; it was eventually put down at Dageraad with terrible vengeance.[11]

The first act of the Commissioners was to draw up regulations for the management of the estates and slaves. They ran to seven closely printed pages and covered such matters as providing 'a copious and permanent supply of native provisions for the slaves'; guaranteeing 'their rest on the Sunday'; supplying them with 'abundant and comfortable clothing'; keeping their 'houses in proper repair'; making 'the preservation of their health, and their due medical treatment in sickness, the object of special care and attention'; never employing slave labour 'where cattle or machinery could be substituted'; accepting 'as a fundamental maxim' that making the estates more productive 'was not to be pursued by a culture more extensive or laborious than might be consistent with the most scrupulous regard to the health and comfort of the slaves'; directing 'that the cart-whip in the hands of the driver, as an instrument of compelling labour, should be laid aside'.[12]

These instructions must have seemed to the planters of Berbice a model of subversion not to be endured or by example enlarged. Both the planters and the colonial government struck out against them and not only against the Commissioners but the slaves themselves. On 17 October, 1815 the agent in Berbice wrote to the authorities in London:

> You are aware... of the general prejudice which exists here against the wise and the benevolent system of the Commissioners; and you also know that notwithstanding the seeming support of the Colonial Government, and all our own exertions, several instances have occurred in which individuals have not only attempted, but have actually succeeded in wreaking their vengeance upon the poor people, who have experienced the blessing of that system.[13]

The agitation for the withdrawal of Wilberforce's hand was vigorously conducted and at levels of high influence. To withdraw the 'Berbice Commission' would have been unthinkable at so high a point in the campaign of the Anti-Slavery Movement. Instead, what was sought by the planters was accomplished with all the semblance of propriety. By the Convention between Great Britain and the Netherlands relative to the Colonies of Demerara, Essequibo and Berbice in 1815, the British Government agreed that the estates in Berbice would revert to their former owners – now identified not as the Dutch Government but as the 'Berbice Association'.[14] Wilberforce was aghast, and he and his fellow Commissioners pleaded against this retrogression. They quoted the poignant report of The Revd. John Wray, their ardent representative in Berbice, who had written on 11 January 1816:

> The Dutch here are very prejudiced against everything the Commissioners have done or are doing; and I believe it is the general opinion of well-disposed people that the poor Negroes will suffer very much out of spite. Several of the Negroes came crying last Saturday evening, to know if it was true. They are well aware what must be their fate, if the Dutch become their masters.[15]

Their principal agent had written earlier in outraged distress: "Me thinks I hear the whip sounding again without mercy".[16] But the pleas were to no avail. The Convention with Holland was concluded and the plantocracy returned to the estates in the guise of the 'Berbice Association'. Reform by example was not to be. The planters and the colonial government could not be fought in the lands where slavery flourished. Only emancipation would suffice; and that was a goal for which the Anti-Slavery Movement had to struggle in London.

Berbice, Guyana, would not be fully rid of the blight of slavery for another twenty years, if we take account of the post-emancipation transition to true freedom. In those years the mantle of the Anti-Slavery Movement would pass to more sturdy shoulders than those of the ageing and ailing Wilberforce, but his connection with slavery and Guyana's connection with both would not end. The neanderthal myopia of the planter class was eventually to contribute directly and significantly through its own excesses to the ultimate victory which the Anti-Slavery Movement sought. In the end, Wilberforce's defeat at the hands of the Berbice planters was the signal that his final victory was at hand.

While the planters kept up their implacable opposition to emancipation and the British Government temporised in the face of the growing militancy of the new abolitionists, the slaves themselves moved; and nowhere more effectively than in Demerara. On 18 August 1823, a revolt broke out on two plantations with the demand for immediate emancipation – which they genuinely believed the Crown had approved but was being denied them locally. They were in essence not so very far from the truth. Let Furneaux's account tell the story. Having attempted to negotiate;

> The Governor returned to Georgetown with some loss of dignity and that night 13,000 slaves from 37 plantations joined the rebels. They were badly armed and easily subdued, but while they were in control of their plantations, their restraint was unusual. This clemency was not returned. Nearly 50 slaves were hanged and three were given the dreadful sentence of 1,000 lashes and condemned to be worked in chains, two for the remainder of their lives.[17]

Wilberforce pamphlets calling for emancipation had been circulating on the estates. The local *Gazette* (24 August 1924) did not conceal the planters' wrath:

> Perhaps the intriguing saints at home had a hand in it – if so, they will hear with disappointment and pain that a Superintending and just Providence has frustrated their diabolical intentions.[18]

But the very brutality of the planters in response to the revolt hastened emancipation; most pointedly in the death of the Revd. John Smith, a Nonconformist Minister, on one of the estates where the revolt started. Smith was a consumptive and two months after the revolt, as he was about to return to England for health reasons, he was arrested and charged with complicity. He was vilified by the planters, tried by court-martial, convicted and sentenced to death, though with a recommendation for mercy. The Governor referred the case to England, but before a reply could be received Smith died in prison.[19] The revolt gave the abolitionists what they needed most – a dramatic event with which they could stir instincts of abhorrence, revulsion and shame against the system of slavery; and the Demerara planters had provided a martyr.

On 11 June 1824 the debate on Smith took place in the House of Commons. A fragile Wilberforce testified against the 'scandalous injustice' meted out to Smith, but there were many other champions: Brougham was formidable and Smith's trial was condemned by all save the West India lobby as a tragic parody of justice.[20] But more than the missionary's fate was being debated; in the end, the Demerara Revolt and the 'martyrdom' of John Smith dealt slavery a blow from which it never recovered. Hence John Ely's inclusion of the vindication of the 'Missionary of Demerara' among Wilberforce's triadic achievements.[21]

Most decisive of all, of course, was the fact that the slaves themselves were no longer prepared to wait. Tension was mounting and spreading. A slave revolt had taken place in Barbados in 1816. The year after the Demerara Revolt in 1824 came the turn of Jamaica. In 1831 an insurrectionary movement developed in Antigua. But the climax came with the revolt in Jamaica during Christmas of that year.[22] Eric Williams sums up well the situation that had been reached on the eve of Emancipation:

> In 1833, therefore, the alternatives were clear: emancipation from above, or emancipation from below. But EMANCIPATION. Economic change, the decline of the monopolists, the development of capitalism, the humanitarian agitation in British churches, contending perorations in the halls of Parliament, had now reached their completion in the determination of the slaves themselves to be free. The Negroes had been stimulated to freedom by the development of the very wealth which their labour had created.[23]

On 25 July 1833, as Wilberforce lay dying, the Abolition of Slavery Bill was given its second reading in the House and was assured of becoming law.[24] The 'first-fruits'[25] of their labour were at hand.

Notes and References

1. A.R.F. Webber, *Centenary History and Handbook of British Guiana,* 1931 (Argosy Company, British Guiana, 1931), pp. 125-127, 141; James Rodway, *History of British Guiana,* 3 Vols. (Vol. I: 1668-1781; Vol. II: 1782-1833; Vol III: 1833-1839) (Thomson, Georgetown, 1891, 1893, 1894), Vol. II, pp. 267-268, 274-275.

2. *Report of the Commissioners appointed for the Management of The Crown Estates in the Colony of Berbice,* (1816-1817), *Colonial Papers House of Commons* (No. 30) 1816, 20 May 1816, p.1.

3. Ibid., p. 2.

4. Ibid., p. 3.

5. Earlier in his Lecture Shridath Ramphal had explained how much longer slavery might have persisted: "were it not for the Anti-Slavery Movement, with Wilberforce at its helm and with men like Thomas Clarkson, James Stephen, Zachary Macaulay, Thomas Buxton and the many others in whose name Wilberforce spoke in Parliament; and for the public outcry against slavery that their collective work generated". *Some in Light and Some in Darkness; The Long Shadow of Slavery,* University of Hull. (Third World Foundation, Monograph 12, London, 1983), p.7.

6. *Commissions of the Lords of the Treasury appointing William Wilberforce Esquire, et al, to be Commissioners for the Management of The Crown's Estates in Berbice and on the Continent of South America,* (1809-1812), *Colonial Papers House of Commons* (No. 39) 1812, 23 April 1811, p. 1.

7. Edgar Mittleholzer, *Children of Kaywana,* (Peter Nevil, London, 1952); *Kaywana Blood,* (Secker and Warburg, London, 1958); *Kaywana Stock,* (Foursquare, London, 1962).

8. *Report of the Commissioners appointed for the Management of The Crown Estates in the Colony of Berbice,* op. cit., p. 6.

9. Order in Council of 15 August 1805 (No. 163), (1796-1810) Vol. I *Berbice Laws,* p. 661.

10. "An Act to prevent the Importation of Slaves, by any of His Majesty's Subjects into any Islands, Colonies, Plantations, or Territories belonging to any Foreign Sovereign, State, or Power; and also to render more effectual a certain Order, made by His Majesty in Council on the Fifteenth Day of August One thousand eight hundred and five, for prohibiting the Importation of Slaves (except in certain Cases), into any of the Settlements, Islands, Colonies, or

Plantations on the Continent of America, or in the West Indies, which have been surrendered to His Majesty's Arms during the present War; and to prevent the fitting out of Foreign Slave ships from British Ports". Cap. 52 of 23 May 1806, (1803-1806) 20 *Public General Statutes: 44 Geo. III to 46 Geo. III*, p. 634. Also, John Pollock, *Wilberforce,* (Constable, London, 1977), pp. 189, 201-214; David Brion Davis, 'An Appreciation of Roger Anstey,' in Christine Bolt and Seymour Drescher (eds), *Anti-Slavery, Religion and Reform: essays in memory of Roger Anstey,* (Dawson, Folkestone, 1980), p. 13, commenting on Roger T. Anstey, *The Atlantic Slave Trade and British Abolition 1760-1810* (MacMillan Publishers, London, 1975).

11.   Rodway, op. cit., Vol. I (1668-1781), pp. 171-214; Webber, op. cit., pp. 58-62.

12.   *Report of the Commissioners appointed for the Management of The Crown Estates in the Colony of Berbice,* op. cit., pp. 25-31.

13.   Ibid., p. 20.

14.   Convention Between Great Britain and The Netherlands, relative to the Colonies of Demerara, Essequibo, and Berbice, London, 12 August 1815, (1815-1816) Vol. III *British and Foreign State Papers* 386. Rodway, op. cit., Vol. I (1668-1781), pp. 85-99.

15.   *Report of the Commissioners appointed for the Management of The Crown Estates in the Colony of Berbice,* op. cit., p. 22. John Wray was the first resident missionary under the English. He went to the East Coast in 1808, and nine years later to Berbice, Webber, op. cit., p. 129.

16.   Ibid., p. 211.

17.   Robin Furneaux, *William Wilberforce* (Hamish Hamilton, London, 1974), p. 416. Also, Joshua Bryant, *Account of an Insurrection of the Negro Slaves in the Colony of Demerara* (Chronicle, Georgetown, 1824).

18.   Rodway, op. cit., Vol. II (1782-1833), p. 240.

19.   Furneaux, op. cit., p. 417.

20.   Ibid; pp. 418-419. Also, "Petition, from London Missionary Society: Conduct of Revd. J. Smith at Demerara" (13 April 1982); "Motion respecting the Trial and Condemnation of Missionary Smith at Demerara" (1 June 1824 and 11 June 1824) in (1924) *The Parliamentary Debates,* New Series Vol. II (March 30 to June 25) at 400-408 (13 April 1984), 961-1076 (1 June 1824), and 1206-1315 (11 June 1824).

21.   In 1934, James Montgomery of Sheffield published a small book,

The Bow in the Cloud or the Negro's Memorial, intended to illustrate the evils of slavery and commemorate its abolition. In it is a funeral oration by John Ely 'supposed to be delivered at the grave of Wilberforce', with a passage which represents a synthesis of Wilberforce's life and work: "If on the tombs of victors are inscribed the dates of their victories, a simple date shall constitute the most splendid epitaph of Wilberforce's sepulchre – that of the day when he achieved his great triumph: write upon his memorial stone that one simple date:

THE 25th OF MARCH, 1807

and all shall comprehend its import and admire it as expressive and sublime. Yet many other victories be inscribed beneath that first and signal one – victories achieved partly by his aid, and partly consequent upon that grand preliminary triumph...Inscribe then the tomb of Wilberforce with this threefold achievement:

THE SLAVE TRADE ABOLISHED –
THE MISSIONARY OF DEMERARA VINDICATED –
SLAVERY EXTINGUISHED.

J. Montgomery, (ed) *The Bow in the Cloud or the Negro's Memorial. A Collection of Original Contributions, in Prose and Verse, Illustrative of the Evils of Slavery, and Commemorative of its Abolition in the British Colonies* (Jackson and Walford, London, 1834), pp. 282-299.

22. Eric Williams, *Capitalism and Slavery* (Andre Deutsch, London, 1964), pp. 205-206.

23. Ibid., p. 208.

24. "Ministerial Plan for the Abolition of Slavery" (1833), *Hansard's Parliamentary Debates,* Third Series Vol. 19 (2 July to 25 July, 1833) at 1056-1069; Ibid., Vol. 20 (26 July to 29 August) at 409-411, 783-784.

25. At the commencement of his Lecture Shridath Ramphal had said: "A while after Wilberforce's death, Thomas Hill, in a little poem which he called 'The Grave of Wilberforce', composed at Chesterfield Vicarage, wrote these words:

Conspicuous on his native coast,
The storied obelisk shall boast
The first-fruits of his fame.

That was a reference to the resolve of the people of Hull to erect such an obelisk in commemoration of the public and private virtues of their townsman. The obelisk was duly erected at St. John's Street and is now a Wilberforce shrine in its new location at The Queen's Gardens. But what attracts me so much to these lines of Thomas Hill is the perception that abolition of the slave trade and emancipation itself were but 'the first-fruits' of the struggle against human bondage." *Some in Light and Some in Darkness: The Long Shadow of Slavery,* op. cit., p. 3.

Indenture:
Another Slavery

The unbroken chain of human bondage represented by African slavery, Indian indentured labour and present day 'apartheid' continued to occupy Shridath Ramphal's mind in the years following his Hull Lecture. On 20 January, 1986, when he spoke to the Commonwealth Society of India in New Delhi about his own roots, these and other more intimate elements of continuity were uppermost in his mind. This is an abridged version of his address – to which he gave the title: 'Roots and Reminders'.

The Demerara revolt in 1823 and the spate of West Indian rebellions against slavery of which it was a part were major elements in forcing slavery's abolition; the Revd. John Smith's martyrdom was an important political factor in securing the passage of the Emancipation Act in 1833.[1] But Smith was not the only martyr. The leader of the Demerara revolt, Quamina, was killed in the course of it. His son, Jack, was tried at the summary Courts Martial that followed and was hanged in public; his head, like those of other rebels executed, was stuck on a pole for public viewing; in the words of the local *Gazette,* "as a monument of personal guilt... and a caution against like criminality".[2] That son, however, bore not his father's African name but that of his master – Gladstone.

By 1823, Sir John Gladstone was already a Liverpool

merchant of substantial means with nearly a third of his fortune deriving from slave plantations in Demerara. Frustrated in his own desire to represent the Corporation of Liverpool in Westminster, he was to see his sons, Thomas and William, go there instead and William rise to be one of Britain's great Prime Ministers. Standing as a 'High Tory', William Gladstone came to Westminster as the new member for Newark in 1832 when the abolition of slavery was an inescapable political issue and one which, as events turned out, he had to face immediately. It had been on a Gladstone plantation in Demerara – Success – that the slave revolt of 1823 had started; it adjoined Le Resouvenir, the estate on which the Revd. John Smith had his Chapel. On 14 May 1833, specific charges were made by Lord Howick, formerly Under-Secretary for the Colonies, against the management of another of Sir John Gladstone's sugar plantations – the estate of Vreed-en-Hoop – alleging "that the increase in sugar cultivation was in direct ratio with over-working and loss of life on the part of the slave population".[3]

Thomas Gladstone replied in the House of Commons three days later, but it was not until 3 June that his brother, William, the future Prime Minister, was able to deliver his maiden speech in defence of his father and West Indian sugar interests in general.[4] His most recent biographer, Richard Shannon, describes it as "a peroration pathetically invoking sympathy for the maligned West Indian planters".[5] Eric Williams was perhaps kinder, acknowledging that maiden speech to be a testimony "more to filial feeling than liberal principles.[6] But 'filial feelings' notwithstanding, it was testimony to the same contradiction of "maintaining that all is good when all is bad", as had confused Voltaire's Candide on his arrival in slavery-ridden Surinam.[7] As Hansard recorded, the future Liberal leader

> ...deprecated cruelty – he deprecated slavery: it was abhorrent to the nature of Englishmen; but, conceding all these things, were not Englishmen to retain a right to their own honestly and legally acquired property?[8]

That same year the Abolition of Slavery Act was passed;
but it is worth noting that the slave owners received £20
million – a large sum which in today's value would be
equivalent to at least half a billion pounds – for the loss of
their 'property'. Little surprise, then, that within two years
of emancipation, even before the brutal apprenticeship
system which followed had itself been aborted, the
Demerara planters – Sir John Gladstone foremost among
them – started the search for alternative labour. A Calcutta
firm – Gillanders, Arbuthnot & Co. – had already supplied
Indian labour to Mauritius; they now advertised their cost to
the Gladstones as "not half that of a slave". On 6 January
1836, Sir John Gladstone wrote asking them to provide "a
hundred coolies" for from five to seven years.

The reply was written in what Hugh Tinker, the author of
an outstanding book on the new system of 'indenture', aptly
describes as a 'curiously proto-Darwinian tone'. It reveals
well that though much had changed with abolition, much
remained the same. "We are not aware", wrote the Calcutta
firm, "that any greater difficulty will present itself in sending
men to the West Indies (than to Mauritius), the natives
being perfectly ignorant of the place they go to or of the
length of voyage they are undertaking". And they
continued, half-defending, half-excusing:

> The Dhangurs are always spoken of as more akin to the
> monkey than the man. They have no religion, no education,
> and in their present state no want beyond eating, drinking
> and sleeping: and to procure which they are willing to
> labour.[9]

Satisfied, Sir John Gladstone, now joined by others,
arranged for the transportation of the first indentured Indian
labourers to the West Indies. Two years later, on 5 May
1838, the *Whitby* and the *Hesperus* landed 396 men, women
and children in Guiana, 101 bound for Gladstone's estates,
including Vreed-en-Hoop.[10]

Although this first venture had been sanctioned by the

Colonial Office,[11] the authorities in India were uneasy about any general scheme of immigration and it did not take the Anti-Slavery Society long to recognise the continuum with slavery. The Secretary of the Society, John Scoble, and two other members actually visited Guiana in 1838 and found gross ill-treatment of the immigrants, including those at Vreed-en-Hoop.[12] In 1839 the Government of India prohibited overseas immigration for manual labour;[13] and the following year, despite protests, Lord John Russell told Parliament that he was not prepared to relax the prohibition of 'coolie emigration' to the West Indies:

> I should be unwilling to adopt any measure to favour the transfer of labourers from British India to Guiana... I am not prepared to encounter the responsibility of a measure which may lead to a dreadful loss of life on the one hand, or, on the other, to a new system of slavery.[14]

But Russell's was not to be the last word. The measure, 'Indian indenture', was to come; and with it both the 'dreadful loss of life' and the 'new system of slavery' from which he had recoiled. In 1844, only four years after Russell's rejection of it, the decision was taken by the British Government to support, and theoretically to control, Indian emigration to the West Indies.[15]

It came about because wherever possible the freed slaves fled from the land, or, if not from the land, the master. In 1842 a House of Commons Committee blamed declining production in the West Indies on lack of labour, and declared that:

> the obvious and most desirable mode of endeavouring to compensate for this diminished supply of labour, is to promote the immigration of a fresh labouring population, to such an extent as to create competition for employment.[16]

It was a blatant scheme to force the freed slaves back on to the land and bring wages down.

In the result, between the 1830s and the beginning of World War I, probably as many as two million Indian labourers were transported overseas under the indenture system to work on tropical plantations – over half a million going to French and British sugar colonies. The bulk of the earliest immigrants came from the hill tribesmen, the Dhangurs, described in that early reply to Sir John Gladstone in the dehumanised language of slavery. Later, the main recruiting was in the heavily populated regions of Benares and North Bihar and, later still, among the landless Tamil labourers of South India, many of them already crushed into semi-slavery by high caste landlords.

But first they had to endure their own passage across the *Kala Pani,*[17] the *Black Waters,* their own diaspora, not so unlike that earlier pernicious traffic in human cargo. A Guyanese poet, Arthur Seymour, has described the *Middle Passage* in these terms:

> A ferry of infamy from the heart of Africa
> Roots torn and bleeding from their native soil
> A stain of race spreading across the ocean.[18]

And so, indeed, it was. It remains an apt description of the ferry that was to succeed it, crossing from the heart of India, spreading another stain of race across the ocean.

For three-quarters of a century, in what amounted for the great majority to an 'exile into bondage',[19] the plantations imposed their servitude on the Indian labourers, who were but mute pieces on the chequerboard of world-wide colonialism. Although nominally free, they were little more than slaves. Often their emigration was a result of fraud and outright force.[20] They endured cruel and degrading conditions of work, frequently under the former slave masters or their descendants.

Perhaps the truest symbol of the unbroken chain between slavery and indenture was the tenement range or 'logie' of the inherited 'nigger yard' – the squalid, foul, degenerate, huddled pens that passed for housing for slave and indentured labourer alike. 'Nigger yard', 'coolie yard', 'bound yard', were all one; only the labels changed to match the changing style of servitude.[21] Like the slaves, the Indian migrants were subject to the coercion of the whip, and to the new coercion of criminal law applied for labour offences such as absenteeism and lack of identity documents which were not crimes under the general law. The minimal wages, which were the inducement for the whole vast dislocation, were subject to arbitrary stoppages. Pay was sometimes withheld for years. The 'double cut' was often applied – two days' pay docked for one day's absence; and throughout the eighty years of indentured labour another type of 'double cut' remained the rule: one day's pay fined for every day absent, but with an extra day added to the period of indenture.[22]

A Royal Commission in 1871 described the indentured Indian as trapped by the law, 'in the hands of a system which elaborately twists and turns him about, but always leaves him face to face with an impossibility'.[23] How like apartheid today! In his Foreword to Walter Rodney's *A History of the Guyanese Working People, 1881-1905*, the West Indian author George Lamming sums up the cruel realities of indenture thus:

> Indentured labour was bound labour. It was deprived of all mobility and was therefore condemned to provide that reliability of service a crop like sugar demanded. The planter class, with the full permission of the metropolitan power, had given itself the legal right to deploy this labour as it pleased. As Rodney emphasises here, with great relevance to many a contemporary situation, what the ruling class could not acquire by the normal play of the market forces had now been appropriated through legal sanctions. Indentured Indian labour was enslaved by the tyranny of the law that decided their relations to the land where they walked, and worked and slept.[24]

It is ironic that the death-knell of the virtually world-wide indenture system was sounded in South Africa, where labour conditions are now among the closest in the world to organised slavery. In 1895, the young Gandhi began his lifelong struggle for freedom and decolonisation by opposing the conditions of Indian indenture. As the cause gathered public support in India, Viceroys such as Curzon and Hardinge added their considerable weight in favour of just treatment of Indians overseas. Gandhi's protest was part of the turning of the tide. Indentured emigration to Mauritius was stopped in 1910 and to Natal in 1911; in 1909 free emigration to Malaya replaced indenture, which was ended in Assam in 1913. By 1915, when Gandhi returned to India, indenture had become the central issue.[25]

The last bastions were in the West Indies and Fiji. The revelations of Gandhi's friend, the Revd. C.F. Andrews, and others, about the conditions of Indians in Fiji, and particularly the moral degradation of Indian women, aroused Indian public opinion to such an extent that in 1917 the whole tottering system of indenture was declared at an end.[26] For the generation that came after, as with the Africans after emancipation, there would be a struggle of a different kind; but the process of recovery could begin. Later, in the 1930s, at the end of a sentimental visit to Fiji, C.F. Andrews placed his faith in the powers of recovery of the indentured Indians[27] – a quality which the children of indenture shared with the children of slavery in its cruellest form.

For reasons which will become apparent, mention of C.F. Andrews prompts me to turn to more personal links. On 5 January 1881 – 45 years exactly after Sir John Gladstone's first letter to the Calcutta firm – the sailing ship *Ellora* arrived in Georgetown after a voyage of some four months from Calcutta. Its human cargo was indentured labourers for the sugar plantations of British Guiana. Among them was a widowed mother and her son of nine, bound for that same estate of Vreed-en-Hoop. Her story was already remarkable, and in many respects unique, for this journey across the *Black Waters* was for her a third crossing.

In India, in the early 1870s, bubonic plague – which was to reach epidemic proportions at the turn of the century in the United Provinces – had left this woman widowed. The couple were high caste Brahmins, but poor; and, as so often happened in their circumstances, almost all their children, eleven out of twelve, had succumbed, leaving only one son alive. 'Suttee' (immolation on the husband's funeral pyre) had long been abolished by law, but remained a sacrifice expected of the orthodox. It was a sacrifice the widow was unwilling to make. She took the only other option – return to her maternal home; but it was not a real option. She was treated as an outcast – the approaches to her home swept before her not in welcome but out of rejection, for having committed the terrible wrong of losing her husband. To purify herself, she took her infant son to the sacred city of Benares for both to wash in the holy waters of the Ganges. Benares then, as Varanasi now, was a city to which the forlorn and despairing came, and it was there that the 'arkathis' lurked – the touts employed by the agents recruiting labour for the sugar plantations. The lack of women among indentured labourers was always a major problem and it had by then become the law that 40 women had to be recruited for every 100 men indentured. Places of pilgrimage like Benares offered the 'arkathis' a prime perch from which to prey on unattached women.

To the rejected widow the promise of a new life must have seemed an answer to her prayers. But who knows with what stories she was lured, or how long she believed the journey or the labouring to be – or even where? At any rate to Calcutta with her son she duly went and was recruited for the West Indies – arriving, eventually, in Surinam – Dutch Guiana. Did she, like Candide in Voltaire's satirical fiction, weep on entering Surinam, sensing the abomination of her indenture? We will not know. Almost certainly she would not have known that the right to recruit her had been traded by Britain to Holland in return for a cluster of old Dutch forts built for the slave trade in what is today Ghana.[28] That traffic to Surinam in 1873 was disastrous, 18 per cent of the immigrants dying in the first twelve months after arrival.[29]

But our widow and her son survived. Eventually, she worked out the five-year contract and, no longer bound, took the long journey back to India.

Her family was pleased to see her, but the rules of caste were strict and she found no welcome despite her absence of six years. In fact, in her penance she had sinned still further – by having crossed the *Kala Pani* and lived among unclean meat-eaters. Once again she went with her son to Benares to wash seven times in the Ganges; to be favoured with better fortune. Her late husband's family was, it is thought, of the priestly class, the 'pandas', who administered the sacred Vishnupad Temple at Gaya in Bihar. For a while, as they lingered by the holy river, the boy was apprenticed to a priest, one of the 'pandas' of Benares, and began his training in the Hindu scriptures. But, once again, they encountered the silver-tongued 'arkathis', perhaps this time with a tale of a better life than Surinam had offered – for the British sugar planters had earned a less cruel reputation than the Dutch.

A second time they journeyed to Calcutta and a second contract of indenture. This time, however, our widow had no thought of returning to the village and family that had cast her out so cruelly, not once but twice. Harsh and uncertain as were the fortunes of indenture, she was leaving now for good: to give her young son, in particular, a better chance than he might ever have in a village and a family that did not want them. So it was that, in due season, on the sailing ship *Ellora*, the widow and her son reached Georgetown committed to labour on that same estate at Vreed-en-Hoop that the abolitionists had singled out for attack almost fifty years earlier and with which, under the then ownership of Sir John Gladstone, the whole system of Indian indenture to the West Indies had begun.

The widow fulfilled her contract of labour on the sugar plantations, her son sharing her burden. Before long, however, he was singled out by the missionaries of the Canadian Presbyterian Church to be trained as a teacher and later a 'Catechist' or lay preacher. He was a respected man in the village of Auchlyne in Berbice where he settled; but, despite his vocation in the Christian faith, his identity with the priestly class (that old link with the Vishnupad Temple in Gaya) lingered among fellow Indians who, all his life, called him nothing but 'Maharaj', as they would have done in Bihar. The tradition of teacher which he began was carried on by his son, who became a pioneer of education in British Guiana. It was he, my father, who set down the scant narrative of my great-grandmother's double encounters with the indenture system in which I have my roots; roots entwined with so much that is India's own lineage; roots that impose so many remainders. ?

I disclaim any personal virtue in the chain of events that have led me to this occasion in India. My mother might dissent. In 1929, C.F. Andrews, Gandhi's friend whom I mentioned earlier, visited British Guiana and spent an evening in my parents' humble home in Berbice. He was particularly interested in my father's work in education, especially his campaign for the education of Indian girls. Their discussion, it seems, was continually disturbed by a mewling infant until the old priest took me in his arms, quieted the cries and gave me his blessing. My mother always had hope for me thereafter!

Late in 1983, at the end of the Commonwealth Heads of Government Meeting in New Delhi – the first ever held in India, and held, as events befell, just in time for us to have the privilege of Indira Gandhi's chairmanship – I travelled to Varanasi and the surrounding countryside from where that brave woman and her son had crossed the 'seven seas' three times just over one hundred years ago. I took with me my mother, herself sprung from another transplantation indenture had procured: my own widowed mother going with me back to Gaya. It was a return journey of a kind: not one conceived as an intensive search for roots, but from which came insistent reminders that they were not far away.

As we sat in the garden of the official Guest House in Gaya, my mother talked with the young wife of the District

Magistrate and Collector about the names of vegetables we thought peculiar to Guyana, like 'baigan' and 'bora', only to find that they were similar in this district of Bihar, when even in neighbouring Trinidad they were quite different. We talked too of my friend Guya Persaud – now a distinguished judge in the West Indies – whose parents, we decided, commemorated his ancestral roots in the most permanent of ways – in his name. There was a spirit of belonging in that languid Gaya countryside.

The highlight of my pilgrimage was being received by the 'pandas' of Gaya as a son of the region and admitted to the inner sanctum of the Vishnupad Temple – still one of India's most sacred places. At its centre, encased in solid silver, is a large rock with an indentation worshipped as being the footprint of Lord Vishnu himself. The climax of the visit was being invited to perform a 'puja' at the shrine, which I did with all the awkwardness of a novice, but the humility which the occasion imposed.

My ancestral link with Gaya and the Vishnupad Temple is still a matter of inference and surmise. But there were other links even in that place. At the entrance to the Temple is a bell bearing the following inscription: "A gift to the Bishnupad by Mr. Francis Gillanders, Gaya, 15th January 1790". Francis Gillanders was a collector, a British official, in Gaya in the late years of the eighteenth century.[30] What links were there between this man, who so closely identified with the pilgrims from whom he would have collected the old 'pilgrim tax' as they visited the Vishnupad Temple from all over India, with Gillanders, Arbuthnot & Company of Calcutta, to whom Sir John Gladstone had written that first letter in January 1836?; the letter that, in a sense, brought me from Gaya to Guyana.

As I sought out beginnings across the shifting line that divided Bihar from India's United Provinces, flashes of these strange conjunctures came before me, hints of continuity, glimpses of patterns traced over time as if there is a story still unfolding which is, as yet, only faintly discernible amid the bustle of the present. And some words of Frantz Fanon came back to me, words that might stand for the whole story of servitude illumined by the light of the individual human will to overcome: "It is a story that takes place in darkness, and the sun that is carried within me must shine into the smallest crannies".[31]

The visit to Gaya was inevitably one of many reflections, not least on the strange pathways that led my forebears to Guyana and now led me back to India through a modern Commonwealth that India made possible. Those pathways, in due course, took me from Guyana to London, to occupancy in 1975 of the then official residence of the Commonwealth Secretary-General at 5 Carlton Gardens, St. James's: still the links of continuity. To the month, 142 years earlier, Sir John Gladstone, had bought, and eventually moved to, the address next door – 6 Carlton Gardens.[32] July 1833 was just one month before the Emancipation Bill was passed and before Wilberforce himself passed away. In that same month John Gladstone's son, William, the future Prime Minister, breakfasted with old William Wilberforce in London. [33] I like to think a process of conversion had begun, [34] though his speech in the House of Commons later that morning on the 'Ministerial Plan for the Abolition of Slavery' hardly implied that it had.

As it transpired, he was to have a continuing link to Guiana. In 1839, three years after initiating indenture in Demerara Sir John Gladstone sold the Guiana estates, then worth 'above £50,000'. With the proceeds he set up a trust for his children, including William: Demerara contributing to the future Prime Minister's financial independence, though he protested at the time that "this increased wealth so much beyond my needs with its attendant responsibility is very burdensome".[35] Numbers 5 and 6 Carlton Gardens are now all one; both incorporated into Wool House. For a while, the wheel turned full circle. I, whose ancestors left India for Guyana because of a letter Sir John Gladstone wrote nearly 140 years before, now found myself in London at the address he had chosen for his own retirement. And that wheel is still turning. The Commonwealth Secretariat itself will soon move into temporary quarters while Marlborough House is being restored. My office will then be at 2 Carlton Gardens, across the way from No. 6.

As I speak to you, on a day which is the birthday of the late Martin Luther King, how palpable it seems that the final lesson of this story, and the final challenge, is how to enlarge our perception of a common inseparable humanity; how to ensure that relations with our fellow men reflect our oneness rather than a sense of 'otherness'. It was that 'otherness' which so dehumanised the slave as to make his servitude, in the eye of the enslaver, not a wrong to the slave but a right of the master. It was so, as we have seen, with indenture: "The Dhangurs are often spoken of as more akin to the monkey than to the man". And it has been so throughout the ages; and not just in the servitude imposed by white men on others, for white and black alike, at various moments in history, have been slave owners as well as slaves.

Notes and References

1. *Supra*, pp. 52-54.

2. Local *Gazette* of 4 September 1824. Also James Rodway, *History of British Guiana*, 3 Vols. (Thomson, Georgetown, 1891, 1893, 1894), Vol. II (1782-1833), pp. 243-244.

3. "Ministerial Proposition for the Emancipation of Slaves" in *(1833) Hansard's Parliamentary Debates,* Third Series, Vol. 17 (2 April to 20 May), 1193-1262, 1250.

4. *(1833) Hansard's Parliamentary Debates,* Third Series, Vol. 18 (30 May to 1 July), at 330-337.

5. Richard Shannon, *Gladstone*, Vol. I: 1809-1865 (Hamish Hamilton, London, 1982), p. 46.

6. Eric Williams, *Capitalism and Slavery* (Andre Deutsch, London, 1964), p. 93.

7. Earlier in his Lecture Shridath Ramphal explains: "Slavery was at its

height when, in 1759, Voltaire wrote his satirical commentary on that philosophy of complacency and acquiescence. In one of many unforgettable incidents Voltaire pictured the innocent Candide entering Surinam and encountering a Negro slave lying on the ground. The slave, who has lost both a hand and a leg, tells Candide that this is the 'price paid for the sugar you eat in Europe'. 'Oh Pangloss!', cries Candide, 'this is an abomination you had not guessed; this is too much. In the end I shall have to renounce optimism'. 'What is this optimism?', asks Candide's valet. 'Alas', says Candide, 'it is the mania of maintaining that all is good when all is bad'. And Candide weeps as he enters Surinam". Voltaire, *Candide,* tr. John Butt, Penquin Classics (Penguin Books, Harmondsworth, 1987), pp. 84-86. Also, David Brion Davis, "Slavery and 'Progress'," in Christine Bolt and Seymour Drescher (eds), *Anti-Slavery, Religion, and Reform: essays in Memory of Roger Anstey* (Dawson, Folkestone, 1980), p. 351-366, at p. 351.

8. William Gladstone in the House of Commons on 3 June 1833; (1833) *Hansard's Parliamentary Debates* Third Series, Vol. 18 (30 May to 1 July), 335.

9. Hugh Tinker, *A New System of Slavery. The Export of Indian Labour Overseas 1830-1920* (Oxford University Press for the Institute of Race Relations, London, 1974), p. 63.

10. Dwarka Nath, *A History of Indians in Guiana* (published by the Author, London, 1950), p. 10.

11. An Order in Council of 12 July 1837 (No. 83) legalised Gladstone's action on indentured labour, (1705 to 1859) *Orders in Council,* Vol. 1. Also, Act 5 of 1837 (India) for 'the control of coolie emigration'. Lord Brougham had discovered the Order in Council of 12 July 1837 (due to expire on 1 August 1840); in the course of the debate on Negro Emancipation on 20 January 1838, he described the measure as 'the establishment of a future slave trade'. On 6 March 1838 he made an impassioned and indignant speech in the House of Commons denouncing the whole system of 'coolie emigration'. I.M. Cumpston, *Indians Overseas in British Territories 1834-1805* (Oxford University Press, London, 1953), p. 19 citing from "Importation of Hindoos into Guiana" (1838) *Hansard's Parliamentary Debates,* Vol. 40 (20 February) 1356 and Vol. 41 (22 February to 28 March) 416-476 at 416.

12. Cumpston, op. cit., p. 35 citing John Scoble: *Hill Coolies: a brief exposure of the deplorable conditions of hill coolies in British Guiana and Mauritius and of the nefarious means by which they were induced to resort to these colonies,* (British and Foreign Anti-Slavery Reporter, 11 March 1840).

13. Act No. 14 of 1839 was passed on 27 May 1839 by the Governor-

General's Council prohibiting emigration for the purpose of manual labour and persons carrying out such emigration were liable to a fine of Rs 200 or three months' imprisonment. The 1839 Act was repealed by Act No. 21 of 1844 which in turn was repealed by Act No. 13 of 1864 which consolidates and amends the Law Respecting Emigration of Native Labourers: (1962-65) Vol. IV *Acts of India*, p. 403.

14. Tinker, op. cit., pp. xiv, 71.

15. Tinker, op. cit., p. 52.

16. *Report from the Select Committee on West India Colonies; together with the minutes of evidence Appendix and Index,* 25 July 1842, H.C. 479, pp. 4-5 (paras. 5, 10 and 11); pp. 6-7 (paras. 4, 5 and 6). Also, M. Craton, J. Walvin and D. Wright: *Slavery: Abolition and Emancipation. Black Slaves and the British Empire. A Thematic Documentary* (Longman, London, 1976), p. 334.

17. *Kala Pani* – A term originally used for the penal settlement of Port Blair in the Andaman Islands in the Bay of Bengal. Initially the 'life imprisonment' convicts were sent there; they had no hope of returning due (it was said) to such factors as: moral depression resulting from exile across the seas; ill effects of a new and severe climate; indigestible water; malaria from newly cleared forests; bad housing and want of personal cleanliness. Even when some did return they were so ill and debilitated that they did not survive for long. Later the term came to be used to signify a 'land of no return'.

18. Arthur Seymour, 'First of August', *Selected Poems of Arthur J. Seymour* (Georgetown, Guyana, 1983), p. 12.

19. Tinker, op. cit., p. 60. The system under which the first immigration took place, that of 1845-1848, had consisted of a contract entitling the immigrants to a return passage at the end of five years of residence, or previously, on payment of a proportionate part of the cost of their introduction. The system not only failed to ensure the health and prosperity of the immigrants but when attempts were made to revive the three years indenture the efforts of the planters were devoted to obtaining a longer period of indenture, or, if that would not be granted to enforce some payment by way of consideration for the return passage. See *Report of the Commissioners appointed to Enquire into the treatment of Immigrants in British Guiana,* June 1871, (c.393 and c.393-1, c.393-II), (1871) *Parliamentary Papers Colonial etc. Vol. 2,* (Nos. 8, 8A, 8B) paras. 230, 231.

20. Timothy N. Thomas, *Indians Overseas: A guide to source material in the India Office Records for the study of Indian Emigration 1830-1950* (The British Library, 1985), p. 4: "The journeys were long, for

example that from Patna or Benares to Calcutta taking thirty to forty days, and had the aspect of a forced march. Yet despite such conditions few tried to escape, because it appears that 'Kanganis' placed persons amongst them who kept up the stories of the land of plenty that awaited them overseas".

21.   Ibid., p. 6: "Life on the plantations took its toll of both men and women, who usually arrived in poor physical shape and were not prepared for the rigours of field work. Much of the labour undertaken by the emigrants was as arduous as that of the former slaves and remnants of slavery still remained, such as the coolie accommodation of 'lines' in British Guiana still bearing the title of the 'Nigger Yard'."

22.   Tinker, op. cit., pp. 186, 188-189.

23.   Ibid., p. 224. Also, *Report of the Commissioners appointed to Enquire into the Treatment of Immigrants in British Guiana,* June 1871, op. cit.

24.   George Lamming, Foreword to Walter Rodney, *A History of the Guyanese Working People, 1881-1905* (John Hopkins University Press, London, 1981), p. xxii.

25.   Tinker, op. cit., pp. 334-366. Also, C.F. Andrews, (ed) *Mahatma Gandhi: his own story.* (Allen and Unwin Ltd., London, 1930), pp. 192-193; *The Collected Works of Mahatma Gandhi* (Delhi, 1958), Vol. I: 1884-96, cited in Tinker, op. cit., pp. 283-284.

26.   Tinker, op cit., pp. 346-57.

27.   Ibid., 381.

28.   Ibid.

29.   Ibid., pp. 112-115.

30.   P.C. Roy Chaudhury, *Bihar District Gazetteer: Gaya* (Patna, 1957), p. 95

31.   Frantz Fanon, *Black Skin White Masks,* tr. by Charles Lam Markmann (MacGibbon and Kee, London, 1968), p. 29.

32.   Shannon, op. cit., pp. 59-60.

33.   Ibid., p. 277.

34.   Compare the later Gladstone of the 'Midlothian Campaign': "Remember the rights of the savage, as well as we call him. Remember that the happiness of his humble home, remember that the sanctity of life in the hill villages of Afghanistan among the winter snows, is as inviolable in the eye of Almighty God as can be your own. Remember that he who has united you together as human

beings in the same flesh and blood has bound you by the law of mutual love; that that mutual love is not limited by the boundaries of the Christian civilisation; that it passes over the whole surface of the earth, and embraces the meanest along with the greatest in its unmeasured scope". M.R.D. Foot, *Midlothian Speeches 1879* (Leicester University Press, 1971), p. 94.

35. Shannon, op. cit., p. 99.

In that sense of being that derives from within and is assured and unchanging, I have been a West Indian from the first moments of my rational awakening. The land of my birth, my country that I was privileged to help bring to sovereign statehood, commands my devotion and my loyalty; but in a further dimension of belonging, the West Indies is, also, my native land. I trust that I am not, in this regard, a member of a vanishing tribe.

Shridath Ramphal*

Chapter 2

West Indian Nationhood

Perspective II   78

Why Federation Failed   82
(Lagos, 1976)

Nationhood: Myth, Mirage or Mandate?   93
(Port-of-Spain, 1971)

The Case for Political Unity   102
(Port-of-Spain, 1971)

* On receiving an Honorary Degree of Doctor of Laws at the University of the West Indies, St. Augustine, Trinidad, 28 January 1978.

Perspective II

Guyana had opted to stay out of the Federation of the West Indies which was agreed in 1958 by ten of the West Indian islands, including Trinidad and Tobago. The decision not to participate in the Federation was due largely to the objection of the leaders of the Indian community which, by the late 1950s, was the single largest group and almost half the entire population.

One of the Indians most strongly supportive of Guyana's participation in the Federation was Shridath Ramphal's father, J.I. 'Jimmy' Ramphal, who served in the Legislative Council between 1954 and 1957. He took issue with those who described, as 'dumping', the migration of people to Guyana which might occur from the other West Indian states of the proposed Federation. He advanced the view that Guyana "shall have lost paradise if we do not enter into Federation".[1]

Shridath Ramphal had chosen 'Federalism in the West Indies' as the subject of the dissertation for his Master of Laws Degree in London in 1952. When the West Indian Federation was being formed, despite Guyana's refusal to participate, Ramphal went to the Federal Capital in Trinidad to work for the Federal Government first as Legal Draftsman, 1958-59, and then as Assistant Attorney-General, 1961-62. He was criticised for doing so by groups within the Indian community in Guyana.

But Ramphal considers federalism to be a fundamentally important instrument "for enlarging the capacity of new states, whether absolutely poor or relatively poor, to survive in a world in which old, large and relatively rich states are themselves integrating for survival". Small states, he says, "must enlarge the prospects of federalism by miniaturising the potential for separatism".[2] In 1958 he was convinced that The West Indies Federation provided a genuine opportunity for large-scale advancement of the disadvantaged and dispossessed of the entire region, including the Indian community in Guyana.

The Federation did not last long – less than four years after it began, it ended. According to Arthur Lewis, the Nobel prize-winning West Indian economist, "the Federation was destroyed by poor leadership rather than by the intractability of its own internal problems".[3] Shridath Ramphal was actually drafting the Constitution for the Independent West Indian Federation when it collapsed in 1962 to make way for the independence of twelve separate Caribbean states. None of the twelve had a population of more than two million and the majority had less than 100,000 inhabitants; few possessed sufficient resources to be economically independent and the majority were heavily dependent on external aid. Ramphal left the region deeply disillusioned.

But Shridath Ramphal's heart remained in the West Indies. After a Guggenheim Fellowship at Harvard in 1962-63 and law practice in Jamaica in 1963-64, he returned to Guyana in 1965, accepting the invitation of Forbes Burnham to take up the post of Attorney-General and see the country through to Independence. With Guyana's independence in 1966, he took charge of the new country's foreign affairs. It was as Attorney-General and Foreign Minister that he did most of his work in the Caribbean in the ten years that followed. But the fact of Guyana's independence and the independence of other states in the Caribbean did not blur Ramphal's vision of a united West Indies; indeed, the realities of independence strengthened it. As early as 1971, he was saying to Caribbean peoples as much as to their Governments:

> Side by side with the psychological lift that the new status has given and the new opportunities for practical change it has provided, comes the acknowledgement, however reluctant, that decolonisation is not enough; that the reality of independence derives not from constitutions but from strength; that while it is good to possess the right of choice, it profits us little when we are faced with barren options – when both our freedom of choice and our range of choice are conditioned by external forces which we are powerless individually to influence, much less to control... we may have to contribute sovereignty in order to gain economic independence.[4]

Over the period 1968 to 1975, Ramphal became what Eric Williams called a "labourer in the vineyard"[5] of West Indian integration and the Caribbean Chapters of this book record his urgings for deeper integration arrangements. They record as well the progress that was made on many fronts, particularly in the course of collective self-reliance which governments adopted with a view to securing larger gains from their own production and better returns from their external economic relations. In 1968, the Caribbean Free Trade Area (CARIFTA) was established and from it grew the Caribbean Community and Common Market (CARICOM) in 1973.[6]

Ramphal never ceased his advocacy of political unity in the West Indies. In 1971, with the Grenada Declaration, he came close to actually securing a process for establishing "a new state in the Caribbean", starting with Guyana and five of the island states but directed towards "creating a West Indian nation of which all the people of the West Indies may one day be a part".[7] But, as in that case, he was not always successful in persuading governments to take the practical steps which would lead Caribbean countries to nationhood.

R.S.

Notes and References

1. *British Guiana in War-Time: A Bi-Montly Wartime Series,* Vol. 1, No. 3, 15 August 1941.

2. *Infra,* p. 90.

3. W. Arthur Lewis, Epilogue in John Mordecai, *The West Indies: The Federal Negotiations* (Allen and Unwin Ltd., London, 1968), p. 461.

4. *Infra,* p. 96.

5. Inscription in the personal presentation copy of Eric Williams, *Columbus to Castro: The History of the Caribbean 1492-1969,* (Andre Deutsch, London, 1972).

6. The Caribbean Community and Common Market (CARICOM) was established by the Treaty of Chaguramas on 4 July 1973.

7. From the preamble to the Grenada Declaration which appears in this volume as Appendix A.

Why Federation Failed

Shridath Ramphal was actually engaged in the drafting of the Independence Constitution of The West Indies – the Federation of The West Indies that was to become independent on 31 May 1962 – when the Federation collapsed and the West Indian territories opted for independence on a separate basis. Fourteen years later, on 10 May 1976, Ramphal was invited to give the keynote address at an International Conference on Federalism held in Lagos as Nigeria sought out the appropriate constitutional forms of what was to be the short-lived Third Republic. In his address, 'Federalism for Nigeria', he drew heavily on his West Indian experience in highlighting the conditions needed for federalism to succeed.

The Americans have long ago registered patents for federalism. Certainly, many a constitution has been inspired by the federal traditions of the United States, and the maturing of federalism throughout the many lands that have adopted it owes an immeasurable debt to the American experience of nearly 200 years of the working of the Constitution of 1787. It is worthwhile recalling, however – and as a West Indian myself I may perhaps be forgiven for recalling it – that almost a century before the Philadelphia Constitution, federalism was already influencing experiments in governmental organisations in the Western hemisphere – in the scattered Leeward Islands of the Caribbean.

Starting with a consultative body comprising representatives of the various island legislatures, a General Assembly of the Leeward Islands came into being in the 1680s and soon developed the character of a federal council legislating on matters of common concern. Between 1690 and 1705, for example, it passed some fifty-five separate Acts including an organic instrument – an Act of 1705 entitled, in language essentially federalist, "An Act to settle General Councils and General Assemblies for the Charibbee Islands in America and to secure to each particular Islands their own peculiar Laws and Legal Customs".[1] The experiment, however, was brief and by the 1720s the emphasis in legislative activity had shifted back to the separate island Councils – a shift which appears to have coincided with the departure of the Governor who had boldly established the Assembly. Not for the first time in the history of federalism, its fortunes may well have turned on the commitment of the leadership to its efficacy.

The experiment, however, had pointed to the value of federal approaches, and it is interesting that in 1721 the Council of Trade and Plantations in its *Report upon the state of Her Majesty's plantations in America,* should be recommending that the Leeward Islands' precedent should be adopted for the American colonies. "In order", said the Report, "to render the several provinces on the continent of America from Nova Scotia to South Carolina mutually subservient to each other's support, the whole ought to be put under the Governorship of one Lord Lieutenant or Captain-General as is the present practice in the Leeward Islands where each Island has a particular Governor but one General over the whole".[2] It is tempting to speculate how different the history of North America, and perhaps of federalism, might have been had this recommendation been implemented.

Not so long ago, a team of scholars under Tom Franck, working at the Centre for International Studies at New York University, conducted an enquiry into 'the requisites for successful federalism'.[3] They carried out, in effect, a post-mortem on four attempts at regional unification through federalism: the West Indies, East Africa, Malaysia and Rhodesia/Nyasaland. They considered the role played by the Constitution and its formula for dividing power between the centre and the units. They examined the relative importance of such non-constitutional factors as region, culture, language and distribution of resources. They tried to discern the weight to be given to personal and psychological factors: charisma, commitment, friendship, rivalries and personal ambitions. Their findings – which, as careful scholars, they described as "tentative hypotheses" – are illuminating and, in my view, convincing.

The principal cause of failure or partial failure of each of the federations studied was not to be found, they discovered, in an analysis of economic statistics or in an inventory of social, cultural or institutional diversity. It could only be found "in the absence of a sufficient political-ideological commitment to the primary concept or value of federation itself".[4] In each case, this commitment to the federal ideal as a primary goal was shown not to exist at the moment of federation and not to have been generated subsequently.

They found that the presence of certain secondary factors such as a common colonial heritage, a common language, the prospect of complementary economic advantages, were useful, even necessary, but were not sufficient to ensure success. Their value lay in their capacity to engender a common commitment to the primary goal of federalism; in fact, they were not enough to engender or to sustain that commitment. And the analysis pointed also to the fact that if the only commitment is to short-term goals, federal institutions survive only so long as those goals continue to be important; once they are attained, their very achievement – for example, the securing of independence – becomes a factor making for disintegration. Their inference from all this was as follows:

For a federation to be able to resist failure, the leaders, and their followers, must 'feel federal' – they must be moved to think of themselves as one people, with one, common, self-interest – capable, where necessary, of over-riding most other considerations of small-group interest. It is not enough that the units of a potential federation have the same ideal of 'the Good' but that 'the Good' for anyone must be consciously subordinate to or compatible with 'the Good for all'. This, then, is tantamount to an ideological commitment not to federation only as means – such as, for example, a means to gain independence or financial stability, to utilise secondary or tertiary factors – but to federation as an end, as good for its own sake, for the sake of 'answering the summons of history'.[5]

I find the analysis convincing, and its relevance to the Caribbean compelling. Nor is this a phenomenon recently emerged. Over two hundred and fifty years ago, in 1722, Pere Labat, writing about his travels among the islands and states, invoked that identity, so palpable to him, in support of the common destiny to which he saw us all committed as part of an even wider Caribbean. He wrote:

I have travelled everywhere in your sea of the Caribbean from Haiti to Barbados, to Martinique and Guadeloupe, and I know what I am speaking about... You are all together, in the same boat, sailing on the same uncertain sea... citizenship and race unimportant, feeble little labels compared to the message that my spirit brings to me: that of the position and predicament which History has imposed upon you... I saw it first with the dance... the merengue in Haiti, the beguine in Martinique and today I hear, *de mon oreille morte,* the echo of calypsoes from Trinidad, Jamaica, St. Lucia, Antigua, Dominica and the legendary Guiana... It is no accident that the sea which separates your lands makes no difference to the rhythm of your body.[6]

In many ways, those 250 years since Labat sailed the Caribbean should have strengthened the awareness of a common identity and developed among our people an instinct for unity. A common experience of British colonial authority and, in later years, a common struggle for release from it, were conducive to a sense of community. A broadly identical environment, propitious to the flowering of the cultural traditions of its transported people, contributed to the development of a socio-cultural unity. Joint patterns of colonial administration, supportive of a broadly uniform legal and political system, produced in the region a common legal-political framework; transmitted traditions of the rule of law and of parliamentary democracy passed into a West Indian ethos.

But there were other aspects of that common experience – there was another side to the common inheritance. Separatism was the hand-maiden of colonialism in the heyday of empire in the West Indies. Even when administrative convenience dictated to the Colonial Office, as it often did, the case for unified administration, an entrenched plantocracy successfully frustrated innumerable efforts to make federalism a factor in the region's future.[7]

Those separatist forces had to be confronted if colonialism itself was to end. Inevitably, West Indian politicians of the 1930s who were in the vanguard of the movement for constitutional reform sought in political unity the kind of collective strength which hitherto they had lacked in their futile solitary assaults on the colonial system.

The truth is that the West Indian Federation foundered because of the absence of a sufficiently strong and pervasive political commitment to the primary concept or value of federation itself; it foundered because of the absence of an ideological commitment to the concept of West Indian nationhood. The goal was release from colonialism; it had not yet become regional self-determination for the West Indian people. There had not emerged that paramount commitment to federalism as the hand-maiden of nationhood which was essential to the survival of federal institutions.

How to marry expectation with reality, how to create a larger field for ambition, how to overcome the disadvantages of being too small to be heard in a world where silence means stagnation, how to make a real culture and a real unity out of all the richness of our diversity, how to show the world that differences of origin and colour can come together on a level of tolerence and oneness, how to overcome distance and poverty; these are the challenges that federation faces and may meet to make a worthy end.[8]

Thus spoke the most inspired advocate of West Indian federalism, Norman Manley, who might so easily have become the father of the West Indian nation. Yet, when the moment to lead the nation came, political realities at home constrained this great man to stay at home, to decline the mantle of regional leadership and, ultimately, to take his island state to a separate independence.

This is not to say that identity and commitment cannot grow. In most of the great federations that, indeed, has been the process. The American colonists began with great advantages. John Jay, later to become the first Chief Justice of the United States, perhaps described them best:

Providence has been pleased to give this one connected country to one united people – a people descended from the same ancestors, speaking the same language, professing the same religion, attached to the same principles of government, very similar in their manner and customs, and who, by their joint counsels, aims and efforts, fighting side by side through a long and bloody war, have nobly established general liberty and independence.[9]

It was a blessing, however, as the Franck Study has pointed out, that their union, even in the imperfect form of the Confederation, came into being immediately before separate sovereignties had time to crystallise and the memories of the common strugle began to fade. It is true that most of those whom the Founding Fathers described, perhaps euphemistically, as "We, the people of the United States" would not at the time, if asked their country or nation, have answered 'American'; but rather 'Carolinian', 'Virginian', 'Pennsylvanian', 'New Yorker' or 'New Englander'; but it is equally true that out of their sense of community and, more especially, their recent comradeship in struggle, they were committed to becoming Americans – and their leaders passionately so.[10]

It is that kind of general consensus about nationhood that must exist at the time of the federal compact or develop quickly thereafter. That is the real pre-requisite for the success of federalism. And it is a consensus that must be sustained if it is not to be weakened by the pulls of separatism or by the opposite forces of a nationalism that demands unity not in federalism but in union. No one has better expressed this than Pierre Trudeau of Canada, writing some time before the mantle of leadership was placed upon him, but programming, as he did so, a philosophy by which he lived in office:

> It is, of course, obvious that a national consensus will be developed in this way only if the nationalism is emotionally acceptable to all important groups within the nation. Only blind men could expect a consensus to be lasting if the national flag or the national image is merely the reflection of one part of the nation, if the sum of values to be protected is not defined so as to include the language or the cultural heritage of some very large and tightly knit minority, if the identity to be arrived at is shattered by a colour-bar. The advantage as well as the peril of federalism is that it permits the development of a regional consensus based on regional values; so federalism is ultimately bound to fail if the nationalism it cultivates is unable to generate a national image which has immensely more appeal than the regional ones.[11]

These are all real issues on which Canada has taken courageous decisions designed to sustain the national consensus and preserve Canadian federalism.

It is said that most marriages last if they survive the first seven years. I do not know the comparative statistics for federations; but the principle is the same – the early years are the most testing ones. Whether it be seven or seventeen or seventy years that federalism needs to secure nationhood, it is in those formative years of nation-building, while the institutions of federalism develop strength and character and while the people of the federation enlarge their commitment to federalism itself and drive the foundations of their nationalism deep into it, that federalism stands most in need of protection against secessionist dangers. But these dangers are compounded, and the threat immeasurably enlarged, by two very different factors relevant to many of the federal experiments of the post-war era – the democratic system and pervasive poverty.

It is idle to pretend that societies do not pay a price for democracy. For most of us it is one willingly paid; but it is foolhardy not to count the cost and to seek to minimise it. And this cost is greatly heightened when the new federal democracy is a developing country counted among the world's poor; for poverty reduces, and sometimes denies altogether, the capacity of the federal state to sustain conditions propitious to consensus. Poverty of these dimensions, although largely irreducible through national programmes only, nevertheless quickly breeds discontent and disaffection which sooner or later develop a focus directed to federalism itself. In the new federal state committed to democratic institutions and embattled by siege conditions of under-development and poverty, the search for solutions to social, political and economic problems all too readily turns to separatism; the right of dissent all too easily finds expression in secessionist movements threatening the new state with disintegration into as many fragments as there are ambitious individuals – or, at least, as there are disaffected groups susceptible to their manipulations. To minimise these dangers and to guard federalism through these early years must be a primary charge not merely upon the institutions of federalism once they have been established, but upon those who plan for them.

One approach to this problem is consciously to seek to build into the political commitment to federalism, as part of the ethos of nationhood, the acceptance that political differences and dissatisfactions do not provide justification for the disruption of federalism itself. A start can be made by renouncing a facile romanticism that automatically equates secessionist movements with the pursuit of self-determination and makes a consequential appeal to the Charter of the United Nations. It needs to be recalled and articulated that Resolution 1514(xv) on the Granting of Independence to Colonial Territories and Peoples specifically enjoins that:

> Any attempt aimed at the partial or total disruption of the national unity and the territorial integrity of a country is incompatible with the purposes and principles of the Charter of the United Nations.[12]

Self-determination in the context of the Charter and of the Resolution (which delineates the work of the Committee of 24) is concerned with the process of decolonisation – it is not directed to the disruption of new states through the facilitation of processes of fragmentation. Nor am I convinced that Resolution 2625(xxv) on the Principles Governing Friendly Relations Between States [13] carries this matter further.

I have ventured to put the case for the rejection of an automatic linkage between secession and self-determination rather higher than some may expect to find it. But if federalism is, indeed, one of the instruments for enlarging the capacity of new states, whether absolutely or relatively poor, to survive in a world in which old, and large, and relatively rich states, are themselves integrating for survival, we must enlarge the prospects of federalism by miniaturising the potential of separatism for endangering it through too ready an appeal to secession. This is not to resile from the obligation to sustain a national consensus for federalism; it is to ensure that the dialogue, even the argumentation, by which it is sustained does not easily threaten the national integrity – does not endanger, *ab initio,* the primary political commitment to federalism itself.

And this brings me to my final and related point; which is that the principles of federalism are constantly becoming more relevant to our global society as interdependence passes from mere perception to an international actuality. The truth is that the acknowledged 'non-system' of our current global international structure makes it necessary for us to develop new approaches (as well as, perhaps, new structures) responsive to our insights of interdependence. We may, indeed, require a system capable of maintaining the unifying philosophy of 'one world', yet accommodating and giving voice to that world's complexities. We may need, in fact, as has already been suggested in the context of a new world development system, an international order which would follow a federal model operating on multiple levels and locating decision-making and operational responsibilities as close as possible to regional levels. It is an order which, building on the realities of regionalism, would draw inspiration from federalism itself.

Notes and References

1. *Acts of the Assembly of the Charibee Leeward Islands, (1692-1730)* No. 28 of 1705. Also, S.S. Ramphal 'The West Indies: The Constitutional Background to Federation', *Public Law,* Summer, 1959 (London), pp. 128-151.

2. Council of Trade and Plantations, *Report upon the state of His Majesty's Plantations on the Continent of America,* 1721 (CO324/10), p. 429.

3. Thomas M Franck, Gisbert H Flanz, Herbert J Spiro and Frank N Trager: *Why Federations Fail: An Inquiry into the Requisites for Successful Federalism* (Studies in Peaceful Change No. 1, Center for International Studies, New York University, New York, 1968).

4. Ibid., pp. 173-174.

5. Ibid., p. 177.

6. Gordon K Lewis, *The Growth of the Modern West Indies* (MacGibbon and Kee, London, 1968), p. 46 quoting Pere Labat, from F Jean-Baptiste Labat, *Nouveau Voyage aux Iles de*

l'Amerique (Theodore Le Gras, Paris, 1722). An English edition of Pere Labat's work is the Translated and Abridged edition by John Eaden as *The Memoirs of Pere Labat 1693-1705* (Frank Cass and Co Ltd, London, 1970).

7. S.S. Ramphal, op. cit., p. 133.

8. S.S. Ramphal, 'Federalism in the West Indies', (1960) 6 Nos. 2 and 3 *Caribbean Quarterly,* p. 229 quoting Norman Manley.

9. James Madison, Alexander Hamilton and John Jay, *The Federalist Papers* (Belknap Press, Cambridge, 1961), No. II, p. 91.

10. Franck, Flanz, Spiro and Trager, op. cit., p. 185.

11. Pierre Elliott Trudeau, 'Federalism, Nationalism, and Reason' in *Federalism and the French Canadians* (Macmillan, Toronto, 1968), p. 193.

12. UNGA Resolution 1514 (xv), 14 December 1960, para. 6.

13. UNGA Resolution 2625 (xxv), 24 October 1970.

Nationhood:
Myth, Mirage or Mandate?

By 1971, the Caribbean regional integration movement was well advanced. Ramphal had played central roles in its progress – in conceptualising, drafting, negotiating: all his contributions underpinned by a passionate belief in the compulsions of West Indian nationhood. He argued strongly the need to respond to these demands of political unity in opening a series of public lectures on 'Caribbean Perspectives', sponsored by the Institute of International Relations of the University of the West Indies in Port-of-Spain, Trinidad, on 20 May 1971. His warning against 'the danger of fragmentation' and his pleas for 'the creation of machinery for regional peace-keeping' and 'the dismantling of separatism' have continued to have practical significance to the Caribbean.

The London Conference of 1961 had selected 31 May 1962 as the date for the Independence of The West Indies.[1] Even as we ended that cheerless Conference, we were conscious that it was an independence that might never dawn; and so, indeed, it transpired; for that last day of May in 1962, which should have seen the beginning of the new West Indian nation – was to be the last day of the dissolved Federation. Hard on the heels of the dissolution (on 6 August 1962) – some thought indecently soon after the funeral rites –

Jamaica embraced independence. Less than a month after (on 31 August 1962) Trinidad and Tobago, pursuing an inexorable subtraction,[2] followed suit. Four years later – years marked by bitterness and lost opportunity – Barbados moved on to independence (on 30 November 1966), leaving the Leeward and Windward Islands to an uncertain and problematical constitutional end. Just six months before Barbados' independence, my own country, Guyana, which had chosen to stand aside from the Federal experiment, with that smugness which is often the mask of indecision, itself moved on to independence (on 26 May 1966) – estranged in no small measure from the Caribbean it had deserted. Belize, meanwhile, was steadily proceeding towards self-determination, bearing on its back the burden of an intractable boundary dispute; and the Commonwealth of The Bahamas had itself begun to move toward truly representative Government and a new West Indian identification.

The constitutional scene of the 1970s is thus a complete transformation of that in which federalism had emerged in the 1950s as the possible answer to improbable local self-government. The island nationalisms that had been burgeoning since the 1930s and that ultimately destroyed the Federation in their assertiveness, have found fulfilment in the independence of the larger states. In the Leeward and Windward Islands what was attainable on an island basis was, of course, less than immediate independence, and found expression in the phenomenon of Associated Status.[3] But it was characteristic of the prevailing mood that this new constitutional form should have been widely celebrated throughout the region as the achievement of self-determination; indeed, in one state, it was officially proclaimed as "Independence in Association".[4] The Bahamas is now poised for independence in its more conventional form; as, also, is Belize.[5] In each case it is a matter of timing; and the timing is in the hands of the local leadership.

It may be the case that West Indian unity can only emerge

in an effective and permanent form out of conscious sacrifice; and that, therefore, it cannot be achieved in these terms until that autonomy which must in part be sacrificed is itself secured. Perhaps, this was why a federated West Indies which was accepted in Montego Bay in 1948,[6] when it seemed to be the only means of satisfying the local national ambition, was no longer supportable in 1961 when it could be presented as frustrating that narrower nationalism. Now it is all different. What was attainable as separate states has been achieved. We have been equipped with the conventional form of independence. We have acquired what Professor Gordon Lewis calls "the paraphernalia of sovereignty",[7] and have done the fashionable and the necessary things. And to a substantial degree this is as true of the Associated States as it is of the rest of us.

To the extent, therefore, that we have needed the psychological reassurance of independence before creating that unity which Norman Manley so perceptively described as "a wider field for ambition",[8] that need has been fulfilled. Our flags, our anthems testify to our independence. Our votes in the United Nations, our separate Embassies abroad, proclaim our sovereignty, as they do our separateness, Hereafter, the decisions are our own and we alone shall be responsible for the regional implications of those decisions that we take – as we alone shall be responsible for the local implications of those decisions that we fail to take. To those who accept a Freudian analysis of the failure of federalism in the 1960s, we can present today a new West Indies released from the inhibitions of a thwarted island nationalism and well equipped, or at least better equipped, to adjust to the need for a more mature West Indian nationhood. The psychological environment of the West Indies of today must, to this extent, be more propitious for the growth of an effective and a lasting unity and the acceptance of a regional identity based upon it.

The next factor which I see as contributing toward West Indian nationhood is the actual experience of independence and of Associated Status. How satisfying, other than in psychological terms, has been the new status? There has been, of course, a substantial area of satisfaction. The processes of nation-building, which have been at work throughout the region and which have given the West Indian a new spirit of self-reliance and fostered a new confidence and self-respect, could never have been invoked save through the forms of self-determination. Whatever may be our particular asessments of the pace and quality of change, no West Indian will seriously deny that important advances have been made in the social, political and economic fields in the post-independence period in all our states, and that they would never have been made under colonial auspices.

But the new status has made a contribution of another, almost opposite, kind; it has dispelled the illusion that self-determination, by whatever name called, provides a magic key to a better life for our people. Side by side with the psychological lift that the new status has given and the new opportunities for practical change it has provided, comes the acknowledgement, however reluctant, that decolonisation is not enough; that the reality of independence derives not from constitutions but from strength; that while it is good to possess the right of choice, it profits us little when we are faced with barren options – when both our freedom of choice and our range of choice are conditioned by external forces which we are powerless individually to influence, much less to control, and which we would be foolhardy to ignore. It is ironic that having fragmented to satisfy a primal instinct for freedom, independence in isolation has served to emphasise our need of each other. It is a paradox that we may have to contribute sovereignty in order to gain economic independence.

An indispensable attribute of nationhood is the capability to maintain the state intact against forces making for fragmentation and to maintain within the state peace and lawful government. I do not speak, of course, of a capability for repression or even imply qualification of the right of dissent. Protest movements anywhere have less to fear from a strong democracy than from a weak oligarchy. What I speak of is that capability which is essential if states are not to degenerate into anarchy or disintegrate into fragments. This is why today what stands in the way of the exercise of the option for independence by each Associated State is more often an unspoken anxiety about the needs of internal security rather than of external defence. And are these considerations not relevant even to the independent states?

In Caribbean countries, as in every democratic state, there will always be political dissatisfaction with the policies of governments. But the geography of the Caribbean introduces two special factors. In the first place, it increases the probability that separate communities – particularly island communities within multi-island states – will have peculiar areas of dissatisfaction. In the second place, it makes it more likely that these differences will exert fissiparous tendencies as they become more acute. In an archipelago, the search for solutions to political problems all too readily turns to separatism and finds expression in secessionist movements. To minimise these tendencies and to prevent the further fragmentation of the region must surely be a primary responsibility of our time. The Wooding Commission on Anguilla has rendered a valuable service by drawing attention to the consequences of further fragmentation in the region. It is good to remember what they said:

> Fragmentation would make the subversion of lawful authority on any one island easier; it would make the preservation of its sovereignty more difficult; and it would make the task of providing an acceptable standard of living for the population of the islands beyond the capacity of most. Moreover, the West Indian territories are geographically within easy reach of the great and expanding economic giants of the American mainland and for this reason are exposed to the risk of being overwhelmed by them and so losing the opportunity for political and economic self-fulfilment. This risk is increased when tiny islands, lacking the resources to support even administrative structures capable of meeting their own needs, seek to create or maintain an independent existence.[9]

The Commission recorded the manifest concern over fragmentation and its consequences that they found among the governments of the region. But they also found that this expression of concern had not yet been followed by determined efforts to guard against the consequences. Unless Commissions of Inquiry into secessionist attempts are to become an annual ritual in the Caribbean, it is time that we undertook such efforts and pursued them with resolution. In doing so, let me suggest two pre-requisites to success. First, a regional acknowledgement that political differences and dissatisfactions do not provide justification for the overthrow of lawful government or for the disintegration of states through unconstitutional action. This is the area of ideas. Governments, political parties, groups involved in public affairs and the people of the Caribbean generally must articulate the concept so that it becomes a part of the political ethic of the region.

The second pre-requisite is that, within the region and available to every state, must be the means by which the violent or otherwise unconstitutional overthrow of governments, whether through secessionist movements or otherwise, can be prevented. This calls for the creation of machinery of practical co-operation in matters of security. In short, it calls for the creation of machinery for regional peacekeeping. If it be the case, as I suggest it to be, that it would impose an intolerable burden on the Associated States to carry separately a physical capability necessary for the maintenance of the state's territorial integrity, the only alternatives are recourse to assistance from outside the region in times of extremity and crisis or regional security machinery. The former is, of course, not a real alternative, for such assistance will always carry with it the stigma, and the danger, of external interference. But by the same token, if we reject that course and do nothing about assembling a regional alternative, we merely pander to the forces of fragmentation and invite the dethronement of constitutionalism in the Caribbean.

It is, I suppose, conceivable, although it will surely be

extremely difficult, for regional security machinery of the kind I have mentioned to be created on the basis of our present separatist political arrangements. What is obvious is that such machinery will function best if assembled under the roof of regional political unity; if, in fact, it were seen as one of the attributes of Caribbean nationhood.

One of the impediments to progress toward integration is the absence of an ideological commitment to regionalism. But the difficulties encountered also have their origins in the realities of separatism. These realities are forever contending for supremacy over the needs of regionalism and eroding our regional commitments as fast as they are made. There is only so much that can represent a common factor of advantage in regional arrangements. Beyond that point, and if commitment to regionalism is to prevail, we shall have to dismantle the realities of separatism.

We cannot reach our goals of integration, much less of nationhood, if each of us must weigh every regional enterprise in the scales of local self-interest. It is not, for example, that an 'open skies' policy may not promote the local interests of a particular island; it is that what will best serve the interest of the West Indian community should prevail. It is not whether an enlargement of the Free Trade Area would not assist industrial expansion in another; it is that what maximises the benefits of free trade for the entire region and advances us to our agreed objectives should predominate. But so long as our governmental structures are separatist so long will most governments feel obliged to make local self-interest the touchstone of regional action.

I submit that the time is at hand to explore all the possibilities of achieving a realistic West Indian nationhood. In our perspectives for the Caribbean let us fix on the horizon, as a distant light that beckons us, the Republic of the West Indies. Let this be our vision of the future. Some will say that our three hundred years of inconclusive association establishes West Indian nationhood as a part of our mythology – a myth in the folklore of the Caribbean.

Others, grown cynical with the frustrations of the past and the particular disillusionment of the federal experiment, will urge that it is no more than a mirage, a unity that will forever be in sight but yet ever out of reach.

I suggest to you that West Indian nationhood can be both real and attainable and that to make it so has become a mandate of history to our generation. To the carrying out of that mandate we must bend our energies now – without dogma, without preconditions, without unalterable formulae, without non-negotiable positions, with a willingness to search for the right means, with patience in persuasion and with tolerance where we fail to persuade, but with a clear and unyielding commitment to the creation of a West Indian nation.

Notes and References

1. *Report of the West Indies Constitutional Conference,* 1961,held in London, May and June 1961 (Cmnd. 1417) p. 18.

2. Eric Williams' reaction to the Jamaica referendum result: 'Ten minus one equals zero'; cited in John Mordecai *The West Indies: The Federal Negotiations,* (Allen and Unwin Ltd., London 1968), pp. 426-427.

3. Between 1974 and 1983 each of the six Associated States, and the Leeward and Windward Islands moved to full independence.

4. V.C. Bird, Premier of Antigua, 1 February 1967, at the official declaration of Associated Statehood.

5. The Bahamas became independent on 10 July 1973 and Belize on 21 September 1981.

6. *Conference on the Closer Association of the British West Indian Colonies, Montego Bay, Jamaica, 11th-19th September 1947 Part I: Report* (Cmnd. 7291).

7. Gordon K. Lewis, *The Growth of the Modern West Indies* (MacGibbon and Kee, London, 1968), p. 46.

8. S.S. Ramphal, 'Federalism in the West Indies', (1960) 6 Nos. 2 and 3 *Caribbean Quarterly,* p. 229 quoting Norman Manley.

9. *Report of the Commission of Enquiry appointed by the Governments of the United Kingdom and St. Christopher-Nevis-Anguilla to examine the Anguilla Problem* (Chairman: H.O.B. Wooding, Q.C.), November 1970 (Cmnd.4510), p. 57.

The Case for Political Unity

On 16 November 1971 Shridath Ramphal addressed the Caribbean Ecumenical Consultation for Development in Port-of-Spain, Trinidad on the theme of regional unity and the search for a West Indian identity. Earlier that year, the 'Grenada Declaration'[1] had been signed holding out the prospect of a new unified state in the Eastern Caribbean. That prospect was not to be realised; but, Ramphal's reflections in 1971 are among the strongest pleas voiced in the post-independence period for West Indian political union.

I am of the English-speaking states of the emerging Caribbean – of what has come to be called the Commonwealth Caribbean – of what I prefer to regard as the West Indies. For me, the West Indies is the immediate Caribbean; it is the region that comprises the four independent states of Jamaica, Trinidad and Tobago, Guyana and Barbados, the six Associated States of Antigua, Dominica, Grenada, St. Kitts-Nevis-Anguilla, St. Lucia and St. Vincent, the territories of Montserrat and the Virgin Islands and Belize, The Bahamas, the Turks and Caicos and the Cayman Islands. That is what we call the Commonwealth Caribbean – their people are the West Indians of whom I speak. The search for identity in that Caribbean is for me a search for collective strength through unity and for unity through brotherhood and enlightened nationalism.

I start with the premise that the realities of survival on the basis of both political and economic independence, that is survival with self-respect, makes it essential for us to acquire collective strength both politically and economically; that this can only be secured through unity with those nearest to us who recognise a similar need; and that our best prospect of achieving such a unity lies with the countries of the English-speaking Caribbean with whom we already share such a large measure of kinship. Accordingly, it is of this search for identity among the English-speaking peoples of the Caribbean that I speak.

What is there that denies us that over-arching identity which Croat and Serb have found in Yugoslav nationalism, that Walloon and Fleming have found in Belgium, that the Welsh and Scot and English have found in the United Kingdom? In each case, the differing ethnic or linguistic groups had in the beginning, and in some still have, far less in common than the peoples of any two West Indian states. Indeed, in most cases, they had a turbulent history of conflict or of deep dissension. In all of the societies such differences have left their mark on the social, political or even economic scene; but in each, their members have managed to sublimate the differences to an overriding national identity.

What is there that has impeded so natural and so necessary a development in the West Indies? One truth is that, until recently, the people of the West Indies have had no part in the decision-making processes that controlled the consummation of a national identity. It was not surprising that the movement for political unity that emerged in the 1930s was led by West Indian politicians, who saw in the collective strength it would provide an answer to the frustrations they faced in their solitary assaults on the colonial system. The generation of Marryshow, Cipriani and Rawle might, indeed, have led the Eastern Caribbean to nationhood had the wind of change begun to stir even faintly through the corridors of the Colonial Office fifteen years before it did.

It fell to another generation to pursue nationhood through unity; but, by then, the wind had, in fact, begun to blow, and self-determination on a separatist basis was no longer unattainable or even improbable – it was available for the asking. We should never forget that what made the referendum in Jamaica possible was Ian MacLeod's assurance to Norman Manley that independence would be available to Jamaica if, in the referendum, the people of Jamaica answered "no" to Federation. And, in the end, despite all the economic, social and political justifications, three hundred years of separatist existence proved too formidable an opponent to the consummation of a regional identity – once nationhood was possible without it.

Manley's referendum gamble, the revelation by Eric William's Government that '1' from '10' leaves '0' not '9', and the decision by Errol Barrow's Government to break off the dialogue for the 'Federation of the Eight', were, in a sense, the last major decisions of West Indian leaders during the colonial period. The identity of their implications for West Indian unity, to which each asserted a commitment, is truly remarkable. Yet history may come to see them not as decisions against regionalism or in rejection of a West Indian identity, but as agonising decisions for self-determination on an island basis which, while declining consummation of a regional identity through political union, nonetheless specifically avoided repudiation of that identity. Inevitably, however, those decisions threw up barriers, of a political nature for governments and of a psychological nature for people, in the path of the continuing pursuit of a West Indian identity to its logical conclusion. Some of these impediments still remain, although less so in the Eastern Caribbean than elsewhere in the region.

But the coin of independence has another side which exposes the harsh realities of independent existence in a world in which nations remain motivated by the pursuit of national self-interest and which increasingly has little time or place for fractional communities. Self-determination may guarantee the forms of political independence and may invest the new state with the trappings of equal international status; but it does not take the new states long to recognise that the *modus operandi* of the international system deprives these guarantees of much of their practical content; that political independence is a shibboleth without economic strength and economic independence, and that equality of status, even in the United Nations, is more formal than real save on those rare occasions when important issues are decided not by consensus of the major powers but by votes of the Assembly – and, even then, small states vote under peril of reprisals. And so it is that that very independence which was the occasion for the dismantling of West Indian unity now provides its own compulsion for its reinstatement.

In all the circumstances, it is hardly surprising that efforts to strengthen West Indian unity at several levels have been pursued with increasing momentum in recent years. Essentially, they have taken the form of efforts to promote a programme of West Indian economic integration through a Free Trade Area, a Development Bank and a Regional Secretariat. CARIFTA, with its Agricultural Marketing Protocol, and the Caribbean Development Bank were established to increase the options for development of all their member states – now the entire English-speaking Caribbean from Belize in the West through Jamaica and the Eastern Caribbean states to Guyana in the South. Both institutions proceeded on the acknowledgement that their member states possessed a community of interests and were prepared, through programmes of economic integration, to advance the development and prosperity of the entire region – placing priority on the urgent needs of the Associated States.

It is already clear, however, that not all have entered these institutions with the same level of commitment to the objectives of integration or with the same readiness to give as well as to get. The result is that the integration programme is gradually being forced into a cul-de-sac where we shall all mark time at the stage of internal free trade. We shall not advance to the goal of an economic community without agreeing on a rational policy towards foreign investment which will harmonise fiscal incentives policies; on a rational approach to the location and regional integration of industries which will spread the benefits of industrialisation around the region; on a rational policy towards agriculture which will make our production complementary instead of competitive; on a common external tariff through which we can deal as an economic unit with the rest of the world.[2]

If we fail to agree on all these, or even to commit ourselves to them, there is, indeed, a danger – and it is a real and pressing danger – that we may not only fail to achieve our objectives but also, through protracted and increasingly angry argumentation, impair that measure of identity which was our starting point. We need to remember this when critics of attempts to advance the case for political unity urge us to proceed instead with economic integration – mindful as they must be of the impediments to progress in this direction. I submit that the demands of economic integration reinforce the case for political unity; that the realities of separatism and the political constraints which they place on regional decision-making require us to evolve appropriate forms of political unity or face the erosion of the institutions of mutual assistance we have so far established.

But there is another reason why the search for West Indian identity must be pursued to its logical conclusion with increasing urgency. The demand for social and economic change reverberates through all our West Indian states. It is a demand for social equality and for economic justice; it is a legitimate demand; it is a demand that arises out of disaffection with the established order and out of resentment of its many inequities. It is, therefore, a demand that we must be prepared to meet and must be capable of meeting effectively; and it is at this level of effective response that it poses the challenge of nationhood.

The demand is bound up with such questions as ownership and control of West Indian resources – whether they be on or beneath our soils or in or below the waters adjacent to our coasts; our right to be more than primary producers for the industrialised societies of the world; our access to world markets on just bases; the terms of bilateral and multilateral aid in redress of our legacy of under-development. I contend that only through a West Indian identity that has found fulfilment in political unity – in a unity that places decision-making, at least in our dealings with the outside world, in a single regional entity – can we maximise our all too slender chances of meeting the demands for change that lie behind the protest movements of the region, including, as they do, the demands for employment and a better quality of life. I take it to be axiomatic, although it seems to be all too frequently forgotten, that a West Indian identity that does not stand on a regional base of social equality and economic justice does not rest on sure foundations and will not survive the stress of internal social upheaval and the shifting sands of uneven regional development.

This means, of course, that the movement for political unity will meet with resistance. It will meet with resistance from two sources mainly – both opposed to constructive change, although for very different reasons. It will meet with resistance, first of all, from the blind reactionaries; and it will meet with resistance from the blinkered revolutionaries. The resistance of both is not peculiar to the West Indies nor even to our generation. Nearly two hundred years ago a great West Indian who made his contribution to the political union of another society – Alexander Hamilton[3] – had issued in the very first of the *Federalist Papers* a similar warning to his compatriots in relation to the federal experiment on which they were embarking:

> Among the most formidable of the obstacles which the new constitution will have to encounter may readily be distinguished the obvious interest of a certain class of men in every state, to resist all changes which may hazard a diminution of the power, emolument and consequence of the offices they hold under the state establishments; and the perverted ambition of another class of men, who will either

hope to aggrandise themselves by the confusions of their country, or will flatter themselves with fairer prospects of elevation from the sub-division of the empire into several partial confederates, than from its union under one government.[4]

Many who have a vested interest in the *status quo* and have not the vision to recognise that it must change, and that it is right that it should, will deplore movement toward political unity, will seek to intimidate the community by imaginary or exaggerated dangers which they will claim to be inherent in it, will ascribe false and calumnious motives to its proponents, and, through manipulation of such elements of the communications media as they control, will foster fear and resentment of these developments among the people of the region. These are substantial opponents, and the burden of contending with them must rest primarily upon the political leadership. If that leadership lacks commitment to political unity, it will lack resolution in standing firm before these critics. But the victories which this irresolution brings will be short-lived; for the voices crying out for change will not be stilled. Protests will grow louder and the forms of protests will, in the end, sweep all before them – critics and supine governments alike – and, through chaos and anarchy, set back the progress which unity should have helped to yield.

There will be critics, too, on the other side; critics whose business is contention, who batten on the social and economic injustice of our societies and who lose their capacity for revolutionary posturing when the processes of change redress those wrongs. These, too, will criticise. They will worry about the new strength that unity should provide – for they function most successfuly in societies that are weak.

And there is a third category of critics for whom we must be prepared – those from within the family who have chosen not to pursue their West Indian identity to the point of political union. It is sadly the case that not all such states will be willing to say, like some: "You have our blessing, brothers. We cannot join you now. Proceed with your great enterprise. We hope one day to dwell among you." Uncertainty all too often prompts states, like people, to denigrate developments from which they have freely chosen to stand aside as if, still questioning their judgement, they need further justification for declining to exercise the option to partake. And so our brothers who do not join us, or at least some of them, may be uncharitable in these ways.

How can these obstacles be overcome so that we may pursue our search for a West Indian identity to its logical end in nationhood?

First, I submit, we must have a commitment to the primary political ideal at the level of the political leadership, a commitment to the ideal of nationhood, and a capability on the part of that leadership to generate that commitment throughout our communities.

Secondly, we must be ready to act in pursuit of that commitment along with those within the region who share that commitment and resolution. But, in so acting, we must make it clear that we proceed on no basis of divisiveness or of exclusion and that we seek to build a mansion wherein all West Indians may dwell.

Thirdly, while ready to pause in the interest of a wider unity and tireless in pursuit of consensus, we must be wary of the tactics of filibuster which seek to deprive advance of its momentum.

Fourthly, while it is the responsibility of governments to initiate action, it is essential that the people of the region shall not merely be fully informed but fully involved in the processes of decision-making on the forms of political unity.

Fifthly, it must be our responsibility to ensure that those forms of unity do not merely institutionalise social inequality and economic injustice but improve our capability to redress them and provide machinery that will make an obligation to do so effective.

Sixthly, in our search for the forms of political unity, let us be uninhibited by traditional federal stereotypes. The uniqueness of our situation may well demand new techniques and new constitutional forms. And let us not think only in terms of super-structures, for we may well have to dismantle before we can rebuild.

Finally, let us have confidence in ourselves as we proceed with this creative task whose beginning awaits only our resolution.

Notes and References

1. The text of the Declaration as amended by Signatory Caribbean Heads of Government in November 1971 is reproduced at Appendix A.

2. See, generally, *The Caribbean Community in the 1980s,* Report by a Group of Caribbean Experts, (Commonwealth Caribbean Regional Secretariat, Georgetown, 1981).

3. Born in Nevis, in 1757, Hamilton left the Caribbean when a boy of 15 and went to New York where he served during the War of Independence as a Captain. A mere eight years after leaving the West Indies, at 23 (1780) he was expressing the conviction that the Articles of the Confederation needed drastic overhaul in the direction of strong central authority. He became a champion of federal union, joint author of the *Federalist Papers* and one of the architects of the American Constitution.

4. James Madison, Alexander Hamilton and John Jay *The Federalist Papers,* (Belknap Press, Cambridge, 1961), No. 1, p. 87.

It is a token of the importance we have attached to the consultations which begin today that I and my colleagues from the Caribbean and the Pacific states should have come from across the oceans to be with you in Dar es Salaam... we are here because we have shared with Africa a history of European colonialism – a colonialism that, in its beginnings, took us from Africa and Asia to a Caribbean designed and organised to contribute to the wealth of Europe. It was a shared experience born out of kinship with Africa and Asia.

*Shridath Ramphal**

Chapter 3

A Wider Unity

Perspective III   112

Building ACP Unity   116
(Georgetown, 1975)

A New Relationship with Europe   122
(Brussels, 1973)

The Challenge of Unity   131
(Dar es Salaam, 1973)

Lomé: A Promise to be Fulfilled   135
(Lomé, 1975)

* Addressing the Conference of African Trade Ministers, Dar es Salaam, Tanzania, 1 October 1973.

Perspective III

The Caribbean Community (CARICOM) was inaugurated in August 1973 – a high point of Caribbean regional integration. At almost the same time, the dialogue began between the European Community and African, Caribbean and Pacific countries that would lead to the Lomé Convention. That conjuncture was to be of great practical significance. Shridath Ramphal was one of the main architects of Caribbean initiatives to develop closer links with other developing countries recognising, as he did at an early stage, that each such "process of unification added a new dimension to the quest of the Third World for economic justice through international action".[1] He was particularly conscious of the impetus which international economic realities gave to Caribbean regional integration and the significance for 'community' in the Caribbean of the far-reaching negotiations with Europe that now lay ahead[2] – ones in which he was to play a critical role.

Britain's accession to the Treaty of Rome in May 1972, giving it membership of the enlarged EEC, caused genuine fears among Commonwealth countries about market access for their products. But by far the most vulnerabe countries were those of Africa, the Caribbean and the Pacific which traditionally had exported most of their products to Britain under tariff preferences or other special arrangements. The Treaty of Accession promised them negotiations with the enlarged Community for a special economic relationship.[3]

Ramphal was convinced that negotiations between separate groups of African, Caribbean and Pacific (ACP) states and the EEC would result in severe disadvantage to the developing countries. A particular problem was the distinction the Europeans sought to sustain between the Francophone 'Associates' grouped under the Yaounde Convention and the Commonwealth 'Associables' covered by the Treaty of Accession. He was troubled, moreover, by the negotiating straight-jacket imposed by the 'options' in Protocol 22 of the Treaty of Accession and EEC overtures for a free trade area arrangement involving 'reciprocal preferences'.[4] In his view, only a united front by all the ACP states would allow such a collection of economic 'Lilliputians' to contain the bargaining power of a European 'Gulliver'.

The task of unification of the ACP began in August 1972 in the Cabinet Office of Guyana's Prime Minister, Forbes Burnham, when Ramphal brought Foreign Ministers from Caribbean and African states from an outdoor reception at the Prime Minister's residence to talk informally about the prospective negotiations with the EEC. The Ministers were in Guyana for the first full Ministerial meeting of the Non-Aligned Movement convened in the Western Hemisphere. Prior to the meeting, Ramphal had told his Caribbean colleagues on the Council of Ministers of the Caribbean Free Trade Association (CARIFTA) that he intended to make use of the occasion to talk with Commonwealth Ministers in the Non-Aligned Group "to see if we can get other people to pool their resources with ours in relation to the negotiations that lie ahead."[5] In the event, the group (eight Caribbean and African Ministers) agreed to co-ordinate their positions and to devise a joint strategy for the negotiations.

One year later, on 26 July 1973, the ACP-EEC Conference opened in Brussels. Much had been achieved by way of a political mandate for the three groups to negotiate a unified relationship; but Shridath Ramphal, as spokesman for the Caribbean group which was spear-heading ACP unity, felt that their fledgeling unity lacked the symbolism of a single spokesman. He convinced his Caribbean colleagues that the demonstrated unity of the ACP group should be "symbolised and formalised" by a single presentation to be made by the Chairman of the African group. The proposal was accepted by the ACP as a whole and, thereafter, the ACP negotiated neither as 46 individual states nor as three regions but as one group with one voice. New ground was broken in international relations as a large section of the developing world, for the first time, took on a powerful group of developed countries and successfully negotiated a comprehensive and innovative regime of economic relations which, in Ramphal's words, "though falling short of the ACP's aspirations, far exceeded the original intention of the EEC".[6]

Shridath Ramphal's last major act in Guyana before leaving to take up the post of Commonwealth Secretary-General in 1975 was to chair a meeting of ACP Ministers whom he had invited to Guyana to discuss the unity of the ACP. The result was the Guyana Accord establishing the ACP as an entity in its own right, separate from the Lomé Convention.

The next Chapter shows the way in which Ramphal helped to forge a unity which has so far endured among African, Caribbean and Pacific states and so secure the promise of important dividends in aid and trade from the EEC under the Lomé Convention. Over the years, the Convention has not fulfilled its full promise, largely because the EEC countries backtracked on the spirit of their commitment to the ACP Group; but the significant achievement remains, namely, that for the first time arrangements between developed and developing countries were "genuinely negotiated rather than unilaterally imposed."[7]

R.S.

Notes and References

1. Shridath Ramphal, Introduction to *The ACP/EEC Negotiations: A Lesson in Third World Unity*, (Guyana, 1975), p.5.

2. Shridath Ramphal, *The Prospect for Community in the Caribbean* (Guyana, 1973), an address at the Royal Commonwealth Society, London, 22 January 1973.

3. For the *Treaty of Accession* see, Cmnd. 4862-I and 4862-II.

4. Shridath Ramphal, Introduction to *The ACP/EEC Negotiations*, op. cit., p. 7.

5. Ibid., p. 5.

6. Shridath Ramphal, 'Rekindling the Spirit of Lomé', *Lomé Briefing*, No. 1, 1983; NGOs to the European Communities, Brussels.

7. Ibid.

Building ACP Unity

In June 1975, before leaving Guyana for London and the Commonwealth Secretariat, Shridath Ramphal set down in an 'Introduction' to a booklet published by the Ministry of Foreign Affairs in Georgetown an account of the process by which the grouping of African, Caribbean and Pacific countries (the ACP) came into being and negotiated the Lomé Convention with the European Community. In many respects, it was the story of a journey from Georgetown to Lomé – one to which he had contributed much. At the journey's end, he was at least as proud of having helped to forge ACP unity as of the result of the negotiations themselves. The account below tells a remarkable story of Third World success in forging and sustaining unity against the odds.

As the 46 ACP states prepare to move from the negotiation of the Lomé Convention to its implementation and development, it may be useful to recall the various stages of the process of unification of the ACP – if only because of their relevance for the programme of sustained unity that must be undertaken if the promise of the Lomé Convention, in terms of both immediate benefit and potential for improvement, is to be fufilled.

At the *ad hoc* discussions in Georgetown in August 1972,[1] it was agreed that a team of Caribbean officials would visit Commonwealth African states for more comprehensive technical discussions. That CARIFTA mission went in September 1972 to East and West Africa, holding talks in Arusha with officials of the East African Community and with their counterparts in Lagos, Accra and Freetown – apprising their colleagues of the preparatory work already being undertaken in the Caribbean. What was clearly needed, however, was concerted action among African states, and at Lagos, Nigeria, in February 1973 a start was made in this direction with a meeting of Commonwealth African Ministers hosted by the Government of Nigeria. It was characterised by a bold and purposeful approach to the questions whether there should be negotiations with the EEC and, if so, on what basis, and with what objectives.

At Lagos, it was agreed that a further meeting of Ministers should be convened in Nairobi to pursue these issues; but, building on the international links forged earlier in 1972, the Lagos meeting authorised a team of Commonwealth African Ministers to visit Georgetown to hold discussions with Caribbean Ministers at CARIFTA headquarters. This meeting, held on 19 March 1973, provided an opportunity for a comprehensive exchange of views on the approach to any negotiations with the EEC and on the essentials of any possible relationship. A refusal to be confined within the negotiating straight-jacket imposed by the 'options' in Protocol 22 to the Treaty of Accession and a determination to resist European overtures for a free trade area arrangement involving 'reciprocal preferences' emerged clearly and with unanimity from these discussions. Caribbean officials were invited to attend the Nairobi meeting as observers and did so in continuation of the inter-regional dialogue that was now fully established.

The Nairobi meeting allowed the governments concerned to further elaborate and refine their approach to the negotiations and it prepared the ground for the next major step forward – namely, a deepening of the dialogue to encompass a political mandate for Africa as a whole to negotiate a unified relationship. Until these developments, the AASM states – the 'Associates' – were preparing for the renegotiation of the Yaounde Convention (due to expire at the end of 1974) and there was a real danger of the perpetuation throughout the negotiations of the separateness – and, indeed, the potential conflict of interest – which the status of 'Associates' and 'Associables' tended to imply and develop.

As these separate preparations unfolded it became clear that a wider African unity was the prerequisite to any effective negotiations with the EEC. This was accomplished at Abidjan, Ivory Coast in May 1973 at a Ministerial meeting convened under the auspices of the OAU. Out of that meeting came a united African approach to the negotiations – an approach founded on the 'eight principles' hammered out as the essential requirements of African states. At Addis Ababa, around the middle of the month, these principles were endorsed by African Heads of State at the Tenth Anniversary Summit Meeting of the OAU. They were to become the cornerstone of the negotiating structure erected by the ACP in Brussels.

All this had taken place against the background of not inconsiderable pressure from the EEC for the urgent commencement of negotiations and for their being channelled into the pre-determined contours of Protocol 22 – contours that themselves tended to highlight distinctions between the 'Associates' and 'Associables'. As it transpired, these divisive 'options' under Protocol 22 (for inclusion in a revised Yaounde Convention, for a separate Arusha-type Convention under Article 138 of the Treaty of Rome, or for a simple Trade Agreement with the Community) were never exercised by the 'Associables' – despite Community mythology to the contrary. What eventually emerged at Lomé was the *sui generis* Agreement for which the ACP initially contended.

At Brussels in July 1973 the first meeting took place between the Ministers of the African, Caribbean and Pacific states and the Ministers of the Community. For the Europeans, it was the beginning of the negotiations; for the

ACP it was 'talks about talks'. But whether it was the one or the other, a much more significant trend was discernible – a trend which the negotiations later confirmed and which had a decisive influence on their outcome. The European statement, relying heavily on generalisation, if not indeed on ambiguity, bore all the marks of internal Community conflict; the ACP statement – three separate statements delivered by spokesmen of Africa ('Associates' and 'Associables' making a single speech), the Caribbean, and the Pacific – revealed clearly perceived objectives and bore all the marks of internal co-ordination and consistency. It was really at that moment of revealed unity that the ACP was conceived; for although the Brussels meetings with the European Council of Ministers had been preceded by a caucus of the 'Associates' and 'Associables' at which a united African group approach had been laboriously worked out, it was the demonstrated effect of unity achieved that provided the catalyst for unity resolved.

From that time onward there was no turning back to separateness. At the next joint ACP/EEC Ministerial Meeting in Brussels in October 1973, the ACP case presented by three voices in July was now urged by one voice – that of the then current Chairman of the African group. This was in response to a specific Caribbean offer that the demonstrated unity of the ACP Group be symbolised and formalised by such a single presentation. Thereafter, throughout the discussions, the ACP never negotiated otherwise than as a group and spoke always with one voice. It was often an African voice, sometimes a Caribbean or a Pacific voice; but always a voice that spoke for the ACP.

Such sustained unity naturally called for immense preparatory work. In large measure, this was done by the ACP Ambassadors in Brussels, meeting in regular session. Their monumental efforts prepared the ground for ACP Ministerial Meetings held successively in Dar es Salaam, Dakar, Kingston and Accra at which ACP positions and approaches were discussed and settled. Kingston, Jamaica, represented a high point in ACP solidarity. Hitherto, meetings with the EEC Ministers had all taken place in Brussels. It was important to the ACP that this pattern of movement to Europe be broken and, in July 1974, the next Joint ACP/EEC Ministerial Meeting convened in the Caribbean. ACP unity was both manifest and insistent and the negotiations moved forward appreciably, but with discernible signs of mounting Community resistance to some of the more 'sensitive' demands of the ACP – such as those on 'rules of origin', or the character of 'MFN treatment', or access for products covered by the Community's 'Common Agricultural Policy'.

Meanwhile, the ACP had been developing its machinery of unity. Reference has already been made to the Committee of Ambassadors in Brussels and the Meetings of ACP Ministers. Underpinning all these was the *ad hoc* Secretariat of the ACP Group headed by an Executive Secretary, supported by staff permanently based in Brussels and supplemented by a continuous flow of ACP technicians working closely with it. Nothing did more to forge the ACP into a disciplined united working group at all levels than this regime of joint effort directed towards concerted goals.

In the end, at the final negotiating session in Brussels, the Ministerial spokesmen of the ACP on whom rested the responsibility of negotiating with European Ministers on behalf of the entire Group, came from such varied backgrounds as Gabon (Financial and Technical Co-operation), Mauritania (Institutions, Establishments, etc.), Guyana (the Trade Regime), Fiji and Jamaica (Sugar) and Senegal (Co-ordinating ACP Chairman).

The unity of interests of the ACP became more manifest as the negotiations lengthened and – as was clearly revealed in the ultimate stages when rum, a product of interest to only one region, the Caribbean, threatened to frustrate the eventual consensus, neither regional nor linguistic affinities – neither separate national interests nor past associations, neither personalities nor cultural patterns were allowed to supersede the interest of the Group as a whole.

The Lomé Convention is not perfect. It does not meet all the aspirations of the ACP as a significant segment of the developing world. But it is a point of departure in the relations between the developing and the developed states. That it is such an innovation and represents such a promise derives in the main from the process of unification described above – a process that brought together 46 developing states in a uniquely effective manner to meet the challenge of negotiating with the European Economic Community – a significant segment of the developed world that had itself so rightly turned to integration in answer to the challenge of survival.

Notes and References

1. See Perspective III, p. 113.

A New Relationship With Europe

On 26 July 1973, the first meeting took place between Ministers of African, Caribbean and Pacific states and of the European Community. Shridath Ramphal spoke for the Caribbean as a whole in a speech that was to set the tone for much that followed in the negotiations – as in the rejection of the concept of 'reciprocity'. Of special importance to him, however, was preparing the ground for the unity that was to emerge between the African, Caribbean and Pacific countries.

The lands whose coasts are washed by Caribbean waters are no strangers to Europe – Spain, Holland, Britain, France and Denmark have, in their time, shaped the course of our history and the destinies of our people. Indeed, given the vagaries of the trade winds and the vicissitudes of metropolitan power, I might well today have been addressing you in some other of the official languages of the Community. Long before the 'scramble for Africa' began, the islands of the Caribbean were regarded as the prizes of European wars of the seventeenth and eighteenth centuries – prizes that frequently changed hands as fortunes ebbed and flowed in those more leisured contests. These rivalries, these conflicts, have left their mark upon our region, so that while today I speak on behalf of the English-speaking states, there are other Caribbean states speaking Dutch and French that are already within this Community. Perhaps history, in its inexorable logic, is moving through these present responses to unity in Europe to redress within our region the fragmentation which is the legacy of those earlier rivalries.

For our own part, we have not been unmindful of the lesson of your successes in economic integration and, as I speak today for the Caribbean, it is on behalf of states that have already survived the first quinquennium of the Caribbean Free Trade Association and that, on 1 August, in a few days time, will inaugurate the Caribbean Community and the Caribbean Common Market. We are proud that these efforts permit us today to approach our discussions with Europe as a dialogue between one economic community and another – disparate as we might be in size and strength, but equal as we are in the resolve to achieve, through the processes of economic integration, the strength through which we can improve the quality of life of our people and contribute to like improvement in the lives of others.

These reasons inform the decision which we have communicated to you that it is our intention to negotiate with the Community as a group – a group which includes both the four independent states of Barbados, Guyana, Jamaica and Trinidad and Tobago, and the eight remaining member states of the Caribbean Free Trade Association – the non-independent states of Antigua, Belize, Dominica, Grenada, St. Kitts-Nevis-Anguilla, St. Lucia, Montserrat and St. Vincent. The temporary difference in the constitutional status of the two groups of states has not prevented the evolution and implementation of meaningful economic integration arrangements within our region. It is a token of our earnest in this regard that we have chosen to sit together at this table under the single label of the 'Caribbean Countries'. In so doing, it is an important part of our purpose to ensure that any future relationship with this Community will be such as to facilitate and enhance – and in no way to retard or diminish – the processes of economic integration within our region.

Those Caribbean countries which are not yet independent

are currently entitled to the status of 'Associates' under Part IV of the Treaty of Rome. Associated as they are with the independent countries in our programmes of regional economic integration, they have chosen to participate in the forthcoming negotiations as an integral part of the group of Caribbean countries with a view to establishing a satisfactory group relationship with the Community. I wish to make it clear, however, that such participation is entirely without prejudice to their present entitlement.

But other considerations of solidarity will mark our approach to the negotiations ahead – considerations deriving from our resolve to pursue with the states of Africa that sit around this table, whether they be already in association with the Community or not, and with our colleagues from the islands of the Pacific, the maximum co–ordination and unity of effort. To that end, we have been mandated by our Heads of Government.

As the first measure of that solidarity, let me say on behalf of the Caribbean states that we identify ourselves fully with the presentation just made for Africa by our good friend, the Commissioner of Trade from Nigeria, and for the Pacific countries by the distinguished Prime Minister of Fiji. We share the aspirations and the objectives to which they gave expression, and we share also in those approaches to the negotiations which they laid out before the Council as the way along which a durable arrangement may be developed between the African and Pacific states and the Community. If, in what follows hereafter, I traverse the path they had already cleared, let that reiteration serve to confirm the identity of our objectives and of our resolve to attain them in the interest of our respective peoples.

Let me say straight away, Mr. President, that we are grateful to you and to the Community, on whose behalf you spoke yesterday, for the care with which that presentation was prepared. And if it be the case that, on occasion, that care so far spilled over into caution as to deprive the Community's proposals of those qualities of dynamism and innovation for which we looked, we temper our disappointment with the reflection that it was but an initial presentation.

Mindful of these considerations, we are specially grateful that you should have specifically invited from us an indication of our policies on the questions which are likely to arise in the course of the negotiations; and we note that you were careful to say that, before adopting a position on them, the Community awaits these indications with particular interest. These observations encourage us to believe that the Community's approach to the negotiations is not doctrinaire but open–minded; and they encourage us also to recognise that it would be in the interest of our future work together for us to respond to the Community's presentation with frankness and without diffidence. It is in that spirit that we approach these proceedings today.

First of all, we interpret the statements made yesterday to mean that in its approach to the negotiations the Community is not hide–bound by existing stereotypes but is willing to formulate new models best capable of meeting current realities and reflecting contemporary ideas. In what I have to say, it will be clear that we have many reservations on the character of the model put forward; but, so long as our negotiations are conditioned not by the precedents of a passing era but by a resolve to identify a model of arrangements more relevant to the needs and the mood of the 70s and beyond, there is no reason to doubt our joint capacity to devise it.

For our own part, we recognise the Yaounde and Arusha Conventions as part of the historical development of the Community's relationships with developing states.[1] We do not regard them as necessarily determining the character of the relationships that will succeed them. We seek from the Community arrangements for co–operation in the area of trade and economic development that are just, enlightened and effective – arrangements informed by past effort and experience but determined by their conformity to the criteria we establish for relationships of the future. For these reasons, we believe it would be more helpful for us to begin afresh in our search for satisfactory models and, as we begin that search, for us to convey to the Community our ideas on some of the more important elements of which they must be compounded.

As regards trading arrangements with the Community, we do not consider it to be appropriate that the negotiations should proceed on the concept of a free trade relationship;[2] and we reject entirely the notion that the price of duty-free entry into the Community for the main products of developing states with whom the arrangements are concluded should be the reciprocation of trade benefits. Reciprocity between those who are unequal in economic strength is a contradiction in economic terms. In contemporary international economic relations, Aristotle's dictum that 'justice requires equality between equals but proportionality between unequals'[3] must surely mean that, as between those who are unequal in economic strength, equity itself demands non-reciprocity.

It is surely unarguable today – having regard to developments in the UNCTAD, indeed, having regard to the spirit of Part IV of the GATT – that in any arrangements between the Community and the developing countries covered by Protocol 22,[4] the latter should be obliged to grant reciprocal tariff-free entry to the Community. We hesitate to believe that the Community seriously seeks such entry and we can see no rational basis on which we should be required to grant it in the context of arrangements intended to promote our economic development.

Let me turn now from these fundamental aspects of the arrangements with which the negotiations will be concerned and touch briefly on some of the features of the economic life of the Caribbean; for, in the end, no set of arrangements, no form of relationship, can be either effective or durable unless they take account of these realities of our region and of their impact upon the lives of our people.

The first of these realities is that almost 300 years of a colonial experience have left our economies heavily dependent on our agricultural and agro-based exports to metropolitan Europe, and upon those special tariff and non-tariff arrangements which, over the years, have been devised to maintain and guarantee the availability of these products for these markets. The availability of adequate export volumes of these products, particularly sugar, bananas and citrus – to name the three most important – is essential not only to enable us to continue to earn a significant part of our foreign exchange but also to prevent already high unemployment levels from escalating even higher.

Put very simply, our heavy rates of unemployment throughout most of our countries ranging between 15 per cent and 25 per cent of the labour force – constitute a formidable economic and social problem whose implications for stability within the region can only be dangerously enlarged by our failure to secure arrangements for equivalence of access to the market of an enlarged European Economic Community that now includes the United Kingdom. Indeed, one could truly say that the present levels of unemployment in the Caribbean would blow the lid off most European societies.

In many countries of the Caribbean region – particularly in the smaller islands – bananas and sugar are of transcendent importance not only in total export earnings but also for employment. Indeed, in many of the smaller states, if the present UK market arrangements for these two commodities were not to be replaced in the context of the enlarged Community by arrangements giving at least equivalent advantages, not only would export earnings and employment be severely affected, but the entire economy could be disrupted to the point of virtual collapse. Even where, as in some of the larger states of the region, export earnings from bananas and sugar may not account for a very high proportion of total foreign exchange receipts, these commodities are of great significance in the already desperate overall employment situation.

In our effort to free ourselves fron a mono-cultural economy, to diversify our production structure and to improve that desperate unemployment situation, we have had to face the reality that, with limited room for manoeuvre, no country can transform the structure of its economy overnight. We have been promoting the development of exports of new, non-traditional, agricultural products and the growth of the manufacturing sector through a development strategy which not only promotes import substitution at the regional level but also the growth of exports for extra-regional markets.

In communities as relatively small as ours, such an outward-looking economic strategy is essential to development; but, in present conditions, it leads to the reality of a constantly enlarging need for access to the markets of the developed world. Put simply, this means that if we are to have a chance of redressing the economic imbalance that has been the heritage of our relationship with Europe, our processed and semi-processed agricultural products and new production of manufactures and semi-manufactures stand urgently in need of access to the market of the Community.

But diversification cannot be confined to the development of new agricultural products or to manufactures alone. No less urgent is the need for the exploitation of our natural resources, including our mineral resources – in particular, oil and bauxite – under conditions which, consistent with our national sovereignty, draw upon the technology and markets of the developed world and, increasingly, of Europe. All such development requires, as a pre-requisite, access to external development finance on favourable terms – finance which is an essential supplement to our own national and regional efforts in mobilising financial resources. If such development is to become a reality, we need access to the

th Ramphal in Marlborough House, headquarters of the Commonwealth Secretariat, across the way from 6
Gardens where Sir John Gladstone retired after selling his plantations in Guyana

Paid 1/-

Form 34

Ord. 18 of 1891
Section 191.

Trip : CERTIFICATE OF EXEMPTION FROM LABOUR.

BRITISH GUIANA.

I hereby certify that the undermentioned _East Indian_ Immigrant

has completed _his_ Term of Service under indenture on Plantation

Vreeden Hoop

Name of Immigrant	...	_Ramphul_
Father's Name	...	_Moorli Sing_
Sex	...	_male_
Age on Arrival ...	...	_9 years_
Height	...	
No., Ship and Year of Arrival		_278 Ellora 1881_
Date of Indenture ...	...	_5 Jany 1881_
Bodily Marks ...	...	
Number of Certificate	...	_1508_
Date of Issue ...	...	_8 Nove 1932_

Dated this _8th_ day of _Nove_ 19 _32_

Signature :- _Ramphul_

_~~~~~~ s._

Immigration Agent. General

IMMIGRATION—No. 25.

[OVER

Daniel Ramphal's certificate of 'release from indenture'. This is a copy of the original document, hence the date of issue is given as 8 November 1932, but he had been released many years before

th Ramphal's grandfather, Daniel, who at the age of 9 was indentured along with his mother on plantation en-Hoop in British Guiana

Shridath Ramphal's parents J I 'Jimmy' Ramphal, a pioneer of education in Guyana, and Grace Ramphal

From Columbus
to Castro:
The History
of the Caribbean
1492—1969

ERIC WILLIAMS

Eric Williams

my dear Sonny

We are both labourers in the vineyard.
It is in this spirit that I send you this work.

Bill

André Deutsch

With Guyana's Forbes Burnham and Algeria's Foreign Minister Abdelaziz Bouteflika at the August 1972 Non-Aligned Foreign Ministers meeting in Guyana

Ramphal with Henry Kissinger, then US Secretary of State, in 1974. Earlier Ramphal had argued against Kissinger's plan to develop a community of the western hemisphere between the US and Latin American and Caribbean States, but excluding Canada and Cuba. Kissinger withdrew his plan. (Max Machol)

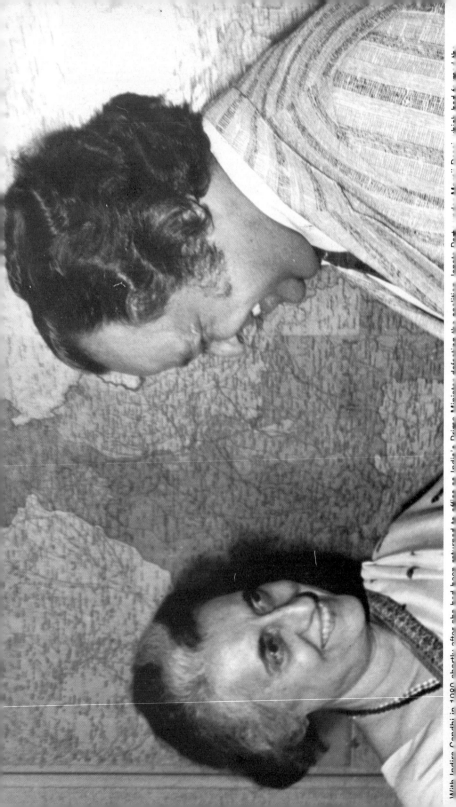

With Indira Gandhi in 1980 shortly after she had been returned to office as India's Prime Minister defeating the coalition Janata Party under Morarji Desai, which had forced the

Robert Mugabe, Zambia's Kenneth Kaunda and Joshua Nkomo in Shridath Ramphal's study during the 1979 Lancaster House Conference on Zimbabwe's independence. Over Mugabe's right shoulder is a portrait of Ramphal in his lawyer's wig and gown. (Time Inc.)

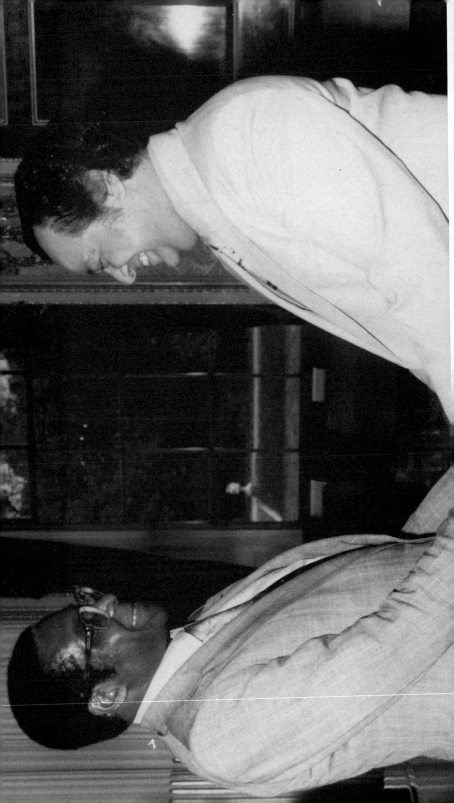

March 1987, Shridath Ramphal presented South Africa's Bishop Desmond Tutu to the Queen at a onwealth Day reception at Marlborough House

Shridath Ramphal,

Love,
from a nation
that adores you for
caring so much.
Winnie Mandela

Ramphal is the Chairman of the Committee which awarded the 1985 Third World Prize to South Africa's Nelson and Winnie Mandela. In 1986, during the visit of the Eminent Persons

Shridath Ramphal and Willy Brandt presenting the 'Brandt' report on 'Development' to US President Jimmy Carter in Washington. (UPI)

Ramohal with Pierre Trudeau, then Prime Minister of Canada, at Kaieteur Falls in Guyana. Trudeau was one of Ramohal's strongest supporters at his election as Commonwealth

In 1981, during the Commonwealth Summit in Melbourne, Ramphal was awarded the Order of Australia. The presentation was made by the Queen on board the Royal Yacht Brittania. On the left of the photograph is Malcom Fraser, then Australia's Prime Minister

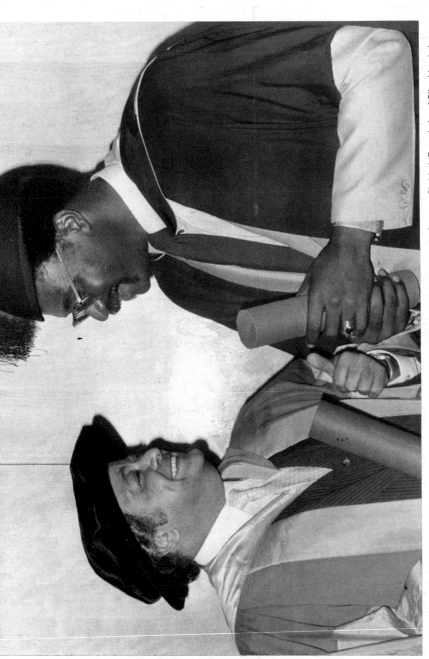

Receiving Honorary Doctorates from the University of Hull in 1984 – sons of slavery and indenture in Guyana, Shridath Ramphal and Clive Lloyd, former West Indies Cricket Captain. On that day an Honorary Doctorate was also awarded to noted West Indian writer, Trinidad-born C L R James

European Development Fund, to the European Investment Bank and to other sources – both public and private – of EEC development finance, on terms which do not compromise our national dignity and self-respect.

Finally, in the catalogue of realities, let it be recognised that for countries of our limited size and resources, regional economic integration is an indispensable element of our development strategy. We need to create a wider and more adequately protected regional market, and we need to co-ordinate the development of our natural resources for the economic advancement of our individual countries and of the region as a whole. Any arrangements for co-operation in the area of trade and economic development which we may evolve with the Community must be such as not to hinder but rather positively to promote the processes of economic integration in the Caribbean.

A Europe that has made economic integration the corner-stone of its own philosophy could hardly, in its relations with developing states, do otherwise than actively assist them in adapting that philosophy to their own even more urgent needs. It would be a supreme irony if the integration of Europe were to be made the occasion for the economic disintegration of the Caribbean region which the colonial experience has already fragmented to the point of absurdity.

Notes and References

1. The first Yaounde Convention associating 18 states in Africa (including Madagascar) with the (then) six states of the EEC came into force in June 1964 for five years. It covered trade arrangements (entailing reciprocal preferences) and financial and technical aid, and also incorporated the second European Development Fund. Yaounde II was signed in July 1969 between the AASM and Mauritius on the one hand and the Community on the other. It ran for four years from January 1971 and included the third European Development Fund. In 1966, Kenya, Tanzania and Uganda signed an Association Agreement with the EEC in Arusha. It was never

ratified but a second Agreement essentially limited to trade arrangements, which became known as the Arusha Convention, was signed in 1969 and became operational in 1971.

2. As had occurred under the Yaounde Convention.

3. Aristotle, *Ethics*, tr. J.A.K. Thomson, Penguin Classics, (Penguin Books, London, 1987), pp. 179–184.

4. *Supra*, p. 108. Protocol 22 of the Treaty of Accession concerned the three alternative commercial arrangements which the EEC offered to the 20 independent Commonwealth countries of sub-Saharan Africa, Caribbean and the Pacific (the 'Associables'). The alternatives offered were (i) to join a Yaounde–type Convention; (ii) to negotiate one or more special Conventions of Association comprising reciprocal rights and obligations; or (iii) to negotiate a general trade agreement. The ACP rejected all three.

The Challenge of Unity

Early in the ACP-EEC negotiations, the ACP countries took advantage of a Conference of African Trade Ministers in Dar es Salaam, Tanzania to further co-ordinate their positions. Shridath Ramphal addressed the Conference on 1 October 1973, making a stirring plea for the unity and solidarity of the ACP group. From the next ACP/EEC Ministerial Meeting later that month in Brussels, the African, Caribbean and Pacific countries never again negotiated other than as a single group speaking always with one voice. In the final negotiating session leading to Lomé, Shridath Ramphal was the ACP spokesman on what was to become the Lomé Convention's central Trade Regime.

At all levels and in all forums it is an essential element of Caribbean endeavour that we should maintain and secure the largest possible area of unity with an Africa that is itself united – a unity which will give us strength and through which, in turn, we may be able to contribute in due measure to the strength of Africa. It was, therefore, most natural to us – as we faced the unfolding of new relationships with a Europe that had forged for itself a new strength through a new unity – that we should seek to co-operate with the states of Africa, all of Africa, who faced a similar challenge. We have greatly welcomed the opportunities for co-ordination of approaches to the negotiations with the European Economic Community that recent developments have provided -- whether through Caribbean initiatives or initiatives of African states – both Associates and Associables.

We were with you at Lagos in July; and we were witness to the unity you forged then as the essential instrument of securing, in the negotiations with Europe, arrangements consistent with the demands of Africa for a just, enlightened and progressive relationship. We have been greatly moved by your Resolution of Lagos welcoming our continued participation in these consultations. And we were with you in Brussels as that instrument of unity demonstrated in so dramatic a way the strength of Africa and the strength of all the Associate and Associable States as we took the first step together in the negotiations.

We hope that our own contribution at Brussels from the base of unity which we have secured among ourselves in the Caribbean states – through the unity of the Caribbean Community and the Caribbean Common Market into which the Caribbean Free Trade Area has evolved – were worthy complements to Africa's united presentation on that occasion. It is our considered belief that the united front presented to the Community on behalf of the African, Caribbean and Pacific states has dramatically altered the balance of negotiating strength around the Conference tables of Brussels and has provided the peoples of the developing world there represented with a new – perhaps a unique – opportunity of securing in negotiations with the developed world just and satisfactory arrangements.

We are confident that so long as we remain resolute in our positions, steadfast to our principles, refusing to be divided among ourselves or between our regions, we can and will secure those objectives which, together, we communicated to the Community in the name of our people. We owe it to them not to lose by default or by division the negotiating strength we have achieved. If our collective presence here is to be symbolic of anything, let it be symbolic of our continued unity of approach to the negotiations and of our steadfastness in maintaining it. In our joint effort, you may count on the Caribbean being resolute and unwavering.

We live in a time when the super–powers remind us continuously of the detente they have achieved between themselves. It is a detente we must welcome as a part of mankind, for anything which reduces international tension advances the interest of all men. But as we remind them, it is a detente which leaves untouched many festering areas of international tension, most of them in the Third World, but, most of all, it is a detente which leaves unreconciled the crisis of economic relations between the developed and the developing world which today threatens the international community as gravely as any other single issue. Detente, if it is to be meaningful to the totality of human relations, must encompass this issue also.

In the negotiations with the European Economic Community, the more than forty member states of the developing world engaged in them and the nine member states of Europe have an opportunity to create an environment of detente in this critical area of international economic relations. But, as power speaks out of the barrel of a gun, so detente issues out of the strength of negotiating positions. If we are to secure that detente, if we are to establish with Europe a new regime of economic relations which can redress the effeteness of a faltering international development strategy and serve as a model of relations between developed and developing countries, it will depend on the strength of our negotiating position when we talk again in Brussels on October 17th. And that strength will depend on the unity we sustain here in Dar es Salaam and commit ourselves to sustaining around the conference tables of Brussels.

The obligations we owe, therefore, in response to the challenge of unity which the President of Tanzania has so clearly and so inspiringly identified, are obligations not only to our own people and to each other, but obligations also to all the developing world and to human society generally. The best tribute we can pay to President Nyerere, the most tangible expression of our gratitude to him, is to discharge these obligations with courage and to demonstrate to Europe that the unity within our regions, whether of Africa, or the Caribbean, or the Pacific, is a unity that is real, and pervasive and lasting, and that our several regions are themselves united in the demands we jointly make of Europe for just, enlightened and effective arrangements.

Lomé:
A Promise to be Fulfilled

On 28 February 1975, nineteen months after the start of talks in Brussels, Ministers of the ACP and EEC countries met in the capital of Togo to sign the Lomé Convention. In speaking on behalf of the ACP group at the signing ceremony, Shridath Ramphal underlined that what had been achieved was a lesson for developing countries in the essentiality of unity – and he warned that the Convention was merely a promise of a new relationship with Europe which would be fulfilled only if that unity was sustained.

The fact that today, at the end of these negotiations, I speak, as one of three, on behalf of the ACP states is testimony to an even more ample fulfilment of the ambition for unity dimly perceived and cautiously advanced at the start of the negotiations. More ample, because what has emerged is the unity of all our states across regions and oceans and continents. If these negotiations had produced no more than this, its achievement for us would be recompense enough. Indeed, there were moments when that unity brought us a premium satisfaction which I know our European friends would not deny us – moments when it seemed that the unity, or at least the unanimity, of the 46 ACP states was more real than that of the Community of Nine.

I venture to suggest that this reality of unity – tested as it has been in these negotiations – is of the most immense importance, not merely for the strengths it brings to our group of states and, therefore, to the operation of the Convention, but for the new dimension it contributes to the efforts of our generation to evolve the structures of an interdependent world society.

Our negotiations have fully confirmed and employed that capacity to create, to innovate, to devise more just and more relevant mechanisms of co-operation. Certainly, in conceptual terms and, indeed, in terms of the structures of co-operation, we might be tempted to claim, in the lofty language of Pericles in his polemic to the people of Athens, that by the Convention of Lomé 'we do not imitate – but are a model to others'.[1] For us, this too is a major cause for satisfaction; for throughout the negotiations we have been conscious of their relevance to the evolution of a new model of relationships, operable not only between ourselves and the Community, but universally applicable between developed and developing countries the world over.

We have been determined, and remain determined, to ensure that the Convention contributes to the realisation of the aspirations of the international community for a New International Economic Order – aspirations of which we speak without apology and without qualification; for we believe that upon their fulfilment rests a major hope for the future of our planet.

This is why, as we recorded in our Resolution at Accra when adopting the draft Convention, we see this moment of signature not as history's terminal station but as a mere transit stop, not as an end of the journey but as the beginning of a new phase – one of co-operative effort between our states and the Community devoted to ensuring that the Convention is, indeed, a vehicle for the progressive development of our economic relations with Europe and for the fulfilment of those over–riding aspirations that are of importance to all mankind. For the securing of that development and the fulfilment of those aspirations we must be ready to strive with endless resolution. If, to some, such a quest may appear Herculean or such a resolve untimely, let me invoke the exhortation of a great poet of the Community: "Ah, but a man's reach should exceed his grasp – or what's a heaven for". [2] The Convention's growth capacity both justifies and mandates so noble an ambition.

And it is essential in specific, no less than in general, terms that we do strive to ensure that this Convention, in the fulfilment of its potential – and it is in its potential rather than in its text that its great value lies – is true to the ideals of co–operation which it proclaims. It would be an essay in self-deception for us to believe that the document we sign today fulfils all those ideals, and it would be a dangerous pretence for us to imply that it does. We do honour to this occasion of genuine pleasure with more integrity, and with a truer promise of understanding in the days ahead, if we are as candid in expression of our disappointments as we are forthcoming in expression of our satisfactions.

Meanwhile, what we have achieved together is a notable advance for which Europe and our 46 states may, indeed, take credit – credit both for what it promises for ourselves in terms of economic co-operation between our states and for what it offers to the world within the framework of the wider search for international consensus for the conditions for human survival.

For the rest, let us here, at the level of Ministers, commit ourselves to pursuing these practical tasks by sustaining a political will to make the Convention of Lomé a document that years hereafter we will be proud to have signed this day.

Notes and References

1. Thucydides, *History of the Peloponnesian War,* tr. Rex Warner, Penguin Classics (Penguin Books, London, 1987), p.145.

2. Robert Browning, 'Andrea del Sarto' in *Browning: Poetry and Prose*, selected by Simon Maxwell-Smith (The Reynard Library, Rupert Hart-Davis, London, 1950), p.330.

The non-English speaking states of Latin America must accept that there is now a new community of Latin American states of which the Caribbean is a sub-region, and they must accept this not reluctantly and with reservation, but warmly and with enthusiasm – conscious of the new strengths and the new opportunities which the enlargement brings. And the Caribbean must accept involvement in Latin America as an integral part of the enlarged community.

*Shridath Ramphal**

Chapter 4

The New Latin America

Perspective IV   140

The Realities of Inequality   144
(Tlatelolco, 1974)

The New Latin America   150
(New York, 1974)

A Caribbean Basin Initiative   156
(New York, 1974)

* Addressing the Center for Inter-American Relations, New York, 2 April 1974.

Perspective IV

In geographical terms the English-speaking Caribbean has always been part of Latin America, but centuries of domination by rival imperial powers, imposed language differences, and an inherited system of no trade, no direct communication by sea or air and no cultural or intellectual exchanges left the two neighbouring groups not only estranged but suspicious of each other. Thus, while Latin America and the Caribbean are regarded by the rest of the world as one region, they see themselves as separated by the five different languages, cultures and political traditions established in the area by vying colonial powers.

Many of the countries of Latin America and the Caribbean also have similar natural resources which each has developed independently and is marketing competitively. Since the 1950s, there has been much discussion about 'integration' in Latin America and the Caribbean. However, the most significant result of these discussions was the separate development of economic integration in Latin America on the one hand and the English-speaking Caribbean on the other.

Apart from competition in trade, the countries of Latin America and the Caribbean also compete with each other for aid and investment. When the Caribbean Basin Initiative (CBI)[1] of US President Ronald Reagan was announced in 1982, Central American and Caribbean reaction to the scheme was characterised more by competition for benefits than by co-operation to ensure that their best interests were served. There was not one meeting among the proposed beneficiary states to devise a strong, unified approach to the American proposals. In the event, the CBI brought little tangible benefit to the Caribbean Basin countries and the bulk of its aid funds was spent on military equipment for El Salvador and Honduras.

A drive for influence in the region by the United States and the Soviet Union currently feeds further division not only between Latin America and the Caribbean, but also among countries within each group. Ample evidence of the rivalry in the area between the two super-powers are the invasion of Grenada in 1983 by the United States and the current involvement of both the Soviet Union and the United States in supplying arms and military advisers to opposing sides in Nicaragua.

The Organisation of American States (OAS), whose membership includes the United States and all of the independent Latin American and Caribbean states except Guyana and Belize,[2] has played virtually no role in security arrangements in the region. This is largely because the United States discourages such a role, interpreting it as an obstacle to its desire to intervene militarily in states when it considers its interests are threatened. The Rio Treaty, which is the closest arrangement that the OAS countries have to a security agreement, is perceived by the English-speaking Caribbean countries more as the means for intervention in a signatory state than as a source of security; consequently, few of them have adhered to it.

Cuba is a further dimension to the problem of political co-operation in Latin America and the Caribbean. Some Latin American countries have diplomatic and other relations with Cuba but many of them harbour suspicions that Cuba wishes to export its revolution to their countries. Similar sentiments exist among Caribbean countries. However, in 1974, four English-speaking Caribbean countries (Barbados, Guyana, Jamaica and Trinidad and Tobago) simultaneously established diplomatic relations with Cuba. It was a bold course which effectively broke the Latin American diplomatic embargo of Cuba. Shridath Ramphal, as Guyana's Foreign Minister, played a central role in this development. The process of normalisation of relations with Cuba has suffered a set-back in recent years starting with the breaking-off of diplomatic relations by Jamaica when the right-wing government of Edward Seaga took office in 1980.

Shridath Ramphal, always sensitive to the benefits of unity, was one of the first to appreciate that neither Latin America nor the English-speaking Caribbean would be free of the eye of the American eagle or the squeeze of the Russian bear unless they built up a framework of meaningful co-operation among themselves. Throughout the early 1970s, he urged the two groups to come to terms with each other.

But his perception of the need for Latin American and Caribbean co-operation did not relate solely to security and freedom from super-power hegemony. In his view, the identification of the English-speaking Caribbean countries with Latin America combined with their ethnic and other links to Africa and Asia could play a bridging role between the continents of the Third World and so strengthen their solidarity in international bargaining in the economic and political fields.

Ramphal recognised that given their endowment of important natural resources and their considerable intellectual talent, Latin America and the Caribbean could be one of the strongest regions of the world. The speeches in this Chapter demonstrate that he had begun to point the way to close and meaningful links between the two groups. But his words fell upon ears that were either too concerned with the reaction of external powers to such a development or too rooted in their own traditional prejudices to respond effectively.

Thus, while individual countries of each group have

deepened bilateral relations and some Latin American countries, particularly Mexico, Venezuela and Colombia, have contributed to development of the English-speaking Caribbean through the provision of funds to the Caribbean Development Bank, the two groups are not much closer today than they were in the mid 1970s.

R.S.

Notes and References

1.   Properly called the Caribbean Basin Economic Recovery Act, the CBI actually came into force on 13 September 1983. While the Act designated all Central American and Caribbean countries as beneficiaries, it stipulated that they each had to apply for such status and, among other things, should not be 'communist'. Cuba, Grenada, Guyana and Nicaragua did not apply. However, after the 1985 US invasion, Grenada became a beneficiary state and, in 1987, Guyana, whose relations with the US improved after 1986, applied for 'beneficiary' status. Originally, the scheme was intended to provide 12 year duty-free access to the US market for products from the Caribbean Basin but, after intense lobbying by groups seeking to protect US goods from competition, many products of vital importance to the Caribbean were either denied duty-free access or were placed under quota restrictions. The CBI also granted tax concessions to US firms that set up subsidiary manufacturing companies in Caribbean countries which entered into a double taxation agreement with the US. Throughout 1987, Caribbean leaders voiced great dissatisfaction with the CBI.

2.   Belize and Guyana were precluded from joining the OAS by virtue of their border disputes with Guatemala and Venezuela respectively, both of which were already members. An amendment to the Charter was proposed in 1987 to permit their membership by 1990.

The Realities of Inequality

In February 1974, at the Opening Session of a Conference in Tlatelolco, Mexico, on 'The Role of the Hemisphere in the International Community', United States Secretary of State Henry Kissinger proposed the creation of 'A Community of the Western Hemisphere'. Latin American Ministers rejected the proposal largely on the basis of the interventions of Guyana and Venezuela in opposition to it. The exclusion of Canada and Cuba from Dr. Kissinger's 'Community' disturbed Shridath Ramphal; but he was also concerned with the larger question of United States hegemony which he saw as the inevitable result. 'Community' in the Hemisphere was out of step with the reality of extreme inequality. The Kissinger proposal was eventually withdrawn at the same Conference.

I suggest that the first requirement of our dialogue, in so far as it concerns future hemispheric relations, and, indeed, as it concerns the role of the Hemisphere in the international community, is a frank acknowledgement of contemporary realities and an avoidance of the danger of looking to the future with habits of thinking relevant only to the past. And, of course, the essential reality is the reality of change. These changes are many and many-faceted; all of us know them too well to justify a narration. I mention only a few that seem specially relevant to our dialogue.

The first is the series of changes that have occurred within

Latin America itself, prominent among them being the change which has occurred in the composition of the Latin American community. Within the last ten years the English-speaking states of the Caribbean, newly come to independence, have joined the family of American states. We have joined ready, indeed anxious, to identify with Latin America, to contribute to the evolution of its institutions and to assist in the formulation of programmes for the achievement of those objectives and aspirations which are common to all our peoples. I hope that our involvement has, indeed, contributed to the achievement of these regional objectives; I know that the involvement has enriched our national lives.

But beyond these changes in numbers and character, Latin America has been living through a period of revolutionary change in social, political and economic action. They have been years of courageous experimentation, years of great achievements – and some failures – years of progressive change for the greater part, and years whose experiences have brought to Latin America a new confidence. They have been years, also, that helped Latin America to look beyond the Hemisphere and to acknowledge its common cause with the rest of the developing world – to forge new links with the states of Africa and Asia, themselves new to independence. And over these years, as a result of co-operation at inter-regional and at international levels, there has begun to emerge through the group of developing countries – a group now grown from the 'seventy-seven' to the 'ninety-six'[1] – an influence, I do not say a force, that cannot be entirely discounted.

Recent years alone have given ample manifestation of this sense of joint endeavour and shared responsibility with the Third World. The meeting of the Group of 77 at Lima in 1970, the meeting of UNCTAD III in Santiago in 1972, and, later that year, in my own capital of Georgetown, the meeting of the Foreign Ministers of the Non-Aligned group of countries, were symbols of a new Latin America whose vision reached out beyond Hemisphere.

The United States had already moved beyond the era of the thirties – beyond being the power-house of the 'new' world only tentatively and reluctantly involved in the affairs of the 'old'. It was a movement from isolation to involvement – a movement that rapidly drew the United States into an activist role as one of the world's major powers, pursuing the highest ideals and objectives of internationalism and, through those processes, broadening its area of concern and its areas of action – sometimes, let it be admitted, to our chagrin – to the furthermost corners of the globe.

It is an internationalism which, acknowledging an understanding of the finiteness of the earth's resources and the potentiality for human extinction of man's technology, has already led – largely through the instrumentality of our colleague Dr. Kissinger – to a limited detente among the major powers and which promises, through co-operation with all nations, to move from co-existence to global community.

The joint result of these developments is that for both of us, for the United States and for Latin America, the priorities of the post-war years have changed in fundamental ways. No longer is it true for any of us – for the United States or for Latin America – that hemispheric affairs constitute the dominant features of our external relations. Indeed, if we are to be honest with ourselves, no longer is the hemispheric dimension even the most important feature of those relations. The truth is that we have entered an era in which the world is moving away from an international system structured on the basis of geo-political considerations to one increasingly determined more by economics than by geography. In the result, as the United States reaches out into Europe and beyond, so Latin America is forging new ties with the rest of the developing world.

The concept of the Hemisphere as a political and an

economic unity has ceased to possess its old relevance. So far, indeed, is this so that it should be a real question for us now whether it may not, in the world of the 1970s, have lost its validity also. Can we, in any event, conceptualise it except in terms of a Hemisphere that is all-embracing, that includes all the states of Latin America – those like Cuba not with us here, and those still to come to independence? But, beyond Latin America, can we conceive of Hemisphere today in a context which does not specifically include the great hemispheric nation of Canada? We have only to raise these considerations to highlight the need for us to examine critically the very concept of Hemisphere – and to do so both in relation to United States/Latin America relations and in relation to the organisation of the affairs of the international community.

But there are other constraints of which we need to be mindful; and the most fundamental of these is the reality of inequality between the United States and the states of Latin America. It is not merely that the United States is one of the world's great super-powers. It is not merely that the United States is a large trading market; it is that the United States is the world's **largest** trading market. It is not merely that the United States is a rich developed country; it is that the United States is an economic giant, even in a world that knows other giants.

And these are only some of the realities of inequality; they need only to be catalogued for their enormity to be apparent. Indeed, as Dr. Kissinger himself said in his public address yesterday, so great are these disparities that almost any course of action, in almost any field, that the United States pursues, possesses the potentiality of impinging upon Latin America in one respect or another. What difficulties does this condition of gross inequality create for relations between the United States and the States of Latin America?

Centuries ago, indeed a whole age ago, Aristotle perceived the fundamental problem of relations between unequals when he propounded his dictum to the effect that 'as between unequals, equity itself demands non-reciprocity'.[2] The dictum holds true today, and is at last being acknowledged to be true by the new European Economic Community in its relations with the developing world. And it is a dictum whose validity has been reflected as well in the indications that were given yesterday by Dr. Kissinger that the United States is ready to proceed on the basis of generalised preferences without demands for reciprocity – even though, alas, the concept of reciprocity seemed to have crept back into his presentation in relation to the multilateral trade negotiations.

But my point is that Aristotle's dictum has application beyond the field of economics, and that we would do well to acknowledge its validity in these areas also. Is it not true that all history bears out the proposition that at the level of political relations between states of unequal strength, unity has invariably involved hegemony? And does it not follow that, as between unequals, community might so easily imply dominion? Do not the political realities of our time dictate that even the possibility of such an unintended implication should make us pause and approach the concept of a Community of the Western Hemisphere with caution and with reserve?

May it not, indeed, be the case that we should better promote and secure the spirit of community in our relations if we are to eschew not only the formalisation but even the rhetoric of a Community of the Western Hemisphere? Let us not be unmindful of our critics outside who would wish to distort the true spirit of our dialogue of Tlatelolco and condemn us, wrongly, for making a Yaounde or, worse still, a Warsaw, of this great capital of Mexico City.

And none of this is to say that vast areas of co-operation and collaboration do not lie before us in many fields arising out of the special relations which history and geography and sentiment justify. As we look upon the vistas opening before the United States and Latin America, as we begin with new attitudes and a new spirit the dialogue we have commenced this week, we cannot but be impressed with what is attainable in practical terms.

Nor does it mean that there is not an ennobling role that awaits Latin America in the international community. Just as the political independence of Latin America helped to inspire and sustain the states of Africa and of Asia as they struggled for and won their political independence, so today the economic nationalism of Latin America and its cumulative expertise and militancy in the struggle for economic independence can help these new states, and, in turn, be helped by their solidarity, in the joint endeavour to change the international economic system and render it more just and equitable for all the people of the developing world.

It is a contribution, I venture to suggest, that Latin America is specially well placed to make. And it is a contribution not only in the area of expertise but in the still wider area of building bridges of understanding to the peoples of the other regions of the world – bridges which must themselves help to lead us all to the creation of that planetary community which must be our ultimate destiny.

Notes and References

1. Membership of the Group of 77, established by 77 developing countries in 1963, increased further to 127 by 1987. The Group is still referred to as the 'Group of 77'.

2. Aristotle, *Ethics,* tr. J.A.K. Thompson, Penguin Classics, (Penguin Books, London, 1987), pp. 179-180.

The New Latin America

On 22 April 1974, Shridath Ramphal spoke at the Centre for Inter-American Relations in New York. His address was against the background of the Caribbean having moved toward economic integration with the formation of CARICOM, and playing a leading role with African and Pacific countries in the negotiations with the European Community on an aid and trade agreement. This address, inspired by these successes of Third World co-operation, was at once a reminder to the Caribbean of its Latin American connection and a summons to Latin America to recognise that the independence of Caribbean countries had inaugurated a 'New Latin America', one which had a potential for contributing to the creation of a more just international economic system.

A new role for the Caribbean in Latin America must relate directly to its situation as a part of the Hemisphere and to the circumstance of change in the affairs of the Hemisphere. During the colonial period, links between the Caribbean and the Spanish-speaking and Portuguese-speaking states of Latin America were tenuous indeed. Simon Bolivar, it is true, had found refuge in Jamaica,[1] and West Indian labour helped create the Panama Canal. Links of a kind there were between Venezuela and Trinidad across the twelve miles of the Gulf of Paria and from time to time in Guyana a continental destiny beckoned. But these were isolated, almost accidental, points of reference. They were scattered incidents of geography; they did not represent an identification with Latin America and only barely an awareness of its relevance.

Colonialism turned the face of the Caribbean away from Latin America to Canada with whom, under a system of imperial preferences, substantial trade developed and with it important links of communication; to the United States, in which many a West Indian sought training and opportunity, despairing of the lack of both at home; and, of course, within the Hemisphere, it was with Canada and with the United States that West Indians shared a common language. But these contacts themselves were peripheral, for it was to the United Kingdom mainly that West Indians turned their gaze when they looked outward.

It was Britain, after all, that was the administering metropolitan power. It was in Britain, for the greater part, that all our professionals were required to qualify. Throughout most of the area until, indeed, quite recently, North American professional qualifications were unacceptable to the colonial administrations of the West Indies – with the almost singular exception of qualifications in dentistry. In over 150 years of legal development, I was the first Guyanese lawyer – if not, indeed, the first practising West Indian lawyer – to be exposed to institutions of legal learning in the United States, and that in the nature of a sabbatical. Latin America was entirely alien. French, not Spanish, was the foreign language taught in our schools. It was to London, not to Rio or Caracas, that those few West Indians who could travel went on their vacations.

With independence, change was both necessary and inevitable. Released from the psychological no less than from the legal constraints of the colonial relationship, West Indians turned readily, almost eagerly, to the challenge of new friendships and to the involvement of the Caribbean with Latin America. But from the beginning, to West Indians, it was a process of involvement not of absorption. If I could use the analogy of another post-colonial process of integration with neighbouring states – for the West Indies in relation to Latin America, as for Britain in relation to Europe, it was a question of membership of an enlarged Community.

With the addition of the Caribbean, Latin America has acquired a new dimension, and the most urgent need is the recognition that this enlargement requires mutual adjustment to the realities of the new situation. If the old Latin America and the old Caribbean go on thinking about each other in habitual ways, the new Latin America that integrates the two will not be realised, and where there should be harmonious growth and the development of new strengths there will be tensions and new weaknesses born out of division. The essential need, therefore, is for clear perspectives of the realities of the Latin American scene in the 1970s.

The non-English speaking states of Latin America must accept that there is now a new community of Latin American states of which the Caribbean is a sub-region, and they must accept this not reluctantly and with reservation, but warmly and with enthusiasm – conscious of the new strengths and the new opportunities which the enlargement brings. And the Caribbean must accept involvement in Latin America as an integral part of the enlarged community mindful that while it has a contribution to make, especially at this time of transition in the affairs of Latin America and the Hemisphere, it is a contribution that must be made by working as a member of the new Community and not by mere association from outside.

In the decade since independence there has not been enough articulation of these mutual needs and reciprocal obligations, although I suspect that both the Caribbean and the old Latin America have been steadily groping toward these perceptions. An almost accidental exchange at the Washington Foreign Ministers' Conference – the second in the series of dialogue meetings – may have helped us to reach new understandings on this matter.[2] The communiqué issued at the end of the first dialogue meeting in Mexico – the Declaration of Tlatelolco – spoke consistently of "Latin America and the Caribbean". At Washington, as the final communiqué was being considered, the question was raised whether this was not a verbal perpetuation of distinctions that no longer existed. Some Caribbean delegations saw value in retaining the nomenclature, if only to emphasise the character of the Caribbean as a sub-region of Latin America; others were less concerned about the label than with the contents of the new integration package. In the end, we agreed that we shall henceforth speak of one Latin America – mindful that it was an enlarged Community with new dimensions and a new potential, a Community of which the Caribbean sub-region is an important element.

It is as well that we did so, for this nomenclature reflects more precisely our objective of a coherent and cohesive grouping of Central and South American and Caribbean states even if, perhaps not unnaturally, we are still in the process of advancing in that direction. To the attainment of that goal, the Caribbean has its particular contribution to make. Our role, therefore, at this time of transition in the affairs of the Hemisphere, is to become fully involved in, and not just to be loosely associated with, Latin America – to be part, and an important part, of a new and enlarged Latin America.

But the new Latin America must be new not only through enlargement of its membership; it must be new also in more fundamental ways. In the main, it must be an outward-looking Latin America. In particular, it must be a Latin America that confirms and strengthens its identification with the Third World, rejecting an image of the Western Hemisphere as a monolithic unit. It is important, however, that Latin America's identification with, and its role in, the Third World should be sustained and not occasional, should be pervasive and not limited to special issues, should be unambiguous and unapologetic, should be understood as inevitable and welcomed as constructive. It is an identification and an environment that will, of course, de-emphasise 'Hemisphere'; but it should not on that account be seen as harmful to the growth and strengthening of hemispheric relations. Indeed, far from signifying indifference to hemispheric relations, it is the logical consequence of developments elsewhere in the Hemisphere.

If, at the political level, and with the avowed objective of helping to secure and maintain international peace and security, the United States has moved from isolation to super-power involvement and from Western alliance to Eastern detente, why should it be surprising that at the economic level, and with the avowed objective of securing a more just international economic system, Latin America should have moved beyond the relative isolation of the inter-American system to play a major role in the efforts of the developing countries for economic change? And it is a major role that Latin America is playing. Latin American economic nationalism has inspired the struggle of the Group of 77 countries. Latin American states are now in significant numbers, playing a central role in the Non-Aligned Movement and particularly so since the Georgetown Conference of Foreign Ministers and the Action Programme for Economic Co-operation between developing countries that was there formulated – with substantial contributions from Latin American member states.[3] It can hardly be otherwise; for Latin America's aspirations for social and economic justice can be secured only by action within the international community generally – not by action merely within the Hemisphere.

An urgent need exists for an understanding of these realities not only by Latin America but by the rest of the Hemisphere – and especially by the United States. The Caribbean can help to strengthen these perceptions within Latin America and can contribute to advancing the change in outlook which they demand. We are, in a sense, well placed to do so because of our more recent and more direct links with the rest of the Third World – with the countries of Asia and of Africa from which we are but three generations removed, and with whom we have had a shared experience of colonialism and of the struggle for freedom. The Caribbean can be the bridge for the new Latin America to cross the South Atlantic and the Indian Ocean.

In fact, the matter can be put much higher. An outward-looking Latin America is essential to the lasting integration of the Caribbean into Latin America; for we will not be integrated in any effective way unless the enlarged Latin America is simultaneously integrated into the Community of developing states. In the long run, success in advancing the identification of Latin America with the rest of the Third World will greatly influence the quality of Caribbean involvement in Latin America. Another role for the Caribbean is, as we seek to be a part of an enlarged Latin America, to simultaneously help Latin America to look beyond Hemisphere.

Notes and References

1. Salvador de Madariaga, *Bolivar,* (Hollis & Carter, London, 1952), p. 263.

2. Meeting of Foreign Ministers of Latin America, Caribbean Countries and the United States of America, in Mexico, 21-23 February 1974. See 'The Realities of Inequality', *Supra,* p. 144.

3. *The Action Programme for Economic Co-operation between Non-Aligned and other Developing Countries* formulated at the Ministerial Meeting held in Georgetown in 1972 and elaborated and endorsed at the Algiers Summit in 1973.

A Caribbean Basin Initiative

Eight years before President Reagan announced his 'Caribbean Basin Initiative' (CBI) under which the United States offered additional aid and improved trade terms to ideologically acceptable Caribbean Basin countries, Caribbean Heads of Government had accepted a proposal from Shridath Ramphal that a meeting of Heads of Government of 'Caribbean Basin' countries should be convened. On 4 October 1974, at a meeting at the United Nations in New York of Foreign Ministers of the countries of the Caribbean Basin, including Cuba, Ramphal introduced the proposal on behalf of the six independent Caribbean Governments. The proposal was well received; but, it fell victim to faint-heartedness and inertia. In the light of subsequent events in the Caribbean and Central America, this earlier proposal for an authentic coming together of all the developing countries of the Caribbean Basin was clearly not ahead of its time in terms of need.

Our Hemisphere is in transition. It is a moment in the history of Latin America when new bases of fraternity are being forged with great success between those states that pioneered the way to independence more than a century ago and those of us for whom victory came much later. Among the most vital of these elements of change are the acceptance by the English-speaking peoples of the Caribbean of their Latin American heritage and identity, the acknowledgement by the rest of Latin America of the new and valuable dimension which these states bring to that heritage and that identity, and the emergence from these new perceptions and relationships of new strengths as, together, we seek to evolve our joint Latin American destiny. Today, for the first time, it is truly all of Latin America that proclaims: 'para nosotros la patria es America Latina'.[1]

While these changes affect all of Latin America, the Caribbean Basin is the crucible in which the quality of the new developments will be assayed. It may be, indeed, the crucible in which that common Latin American destiny will be first shaped. A convocation of the statesmen of our area at this moment of transition will be at once an acknowledgement of the vitality of these processes of change, a symbol of our joint commitment to their successful consummation and a recognition of the special role that falls to the Caribbean area in ensuring that success.

Our world is in transition. Old alliances are dissolving, old assumptions of mutual interest are losing their validity. Latin America, which for so long has given emphasis to a hemispheric destiny, is looking outwards to the new countries of the developing world and forging with them durable bonds of understanding and co-operation – bonds that link Latin America with Africa and with Asia in particular. The vision of Henri Christophe is the dynamic of our time.

The Caribbean Basin, itself the melting pot of many races, represents in a unique way this new convergence of Latin America with the Third World – a multilingual area; an area that brings together and moulds the indigenous peoples of the region and those of us whose ethnic origins lie beyond the Americas in Africa, in Asia and in Europe; an area pluralistic in political ideology and in forms of government; but, in its totality, a region committed to progressive change and to contributing in no small measure to the joint struggle of the developing countries for a new and more egalitarian world community. A convocation of the statesmen of our area at this time must be both a symbol of our unity in diversity and a reaffirmation of commitment to the wider causes in which we have enlisted with the peoples of other developing lands.

And the moment seems propitious for such a coming together for a reason of more pressing Caribbean concern. The sea which is our common geographical experience is also a dividing sea. The understandings and rapport that now characterise our relationships within the area have come out of the experience of working together in the councils of the Hemisphere and of the world. They do not arise by instinct, and will not be sustained save by endeavour. Inevitably they rest upon too narrow a base of contact. Except for occasional friendships of long standing, or the opportunities of particular visits, the political leadership within the Caribbean Basin is deprived of these opportunities of systematic consultation out of which emerges that intimacy and 'simpatia' so often critical to maximising the gains of unity. A convocation of the political leadership of the area now and hereafter will, we believe, make a notable contribution to the strengthening of the harmonious relationships already emerging between our states.

Finally, and as important as any other justification, a conference of the Heads of State or Government of the Caribbean Basin will help to symbolise for the people of our area these new emerging relationships, the new strengths that are developing out of our joint endeavours, and the new Caribbean identity which is the concomitant of the past we have shared and the future which binds us together. All these reasons, we firmly believe, constitute a mandate to us for the convening of the consultation we have suggested.

The Caribbean of which I have been speaking is not, of course, a mere cartographic expression. It is not, for example, an area that can include the United States with whom, at another level, we seek to pursue with seriousness and in friendship a new dialogue of constructive relationships between all the states of the Hemisphere. Nor can it include automatically those territories, geographically within the Basin, for whose international relations governments external to the area are the ultimate arbiters. It is, as we see it, a consultation between the political leadership of the free, independent, developing states of the Caribbean Basin.

We believe that all the reasons which seem to us to command an early consultation of the kind we are suggesting will in themselves provide material out of which will come substantial achievements. We need not, as we see it, contemplate an agenda of major dimensions touching all the issues on which, in common with the rest of Latin America, we are now engaged in dialogue at the level of the Hemisphere or of the international community.

We believe that there would be great value in endeavouring to formulate, in broad terms, a concept of the Caribbean Basin as an area of tranquility, of justice and of progress.

Notes and References

1.   Jose Marti: inscribed on the Marti Monument in Havana, Cuba.

We are pleased that the Caribbean has contributed 'Sonny' Ramphal to the Commonwealth and to the world. We are persuaded, however, that because his roots are firmly embedded in the Caribbean, it is essential that persons like him be given ample scope to keep in touch with the Caribbean and to keep the Caribbean in touch with him...the emerging view of the Caribbean as a major arena of international political conflict is adding a new and disturbing dimension to the lives of the ordinary people of the region. It is in the interest of our people that whosoever speaks or acts for the Caribbean should bear in mind that the Caribbean is, after all, our home.

Dr. A.Z. Preston[*]

Chapter 5

Caribbean Options

Perspective V   162

To Care for CARICOM   167
(Montego Bay, 1975)

The Lure of 'Realpolitik'   177
(Port-of-Spain, 1985)

[*] Vice Chancellor of the University of the West Indies, introducing Shridath Ramphal before his lecture *The Lure of Realpolitik,* Port-of-Spain, Trinidad, 13 May 1985.

Perspective V

Shridath Ramphal left the Caribbean in May 1975 to take up the post of Commonwealth Secretary-General. In his parting words to the governments of the Caribbean Community, he urged "an activist programme of economic integration"; the way forward, he reminded them, did not lie "merely in protestations and asseverations of commitment".[1]

But between 1975 and 1982 some Caribbean leaders were engaged in such intense personal rivalries and conflicts that it proved impossible even to hold a Heads of Government Conference. In the same period, the trade policies adopted by several countries – mainly in response to major economic problems at home – considerably eroded the spirit if not the letter of the CARICOM Treaty.

In the 1975-82 period, major political differences had also emerged in the region. 'Ideological pluralism' which had been accepted within CARICOM in the past was being rejected, particularly by the Prime Ministers of Jamaica and Barbados, Edward Seaga and J.M.G. 'Tom' Adams. Seaga's Jamaica Labour Party had replaced the government of the socialist oriented People's National Party of Michael Manley in 1980 and the new Prime Minister's first international appearance was on the steps of the White House in Washington where US President Ronald Reagan pledged to help build a bastion against communism in Jamaica. 'Tom' Adams had come to power four years earlier, defeating the veteran Errol Barrow at the polls. Barrow had been a close personal friend of both Manley and Guyana's Forbes Burham; Adams pulled close to Seaga and distanced Barbados from Guyana.

In 1979, after years of abuse of office and gross human rights violations, the Government of Eric Gairy in Grenada was overthrown by a group of intellectuals led by Maurice Bishop. This was the first coup d'etat in the Caribbean, albeit bloodless and popular. It created great anxieties among Caribbean governments. The United States refused to recognise the new Grenada Government, which openly talked of fears of invasion and, much to the chagrin of Seaga and Adams, turned to Cuba for help including the provision of military equipment.

When the thirteen CARICOM leaders did meet in Jamaica in 1982, eight of them had not attended a summit before. What was striking about the meeting was that, although it was the first gathering of Caribbean leaders in seven years, Seaga and Adams were more interested in fragmenting CARICOM than consolidating it. Deeply unhappy with the socialist policies of Guyana and the revolutionary government in Grenada, Seaga and Adams canvassed the idea of dissolving CARICOM and replacing it with CARICOM II which would exclude Guyana and Grenada. In the event, they could not muster sufficient support for their initiative and were forced to abandon it. But relations among the CARICOM leaders did not benefit from the Jamaica meeting.

In 1983 came tragic events in Grenada. First, the brutal murder of Maurice Bishop and some of his Cabinet colleagues on 19 October, and the establishment of a military regime under Hudson Austin. Second, the invasion of Grenada on 25 October by the United States supported by Jamaica, Barbados and the countries of the Organisation of Eastern Caribbean States,[2] even though, at a meeting of CARICOM Heads of Government in Trinidad just three days before, it had been agreed that no military action would be taken.

While his office was in distant London, Shridath Ramphal was never far from developments in the Caribbean. Although Caribbean leaders had failed to hold a CARICOM Heads of Government Conference between 1975 and 1982, he had seen many of them at Commonwealth Summits: in London in 1977, Lusaka in 1979 and Melbourne in 1981; and had constantly encouraged revitalisation of the integration process. He had been invited to attend the 1982 and 1984 CARICOM Summits and took part in the deliberations of the Heads of Government.

Ramphal had deplored the Bishop coup d'etat and had set up a West Indian Advisory Group with whose help he hoped Bishop could be persuaded to hold early elections. But it was the invasion and its support by some Caribbean leaders that caused him the greatest anguish. Throughout the crisis he worked round the clock trying to avert external intervention by talking to Caribbean leaders including the Governor-General, Sir Paul Scoon, by telephone.

The subject of Grenada dominated the New Delhi Commonwealth Summit which convened 29 days after the US-led invasion of the island. Earlier, the UN General Assembly had strongly condemned the invasion.[3] Ramphal tried hard, but without success, to persuade the leaders of the Commonwealth Caribbean countries which had participated in the invasion to accept a Commonwealth civilian presence in place of US forces. Moreover, he secured the establishment of a Commonwealth Expert Group to examine the problems of small states. Their Report[4] became a guide for action by the international community in relation to small states; but, largely because they remain preoccupied with day to day economic survival, the small states themselves have so far failed to implement the recommendations of the study.

In 1971, twelve years before the Grenada invasion,

Shridath Ramphal had tried to get Caribbean Governments to accept that "the creation of machinery for regional peace-keeping must be the means by which the violent or otherwise unconstitutional overthrow of governments, whether through secessionist movements or otherwise, can be prevented". If there is no regional machinery, he warned, "the only alternatives are recourse to assistance from outside the region" – but "such assistance will always carry with it the stigma, and the danger, of external interference".[5] Grenada demonstrated how right he was. Today, the military influence of the United States is evident through most of the region in joint training exercises with troops of several Caribbean countries; but no regional security machinery is in place, not even among the seven OECS countries and Barbados which, in October 1982, signed a Memorandum of Understanding, entitled 'The Regional Security System', calling for co-operation in assisting each other in national emergencies.

In the immediate aftermath of the Grenada invasion the mood of the Caribbean changed significantly. The spirit of independence that had characterised the 1970s appeared to wane; there were fewer assertions of the right of Caribbean countries to pursue a course of their own choice; there was a greater readiness to make an accommodation with the so-called realities of power.

R.S.

Notes and References

1. *Infra,* p. 183.

2. The Organisation of Eastern Caribbean States was established on 18 June 1981 by the Treaty of Basseterre. The signatory states are Antigua and Barbuda, Dominica, Grenada, Montserrat, St. Kitts-Nevis, St. Lucia, St. Vincent and The Grenadines.

3. UNGA Resolution 38/7 of 2 November 1983.

4. *Vulnerability: Small States in the Global Society,* Report of a

Commonwealth Consultative Group (Commonwealth Secretariat, 1985).

5. *Supra,* Chapter 2, p. 80

To Care for CARICOM

Shridath Ramphal's last speech in the Caribbean before assuming office as Commonwealth Secretary-General was at a Dinner held in his honour at Montego Bay, Jamaica on 5 July 1975. His address was a cri de coeur: "To Care for CARICOM"; his sentiments have relevance to regionalism worldwide. They were to find manifestation in many aspects of his work at the Commonwealth Secretariat in the years ahead.

I have been the beneficiary of the efforts of many: first of all, of the efforts of another generation of West Indians who, despite a barely rudimentary regional communications system – but, who knows, perhaps because of it – developed a perception of identity and an instinct for unity which could only have emerged in those unpropitious years from a profundity of faith and commitment.

Men like Marryshow and Grantley Adams, Norman Manley and Eric Williams, and the many others who worked around them to nurture and develop the West Indian identity which is our birthright but which the geo-political environment of an archipelago so easily places in forfeit; these men inspired us by their faith and confidence in West Indian unity and obliged us by their service in the cause of West Indian regionalism to continue the journey they had begun. They were in a real sense the creators of our faith. If my contributions have been of any value, it is because they were founded upon that inheritance – upon an unshakeable faith in our West Indian destiny.

Those who went before us travelled, as we all know, a path strewn with hazards. They stumbled and sometimes fell. The journey was often halted and sometimes the course itself was changed; yet, despite this, the history of the West Indies for nearly a century now has been one of steady emergence and consolidation of a West Indian identity and relentless progression toward West Indian unity.

There have been many times in the past, and in the not too distant past, when faith in West Indian regionalism and commitment to a continuing programme in fulfilment of it could only have been sustained by an overview of history – lifting our sights above the seeming disarray of the prevailing regional scene. It is not so different today; for our times are compounded of the conflicting elements that derive from what is contemporary and what is ultimate, from what is transient and what must be lasting, from the perspective of history and the reality of change.

The reality is that the decade between 1965 and 1975 has been a decade of progress in West Indian regionalism unmatched in the entire history of the Caribbean. Have we not, out of our own circumstance and resources, built brick by brick an integration movement that is generally hailed as the most successful of its kind in the developing world? From its tentative, perhaps adventurous, beginnings with the Agreement of Dickenson Bay,[1] have we not evolved from a notional Free Trade Area of three to a full-fledged functioning Economic Community of twelve? Have we not founded our Regional Development Bank and established the Secretariat of our Community? Have we not multiplied twenty-fold our areas of co-operation and of co-ordination? Have we not, indeed, transposed the question of regionalism from one of concept to one of function – from 'if' to 'how'? Let us not in our arguments about the mechanics of 'how' put into issue the principle of 'if'; and let us not in our pre-occupation with those mechanics lose sight of the grandeur and the significance of what we have constructed.

We have just emerged from two years of active involvement in the most intensive economic negotiations which any group of Third World countries has ever conducted with the developed world[2]. Throughout those negotiations with the EEC, the Caribbean worked and spoke as a single entity. Barbados and Guyana, Jamaica and Trinidad, were represented through their Ministers and Ambassadors and officials; but it was the Caribbean that spoke and it was a Caribbean position that was advanced. And let it not be forgotten that it was that manifest Caribbean unity within the councils of the 'Associates' and 'Associables' that helped greatly to inspire and sustain the unity of the ACP itself. Without that example from within – a Caribbean example – the unity of the ACP may never have been attainable.

But as the example of success promotes, so the example of failure erodes, achievement. The truth is that our successes over the last ten years have now imposed upon us responsibilities beyond those which we owe to our own region. Economic integration of the Commonwealth Caribbean has become an essential element of the widening patterns and prospects which will themselves be diminished by any weakening of our structures or any slackening of our commitment.

And have we not out of this decade of effort created an environment of functional unity within our region which gives strength to our political leadership as it contributes to the urgent issues that concern the even wider international community? Jamaica, Trinidad, Guyana, Barbados, Grenada – the States themselves, their Prime Ministers and Ministers – are all strengthened in the councils of the international community – within the Movement of Non-Aligned Countries, within the Group of 77, within the United Nations itself – by the base of regionalism from which now they speak and act.

At the 1973 Algiers Summit Meeting of the Non-Aligned Movement, Guyana and Jamaica made a single presentation through the Prime Minister of Jamaica. Within the Councils of the Commonwealth in Jamaica in 1975, it was always a Caribbean presentation whatever the voice that spoke it – a presentation greatly reinforced by its multiple authority. Increasingly, at the United Nations, through functional arrangements between our Ambassadors, our presentations are co-ordinated and unified – a working example of co-operative self-reliance in advancement of national and regional objectives. What then are the lessons and mandate of this experience? It must be a command surely to consolidate and strengthen what has been achieved and to guard it securely against erosion.

But the process of consolidation and strengthening is a dynamic, not a static, one. To consolidate and strengthen our integration structure we must respond actively to three separate elements of demand. First of all, we must respond to the mandate of care which our commitment to regionalism imposes. Next, we must respond to the self-generating momentum of integration. Finally, we must respond to the environment of global and regional change within which our integration movement is obliged to function.

As to the mandate of care, we must remember that just as a house does not a family make, but the quality of relationships under the roof give it the character of a home – so a Treaty does not a Community make, but the quality of relationships between its member states give life and constant freshness to the formal ageing parchment.

Caribbean economic integration, CARICOM itself, is the product of a massive effort to preserve patience in negotiation and goodwill and understanding in regional development. It will not survive if we abandon patience in the pursuit of consensus or allow petulance or, more so, suspicion, to displace goodwill and understanding. Regionalism is a plant of tender growth. It must be nurtured and cared for or its early blooms will fall, and the tree itself will wither and die. The true measure of our desire that it should flourish is the quality of our attentiveness to its survival and growth.

A consequence of our relative success over the last ten years is a readiness to believe that unity is our natural state – one which will subsist despite ourselves. It is a dangerous falsehood. A history of colonialism and the geography of a scattered archipelago deny its validity. The natural state of our Caribbean is fragmentation; without constant effort, without unrelenting perseverance and discipline in suppressing instincts born of tradition and environment, it is to our natural state of disunity that we shall return.

Each generation of West Indians has an obligation to advance the process of regional development and the evolution of an ethos of unity. Ours is endeavouring to do so; but we shall fail utterly if we ignore these fundamental attributes of our West Indian condition and, assuming without warrant the inevitability of our oneness, become casual, neglectful, indifferent or indisciplined in sustaining that process and that evolution.

This imposes upon all of us – governments, trade unionists, manufacturers, consumers, our academics, our mass media – a mandate of care for our integration movement. Let us have dialogue, not confrontation; let our debates be frank without being angry, penetrating without being strident, and let them take place around our conference tables. Particularly as governments, let us communicate through constitutional channels and not via the regional mass media; above all, let us, as joint custodians of our regional destiny, show mutual respect for each other. The intimacy of Community does not give licence for public deviation from those norms of diplomatic comportment that we respect in our relations with other states.

And, lest I appear to be striking a 'holier than thou' posture, let me say quite unequivocally that each of us has, from time to time, been guilty of some lapse in these respects. In the busy rush for development, in the conscious- ness of our own commitment to regional goals, we some- times forget to pause, to inform, to consult, to reassure, to co-ordinate with our Community colleagues. There is no malice in the omission; but, in these formative years – as in early love – even innocent thoughtlessness can be a major offence. To care for CARICOM must become a way of life.

I have said, also, that we must respond to the self- generating momentum of integration. No matter how much care and consideration we demonstrate, CARICOM itself will not survive merely by standing still. It will survive only if we generate the political will to constantly renew it with relevance to the aspirations of the West Indian people and to pursue a continuous process of upgrading the mechanisms of integration so as to ensure their potential for fulfilling the practical needs of the West Indian region.

Let me merely recall – for we dare not forget or, mindful, be complacent over – such omissions from our catalogue of successes as derive from no regionally-integrated industry, no regional airline, no co-ordination of economic planning and development strategies, no common policy on foreign investment, and no sufficient co-ordination of foreign policies.

I am absolutely convinced that, sooner or later – and it may be later, though it should be sooner – we will find it essential to return to the conceptual framework of the Grenada Declaration[3] – limited, as it was intended to be limited, to the exploration of forms of political association in the Eastern Caribbean.

An effective start in this direction would be a process of unification among the LDCs;[4] and, if a way must be found between the need of the smaller islands for a helping hand over and through independence and their fear of dominion from whatever quarter, why can we not explore the potential of CARICOM itself to provide that collective supplement to self-determination? The metropolitan presence in the Eastern Caribbean must end, and it is in no one's interest that that end be long delayed. It is up to CARICOM, and in our community's interest, to ensure that, as that presence passes, it leaves not a vacuum attracting replacement but political, social and economic structures that have a chance of supporting the essentials of sovereignty.

I believe it to be essential to the future of CARICOM that within the region we have the clearest conception of where we are going as a Community. I have long believed, and often said, that the greatest danger that faces the process of integration in the region is that of widening our Caribbean Community at so early a point in its formative stage that we impair our prospect of deepening the process of integration itself – the determination 'to consolidate and strengthen the bonds that have historically existed among their peoples'. It is the first sentiment in the Preamble to the Treaty of Chaguaramas. It is the basic motivation of the process of Caribbean economic integration. It lies at the heart of our ideology of Community. We know that the processes of integration have still to be deepened. We must ensure that the potential for deepening is in no way diminished.

But our Community lives within a wider Caribbean – within a region of interlocking circles. It is a Caribbean that also includes Surinam and Guadeloupe and Martinique and the islands of the Dutch Antilles – communities that have had a recent experience of a European colonial relationship. It is a Caribbean that includes Haiti and the Dominican Republic, Cuba and Puerto Rico – island communities of the Caribbean with whom there are socio-economic no less than geo-political points of reference with our States. It is a Caribbean that cannot ignore the reality of the States of South and Central America which share in the heritage of the Caribbean Sea and which are intent upon pursuing a destiny within it. All these are parts of that wider Caribbean; but at the heart of even that Caribbean lies our Community; and just as it is important that we acknowledge the realities of our Caribbean environment in these wider terms, so it is crucial that we consolidate and strengthen, through our Community structures, the bonds which have historically existed among our people.

It must be possible to ensure the consolidation and strengthening of those bonds contemporaneously with enlarging our contacts and improving our machinery of co-operation within that wider Caribbean and, indeed, within the new Latin America of which we are now a significant sub-region. There must be no confusion in our minds or in our methods. We do not of necessity face a choice between our Community objectives and enlightened relationships with our Latin American neighbours. What is needed is a clear appreciation of priorities. The economic integration of the Commonwealth Caribbean and the development of the Caribbean Community, the consolidation and strengthening of CARICOM, must be a matter of paramountcy in all our regional and hemispheric relationships.

To that end I believe it can materially assist in removing misunderstanding within our Community, and perhaps also in discouraging premature advances from without the Community, if we were to resolve that full membership of the Community and the Common Market would remain closed to present members – and, of course, to The Bahamas, for whom special arrangements exist – for a determinate period of time. This still leaves room for special forms of liaison and association with appropriate states – and I think particularly of a new country like Surinam – but it would serve the dual purpose of guaranteeing a period for the deepening of the process of integration and of dispelling anxieties and misunderstandings that relationships, which are inevitable between CARICOM member states and progessive regimes in the wider Caribbean area, are likely to erode the processes of integration. Let us remove such misgivings by foreclosing the opportunity for dilution of the West Indian character of our integration process during its formative years just as we had earlier done with the same intent, and must continue to do, in order to perserve the

West Indian character of our Caribbean Development Bank.[5]

I do not despair for CARICOM. West Indian politicians, like West Indian cricketers, have a boundless capacity for sustaining an atmosphere of breathless excitement. They may sometimes fail; but they more generally succeed. The team is seldom as vulnerable as the score – or as the commentary – suggests. I am confident that we shall overcome current misunderstandings and difficulties; but I am certain that the way forward lies in an activist programme of economic integration and not merely in protestations and asseverations of commitment. If that is all we do, we shall be engaging in a kind of verbal political jogging – the semantic activism of marking time – and we will find that, far from remaining at our present point, we shall have slipped backward; for as we engage in our jogging, the rest of the world will be sprinting by. In our commitment, therefore, let us remember the way of performance – and the urgent need to take it.

Notes and References

1. In July 1965, talks held between the Premiers of Barbados and Guyana on the possible establishment of a Free Trade Area in the Caribbean resulted in the announcement in July of that year of definite plans to establish such a Free Trade Area. This was carried further in December of the same year when the Heads of Government of Antigua, Barbados and Guyana signed an Agreement at Dickenson Bay, Antigua, to set up the Caribbean Free Trade Association. See generally, *CARIFTA and the New Caribbean*, Ch. 2 'From Federation to CARIFTA, 1962-1968' (Commonwealth Caribbean Regional Secretariat, Georgetown, 1971).

2. ACP-EEC negotiations which concluded with the signing of the Lomé Convention in January 1975. See, *Supra,* Chapter 3 for a full treatment of this subject.

3. Appendix A.

4. 'Less Developed Countries': The CARICOM Treaty and in the Caribbean Free Trade Agreement before it, provided for two categories of benefits favouring the LDCs who were the smaller island countries (now members of the OECS) and Belize.

5. The Caribbean Development Bank was set up in October 1969 and started its operations in 1970. The Bank's role is to provide funds for development to all the CARICOM member states but with particular attention accorded to the 'Less Developed Countries' (LDCs). The 'More Developed Countries' (MDCs) have, in addition, voluntarily offered to give preference to the LDCs where the Bank's 'soft loans' are concerned. See *CARIFTA and the New Caribbean*, op. cit., Ch. 23.

The Lure of 'Realpolitik'

Ten years after leaving the Caribbean, Shridath Ramphal spoke in Port-of-Spain, on 13 May 1985, on the theme of economic and political options for the region. The address was delivered against the backdrop of his own sense of disappointment with the integration process and an uneven record of development in the region. More pointedly, however, it was in the context of events in Grenada and Central America and the current policies of the United States Administration. His speech in the Distinguished Lecturer Series sponsored by the Institute of International Relations of the University of the West Indies was a warning to the countries of the region against the lure of 'realpolitik'.

History never writes on a clean slate. The future will never be free of the present, any more than the present can be released from the past. These are universal truths – realities which even an idiosyncratic Caribbean must accept. As I reflected on what I might say to you about options for the Caribbean, I thought inevitably about the degree to which those options are conditioned by what we are and what we have been; by where we are and whence we have come. We truly cannot avoid looking both before and after. Nor can we, I think, avoid a measure of pain and sadness even when we contemplate what has been best in the region to date and our brightest hopes for the future. Permit me, then, that glance before.

It might have been the case that this year, 1985, the West Indies – with its capital in Port-of-Spain – would have been celebrating 23 years of West Indian independence; perhaps planning for the Silver Jubilee of the Federation in 1987. I wonder what would have happened had Jamaica's referendum gone the other way or if, perchance, there had been no referendum. What would have happened had the decisions taken at the 1961 Lancaster House Conference, which settled outstanding details of the federal system and fixed the date for the independence of the Federation, not been frustrated by the 'No' vote in that referendum? Perhaps some other intervention would have changed the region's federal destiny; but perhaps not.

What would have been the political environment of the region over the ensuing 23 years? What, for example, would have been the course of events in Grenada? Would the collective will of the region and the political, if not the constitutional, authority of the Federal Government not have curbed, or at least constrained, Eric Gairy's excesses? And even if it had not, would it not have precluded, or at least actively put down, the Maurice Bishop coup d'etat that was itself a response to those excesses? The Federal Defence Force, by then well established with land, sea and air units, and with the Federal Government's authority behind it, would have had a legal duty to come to the aid of the civil power in a constituent territory – whatever the political judgement about the quality or standing of the local government.

Might it not on the whole over those years have been a more stable region? – though a region, no doubt, with its quota of quarrels arising out of relations between the Federal Government and those of constituent territories; quarrels of the kind all federal systems face. But would we, too, not have matured, as others have done, in our judgement that federalism was the rock upon which the region and the region's hopes must be founded and have developed the will to make it work through understanding and accommodation?

And what would have been happening to the people of the Caribbean? Would they, too, not have shared in this wider field for ambition? Would they not have sensed greater scope for contributing, for sharing in the process – the harder but more exciting process – of building the West Indian nation? Would young people have grown more confident of a future here in the West Indies, less 'transient' as West Indians, despite the initial constraints on 'freedom of movement'? Would all this have helped to keep within modest proportions the region's brain-drain to the metropolitan centres of Britain, Canada and the United States, with some, at any rate, of our best people sensing the prospects of a rewarding future in the wider region that was their country now?

But, all that is behind us. I have indulged these speculations not to urge that we retrace our steps but to recall what might have been. From among the best of what might have been are elements that may still be within our grasp without federalism.

As the present comes out of the past, so for the West Indies it has emerged from the rejection of the federal option, and the future has to be erected on that present: a present built upon the less rigid foundation of regionalism. Having rejected federalism – or, at least, having let it slip from our grasp – regionalism became a necessity, and we have spent the last 23 years – not always with total conviction – making a virtue of it. That effort, the evolution of the Caribbean Community, has been on the whole a triumph of practicality over inclination – the compulsions of mutual interest in regional integration overcoming our natural archipelagic instinct for contrariness and fragmentation.

But to speak of a triumph is not to ignore the struggle. Indeed, it is to underline it. And a struggle it was and has continued to be from CARIFTA to CARICOM and in the evolution of CARICOM. Barrow, Bird and Burnham deserve much credit for having the will to make the start at

Dickenson Bay in 1965.[1] It was a bold venture that might have died at birth had a sense of shared benefit from regionalism not prevailed. If there is one lesson that emerges from the story of the beginnings of CARIFTA, it is the importance of being willing to embark on the journey toward regional goals even if the entire region is not yet ready. But they must be genuine regional goals along a path that leads to ever widening unity. The region then will come. Certainly it was so with CARIFTA, and those who began were wise enough to wait just a while, particularly for Trinidad and then, later, for Jamaica. They were heady days, those early years of regionalism. I was privileged to play a part in their unfolding and can speak from personal recollection of the sturdiness of the commitment to deepening it. The very fact that there was argument at one stage with Jamaica over whether what we had embarked on was regional integration or co-operation merely, is testimony to that sense of purpose, for it was the goal of integration that prevailed. But it remained a constant struggle for everyone to rise above short-term national interest. Yet rise we did – at least from time to time.

Nothing better illumines this vintage period of Caribbean regionalism than the joint recognition of Cuba by the four major countries of the region simultaneously in 1972. It was an act rooted not in ideology but in practical regional considerations and the refusal of Caribbean countries to be pawns in a super-power game. So Cuba attended the Non-Aligned Foreign Ministers' Meeting in Georgetown in 1972 – its first appearance outside the United Nations at an international gathering within the Hemisphere. Its Foreign Minister, Raoul Roa, brought with him authority to conclude with Guyana a formal diplomatic agreement. Guyana's response was welcoming, but counselling deferment to give time for the Caribbean as a group to act in concert. Guyana was ready to proceed and told its CARICOM partners so. Within months, Barbados, Jamaica and Trinidad and Tobago joined Guyana in formally concluding in Ottawa that historic agreement. Latin American participation in the embargo against Cuba was over. And because all this was done in the context not of alignment with East or West but in a framework of non-alignment, it too won for the region only respect.

I do not mean to imply that the Caribbean in these years was without differences. The differences were real. Some governments were to the left of centre; some a shade to the right. But, in large measure, they were differences of emphasis – not ideological rifts.

No backward glance over the post-federal years can fail to take account of the emergence of the Eastern Caribbean islands to independence. When we recall the subordinate role of the Leeward and Windward Islands during the federal negotiations and the querulous LDC/MDC[2] relationships of the CARIFTA and early CARICOM period, it has to be acknowledged that the process of independence through 'associated status' has brought new strengths to the region. Developments such as the OECS have enlarged both confidence and opportunity for the Eastern Caribbean States, and helped to overcome some, though not all, of the problems they face as very small states. But more than that, I sense a more relaxed relationship with what used to be called in a regional context 'the MDCs' – a designation that does not now in all respects conform with reality.

But the gains may go further. Time was when the 'big four'[3] set the pace for regionalism, leaving the others to follow, welcoming and accommodating them, it is true, but in no sense sharing the lead. Today, it is to the OECS countries that the Caribbean may have to look to carry the pace of regionalism. Certainly, it is their new-found sense of unity and self-assurance that helps to hold the Caribbean together and give it the chance to have options as a region. This contribution has not had the recognition it deserves. In the Caribbean of the future, reality may dictate that we cease thinking of 'LDCs' and 'MDCs'. The last ten years have shown that there are strengths and weaknesses everywhere in the region. When better times return for the bigger countries, they must not themselves return to a psychology of superior status.

In a curious way, that early manifestation of regional unity in areas where it mattered most was achieved in an environment within the region that was tolerant of pluralism; tolerant of the shades of difference – ideological and otherwise – among the countries of the region. Ironically, that unity fell away when the environment of the region became unpropitious to pluralism. It might seem paradoxical, but it is really intelligible, that when a group becomes intolerant of the differences within itself, it moves not to homogeneity but fragmentation – the very environment of intolerance encouraging fissiparous trends. The differences tolerated before, and here and there overcome in the interests of joint positions, become now even deeper divisions. And that, in large measure, has been the fate of the Caribbean over something like the last decade.

The region talked much of ideological pluralism but moved away from it; cold-war resonances became louder. As the eighties came nearer, that over-arching tolerance weakened; left-wing movements at home; right-wing pressures abroad; an economic down-turn that reduced options everywhere; an international climate that saw a decline from detente and a resurgence of the Brezhnev doctrine of 'spheres of influence' – all helped to increase stridency within the region on both the left and the right. Maurice Bishop's coup d'etat in Grenada in 1979 was a turning point. Military intervention was its eventual out-turn. We are still too close to those events to assess them conclusively. In the world community, few have changed their minds about them – either among those who were passionately supportive or the many others who felt outraged. All must be content to leave the final verdict to history.

But there are some lessons that it is not too early to draw, particularly from a Caribbean point of view. High among them is the degree to which fear can lead events irreversibly to destruction. Maurice Bishop's fear, for example, of external intervention was clearly a factor in making that intervention more probable. But he was not only a victim of fear, he was a generator of it. For there is no question that both the nature of the regime and Cuba's assistance to it generated fears within the Eastern Caribbean. When history separates the many, many strands and attempts a dispassionate judgement, I should be surprised if this factor of fear does not loom large in the calculus – fear generated from both beyond and within the region.

What is the lesson then? Surely that dogmatism of right or left, from outside the region or from within it, that drives out tolerance and fails to take account of the deepest anxieties its own intolerance generates, will ultimately lead to desperate measures; and, from a regional point of view, make harder the triumph of practicality over inclination. Those tragic events of 1983 are now behind us and a sense of tolerance is coming back. But it would be altogether too simplistic to believe that the path ahead for the Caribbean, and particularly for regionalism, is an easy or obvious one.

What are the alternatives for the Caribbean? There are some options despite the many constraints that operate on Caribbean governments. Against the background I have all too sketchily outlined, there is, I believe, one factor that can be quite decisive in determining how even the region's limited options are, in fact, exercised. I would describe it as 'The Lure of Realpolitik'. The *Oxford Dictionary* defines 'realpolitik' as:

> Politics based on realities and material needs, rather than on morals or ideals.

Politics which responds to needs not principles. The politics of reality, of pragmatism; politics which subordinates all else to perceived short-term interests.

These are, in many ways, the worst of economic times in

the Caribbean. From Jamaica to Guyana, Barbados to Trinidad, and throughout the OECS countries and Belize, these are unpropitious times. Times of special uncertainty and diminished hope for those who at the best of times never had it good. But times of uncertainty and of down-turn for those like Trinidad and Tobago which have enjoyed several decades of relative prosperity. At such times, the lure of pragmatism is almost an element of the instinct for survival. But, like the mirage in the desert, which is also a factor that instinct generates, it is easy to slip from reality to illusion. And it is not merely hard times in the Caribbean that makes realpolitik so attractive an option. It is also the fact that the global environment is encouraging a belief in it as the world once more becomes polarised between the super-powers and captive of their ideological and power contests. Nothing symbolises this more than the resurgence of notions of spheres of influence. It may have been a 'Brezhnev doctrine' in its enunciation, but who can doubt that it holds sway today in Washington no less than in Moscow? – indeed in Washington perhaps even more than in Moscow, reinforced no doubt by an earlier 'Monroe doctrine'.

For whom is this doctrine good? Was it good for Afghanistan? Is it good for Nicaragua? Can it be good for any of the regions within either sphere of influence? There is a reality to being in the shadow of a super-power. Canada and Mexico, Finland and Yugoslavia, can all attest to that reality. But it is altogether another matter to clothe such realities and the constraints they impose with the mantle of legitimacy. The Chinese denounce hegemony and in their picturesque political epithet reject the role of 'running dogs'. Many developing countries look for solidarity and security in the politics of non-alignment. Canada steadfastly asserts her national identity and freedom of economic and political choice. The whole history of Latin America's relations with the United States is a story of resistance of dependency – with greater or less success.

The Brezhnev doctrine has not lacked for application in this Hemisphere. It was interwoven in the 'Alliance for

Progress'.[4] It was the underpinning of Kissinger's 'Community of the Western Hemisphere'.[5] It appears in a benevolent garb in the 'Caribbean Basin Initiative'[6]. Faced with the rising expectations of a generation already saturated with the lifestyles and living standards of the world's richest country, West Indian politicians face inexorable odds. It is more than tempting, it is almost compelling, to take the lure of realpolitik. After all, it holds out the expectation, if not indeed the promise, of security under the United States umbrella from both internal and external threats, the hope of economic and financial assistance in a time of deep recession, and, not least, a sense of being a part of the 'in crowd' at a time when to be on the outside is to feel very exposed. All these must be powerful incentives which it is easy to scoff at if you can afford the luxury of being a spectator, but which are far more irresistible if you have to exercise the option to take it or leave it.

And if this were all that was involved in the politics of realpolitik why should there be resistance? But is this all? Are there not other needs to which the politics of a narrow pragmatism does not respond? What about such old-fashioned concepts as self-determination, freedom, sovereignty, self-respect, the right to determine one's economic and political path to the future? What about the spirit of Chaguaramas, and the primacy of patrimony over power? In accepting the lure of realpolitik can we be sure that the Caribbean would not be turning its face away from these early goals and denying these earlier gains? And if the answer is that it may well be so, must we not question whether 'lying down and rolling over' within your super-power's sphere of influence is, indeed, realpolitik? Is it, in truth, the politics of meeting genuine material needs, or is it merely an illusion of fulfilment?

Take, for example, the new orthodoxy of the market place. Despite occasional rhetoric to the contrary, Caribbean countries on the whole have worked hard to preserve a middle road between statism and *laissez-faire*.

Private enterprise and initiative have a large role to play in the region's economic development. But if this is now to be interpreted as a need to provide complete freedom and unlimited scope for the operations of transnational corporations without any regard for adverse consequences on the region itself, at what price do we buy the new orthodoxy? Must not our first priority in enlarging the role of the private sector in the region be to give emphasis and encouragement to indigenous enterprise and entrepreneurship?

But in many respects, the answer to the question of reality or illusion lies in the wider international environment. And here it is essential to recognise the immense significance of that environment for small states in particular. In a world in which relations between states are rooted in bilateralism, small states have leverage and influence so small that it vanishes altogether. Their weakness is palpable in such areas as trade and finance. They may rely for a time on being among the 'friends' who will be helped bilaterally, but they quickly learn that as times change and they cease to be centres of 'high politics', the very fact of being friends, of being 'good guys', of being 'with us', becomes the reason why bilateral assistance passes them by. Can a small country, then, trapped in a sphere of influence, look to an ethos of internationalism as its economic or political security blanket? Can it look to a world political order founded on principles and rules to save it from being smothered by the paws of the bear or the wings of the eagle? What are some of the realities of that global scene?

The essential case for multilateral co-operation rests on the fact that an increasingly interdependent world, in which the network of economic relations is intensifying, requires such co-operation if we are to pursue expanding opportunities and advance the mutual interest of all nations, Such co-operation implies a sense of shared responsibility for human welfare – a perception of human solidarity. It also implies acceptance of the need to seek consensus in the international community on collective responses to that responsibility. At the heart of multilateralism lies the aspiration for an increasingly democratic world.

Yet, today, multilateral arrangements are under stress and strain. The challenge that multilateralism now faces is nothing less than a questioning of the benefits of international co-operation. It is a questioning encouraged by many factors – some of them rooted in the experience of international co-operation in the post-war era. But it is also, in part, induced by the passage of time which has blurred human memory of how diminished international co-operation brought the world to economic disaster in the 1930s and to near self-destruction in the war that followed. The need for international co-operation "to save succeeding generations from the scourge of war"[7] seemed axiomatic in 1945. It is not everywhere so acknowledged today – particularly within the most powerful countries.

President Truman, opening the United Nations' founding conference in San Francisco's Opera House forty years ago, described its participants as 'architects for peace'. And he went on:

> If we should pay merely lip-service to the inspiring ideals and then later do violence to simple justice, we would draw down upon us the bitter wrath of generations yet unborn...The responsibility of great states is to serve, and not to dominate, the peoples of the world...We can no longer permit any nation or group of nations to attempt to settle their arguments with bombs and bayonets.

What a strange resonance those memorable words have today. How far removed are some countries from the noble heights of principle to which the international system was lifted at the moment of its birth.

Instead, some of those who inspired the UN's establishment seem intent on reversing its evolution. This means miniaturising the UN – scaling it down to reflect the largely unspoken premise that some are more equal than others even under the Charter, ensuring that internationalism does not get in the way of resurgent nationalism and its advancement of crude power. Extremists even talk of emasculating all the agencies that are not under Western control. New York, however, will remain unreformed; the Security Council left inert with the veto intact; the Secretary-General and the General Assembly gradually curbed through budgetary and other strictures. The spirit of internationalism that two wars had evolved into a global ethos by 1945 is not the one that guides decisions in super-power capitals – or those of their compliant allies.

What has all this to do with Caribbean options? Everything! When the Caribbean countries began the process of independence over twenty years ago, a global consensus on international co-operation for development existed and could be made the unspoken premise of policy options. It is doubtful whether that consensus still holds; certainly, it cannot be taken for granted. The alternative to international co-operation is a drift towards a more rigid, fragmented, and power-dominated international environment; a drift away from order, stability, predictability and rules, towards greater arbitrariness, uncertainty and exercise of power; a drift away from the multilateralist trends of the early post-war era; a return to the anarchy of the 1930s. This is the climate in which the Third World generally must now develop its strategy for the future – in which the Caribbean as part of the developing world, a particularly weak and vulnerable part, must explore its policy options.

In this climate, what is the true realpolitik for small developing countries like Caribbean states? Even if we forget principles, where within this environment lies the meeting of real needs? Do the needs of the region not really lie in maximising regional independence in a wholly hard-headed manner, taking account of the reality of super-power politics and the threat to internationalism? Is not that independence necessary to the very survival of Caribbean countries as independent members of the international community? In the interest of the Caribbean people, can the region or any of its parts afford:

- to be for the 'contras' and not for Contadora?
- to be ambivalent about an international regime for the sea and the sea-bed?
- to be equivocal about IMF conditionality?
- to be indifferent on the issue of SDRs?
- to applaud 'constructive engagement' in Southern Africa and not raise its voice for sanctions against South Africa?
- to sit on the sidelines on 'Star Wars' when it knows that a nuclear winter will eclipse the tropical sun?
- to be ambiguous about non-alignment or a silent partner in the G77?
- to be of the South but not for it?
- to profess commitment to internationalism but not stand up for the United Nations?

In every one of these cases, and there are others, the lure of realpolitik will take the Caribbean away from its real self-interest.

And it will also take the Caribbean away from opportunities to preserve options and, therefore, to enlarge hope for its people. Opportunities, for example, provided by our good regional resource endowment – an endowment that can ensure that the shadow of impoverishment does not fall between potential and performance. That resource endowment includes our human resources – a gifted people needing only a propitious environment in which their talents may flourish.

And there are opportunities to enlarge options in the region's historical connections with Canada, in particular, but with Europe and the Commonwealth as well; and by a whole range of new connections with Latin American countries emerging among the newly industrialised. Moreover, the world's political geography may be changing. The threats to internationalism of which I speak may yet forge new coalitions of middle-countries, linking North and South, East and West, defying the pressures for conscription into one super-power camp or the other – Sweden and Austria, Romania and Yugoslavia, India and Nigeria, Brazil and Mexico – countries with no aspiration for dominance but strong enough in themselves and stronger still together, to make a stand against an authoritarian world.

And besides, is it really the case that principle and ideals no longer matter? What do the people, especially the young people of the region – who will, I agree with Arthur Lewis,[8] determine the future of the region – what do they think? What is their realpolitik? A better environment at home almost certainly; but an environment that is home-made in the Caribbean, or one that makes us all, in V.S. Naipaul's[9] phrase, 'mimic men' and women? Are they really for a new dependency, a new colonialism that may acknowledge sovereignty but deny freedom of choice? Is the Caribbean's brave start with independence to be a false start? It is salutary to remember President Reagan's assertion:

> The Caribbean region is a vital strategic and commercial artery for the United States. Make no mistake: the well-being and security of our neighbours in this region are in our own vital interest.[10]

This current perception of the region's super-power offers two possibilities: external domination or internal strength. To a substantial degree, the choice is still ours. Certainly, as a region, our destiny depends on ourselves. Let the present not be seen as a time when we closed our options, abandoning the alternative which was once our goal, that, in Marryshow's compelling words: "The West Indies must be West Indian".[11] And that really is the point: it is still as it always was for the West Indies – in unity lies strength both to perceive our regional needs and to pursue them.

Let me end, therefore, on a note of challenge. There is a difference between making an accommodation with power and welcoming dominion. Reality, pragmatism, may justify the former. They can never require the latter. A realpolitik that responds to the needs of the West Indies requires policies both at home and abroad that strengthen not weaken freedom, independence, self-respect, the right to pursue regional interest as the region sees best; policies that return to the spirit of Chaguaramas. The ultimate option for the Caribbean is whether it is going to preserve a right to have options at all, and a capacity and will to exercise them. One hundred and fifty years after West Indians took their stand for freedom from bondage, are there not lessons from history that not merely guide but compel us?

Notes and References

1. *Supra*, n. 1 on p. 175.

2. *Supra*, n. 4 on p. 176.

3. Barbados, Guyana, Jamaica and Trinidad and Tobago.

4. The Alliance for Progress was the main pillar of US President John F. Kennedy's Latin American policy. It took the form of a multilateral economic development programme established between the United States and 22 Latin American countries by the Charter of Punta del Este in August 1961. Its aims were the maintenance of democratic government and economic and social development.

5. *Supra*, Chapter 4, pp. 144-149.

6. *Supra*, Chapter 4, n. 1, p. 143.

7. Preamble to the Charter of the United Nations signed in San Francisco on 26 June 1945 and brought into force on 24 October 1945.

8. W. Arthur Lewis, 'Epilogue to John Mordecai', *The West Indies: The Federal Negotiations* (Allen and Unwin, London, 1986), p. 462; also, W. Arthur Lewis, *The Agony of the Eight* (Advocate Printery, Barbados, 1965).

9. V. S. Naipaul, *The Mimic Men* (Penguin Books, London, 1969).

10. President Reagan's Address to the Organisation of American States, Washington, 24 February 1982.

11. 'The West Indies must be West Indian' was the slogan which appeared on the masthead of the newspaper, *The West Indian*, published and edited by T. Albert Marryshow in Grenada from 1915.

And what a moral compulsion devolves upon West Indians to yield to none in abhorrence of apartheid and in resolve to stand against it. The spirit of every slave worked and beaten and degraded on West Indian sugar plantations, of every rebel against slavery hanged in the cause of freedom from Guyana to Jamaica, rises up to demand of us that abhorrence and resolve.

*Shridath Ramphal**

Chapter 6

Ending Apartheid

Perspective VI   194

Apartheid: Slavery's Modern Face   199
(Hull, 1983)

Apartheid's Ayacucho   207
(Caracas, 1983)

The End of the Beginning   216
(London, 1985)

Sanctions: The Path to Peaceful Change   225
(Paris, 1986)

Why the EPG is Right   231
(Swaziland, 1987)

The Cost of Political Default in Southern Africa   239
(Washington, 1987)

* *Some in Light and Some in Darkness: The Long Shadow of Slavery,* University of Hull, 24 May 1983 (Third World Foundation, Monograph 12, London, 1983).

Perspective VI

Apartheid in South Africa is many repugnant things, but at its core is a doctrine of racism stripped of all pretence: it has institutionalised the notion that whites are superior to blacks in the legal structure, the social organisation and the economic arrangements of the state. Consequently, the non-white peoples of that sad country are denied basic human rights – economic, social and cultural, as well as civil and political – and are wantonly abused both individually and collectively with the approval of the government. In its doctrine of racial superiority and the naked oppression which flows from it, apartheid is the image of what slavery was in the West Indies. When Shridath Ramphal attacks apartheid it is the human dimension which motivates him – a yearning to see humanity respected and human abuse ended.

His sense of moral outrage against apartheid is shared, in varying degrees, by the majority of the world's people, including an overwhelming number in Europe and North America; and the signs are that this number is increasing every day. Every government today condemns the South African regime for its perpetuation of apartheid, but they remain divided and ambiguous over what practical measures to take in combating it. The Commonwealth has been more involved in the problems of Southern Africa than any other international grouping and, over the period 1975 to 1988 Shridath Ramphal, as Commonwealth Secretary-General,

has played a prominent role in trying to mobilise international support for efforts to bring justice and peace to the area.

In a sense, Ramphal had a foretaste of the problems
involved in mobilising a unanimous Commonwealth
approach to ending apartheid in South Africa when he
tackled the issue of Southern Rhodesia; there, a majority
white regime, led by Ian Smith, had declared the country
independent and instituted petty apartheid arrangements to
keep the majority black population on the margins of
society.

The Commonwealth had twice been on the verge of
fragmentation over the refusal of successive British
Governments to take action to end the illegal
'independence' of Rhodesia and, as Commonwealth Heads
of Government met in Zambia in August 1979, Nigeria
threatened to leave the Commonwealth if the British
Government's attitude persisted.[1] Shridath Ramphal knew
that if this happened other African states would follow suit
precipitating a massive walk-out of developing countries
from Asia and the Caribbean – all, ultimately, to the
detriment of the struggle in Southern Africa. Pulling
together the common threads in the positions put forward by
the main protagonists in the Southern Rhodesia debate at
the Meeting in Zambia, he presented them with points of
agreement upon which they could move forward: central
among them was that a Constitutional Conference should be
called to settle the terms of independence including the
holding of genuine elections based on one-man, one-vote.
The result was the Lusaka Accord and the Conference that
followed at Lancaster House in London.[2]

Throughout the Lancaster House Conference in
December 1979, Ramphal convened what was virtually a
parallel conference of Commonwealth High Commissioners
just a few yards away at Marlborough House – despite the
rising resentment of the British Foreign Secretary Lord
Carrington – to ensure that the British Government kept to
the terms and spirit of the agreement in Zambia. The

Patriotic Front leaders Robert Mugabe and Joshua Nkomo consulted frequently with Ramphal throughout the meeting. But critical to the effective transition from Southern Rhodesia to independent Zimbabwe was the general elections. In keeping with the Lusaka Accord, Ramphal wanted them observed by a Commonwealth mission. After a battle with the British Government, the mission was agreed and the elections returned Robert Mugabe's ZANU PF Party – contrary to Western expectations.

In the years since the emergence of Zimbabwe under majority rule, Commonwealth focus has centred on apartheid in South Africa. Ramphal was among the first to express the view that apartheid is the root cause of the problems of the entire region and at successive Commonwealth Conferences he has tried to promote joint action to end it. The effort continues; but to date, assisted by the refusal of some Western Governments, Britain among them, to apply effective sanctions to sharply and quickly cripple the South African economy, apartheid has tightened its grip within South Africa.

When Britain rejected sanctions at the Commonwealth Summit in The Bahamas in 1983, Ramphal was among those who pushed for the establishment of an Eminent Persons Group (EPG) to go to South Africa. The intention was that the Group would explore peaceful ways to end apartheid by promoting a genuine dialogue between the true representatives of the black community and the government. He had placed much hope in the Mission and was all the more bitter for the failure forced upon it by the South African Government.

Within South Africa itself, time is now running out for a peaceful end to apartheid. The disenfranchised and dispossessed black people have clearly decided that there is nothing more they can lose. Cast out of the areas of their birth and shunted into so-called 'homelands' which are little more than disjointed slums, denied the right to a political voice, victimised by laws which refuse them basic human rights, the blacks – particularly the youth – have chosen to confront apartheid including the soldier's gun which defends it. For the youth the choice is no longer life or death; for them, living under apartheid is no life at all.

The heavily censored news reports emanating from South Africa in early 1988 centred on violence directed at black people by black people. To the uninitiated this gives weight to the argument of the South African Government that a South Africa governed by black majority rule would be destroyed by tribal wars. Shridath Ramphal is among those who know well that similar arguments were made in defence of slavery and indenture in the West Indies and that they are as invalid now as they were then. He also knows that small white oligarchies in the West Indies ruthlessly maintained power over the large majority of people by implementing a policy of 'divide and rule'. Today, in South Africa, the violence of one group of blacks against another is the direct result of manipulation by the South African Government to divide the black community.

And the menace of apartheid has not been restricted within the borders of South Africa. As two writers on the area put it, "South Africa, at war with its own people, is waging war on its neighbours – the independent black-ruled states which have the geographical misfortune to share its borders".[3] The objective of this war is to maintain the dependence on South Africa of neighbouring states – most of which are land-locked – for transportation routes. The war has included military incursions and economic sanctions and every day it intensifies as the South African Government grows more and more convinced that no practical action will be taken against it by the Governments of Britain, the United States, West Germany and France – the countries whose economies are most strongly linked to South Africa.

This Chapter sets out Ramphal's clear analysis of the evils and dangers of apartheid – his is a voice that warns the international community not to delay effective action against apartheid much longer for the consequences will almost certainly be a South Africa in flames – flames, ironically, which would destroy the investments some countries now seek to protect; but flames that could engulf the whole of Southern Africa and threaten world order.

R.S.

Notes and References

1. See Ronald Sanders, 'Is Britain indispensable to the Commonwealth?' *(The Round Table,* Issue 303, July 1987, London), pp. 366-377.

2. For a full treatment of this subject, see David Martin and Phyllis Johnson, *The Struggle for Zimbabwe,* (Faber and Faber, London, 1981), pp. 312-328, and David Martin and Laurence Mark, 'Man Who Saved Rhodesia Deal', *The Observer,* (London), 9 December 1979.

3. Phyllis Johnson and David Martin (eds), *Destructive Engagement: Southern Africa at War,* (Zimbabwe Publishing House, 1986), p. xv.

Apartheid: Slavery's Modern Face

In his Hull Lecture 'Some in Light and Some in Darkness: the Long Shadow of Slavery', Shridath Ramphal followed the course of slavery through indenture to modern-day apartheid as a cruel legacy of human bondage. He made a powerful plea for global action against apartheid which he saw as the legacy of slavery carrying the stain of race into the end years of the century. In July 1985, it was announced that a passage from this lecture would be memorialised in a plaque erected by the Kingston-upon-Hull City Council in the public gardens surrounding the house where the anti-slavery campaigner William Wilberforce was born, dedicated to the honour of Nelson Mandela and called 'The Nelson Mandela Gardens'.[1]

Slavery is more than a system; indeed, for slavery to be formalised by law and institutionalised into a system, a measure of bigotry is essential – often gross, sometimes subtle. In this sense, slavery begins in the human mind, in the distorted manner in which one man looks upon another and makes a perverted judgement enabling him to deny that those enslaved are equal members of one human race. Slavery rests on an assumption of superiority by the enslaver. And it is always 'the other', perceived as consciously different, who is enslaved. In this difference lies the beginning of the denial of common humanity.

The basis of 'otherness' may be religion: European Christians were for centuries enslaved as 'infidels' by the

Islamic Turks and Moors. The difference may be one of class: the West Indian and American plantations were worked in their earliest decades by indentured poor whites or by white criminals. The ruling groups within some African tribes sold their own serf class into the plantation slave trade. The simple distinction between one nation and another, or between one tribe and another, has often been the basis for slavery; which explains why warfare has historically been the most frequent source of slaves.

Race has been a primal reason for 'otherness', with the white race mainly as slave owners and the black race mainly as slaves. But, as we have seen, slavers are nothing if not eclectic; after emancipation, brown men and yellow, Indians and Chinese, made acceptable substitutes. Academics dispute whether the motivation behind the beginnings of plantation slavery in the New World was purely economic, or whether it was from the start racial, as it certainly became. What is clear is that perceived differences of race and colour allowed awareness of 'otherness' to be placed readily at the service of the economic system of slavery. It was dangerously easy, if appallingly unjust, to proceed from the observed reality that most slaves were black men and women to the irrational belief that black men and women were, and should be, slaves.

The history of our own time affords the most complete example of 'otherness' as a reason for enslavement. Nazi Germany used pseudo-scientific theories based on perverted Darwinism to justify the persecution and enslavement of the Jews; for what were the concentration camps but the ghettoes of a vast slave labour force? Even the motto on the entrance gates of one camp, Sachsenhausen, cynically underlined the point: 'Arbeit Macht Frei' – 'Work Makes Free'.[2] But the camps were not reserved only for the Jews, their most numerous victims; within them were to be found any who had opposed themselves by their otherness to the Nazis: political dissenters, members of religious minorities, gypsies, homosexuals, Slavs, prisoners-of-war, even (another irony in that supremely sick system) the mentally ill. Indeed, the category of 'the other' was on the verge of encompassing anyone who was not an Aryan German Nazi, and in the end the psychosis was becoming self-destructive, with the masters forced to look among themselves for their slaves.

That brings us dangerously close to the present; close enough to put us on notice for our own times. Frantz Fanon recognised the totalitarian impulse as springing from the assumption of superiority when he wrote: "It is the racist who creates his inferior", and asked the quesion: "Superiority? Inferiority? Why not the quite simple attempt to touch the other, to feel the other, to explain the other to myself?"[3] No question is more pertinent amid the anomy and anonymity of our multiracial modern cities where it is all too easy to become alienated from one's fellows, to perceive them as strangers, transforming them into the 'others' from whom we can justify withholding what Wilberforce so well described as "that equitable consideration and that fellow-feeling which are due from man to man".[4]

The Martinique poet Aime Cesaire correctly perceived that Nazism was the importation into Europe of a system with which black people were all too familiar, the seeds of which had already been sown by the Europeans themselves. "Before they became its victims", he wrote, "they were its accomplices; that Nazism they tolerated before they succumbed to it, they exonerated it, they closed their eyes to it, they legitimised it because until then it had been employed only against non-European peoples".[5]

It is one of the least pardonable crimes against contemporary humanity that under the label of 'apartheid', false doctrines of racial superiority continue to be employed against its black people. And apartheid is not without its accomplices beyond South Africa; those who, failing to identify with its victims as fellow humans, would tolerate, exonerate, close their eyes to, and legitimate it. Yet apartheid is the most cruel legacy of slavery – carrying the stain of race into the end years of the twentieth century.

One hundred and fifty years after Wilberforce, consider the reality of South Africa: 87 per cent of the land reserved for 4.5 million whites; 20-22 million blacks, 70 per cent of the population, relegated to the remaining 13 per cent of scrub land – denied even the right to belong; legislated out of their own country; deemed to be migrant workers from fantasy 'black homelands'. As with the slavery of the plantation colonies, the laws of apartheid discriminate overtly between one class and another; in South Africa, between the whites and all others, with the totally disenfranchised black Africans the most oppressed of all. As with slavery, apartheid is rooted in 'otherness', the otherness of 'separate development'. As with the slavery, it is the 'otherness' of race that sustains apartheid's evil creed.

Apartheid resembles slavery also in its economic rationale. Its basic motive is to provide a permanent subject labour force kept rigidly separate from the ruling class. The Bantustans, to which every black South African must by law belong, and the townships where the great majority actually live, are nothing other than segregated pools of cheap labour. The mines and farms of South Africa could not function without that labour. And the means of ensuring control and domination of the labour supply is the rigidly-enforced 'pass laws', regulating movement, entrenching insecurity, denying civil liberties, even dividing husbands from wives and children. Pass laws, let us remember, were also a feature of the system of plantation slavery. It was wide protest against apartheid's pass laws which led to the Sharpeville Massacre in 1960: shades of the West Indian slave rebellions of the 1820s and the last-ditch intransigence of the West Indian planters.

Apartheid is another slavery; yet, it is possible to descend through the apartheid system, as through the circles of Dante's hell, to a condition of ultimate repression indistinguishable from slavery at its worst. South Africa rejects every exposé as propaganda – as do its apologists. So let us look to the British press. On 30 March this year a British newspaper reported on the protests of black leaders in Namibia at the token six year prison sentence passed on a white farmer found guilty of battering to death a twenty year old black parole prisoner sent to work on his farm.[6] A photograph produced at the trial showed the farmer holding a chain securing his badly beaten victim. Even the shackles of slavery have been bequeathed to apartheid. The manacles in the Wilberforce Museum are not mere relics to remind us of past evils; they are grim testimony of apartheid's present inhumanites. What we are dealing with here is an imprisoned labour force being worked and beaten to death with impunity.

In 1980 the number of black prisoners working for white farmers was at least 90,000, about one-eighth of the total agricultural work force.[7] After arrest for minor pass laws infringements, many of these forced labourers are directed straight to the farms without trial, under the 'parole' scheme. Others who cannot find employment accept placement on farms by the 'aid centres' as an alternative to deportation to the Bantustans. Another mechanism to achieve the same effect is the 'youth service camp'. The 'aid centres' are administered by the euphemistically-named Department of Co-operation and Development – a new name for the Department of Native Affairs. Even private enterprise mental hospitals have provided contract labour under conditions of brutal compulsion for major national and international companies and for the gold mines, with the patients often paid only in sweets or cigarettes; 11,000 are believed to have been thus abused in 1975; since then an Act of Parliament has prevented the publication of further information.

The true depth of the system is reached in the farm prisons. These are built at farmers' cost and long-term prisoners allocated to each farmer in proportion to his investment; thereafter, the prisoners effectively become the farmers' property. A 1971 advertisement for the sale of grain, wine and sheep mentioned "winery shed and ten convicts" as among the assets. Here, still, is the dehumanisation, the reification, of true slavery. It is a monstrous system, with atrocities, floggings, torture and extremes of sadism a frequent occurrence. Court sentences on anyone charged are often minimal or not even implemented, and the police sometimes aid farmers in their brutality.

In June 1983, 'The Times' (London) carried a report from its 'Own Correspondent' in Johannesburg on the "white man who celebrated his nineteenth birthday by going out and beating a black man to death with karate sticks".[8] He was found guilty of culpable homicide by the Pretoria Regional Court and sentenced to "serve only 2000 hours 'periodic punishment' at the weekends, of which 800 hours have been suspended conditionally for five years. He will be free to continue his job on the railways during the week".

History will record as a twentieth century aberration our failure to show resolution in the completion of this unfinished business of slavery's abolition. How can the future judge the power-brokers of our age, save in terms of hypocrisy and double-standards, when they justify their acquiescence in apartheid in terms of solicitude for 'allies' in the contest between East and West, or simply in terms of national interest in relation to 'trade and investment'? The former is wholly misguided and contradictory and antithetical to the true interests of any who seek the goodwill of Africa. The latter is the modern-day equivalent of what a nineteenth century Parliamentary critic of those who wished to ban slave-grown goods while not attacking the system at source called 'lucrative humanity'.[9] A moral choice is incumbent on all who would trade with apartheid, and there can only be one decision: morality and expediency, humanitarianism and 'policy' demand that South Africa be made to dismantle apartheid. But I go further.

I invite each and every one of you, citizens of Hull and other friends, to question whether any can take pride in the work and achievements of Wilberforce and the Anti-Slavery Movement if, as individuals, as a nation, as a world community, we fail to take a righteous and uncompromising stand against apartheid. By what quirk of logic, what twist of values, can we celebrate emancipation and tolerate apartheid? We tarnish and depreciate the memory of Wilberforce so long as slavery South Africa style flaunts its evil and defies our will to curb it, sensing our resolve to be a fragile thing.

Can any act of commemoration of the historic achievement of 1833 be anything but a charade unless it rouses in us something of the passion of Wilberforce and the 'saints' in renouncing for our world and our time the legacy of slavery that is apartheid? Two hundred years ago the citizens of Hull sent Wilberforce to Westminster. Is there any truer way of commemorating his life of service to mankind than to send out from Hull this year the message that his memory demands: that apartheid is the same 'moral deformity', the same 'crime before God', as slavery is; that it must be viewed with the same detestation, and reprobated with the same boldness as was slavery 150 years ago; that Britain that led the way then must lead the way now; this time reinforced by a Commonwealth which itself became possible because of that first step in acknowledgement of the universality of the dignity of man which Wilberforce and Hull helped Britain to take.

Notes and References

1. *Commonwealth Currents*, October 1983. The passage is printed in italics at pp. 224-225.

2. F.V. Grunfeld, *The Hitler File* (Weidenfeld and Nicolson, London, 1974), p. 318.

3. Frantz Fanon, *Black Skin White Masks, tr. by Charles Lam Markmann* (MacGibbon and Kee, London, 1967), p. 231

4. William Wilberforce, *An Appeal to the Religion, Justice and Humanity of the Inhabitants of the British Empire on behalf of the Negro Slaves in the West Indies* (Hatchards, London, 1823), p. 43.

5.   Frantz Fanon, op. cit., p. 90, quoting Aime Cesaire: *Discours sur le colonialisme* (Presence Africaine, Paris, 1956), pp. 14-15.

6.   *The Guardian* (London), 30 March 1983.

7.   Allen Cook, *Akin to Slavery: Prison Labour in South Africa* (International Defence and Aid Fund, London, 1983), *passim* for this and subsequent paragraph.

8.   *The Times* (London), 6 June 1983.

9.   *(1848) Hansard's Parliamentary Debates,* Third Series, Vol. 96 (22 February), Hutt, at 1096, cited in Eric Williams, *Capitalism and Slavery* (Andre Deutsch, London, 1964), p. 170.

Apartheid's Ayacucho

In 1983 the United Nations Special Committee Against Apartheid held its first meeting in Latin America. Shridath Ramphal was invited to address the Committee in Caracas on 14 September. It was a special occasion since it coincided with the twentieth anniversary of the Committee, the 200th anniversary of the birth of Simon Bolivar and the 150th anniversary of the abolition of slavery. It brought together, therefore, in a particularly pointed way elements that were prominent in Shridath Ramphal's thoughts and work. He used the occasion to summon Latin America to the Bolivarian tradition of struggle for freedom in contributing to the ending of apartheid. Earlier the same year, the Simon Bolivar Prize had been awarded to Nelson Mandela and presented to Oliver Tambo in the presence of six Latin American Presidents. Ramphal conjured up memories of the Battle of Ayacucho, which finally confirmed the liberation of the continent from European dominion, in calling on Latin America to stand with the victors at apartheid's end.

Three anniversaries conjoin this year to give this meeting in Caracas a very special meaning. The first arises from the fact that 1983 marks the end of two decades of the work of the United Nations Special Committee Against Apartheid – twenty years of devoted service to the anti-apartheid cause and the cause of human dignity world-wide. It is a contribution accorded due international recognition at the Committee's Twentieth Anniversary Session earlier this year.

And this year the world, and Latin America above all, is celebrating the 200th anniversary of the birth of Simon Bolivar the Liberator.[1] That the Special Committee in its twentieth year should have assembled in Caracas in the 200th year of Bolivar, is truly in the spirit of the Liberator. This is the city where he began his lifelong campaign to liberate all the countries of South America from colonial rule. It was the seat of the first independent South American government. This gives Caracas a special place in the history of the anti-colonial struggle and makes it a most apt setting for today's historic meeting.

But the link with the Bolivarian tradition is even more direct. In the 'Jamaica Letter'[2] eleven years before the Congress of Panama, Simon Bolivar articulated his lifelong desire for an international gathering of the newly-decolonised states meeting with other world nations to reach decisions on burning international issues. He expressed it in these terms:

> Would to God that some day we may have the good fortune to convene there an august assembly of representatives of republics, kingdoms and empires to deliberate upon the high interests of peace and war with the nations of the other three-quarters of the globe. This type of organisation may come to pass in some happier period of our regeneration.[3]

It was not to come to pass for some 130 years; but Bolivar's vision did near fulfilment with the establishment of the United Nations. Was it not the intention of the founding fathers at San Francisco to endow the world assembly with that power of international arbitration which was first expressed as an essential internationalist principle by Bolivar and stands as his greatest contribution to world order and international law? Is not the United Nations the international equivalent of that additional power with which Bolivar wished to endow the Venezuelan Republic, the moral power to ensure correct behaviour?

And should we not see this Caracas meeting of the United

Nations Special Committee Against Apartheid as an earnest
of the progress made by mankind towards implementing
Bolivar's internationalist principles, and of the
determination of the international community to continue
Bolivar's anti-colonial struggle by eradicating apartheid, the
worst manifestation of colonialism? In 1967 a young
Frenchman, Regis Debray,[4] reminded a Bolivian military
court that Bolivia had been liberated from the Spanish by a
truly international army drawn from every part of South
America and even from Europe. It is time for that same
internationalist spirit, which gave birth to South America's
freedom, to be brought to bear in order to defeat apartheid:
not yet, and let us hope not ever, by force of arms; but by
the unconquerable might of moral power.

Apartheid represents the worst of all colonisations, one
which is not only economic and physical, but also mental,
emotional and spiritual. It is a cancer which gnaws at the
vitals of the human spirit. The strength of African resistance
to apartheid is a tribute to the resilience of that spirit. Just as
Simon Bolivar rose stubbornly from the ashes of defeat to
grasp the laurels of victory, so the opponents of apartheid –
above all the black South Africans suffering under its yoke –
will never cease from their striving until the just goal has
been achieved and the monster of apartheid is no more.

In this year of Bolivar, as a son of Guyana, itself "a piece
of the Continent, a part of the main",[5] I am proud of the
Liberator's role in freeing South America from imperial
dominion. As a Latin American of the Caribbean, I am
proud of the Caribbean's contribution to Bolivar's eventual
triumph: proud of the 'Jamaica Letter', which is both a
political analysis and a blueprint for the future; proud, too,
of the fact that he found ships and support from the
Caribbean Republic of Haiti. A black nation succoured
Bolivar in his hour of need.[6] Now the oppressed black
people of South Africa in their time of travail look to the
nation and the continent of Bolivar for support.

A third anniversary has particular relevance to the

struggle against apartheid. While Caracas was celebrating Simon Bolivar's birth, and marking it appropriately with a prize which Nelson Mandela shared with the King of Spain, ceremonies were taking place elsewhere in the world to mark the 150th anniversary of Britain's Abolition of Slavery Act of 1833 and of the death of William Wilberforce who did so much to bring it about, and to extirpate slavery throughout the world.

It is a poignant fact that the two Liberators, Wilberforce and Bolivar, met in London in 1810, when the British slave trade had already been abolished but when both still had their greatest achievements to come.[7] Bolivar, who grew up as a slave-owner, in 1816 fulfilled his promise to Haiti to declare the slaves free, and he wrote freedom from slavery into the constitutions of Venezuela and Bolivia. The abolition of slavery in this part of the Americas thus predated abolition throughout the British dominions: Bolivar anticipated Wilberforce.

It is a fact, however, that despite the achievement of Wilberforce and his colleagues, slavery is not extinct in the world today. It continues to mock our humanity and nowhere more grotesquely than in the form of apartheid. In truth, apartheid is slavery's modern form – and as cruel and shameful and evil as was slavery before its abolition, or as was the National Socialism that surfaced in Germany fifty years ago with its underpinning of anti-semitism and fascism.

There must be many people in Caracas, in Venezuela, in South America, who are simply unaware of just how horrendous is the human degradation consciously and deliberately perpetuated by the system of apartheid. The institution of slavery was castigated in pre-abolition days as a "moral deformity", and apartheid is the same moral deformity today, beyond comparison with any denial of human rights in any society in the world.

In one way, the situation in South Africa resembles the continuation of a classic colonialism which South America would easily recognise, of a type which South America has long since repudiated by force of arms. In another way, the Pretoria regime replicates more contemporary styles of aggression: the authoritarianism, the arrogance, the brutality of an alien force subjugating the people of an alien land.

And let no one be deluded by South Africa's invocations of cold war attitudes depicting itself as a country under siege from international Communism and as the protector of Western influence. No Western interests can conceivably be served by the oppression of South Africa's peoples under the heinous yoke of apartheid or the continued illegal occupation of Namibia. Let us lay to rest the bogey of a Communist threat to South Africa once and for all. In truth, South Africa is seeking to protect itself against a much more powerful ghost: the spirit of human freedom among South Africa's subject millions.

This is the context in which any talk of an alliance between states on both sides of the South Atlantic must be judged. If any South American government gives sustenance to the Pretoria regime, it will be denying democracy, not combating Communism; it will be setting itself against Africa, not saving Africa from others.

Attitudes to South Africa should be conditioned instead by Bolivar's wise awareness that much of the world "has been, and still is, the victim of its governments. You will note numerous systems of governing men, but always their purpose has been to oppress them".[8] Since Bolivar's time, systems of government in many parts of the world have changed for the better; the decolonisation which he championed became one of the great forces of the twentieth century as well as the nineteenth, as it spread into Asia, Africa and Pacific, with the Commonwealth as one of the results; human freedoms have been infinitely enlarged. Yet the people of South Africa are, indeed, still the victims of their government. From Sharpeville to Soweto the imprint of tyranny remains the same.

Can anyone who takes pride in twentieth century civilisation, or reaps the fruit of it, with good conscience fail to disavow apartheid and fail to do what he or she can, in however small a way, to make a stand against it? The answer is plain: the evil must be contested whenever possible, wherever it manifests itself. And if that human obligation devolves upon all of us, the more pressingly does it weigh upon the disinherited majority of South Africa.

Let us be clear on one thing. Those who struggle against apartheid, who are driven to take up arms against it, are not the ones we ought to condemn as 'terrorists'. They are the counterparts, 150 years later, of the slaves who, in rebellion and uprising throughout the West Indian plantations, threw off their chains and made a stand for freedom. Oppression is no less terrorism because it wears an official uniform. Those who fight for freedom do not become 'terrorists' merely because they cannot form themselves into conventional armies. The real terrorists in Southern Africa are not those who help the oppressed, but the oppressors themselves who command the heights of economic, social, political and military power in South Africa to sustain an evil system of racism that is itself the 'alpha' and 'omega' of terrorism against the human personality. A system that ineluctably will breed its own responses of violent retribution.

For the rest of us, there are a variety of fronts on which the campaign must continue to be fought. Of these, the sporting front is one on which the Commonwealth has campaigned to good effect: in the Gleneagles Agreement,[9] in the Brisbane Code of Conduct, [10] and in the stand of Commonwealth governments, Caribbean governments among them. It is an example this Committee has urged others to follow. But the sporting front is just one; one of the most visible but by no means the most important. The struggle must be waged against arms sales and nuclear collaboration; against trading, financial and commercial links; against the tacit support for apartheid that political and cultural affiliations inevitably suggest.

It is well known that the level of success across these various fronts has been uneven, and the reasons are not far to seek. Major countries with levers of power which can be used to exert pressure on South Africa continue, on the one hand, to plead their preference for persuasion while, on the other, they disclaim effective power to persuade. It is not merely that they recoil from international economic sanctions but that, by the nature and ambience of their relations with South Africa over a wide field, they, in effect, sanction and support the apartheid *status quo*.

Not just the Pretoria regime and its friends abroad but others who misread the signs, sometimes advance the argument that changes are being made in South Africa; that petty apartheid restrictions are being done away with; that sport, to take one example, is now more racially mixed than before. Let no one be deluded. Nothing can be normal in a society so fundamentally abnormal, so antithetically opposed to accepted norms of civilised human relationships. One might as well have looked for normality in Hitler's Germany, or Russia under the shadow of Stalin. Change in South Africa is a myth – the last desperate attempt to present the illegitimacies of apartheid in the guise of concession.

Improvements have been cosmetic only, designed to add a spurious veneer of respectability to surface features while the inner structure of apartheid, the skulls beneath the skin, remain as ugly and frightening as before. The horrifying nature of that inner reality is the message which the Special Committee Against Apartheid is to be commended for conveying so forcefully to the world. That message will ring particularly true here in Caracas, where South American liberties were born. And the heritage of those liberties will be immeasurably strengthened by a determined resolution from this meeting, on behalf of all South America, to do everything possible in concrete ways to extend these fundamental freedoms to the oppressed people of South Africa.

It was a symbol of Latin America's collective commitment to the anti-apartheid struggle that the Simon Bolivar Prize was awarded to Nelson Mandela earlier this year in Caracas in the presence of the Presidents of six Latin American Republics. In accepting the Prize on behalf of Mandela, Oliver Tambo acknowledged that the award and the ceremony would:

> contribute to the deepening and consolidation of relations between Latin America and Africa based on that great vision of international solidarity among other peoples which guided Simon Bolivar as he prepared for the Congress of Panama.[11]

And so, indeed, it has. But, of course, the true and lasting manifestation of solidarity with Africa lies in the practical, tangible measures which Latin America supports and adopts in the framework of the struggle against apartheid. What Africa needs most of all is solidarity from Latin America that translates itself into positive action – solidarity in the tradition of Bolivar.

In each age, the battlefield for freedom is different, but the cause is the same. South Africa is one such battlefield of our own time; let us pray that the battle may be fought with ideas and arguments not with guns; but it must be engaged. In the name of the oppressed people of South Africa the ultimate struggle, the engagement of Ayacucho[12] which will finally vanquish the oppressor, must not be delayed. And Latin America must stand with the victors at apartheid's Ayacucho!

Notes and References

1. Simon Bolivar, the soldier and visionary whose conquests in the name of freedom helped to make today's Third World possible, was born on 24 July 1783 in Caracas, Venezuela, then under Spanish rule. By the time he died in 1830 he had freed not only Venezuela from Spain but also Peru, Bolivia (named after him), Colombia,

Panama and Ecuador, earning for himself the title of 'Liberator'.

2. Written by Bolivar in Kingston, Jamaica, on 6 September 1815. *The Jamaica Letter* is the most widely known of Bolivar's early writings on political and international affairs.

3. V. Lecuna and H.A. Bierck Jr. (eds), *Selected Writings of Bolivar,* 2 Vols. (Bolivarian Society of Venezuela, New York, 1951), Vol. I, p. 118; also Manuel Perez Vila (ed), *Simon Bolivar: His Basic Thoughts* (Presidency of the Republic of Venezuela, Caracas, 1981), p. 79.

4. Contemporary press reports. Also Regis Debray, *Prison Writing,* tr. R. Sheed (Allen Lane, London, 1973), p. 73.

5. John Donne, Meditation XVII, from 'Devotions upon Emergent Occasions' in *Complete Poetry and Selected Prose* (The Nonesuch Press, London, 1972), p. 538.

6. J.B. Trend, *Bolivar and the Independence of Spanish America* (Hodder and Stoughton, London, 1946), pp. 118-119.

7. Ibid., p. 72.

8. 'Angostura Address' in Lecuna and Bierck, op. cit., p. 177; also Manuel Perez Vila, op. cit., p. 95.

9. 'Commonwealth Statement on Apartheid in Sport', (The Gleneagles Agreement, 1977) Appendix B; also in *The Commonwealth at the Summit: Communiqués of Commonwealth Heads of Government Meetings 1944-1986,* (Commonwealth Secretariat, London, 1987), pp. 198-199.

10. In October 1982, during the Commonwealth Games in Brisbane, the General Assembly of the Commonwealth Games Federation approved a new Code of Conduct for national Commonwealth Games Associations designed to give the expectations of the Gleneagles Agreement a practical dimension in the Commonwealth Games context; see *Constitution of the Commonwealth Games,* Appendix A (Commonwealth Games Federation, London, 1983), pp. 39-40.

11. Oliver Tambo, President of the African National Congress of South Africa, on the occasion of the Presentation to Nelson Mandela of the Simon Bolivar Prize, (typescript, Caracas, 24 July 1983), p. 6.

12. Trend, op. cit., pp. 183-186.

The End of the Beginning

The International Defence and Aid Fund for Southern Africa founded in 1966 by the late Canon Collins, now led by Archbishop Trevor Huddleston, has earned an honoured place in the struggle against apartheid's inhumanities. On 10 May 1985, Shridath Ramphal was invited to address the 25th Annual Conference of IDAF in London. He took the opportunity to provide a forthright and unapologetic answer to the question: Why a sporting boycott against South Africa? Eight years earlier, the Commonwealth's Gleneagles Agreement[1] had pointed the way for South Africa's isolation in sport as part of the wider anti-apartheid struggle. But the address went beyond the 'sporting boycott' to hail 'the end of the beginning' of the struggle against apartheid.

In a brilliantly contrived public relations scheme of misinformation, South Africa has gone on the psychological offensive. 'Apartheid' is out; though integration gets no mention. A separate Parliament for Coloureds is in; though given no power; and with none anyway for Blacks. Cosmetic legal changes are everywhere in vogue; meaningful reform is, of course, wholly absent. It is absent because apartheid by definition defies reform.

These simulated winds of change blow not across the solid structures of apartheid but on the sensitive surface of Western public opinion. Apartheid is not being dismantled, it is being repackaged. The grotesque reality remains – but because its hideousness lies revealed, the image must be improved. The harsh realities, for example, of day to day life in the African townships and in the so-called "homelands" are unaffected. The labels are being changed for export, while the grimy product of institutionalised racism remains as sordid as ever.

This pretence of change in South Africa is, of course, a response to the measure of external pressure and internal solidarity which the Anti-Apartheid Movement, including the Defence and Aid Fund, has helped to generate over the years. To this extent, you are justified in being encouraged; but none of us must be deceived or lulled into complacency. The mirror image of the mask of change is the renewal of apartheid. Your efforts, therefore, must be redoubled. In those efforts, the Commonwealth stands with you in the vanguard of the assault on apartheid. It was the Commonwealth that, in 1961, in a move without precedent, pushed South Africa from its fold. It is the Commonwealth that has set its face plainly against racism of any kind, not only in the Gleneagles Agreement[2] and the successive Declarations by Heads of Commonwealth Governments, but in the principled actions of the overwhelming majority of Commonwealth sportsmen and sports bodies.

Yet, in a number of countries, the same questions continue to be asked: Why South Africa? Why sport? Why single out South Africa from the number of countries where human rights abuses take place? Why should sport be used as a lever to bring about change in South Africa, when we continue to play with countries whose human rights records are also abysmal? And why, if sport should make sacrifices, are trade and investment free to flourish? Are we not being selective in our application of morality?

These questions, despite their familiarity and their orchestration, must always be answered; and our responses must be principled, consistent and compelling. And it is important, too, that these answers be repeated, even in an enlightened and sympathetic forum such as your own, for they can never be reiterated too often.

First, it is South Africa, because in that country, and that country alone, a minority racial group clings to power seeking to entrench itself, forever, on a basis that denies every fundamental right and freedom to its overwhelming majority. It seeks, on the basis of colour, to condemn to eternal servitude every one of its non-White citizens even to a point of stripping millions of them of citizenship itself, and forcefully removing many of them to arid wastelands. Denied freedom of movement, of assembly, and of speech, denied the right to participate in political life, denied equality of opportunity, and subjected to arbitrary arrest, torture and detention, 25 million people are kept in a state akin to slavery. And it is curious to reflect that the arguments now heard in defence of such a condition – that the Blacks are better off economically and would prefer the *status quo* to the consequences of equality – precisely echo the arguments advanced by those who opposed the abolition of slavery 150 years ago.

The world does not single out South Africa for special disdain and concerted condemnation. South Africa does that for itself. And daily it reinforces the moral outrage of the world. With all the apparatus of a fascist police state, the White elite do not hesitate to imprison, or even to murder, those within the country who dare to demand to be treated with the dignity that is their birthright. It is South Africa which, with Nazi Germany, has inflicted upon the twentieth century twin monstrosities that for generations to come will blight the record of human endeavour in our time.

And in acting against South Africa no one condones the human rights abuses of other states. These are, and will continue to be, a cause for condemnation. The Commonwealth, I am proud to say, was the first to move against Amin's Uganda[3] when his abuses became so gross that, whatever the line that separates meddling from legitimate concern, we knew it had been crossed. But the gangrenous infection of apartheid must be removed before our body politic can effectively resist other blemishes, not only because of its order of magnitude but because apartheid's persistence in South Africa actually diminishes our moral authority to uphold human dignity anywhere. Moreover, apartheid has now become the root cause of wider dangers in the region – the destabilisation of Angola and Mozambique, the deferral of Namibia's freedom, the enforced diversion of resources that its inhumanities within South Africa impose on African Front-Line States in general.

But why sport? When we look around the world, who can deny that we play sport with some countries whose patterns of human rights are less than worthy? If not with South Africa, how can we play with these others?

Again, apartheid answers its own charges – the degree of evil it represents makes, I believe, a qualitative difference with all other forms of human rights abuse. But there is another, higher reason. Sport is not played between governments, it is played between people. While we may condemn the actions of a repressive government, we do so because of its abuse of its own people, and in the name of their human rights. In playing sport with them, our people can express solidarity and support even as we work to remedy the situation.

By contrast, South African society is so organised that, by its very nature, apartheid controls the structures of sport itself. It decrees that schools be segregated and, once segregated, that they must not compete against each other; Black and White must not grow up together recognising the intrinsic human worth of the other. Apartheid, too, governs access to facilities, who may play against whom, and where, and why. Inter-racial sport, when permitted, takes place under licence or dispensation, and then under the guise of being an 'international' event.

To have sporting contacts with South Africa is in a very real sense, to play sport with apartheid. And as international sporting contact strengthens sport, to play with apartheid is to lend succour and support to the system itself. This is why the international movement to isolate South Africa from sport has attracted near-universal support, and has been such an overwhelming success. As we look at the international sporting calendar, the striking feature is not, as one-sided media coverage may suggest, the number of breaches of the campaign, but that a breach is news because of its exception from the sporting norm. That norm is that South Africa now participates in virtually no international sporting event of any significance whatever.

The occasional 'rebel tour' is mounted, it is true – primed by a system feeling the effects of the sporting boycott. They are so primed because the boycott by sportsmen gives a lie to the line pretoria carries at home; namely, that it is only governments for political reasons who 'posture' against apartheid, but that people generally, and especially White people all over the world, do not share their governments' protestations against apartheid. Ordinary, decent, sportsmen and sportswomen everywhere are telling the people of South Africa, White and Black, this is not so: 'Your system is too sordid for contact'.

In New Zealand today, as a direct consequence of the Rugby Union's decision to tour South Africa – and how sad it is that rugby almost alone among sports insists on demeaning itself – children are turning away from the game; coaches are moving to other games; some school teams, at the insistence of the pupils themselves, are being withdrawn from competitions; and all major sponsors of rugby find it no longer commercially acceptable for their names to be linked with the game. Denied players, coaches and resources and, most importantly, public support, the game can only suffer grievously. A self-inflicted wound made, we are told, in the 'interests' of rugby itself; but how complete an answer to the misguided mandarins of the game.

Yet the question still remains: if a sport embargo, why not also sacrifices by the business community? In practice, of course, trade sanctions are applied, both by a large number of governments and by millions of consumers around the world who, exercising their choice, daily and deliberately, forego produce originating from South Africa. A quite voluntary act of protest. Yet unhappily a number of countries stand aloof, and are conspicuous in their support of the South African economy. So that question remains valid.

The real basis of resistance to sanctions lies in the disingenuous excuse that to implement sanctions would be to hurt most the very people who are already the victims of apartheid. Black leaders within South Africa have strenuously denied this. They know better than most how much they would prefer to see change brought about by economic hardship than through the carnage of civil war – for that, in the end, could be the alternative.

This is not tomorrow's cause, it was yesterday's whose time has come. I recall Canon Collins, in his Lutuli Memorial Lecture in Dublin in June 1970, repeating Lutuli's appeal when he spoke about the Rivonia Trial: an appeal

> to all governments throughout the world, to people everywhere, to organisations and institutions in every land and at every level, to act now to impose such sanctions on South Africa as will bring about the vital necessary change.[4]

That is the authentic voice of Africa. Canon Collins continued:

> This is the objective we should set ourselves for 1971...attacking the fountainhead of this evil as it exists in South Africa we shall be resisting its spread in other parts of the world. In so doing, we shall play a major role in the human struggle for world peace.[5]

The time for sanctions – sanctions carefully selected with a view to maximising their effect – has come.

Resistance to sanctions lies in the cold unfeeling calculus

of money and profit and returns. And it is bolstered here and there by the self-deception, unarticulated for the most part, that White 'kith and kin' could not really be guilty of such atrocities; that South African society is inherently decent, and that if matters are out of hand occasionally, they cannot be substantially to blame. This stubborn sympathy defies the facts, and it comes, too, from countries who, by having enjoyed lengthy social and economic ties with South Africa, are the very economies which have benefited most from the economic deprivations inherent in the apartheid system. They are governments whose policies will not change until an impatient electorate calls a halt.

But people are on the move. In the United States, there are welcome signs that public opinion is waking up to outrage at the charade of 'constructive engagement' – an 'engagement', as we know all too well, during which South Africa has devastated her neighbours, sabotaged international efforts to resolve the Namibian problem and intensified the brutal repression of the Black majority. We welcome our American friends here tonight, and applaud the part they have played in awakening the conscience of their nation. We welcome, too, our friends from New Zealand, whose people in 1981 subjected themselves to not a little brutality in their own efforts to protest the Springbok rugby tour of their country.[6] And we salute the principled actions of the new Government of Prime Minister Lange in its determined opposition to apartheid. We acknowledge, too, the unswerving stand taken by the Government of Australia, where staunch opposition to apartheid has developed to the point where both political parties have demonstrated in courageous terms their commitment to the cause of apartheid's elimination.

Collectively, movements in these three countries, each with long ties of friendship towards South Africa, are, in themselves, grounds for optimism. Today we can see further signs that the days of apartheid really are numbered, one of which has a significance that we have tended to overlook – though, of course, the Fund has not. Until quite recently, under South African labour laws, Blacks were excluded from the definition of "workers",[7] and as such were denied the right to form trade unions. But form trade unions they did, and transnational companies – responding both to international pressure and to domestic economic needs – for the first time began to negotiate with these unrecognised unions, unions beyond the reach of Pretoria as they operated outside the law. Pretoria was driven by the persistence of erstwhile "non-workers" to amend the labour laws, not to extend the limited boundaries of freedom but in an attempt to assert control simply to curtail the unions' political activities. Yet the fact remains that change has been forced – not conceded – and that the Blacks in South Africa have achieved a first and vital platform whose potential for the longer-term struggle is incalculable.

There are signs, too, within that unhappy country not only that Black informers are coming under pressure and so will be reduced radically in their number and effectiveness, but that even the White Afrikaaner, for the first time, is coming to question the long-term outlook for the country.[8] There are also signs of panic in Pretoria – of hasty and muddled decision-making that contrasts starkly with the assured ruthlessness of even a few years ago. Afrikaanerdom is feeling the pressure, and at least some in the laager are showing signs of losing their nerve. These internal processes are nourished by work outside the country, of which the recent awakening of the American conscience is, perhaps, the most significant development.

I do not dare to claim that the end of apartheid is in sight: to do so would be to fall prey to the propaganda designed to demoralise us; but I do declare that apartheid is in retreat and that its destruction is assured. Desperate rearguard action lies ahead that will test the will of the world community and of South Africans within. We must not falter now – we must instead steel ourselves for the final push, remembering how much our efforts on the outside mean to the victims of apartheid in sustaining their morale and their will and determination to resist.

As with slavery's abolition 150 years ago, it will be the conjuncture of the humanitarian support from outside, the modern-day equivalent of Wilberforce and the abolitionists, with the refusal of the victims of apartheid to submit – the assertion by them of their human right to rebel – that will bring about apartheid's end. It is that conjuncture that is in sight. We are not at V-SA day. In the words of Churchill in 1942: "This is not the end. It is not even the beginning of the end. But it is, perhaps, the end of the beginning".[9] The Defence and Aid Fund has helped to make it so and must sustain that effort to the final victory.

Notes and References

1. Appendix B.

2. Ibid.

3. London Communiqué 1985, *The Commonwealth at the Summit: Communiqués of Commonwealth Heads of Government Meetings 1944-86* (Commonwealth Secretariat, 1987), para. 35, p. 192.

4. Canon Collins' Lutuli Memorial Lecture in Dublin in June 1970 about the Rivonia Trial, *Southern Africa: Freedom and Peace,* (IDAF, 1980), p. 36.

5. Ibid.

6. The 1981 tour by the South African rugby team caused deep divisions within New Zealand society, culminating in a decision by the High Court (upheld on appeal) to grant an interim injunction restraining the New Zealand Rugby Football Union from touring South Africa in 1984. *Finnigan and Recordon v NZ Rugby Football Union Inc.* (CS66/85); and *Finnigan and Recordon v NZ Rugby Football Union Inc. (No. 2)* (A 164/85) in (1985) 11 *Commonwealth Law Bulletin* 1173 and 1181. The tour was cancelled as a consequence.

7. Labour Relations Act 1982.

8. In July 1987, 65 prominent Afrikaaner intellectuals, politicians and businessmen met with representatives of the African National Congress in Dakar, Senegal, to discuss the future of South Africa.

9. Winston Churchill, Mansion House, 10 November 1942.

Sanctions: The Path to
Peaceful Change

*"Over the last six months a remarkable thing happened in one
of the saddest corners of our small world. A group of seven
people from five continents, black and white and brown gave
everything they had to offer – integrity, humanity,
compassion, understanding and a wide experience – to
holding back a darkening storm. For a brief moment, the
world – and, pre-eminently, South Africans of all races –
glimpsed a path of negotiation to a more worthy future".*

*That is how Shridath Ramphal began his Foreword to
'Mission to South Africa', the findings of the
Commonwealth's Eminent Persons Group on Southern
Africa.[1] The Report offered a searching look at South Africa
and showed how a catastrophe might yet be averted through a
dialogue for ending apartheid and establishing a genuine non-
racial democracy. Four days after the EPG's Report was
published, Shridath Ramphal, on 16 June 1986, addressed the
World Conference on Sanctions Against Racist South Africa
in Paris.*

The message of the Report is clear: apartheid must end. It
will end; if necessary, through a bloody struggle whose cost
in lives may be counted in millions and whose agonies will
reverberate in every corner of our multiracial world. But it
could end by peaceful means – by a genuine process of
negotiation – once white South Africa accepts that the evil
system by which it has sustained its dominance must end,

and is ready by deeds to bring it about. The Group's account shows with unique authenticity how far the Government of South Africa is from that acceptance and that readiness. It shows, too, that not all white South Africans stand rooted on the banks of the Rubicon; some are ready and willing to cross. And the Group's Report confirms that on the other bank those so long oppressed in South Africa, the victims of apartheid, are ready even now to join in a peaceful process of building a new South Africa in which all its people, black and white, coloured and Indian, will share in fairness and with dignity.

When Commonwealth leaders agreed on the establishment of the Group at Nassau, they saw it as part of a programme of common action. One aspect of that programme was the set of measures against South Africa which they agreed upon as a result of their debate on sanctions. They also agreed that if, in their opinion, adequate progress had not been made towards the objectives of the Accord within six months, they would consider the adoption of further measures, and others beyond them, on a continuing and incremental basis, in order to secure the desired result within a reasonable period.[2]

The task of the Group was to advance the process of change in South Africa "by all practicable means".[3] For the time being, at any rate, their efforts to achieve this by facilitating a process of dialogue among South Africans have been thwarted by the Government. The Group's Report makes it clear that, in the six months of their efforts, there has been no progress towards the dismantling of apartheid and the establishment of a non-racial representative government – the essential objectives of the Accord.[4]

Inevitably, against the background of their findings, they had to turn to the question of sanctions. As they have said in their Report, "against the background in which ever-increasing violence will be a certainty, the question of further measures immediately springs to mind".[5] In my

Foreword to their Report, I draw attention to the fact that whether we speak of "sanctions" or, as the Group has done, of "economic measures", they come to the same thing: effective economic pressure applied particularly by those major economic powers who are South Africa's principal trading partners and to whom it looks for major financial flows; pressure which demands change while there is still time to bring it about by peaceful means.[6]

The Group itself asks the question: "What can be done? What remaining influence does the international community have? What can major states do to help avert an otherwise inevitable disaster".[7]

First of all, they said, the question itself "is not whether such measures will compel change; it is already the case that their absence and Pretoria's belief that they need not be feared defers change".[8] In other words, the absence of sanctions is already contributing to the maintenance of apartheid and the continuation of the *status quo* of violence. Moreover, Pretoria's belief that Western countries will not apply sanctions encourages it to remain obdurate and intransigent. The absence of sanctions is actually right now contributing to the mayhem taking place in South Africa.

So the Commonwealth Group asks, are we "to stand by and allow the cycle of violence to spiral?" Or will we "take concerted action of an effective kind?" Such action – what the Group called "the adoption of effective economic measures against" South Africa – "may offer the last opportunity to avert what could be the worst bloodbath since the Second World War".[9]

Those outside who say that sanctions will "hurt the blacks" simply do not know how intense black suffering already is. It is, in any case, a judgement they have no right to make, when the blacks themselves see sanctions, and any additional suffering they involve, as preferable to the far greater tragedy they would otherwise face. This they said to the Group over and over again.

But the Group goes further. It draws attention to the fact that "the Government of South Africa has itself used economic measures against its neighbours and that such measures are patently instruments of its own national policy".[10] In other words, this Government whose friends plead against international sanctions is itself employing them as a matter of national policy to maintain apartheid and all its terrible consequences through its acts of regional destabilisation.

Understandably, then, since the Government of South Africa is such a skilled practitioner in the effective use of sanctions against others, the Group says it is "convinced that the South African Government is concerned about the adoption of effective economic measures against it".[11] Pretoria's reaction to the Report only serves to confirm this.

But perhaps most conclusive of all is the Group's argument that if the Government of South Africa "comes to the conclusion that it would always remain protected from such (effective economic) measures (against it), the process of change in South Africa is unlikely to increase in momentum and the descent into violence would be acceler-ated. In these circumstances, the cost in lives may have to be counted in millions".[12] Can any challenge to the internatio-nal community be cast in more stark terms? If Pretoria believes that the West, or major parts of it, will not apply economic sanctions, it will not move to dismantle apartheid, and violence that could involve the lives of millions will actually quicken its terrible pace. 'Sanctions' and 'peaceful change' in South Africa have become synonymous. To be against sanctions now is sadly to be for violence on a terrifying scale. Not suprisingly, the Group concludes that "it is not sanctions which will destroy the country but the persistence of apartheid and the Government's failure to engage in fundamental political reform".[13]

I remind you that the Commonwealth Group speaks with unique authority and authenticity. As a Group it held 21 meetings with South African Government Ministers and prolonged dicussions with leaders of political and other organisations as well as with prominent academic, political, religious and community figures within South Africa and outside it.[14]

One final word; and one of hope. As this Report intimately demonstrates, the human spirit survives in South Africa in so many ways. In the courage of young children; in the churches; in the great coalition that makes up the United Democratic Front; among the women who bear some of the heaviest burdens, and women's groups like Black Sash[15] who keep faith with the spirit of caring. But, most of all, its survival is symbolised in the person of Nelson Mandela. The walls of South Africa's prisons confine him; but his spirit soars above them: a spirit of freedom, of nationalism rising above 'group', of courage and resolve that humiliate oppression; a spirit of non-racialism that looks to a democratic South Africa acknowledging black and white as fellow South Africans; a spirit that can release his entire country from bondage.

The human spirit in South Africa is crying out for the world's help, for the world's solidarity. It is proclaiming to all who allow themselves to hear that it is not freedom that white South Africa should fear, but freedom's denial.

It is now only sanctions, effective economic measures – they are the same thing – rigorously applied with a determination to ensure that they compel the dismantling of apartheid, that can now ensure that freedom is no longer denied in South Africa.

Notes and References

1. *Mission to South Africa: The Commonwealth Report. The Findings of the Commonwealth Eminent Persons Group in Southern Africa,*

Foreword by Shridath Ramphal (Penguin Books, London, 1986), p. 13.

2. 'The Commonwealth Accord on Southern Africa', Nassau Communiqué 1985, *The Commonwealth at the Summit: Communiqués of Commonwealth Heads of Government Meetings 1944-86* (Commonwealth Secretariat, 1987), paras. 7-8, p. 269.

3. Ibid., para. 5, p. 268.

4. *Mission to South Africa,* op. cit., Foreword, p. 14.

5. Ibid., p. 140.

6. Ibid., p. 14.

7. Ibid., p. 139.

8. Ibid., p. 140.

9. Ibid., pp. 140-141.

10. Ibid., p. 140

11. Ibid.

12. Ibid.

13. Ibid., p. 137

14. Ibid., p. 20 and Annex 3 at pp. 150-156.

15. "Black Sash" is a women's organisation first formed to mobilise white women to protest against the Pass Laws and is now a non-racial body active in many facets of internal opposition to apartheid.

Why the EPG is Right

In March 1987, the United World Colleges Movement commemorated its 25th Anniversary with a meeting of the International Board at the Waterford Kamhlaba College in Swaziland. Literally surrounded by South Africa, Shridath Ramphal spoke at the College about the Commonwealth's stand against South Africa. 'White elections' in South Africa were only weeks away. Ramphal took the opportunity to urge that 'white' voices be raised in the election debate in support of the Commonwealth's Eminent Persons Group (the EPG) and, more specifically, of the EPG's 'negotiating concept' and the glimpse it offered of a better future for all South Africans. In doing so, he underlined the EPG's acknowledgement of the primary obligation of Pretoria to suspend 'the violence of the apartheid system'.

The real 'root' problem with apartheid is its denial of our common humanity; its repudiation of our oneness as human beings; its crystallisation of evils that have tainted civilisations over the ages into a vile creed of racial supremacy and systems of political, economic, social and cultural organisation designed to uphold it. Apartheid, in this sense, is the modern face of slavery. It calls forth the same moral repugnance that slavery did. It involves the same guilt by association of all who support and sustain it or even acquiesce in it. And it inevitably calls forth the same rebellion in defence of human values: a righteous rebellion against an evil that now taints not just this region but our whole civilisation.

That is why the Commonwealth has taken so strong and so resolute a stand against apartheid and will continue to do so. That is why the Commonwealth has been in the forefront of what I am glad to say is an international movement, a world-wide movement, for sanctions against South Africa, sanctions designed to bring white South Africans to their senses so that they might compel their Government – which, over the years, has remained beyond the pale of reason or persuasion – to recognise that the time has come for change. Harold Macmillan made his 'wind of change' speech in South Africa in 1960,[1] more than a quarter of a century ago. That wind is now blowing with gale force, and still there are those in South Africa who believe that they can hold back the storm.

Right now there is a process of debate and political realignment in South Africa. I hesitate to describe what is going on in that country as an 'election', because an election presupposes a nationwide electorate with all adults having a vote; that, South Africa does not have. But, will it be a real debate? Will it be a kind of referendum among South Africa's whites about the dismantling of apartheid, the true, genuine dismantling of apartheid and the establishment of a democratic system in a united and non-fragmented South Africa? Or will it be, in essence if not in presentation, a debate about the tactics of maintaining white supremacy? Of resurfacing the structures of apartheid so that they look better on the outside, but retain their dungeons within?

The Commonwealth has tried hard to explore with South Africa and with South Africans, Black and White, Coloured and Indian, the path to peaceful change. That is what the Eminent Persons Group was all about. They were offering South Africa a helping hand along that path; and they were specially well equipped to do so. They were people of compassion and understanding, people who knew the worlds of politics and of economics no less than of religion and of social affairs. They were Black and White, from rich and poor countries, from Britain and India, from Canada and Tanzania, from Australia and Nigeria, and from the

Caribbean too.[2] They were not there to tell South Africans what to do. They were there to talk with all South Africans – with the Government, the Black and White communities, with the ANC and PAC in exile, with the UDF, with the trade unions, and with Nelson Mandela in Pollsmoor Prison – to try to find a way forward. And they went quite far down the way of success. For a moment, all South Africans, black and white, had a glimpse of a peaceful path to a better South Africa.

Through its work the EPG won the confidence of enough people of influence within all the communities in South Africa to help a negotiating process to start – provided, only, there was a will on the part of the rulers in Pretoria to take that path. The apartheid regime gave its answer to the EPG in a manner which was in character with apartheid itself. It bombed Lusaka and Harare and Gaborone on the morning the Eminent Persons were to meet the Cabinet's Constitutional Committee for a final answer on its negotiating package.[3] In effect, President Botha's regime was saying to the Commonwealth and to the world in its own crude way that it was not ready for such a journey – because it was not ready to contemplate that journey's end.

In its Report, *Mission to South Africa*, the EPG itself put the matter in the clearest terms when it said:

> ...at present there is no genuine intention of the part of the South African Government to dismantle apartheid... no present prospect of a process of dialogue leading to the establishment of a non-racial and representative Government.[4]

But that is the negative side: the terrible squandering by Pretoria of a unique chance for South Africans of all races to break free of the bonds of apartheid which, in truth, bind both Black and White in different ways but hold them all prisoner.

How right the EPG was to have spoken out so clearly on this critical matter when it reported:

On the issue of violence, we clarified that the steps required of the Government would amount to a suspension of the violence of the apartheid system, and it was only in that context that a corresponding suspension of violence by the ANC was being sought. We had made it clear to the Government that it would be unrealistic and impracticable to expect the ANC to renounce violence for all time, regardless of the success or failure of negotiations, nor would we be prepared to endorse any such demand by the Government.[5]

And Added:

Based on the totality of all that we saw, there was no question in our own minds that the Government's demand (for a one sided 'renunciation' of violence by the ANC) was unrealistic and wholly unreasonable.[6]

Given the escalation of Government repression since last June, the primary obligation of Pretoria to suspend 'the violence of the apartheid system' has only become more palpable and more pressing. And the EPG did not merely put this into their Report; they conveyed it directly to the South African Government in their final communication of 5 June 1986:

Acts of aggression were committed against neighbouring countries on the very morning when we discussed the Negotiating Concept with Ministers. This underlines the essential elements of the concept requiring a suspension of violence on all sides and highlights the unreality of asking others to de-escalate violence before action as proposed by the Group is taken by the Government. A suspension of violence or a commitment to non-violence, if in the Government's view the meaning is the same, would obviously in the present context require a commitment to suspend the violence arising from the administration of apartheid. In addition, in the light of recent events, the Government of South Africa would need to give a firm commitment to desist from further aggression against neighbouring states.[7]

The EPG found much that was hopeful, particularly in the quality of the people that apartheid now excludes from contributing to South Africa's future. The EPG had three meetings with Nelson Mandela,[8] an opportunity given to no other group. In relation to him, they are the only true interlocutors. They found him to be an outstanding, able and sincere person, whose qualities of leadership are self-evident. He was unmarked by any trace of bitterness despite his long imprisonment. His overriding concern was for the welfare of all races in South Africa in a just society. He longed to be allowed to contribute to the process of reconciliation. Not surprisingly, they called for the immediate and unconditional release of Mandela and of all the other political prisoners – a call to which they attached the highest importance.[9]

I cannot go into the whole range of issues that the EPG Report canvassed. But what I do emphasise is the 'Negotiating Concept' which the EPG put to all parties and which they believed, on the basis of those consultations, would have provided a basis for going forward to peaceful change, were it to be accepted by the South African Government itself. The 'Concept' incorporated a framework of specific and meaningful steps towards ending apartheid; steps on the part of the Government and of the ANC and others which the Group believed could ensure negotiations and a break in the cycle of violence.

The Group called for the following action on the part of the Government:

> (a) the removal of the military from the townships, providing for freedom of assembly and discussion and suspension of detention without trial;
> (b) the release of Nelson Mandela and other political prisoners and detainees; and
> (c) the unbanning of the ANC and PAC and the permitting of normal political activity.[10]

From the ANC and others, the Group sought their readiness to enter into negotiations and suspend violence.

As you can see, this was not an abstract proposition. It

had been evolved out of a very detailed process of discussion with all concerned. It represented the belief of the EPG that, if the Government were agreeable, consensus for it could be found. The EPG said as much in submitting it to Pretoria: "It is our view that simultaneous announcements incorporating these ideas might be negotiated if the Government were to be interested in pursuing this broad approach".[11] The Government was not interested; and it proceeded, of course, to bolster its rejection of the peaceful process by a new state of emergency, massive detentions running into many thousands, and a virtual war against the children of black South Africa, a war against children which UNICEF has now documented in all its horrible detail.[12]

But that is not the only war Pretoria now wages. The perverse logic of apartheid requires South Africa to make all of the extended family of Southern Africa victims of its apartheid strategy. It has waged war through proxies on Mozambique and Angola; indulged in aggression against Zambia and Zimbabwe and Botswana; impugned the sovereignty of every neighbouring state, including Swaziland; and is embarked on a crude campaign of economic and political destabilisation of all Southern Africa's states in the front line against apartheid. Apartheid remains the root cause of the most grievous problems facing the countries of this region. It is a crime of immense proportions compounded by Pretoria's arrogance – arrogance well displayed in its recent abductions here in Swaziland, one of whose victims is even now in the appropriately named torture chambers of John Vorster Square[13] – an outrage against both the man himself and the sovereignty of this country.

But must Pretoria's bombing of the EPG's pathway to peace be the end of the matter? Is white South Africa going to permit President Botha's evil regime to condemn South Africa and the entire Southern African region to a calamitous future? It does not have to do so. The EPG's 'Negotiating Concept' remains essentially valid. Are there not white voices ready to say so as this debate in the nature of an election proceeds? Cannot white South African politicians come forward and make a stand for the EPG's formula for peace with justice – a formula we know, and they know, to be workable, if only they will demonstrate the will to make it work? If that 'Negotiating Concept' were to be taken up by the majority voice in white South Africa, it could be taken up by the majority voice in all of South Africa – and the glimpse of a better future that the EPG offered all South Africans could become a reality.

I cannot say that I have a real hope that this is about to happen. But that it can happen means that there is some basis for hope. Here at Waterford you must never doubt that people can turn that hope into reality – people as distinct from governments; people today and people tomorrow; young people and old people; black people and white people; people in South Africa and in the neighbouring countries of Southern Africa. It will take courage and strength to do so, but if both are rooted in principle – in repudiation of apartheid and in a readiness to stand up and be counted on the side of those who struggle against it – and if that courage and strength is bolstered by the resolve of people outside of Africa to stand with those who stand against apartheid, and to make that clear by their actions and by their sacrifices, then hope will become reality, and you in Waterford will one day be proud to be part of a wider region of Southern Africa to which you yourselves will have contributed.

Notes and References

1. The speech was to the South African Parliament in Cape Town on 3 February 1960. See J.D.B. Miller, *Survey of Commonwealth Affairs, Problems of Expansion and Attrition 1953-69*, (Oxford University Press, London, 1974), p. 112. Macmillan's famous phrase about 'the wind of change' in fact first came to Africa in a speech he made in Accra three weeks earlier, when Nkrumah himself qualified the phrase by calling it "no ordinary wind, but a raging hurricane";

Nkrumah, *I speak of Freedom,* (Panaf, London, 1973), p. 203 (footnote).

2. Mr. Malcolm Fraser, former Prime Minister of Australia and General Olusegun Obasanjo, former Head of State of Nigeria: Co-Chairmen; Lord Barber of Wentbridge, former Chancellor of the Exchequer of Britain; Dame Nita Barrow of Barbados, Co-President, World Council of Churches; Mr. John Malecela, former Foreign Minister of Tanzania; Sardar Swaran Singh, former Foreign Minister of India; The Most Reverend Edward Walter Scott, Primate of the Anglican Church of Canada.

3. "On the morning of 19 May 1986, immediately prior to our meeting of the Eminent Persons Group with the Cabinet Constitutional Committee in Cape Town, the South African Broadcasting Corporation announced that the South African Defence Forces had successfully carried out raids upon 'ANC bases' in Harare and Gaborone. It was later announced that a similar raid had been made on Lusaka". *Mission to South Africa: The Commonwealth Report. The Findings of the Commonwealth Eminent Persons Group on Southern Africa,* Foreword by Shridath Ramphal (Penguin Books, London, 1986), p.117.

4. Ibid., pp. 137, 138.

5. Ibid., p. 116.

6. Ibid., p. 120.

7. Ibid., p. 124.

8. Ibid., pp. 152, 155 and 156; see also pp. 67-74. The Group met Nelson Mandela at Pollsmoor Prison, Cape Town, on 21 February 1986 (General Obasanjo alone), and on 12 March and 16 May 1986.

9. Ibid., p. 74.

10. Ibid., pp. 103-104.

11. Ibid., p. 104.

12. *Children on the Frontline: The Impact of Apartheid, Destabilisation and Warfare on Children in Southern and South Africa,* 1987, UNICEF, New York. Also *Summary Report of the International Conference on Children, Repression and the Law in Apartheid South Africa,* 24-27 September 1987, Harare, Zimbabwe, (Bishop Ambrose Reeves Trust, London, 1987; UN Notes and Documents 14/87, October 1987; No. 87-26947). Also, (1987) 13 *Commonwealth Law Bulletin* 1656.

13. Ebrahim Ismail Ebrahim.

The Cost of
Political Default
in Southern Africa

*In August 1986, on the basis of a consideration of the EPG's
Report at the London Review Meeting[1] and in the light of the
earlier Commonwealth Summit at Nassau in 1985, the rest of
the Commonwealth broke with Britain on the issue of
economic sanctions against South Africa. Shridath Ramphal
believed that, in all this, the Commonwealth's credibility,
integrity and capacity to act were on trial. His judgement was
that, in being 'true to itself', the Commonwealth did not
merely survive the trial but emerged from it with new strengths
– in its member countries and worldwide. Within weeks of the
London meeting, the United States Congress passed the
Comprehensive Anti-apartheid Law adopting – against the
Administration's policy of 'constructive engagement' – a
package of sanctions broadly comparable to the
Commonwealth's. On 26 May 1987, Shridath Ramphal spoke
to the Council on Foreign Relations in Washington urging
that it was time for the United States and the West in general to
end what was being perceived, in political and historical
terms, as a policy of appeasement of Pretoria.*

Apartheid is a code word for a number of specific issues
which have their roots in the system. To understand what is
happening in Southern Africa, we must be as conscious of
these issues as of the central evil from which they derive.

They could be variously segmented. I would list them under six heads as issues pertaining to democracy, justice and human rights within South Africa, and decolonisation, dependency and destabilisation beyond South Africa's borders. I do not need, I believe, to argue the case against South Africa on any of these issues; the evidence is palpable, the scale of criminality is horrendous and, for the greater part, the outrage is overt and its perpetrator unapologetic. In its racism, apartheid's transgression of ethical norms is so enormous that history is likely to portray apartheid as our civilisation's gravest moral degeneracy on the eve of the third millenium.

On all these issues the basic values of the American nation, the highest traditions of United States foreign policy, and the most cherished principles of Western society leave little room for argument as to where this country and the West as a whole should stand. And current policy formulations do nod in the direction of such values, traditions and standards in expressing opposition to, and sometimes condemnation of, apartheid and some of its grosser manifestations in South Africa and in the Southern Africa region.

But the burden of my presentation to you is that, in practical and political terms, current responses to this cluster of issues are perceived and interpreted throughout Southern Africa as ranging the United States and much of Western Europe on the side of apartheid. In respect of the United States itself, 'constructive engagement', signalled as this country's essential policy towards Pretoria at the very moment of the strongest internal and external push against apartheid, epitomised this dichotomy. In the eyes of those who bear the day-to-day burden of the apartheid system – whether in the townships of South Africa, in the councils of the ANC or the UDF, with SWAPO in Namibia or the Government in Angola, in Maputo and along the Beira Corridor, in Lusaka, Gaborone, Harare, even in Maseru or Mbabane – the message of constructive engagement seemed clear. Washington was closer to apartheid than to any of those engaged in the struggle against it.

The vigour of Western opposition to economic sanctions against South Africa served only to confirm these perceptions. When a virtual rebellion against the system had broken out within South Africa and those so long oppressed were looking for tangible non-military support for their struggle, in what seemed to them the most effective manner open to the West, namely, sanctions in the spheres of trade and finance, Washington and London, Bonn and Paris found sanctions fundamentally objectionable; some even found them to be 'immoral'.

Such comfort as Southern African opinion has derived has come from the Commonwealth's stand, the United States Congressional action, the policy of Scandinavian Governments, together with 'people action' against apartheid throughout the United States and Western Europe and, in particular, the people-led disinvestment campaign in the United States.[2] These developments have helped black South Africans and African front-liners to believe that the West may yet join in putting an end to apartheid. But even these limited results had to be fought for. An American President's veto had to be over-ridden, the Commonwealth had to face the trauma of breaking ranks with Britain. The perception, therefore, lingers that Western Governments, whatever they say about apartheid, cannot really be counted an ally in the anti-apartheid struggle.

This is ironic outcome, given traditional Western notions that Southern Africa was one of the areas of an East-West contest for minds – and for hearts and souls. Zimbabwe offered the West a great chance of paramountcy in that contest. The Commonwealth effort, through the Lusaka Accord of its leaders and the Lancaster House process it led to in London, opened up immense opportunities in Southern Africa for a positive Western role. Washington helped that process at a critical stage. All this offered real opportunities; opportunities which the West has squandered. Robert

Mugabe did not even want a Soviet Embassy in Salisbury on independence – for reasons, it is true, that were not ideological. But, the antipathy was real. Today, he looks to the Soviet Union for arms in a desperate effort to protect his new country against overt aggression from South Africa. The United States is barely on speaking terms with him; but, even worse, does not seem to understand the sense of disappointment, sometimes downright amazement, with which American policy and practice are viewed from a capital such as Harare.

A neo-war situation now exists throughout Southern Africa. In South Africa apartheid is embattled. The forces against it are the majority black population and some elements of the white community. The recent 'whites only' election has set the stage not for the dismantling but the perpetuation of apartheid. Mr. Botha claims, from about a million whites in South Africa, a mandate to keep in economic and political subjugation something close to 28 million non-white peoples. More blacks stayed away in protest from work and schools on polling day than the whites who went to vote for Mr. Botha. Several thousand children are in custody, their young bodies and minds being bent on the rack of the apartheid system. The world's media, not to mention those who try within South Africa to convey home truths at home, now face a regime of censorship as implacable as that imposed by any Iron Curtain. Mr. Botha is ready to crack down on what he describes as any 'extra-parliamentary' activity against his Government, having first, of course, limited effective parliamentary activity to 15 per cent of the population. Even the pretences of reform have been dropped. It seems clear that there will be no genuine dialogue or negotiation save under intense and sustained pressure.

The war situation extends beyond South Africa itself: a war waged by South Africa in a logical extension of apartheid at home. Pretoria knows that apartheid can only survive in South Africa if the rest of Southern Africa is made so impotent as to be unable to assist financially, politically and militarily in the struggle against apartheid. And so South Africa has embarked on a policy of open destabilisation and intimidation of neighbouring countries – of Zimbabwe, Zambia, Mozambique, Botswana.[3]

Mozambique is in the front-line of the front-line. It is a country whose rulers have turned to the West; but with few, though notable, exceptions – including, I am glad to say, Britain – the West remains ambivalent. Taking over from where Ian Smith's UDI Rhodesia left off, South Africa has conducted through the rebel MNR its own 'contra' operations against Mozambique and continues to do so.[4] And, almost unbelievably, voices are being raised here – in the Congress, of all places – calling for US support for the South Africa-backed rebels.

Is it any wonder that South Africa behaves as if the writ of world order no longer runs in Southern Africa? It indulges aggression at will. It bombed Harare and Lusaka and Gaborone last May as its way of telling the Commonwealth Group of Eminent Persons that it was not prepared to accept their Negotiating Concept – a formula designed to bring all sides to a process of negotiation in the context of a suspension of violence. It bombed Livingstone in Zambia on the eve of the 'whites only' election to demonstrate its virility to the white electorate. It carries out bombings on an *ad hoc* basis within Harare directed at the ANC.

Namibia/Angola is a separate case; but the analysis is not too different. South African aggression precipitated the Cuban presence, and Western policy then became more hostile to that presence than to its cause, and the victim was Namibia. The record of the 'Western Contact Group' on Namibia – after a brave start – became one of continuous inaction and ineffectual dialogue with Pretoria, and, as such, an embarrassment to the very concept of a 'Contact Group' in the South African context. Recent United States policy of supplying arms to Savimbi has only made matters worse for, as much of Southern Africa sees it, that policy places the United States in virtual military alliance with South Africa which is, of course, Savimbi's principal backer and arms supplier.

As the struggle against apartheid intensifies within South Africa, and as the regime's record at home becomes more brutal and flagrant and indefensible, such perceived Western identification with Pretoria inevitably becomes more offensive and more unacceptable. But most serious of all, the identification becomes less deniable. It is one thing to be ambivalent about a great wrong; it is quite another when that wrong becomes a gross and palpable abuse against humanity. There is a point when to abstain is to condone. That point has been reached in relation to apartheid.

At the level of minds, the anti-apartheid struggle has now radicalised black South Africans – especially black South African youth – to a far greater extent than ever before. All this, of course, has happened in the period when the United States was most 'constructively engaged' with Pretoria. It is not yet radicalisation in ideological terms; but, certainly, it is in anti-American and anti-European terms. One has only to recall the difficulties initially encountered, but ultimately overcome, by the Commonwealth's Group of Eminent Persons and those encountered, but not overcome, by Sir Geoffrey Howe's mission on behalf of the European Community,[5] and by your own Secretary of State's Advisory Committee[6] in attempting even to engage the Anti-Apartheid Movement in South Africa in any kind of dialogue, to realise how tenuous is Western credibility in black South African eyes.

The Commonwealth succeeded in reaching the black community because of very special attributes in terms of the range of countries and individuals associated with the exercise. And what our experience demonstrated when they were reached was the essential moderation of the elements that would surface in a post-apartheid South Africa – were they allowed to surface now. Three meetings with Nelson Mandela himself in Pollsmoor Prison, lengthy discussions with every significant political element within South Africa, long meetings with the ANC and with Front-Line Governments, led the Commonwealth Group in its Report, *Mission to South Africa,* to assert that:

> Negotiations leading to fundamental political change and the erection of democratic structures will only be possible if the South African Government is prepared to deal with leaders of the people's choosing rather than with puppets of its own creation. President Botha's recent statements expressing his determination to 'break' the ANC bode ill for the country's future. There can be no negotiated settlement in South Africa without the ANC; the breadth of its support is incontestable; and this support is growing. Among the many striking figures whom we met in the course of our work, Nelson Mandela and Oliver Tambo stand out. Their reasonableness, absence of rancour and readiness to find negotiated solutions which, while creating genuine democratic structures, would still give the whites a feeling of security and participation, impressed us deeply. If the Government finds itself unable to talk with men like Mandela and Tambo, then the future of South Africa is bleak indeed.[7]

And as the time of moderate men runs out in South Africa, the process of radicalisation reaches beyond the country itself. Throughout all the Front-Line States people today have a greater sense of insecurity in both economic and military terms than at almost any time since their countries became independent. Their feeling of military insecurity derives entirely from Pretoria's destabilisation policies, and they know that, whatever the policy mistakes of their own leaders, their economic troubles are greatly enlarged by the need to confront that military threat. For them, too, as for black South Africans at home, Western 'constructive engagement' amounts to a Western embrace of Pretoria.

I have talked personally with young people throughout the Front-Line countries. The strength of anti-American and anti-European sentiment runs higher than I have ever encountered. And it springs essentially from how Western policy is perceived by people – not just governments – in the Southern Africa region. 'Constructive engagement', whether openly avowed as a policy or pursued in practical terms by abstention from sanctions and condescension to Pretoria, is turning Southern Africa, at the level of popular perception, into a vast anti-American, anti-European front. Again, it is not yet an ideological front, but it is assuredly one suspicious and resentful of the West over Southern Africa. Even assuming reluctance on the part of the Soviets to be drawn into the conflict in a major way, this widespread feeling would be a critical development. And it is an utterly predictable and understandable one. And so avoidable.

Can there be any other conclusion than that Western interests in Southern Africa have been heavily damaged in recent years – and damaged by Western policy? Perhaps there are some who believe that nothing matters save to preserve Pretoria as 'a bastion of the free world' in Southern Africa. I would ask, in turn, how could a 'free world' choose as its standard-bearer a regime that is the very epitome of injustice and the very antithesis of freedom not only in Africa but throughout the world? What freedom does this bastion preserve as seen by the people of that whole continent? Is not the most effective bastion of freedom the true friendship of the real Africa – including the real South Africa? Is that friendship not being gravely jeopardised by current policies and practices?

In underlining what I know to be the state of opinion in Southern Africa I do not, of course, overlook other opinions. I know that some question, with sincerity, the effectiveness of sanctions; but I think they would recognise that there is an element here of self-fulfilling prophecy. If you start from the position that sanctions will not be effective and so decline to apply them, there are then no sanctions that could be judged effective or otherwise. And, of course, the effectiveness of the limited sanctions which have managed to secure adoption could be very much greater were they applied more wholeheartedly. It is international consensus as a whole which closes the ring; it is the opting out of the strongest, much more than the impotence of the weakest, that diminishes any sanctions effort and gives apartheid a free ride.

Nor do I overlook the important role that market perceptions of South Africa's economic prospects can play in forcing change on Pretoria. But the forces of the market will themselves be enormously strengthened by the pressure and isolation that arises from sanctions carefully selected and efficiently applied. Overseas confidence in the South African economy has been further eroded in the aftermath of the 'whites only' election. Market forces are sensitive to the strength of governmental policy and public opinion in the West. This is the time for public opinion, governmental action and market forces to interact in harmony to secure movement towards the agreed objectives of ending apartheid and establishing a free, non-racial society in South Africa.

But all these material and strategic considerations apart, is the gravest damage not that at the level of ethics? Why does the United States and much of Western European so readily abandon the high ground on what is, without question, one of the major moral issues of the end years of this century? What damage does it do to its own values and traditions by standing aloof from – or, worse still, against – the oppressed and aggrieved populations of Southern Africa in the struggle against apartheid and the evils that cluster around it?

I have ventured to speak as I have done because I believe those values and traditions to be enduring, and because I believe that there is still a chance to regain that higher moral ground and to reinstate the West in the friendship of Southern Africa. For this chance to be taken, the United States must be seen to be clearly and unequivocally on the side of the anti-apartheid struggle. It must use its considerable influence to secure an end to the cycle of violence – a cycle which begins with apartheid itself – and to ensure negotiations for the end of apartheid, and for political freedom in South Africa.

Notes and References

1. The seven Commonwealth leaders nominated in the Nassau Accord met in London, 3-5 August 1986, to review the South African situation and to consider the EPG Report. In their Communiqué, they warmly commended the EPG for its 'positive and enduring contribution to the efforts to end apartheid and establish a non-racial and representative government in South Africa'. They agreed that Pretoria had taken none of the five steps called for at Nassau; there had not been adequate concrete progress towards ending apartheid, and indeed the situation had deteriorated. See, Communiqué, London Review Meeting, 1986, *The Commonwealth at the Summit: Communiqués of Commonwealth Heads of Government Meetings, 1944-86* (Commonwealth Secretariat, 1987), paras. 5-7, pp. 291-292.

2. By the end of 1987, 135 US companies had withdrawn from South Africa: based on *Investor Responsibility Research Centre Reports* (Washington DC).

3. In 1987, the Secretariat of the Southern African Development Co-ordination Conference (SADCC) estimated that the cumulative cost to nine SADCC member countries on account of South African destabilisation since 1980 had been as high as $30 billion, which is more than their total GDP in 1985.

4. See, Johnson and Martin (eds.), *Destructive Engagement: Southern Africa at War,* (Zimbabwe Publishing House, 1986).

5. Sir Geoffrey Howe visited South Africa in July 1986.

6. The Advisory Committee of 12 prominent Americans was established in December 1985. Its purpose was to examine and recommend to the Secretary of State what United States policy towards South Africa would most effectively influence peaceful change and promote equal rights in that country. It submitted its report on 9 January 1987.

7. *Mission to South Africa: The Commonwealth Report. The Findings of the Commonwealth Eminent Persons Group on Southern Africa.* Foreword by Shridath Ramphal (Penguin Books, London, 1986), pp. 133-134.

As the Secretary-General, to whom its persistence owes so much, has repeatedly told us, the Commonwealth cannot now escape the role which its distinctive composition increasingly places upon it – that of seeking to bridge the ever-widening gap between nations like ours, and the nations so easily left by us obscure in the background...Our one world, which so many divisions make it hard for us to see as one; our world of limited resources, which selfishness and improvidence would have us see as never-ending; such a world surely needs a Commonwealth that, in its very heterogeneity, both bears the load of the past and has the hope of the future. Sir Shridath Ramphal, whom we honour this day, has given new life to this hope, and we are all in his debt.

*The Public Orator, University of Durham**

Chapter 7

Redressing Poverty

Perspective VII   250

A Feudal World   254
(Hull, 1983)

The Other World in This One   262
(London, 1976)

Shadows in the Cave   278
(London, 1981)

The Trampling of the Grass   293
(Addis Ababa, 1985)

For the South, A Time to Think   313
(Kuala Lumpur, 1986)

* On the award to Shridath Ramphal of an Honorary Degree of Doctor of Civil Law, 14 December 1985.

Perspective VII

The issue of development is not one that can be tackled by any single nation, however large and rich in resources it may be. For development is no longer within the preserve of national action only; finance, terms of trade, prices for commodities, access to external markets and even aid are all matters which are fundamental to development but which require international negotiation. Shridath Ramphal understands well this international dimension to development – his learning grounds were his involvement in the problems of development in Guyana, the Caribbean and the Third World generally and his participation in the push for a New International Economic Order during the debates of the Sixth and Seventh Special Sessions of the UN General Assembly in 1974 and 1975.

Thus, when he became Secretary-General of the Commonwealth in 1975, serving a majority of developing countries, he gave high priority to the development issue in the Secretariat's work programme. Apart from the practical ways in which the Secretariat attended to development, such as the provision of technical experts to developing countries, year after year it produced studies on North-South issues[1] based on the work of expert groups assembled by Ramphal from around the Commonwealth. One of those studies, *The North-South Dialogue: Making it Work,* examined the actual process of negotiation between the North and the South and proposed practical steps to enhance it through changes of attitude, style and substance on the part of developed and developing countries alike.

It is well known that Shridath Ramphal played a major role in the work of the Independent Commission on International Development Issues (the Brandt Commission) where, from its onset in 1978, he vigorously articulated the claims of development as an authentic vote from the South. His work on development continued in a direct way between 1984 and 1986 when he served as Chairman of the UN Committee for Development Planning. The three reports[2] issued under his Chairmanship are authoritative arguments for fundamental change in global economic relations.

In his passionate advocacy of the case for development, Ramphal has not hesitated to speak out against the policies of industrialised countries and the international financial institutions, particularly the International Monetary Fund. But, equally, he has not hesitated to call on developing countries to correct their own mistakes both at the policy-making and operational levels. One such call directed to OPEC countries is little-known since it took place in closed-door debates surrounding the UN Sixth Special Session on Development in 1974. As Non-Aligned Ministers met in March in Algiers just before the UN Special Session, the world was reeling from the effects of sudden and sharp increases in the price of petroleum products from the OPEC countries. Ramphal had vigorously defended OPEC;[3] but among the subjects being debated by the Non-Aligned group was a paper on providing 'emergency relief to Non-Aligned countries facing serious and unintended difficulties as a result of the increased price of petroleum products'.

At the meeting, after reminding his colleagues of the support OPEC had received from the Third World, Ramphal warned that oil-importing developing countries were "literally faced with economic ruin and a threat to their economic survival" and he added that while developing nations were paying the cost of rising oil prices, the multinational oil corporations were making handsome profits. He proposed that the OPEC countries impose a $1 surcharge on the price of every barrel of oil to be placed in a fund to offset the burden on oil-importing developing states. He was appointed Chairman of a Ministerial Working Group to hold consultations with the Non-Aligned OPEC countries and eventually submitted the proposal to an OPEC Ministerial Meeting in Quito in June 1974. OPEC promised to consider the proposal but, in the end, did little to relieve the burden on their sister developing states which, in Ramphal's words, had "stood with (them)... without apology and without qualification". Instead they deployed their oil revenues into US treasury equities.[4] Ramphal learned that Third World solidarity was still a "consumption devoutly to be wished".

Ramphal is a member of the South Commission which was established in 1987. The Commission can play an important role in improving the performance of developing countries, in formulating and implementing their national development strategies; in setting up the machinery for genuine South-South co-operation and in devising and fulfilling effective strategies and tactics in North-South negotiations. As the presentations in this Chapter confirm, Shridath Ramphal carries to the work of the Commission not only a deep commitment to redressing underdevelopment but also well considered views on the means to do so.

R.S.

Notes and References

1. See Appendix C for a list of these studies.

2. *Crisis or Reform* (1984), UN Doc. ST/ESA/153; *The Challenge to Multilateralism* (1985), UN Doc. ST/ESA/169; *Doubling Development Finance* (1986), UN Doc. ST/ESA/187.

3. See, *The Energy Catalyst,* Shridath Ramphal's address to the Sixth Special Session of the UN General Assembly on 15 April 1974, (Ministry of Foreign Affairs, Georgetown, 1974).

4. For a full treatment of this subject, including Ramphal's proposals, see Altaf Gauhar, 'Arab Petrodollars', *World Policy Journal*, Summer 1987, pp. 443-464.

A Feudal World

Shridath Ramphal ended his Hull speech in 1983 with a reminder of the world's continuing inequalities. 'Some in Light and Some in Darkness' was still an apt description of the stark disparities between wealth and poverty in human society. The difference between earlier centuries and the twentieth, he argued, is that we are confronted now not with so many separate feudal societies but with a human society that bears the attributes of a feudal state: "Not one state and two people, but one earth and two worlds". The latter, he argued, cannot endure any more than could the former.

When 150 years ago the British Parliament took the final step in the abolition of slavery in lands under British jurisdiction, it was to be the beginning of a wider process of the abolition of slavery world-wide. It was, alas, the beginning also of the colonisation of Africa.[1] Great humanitarian instincts had played a powerful role, even if not an exclusive one, in putting an end to the systematic enslavement of man by man. But neither those instincts nor the religious mandates to which they were a response were a match for the economic forces which underpinned Europe's unseemly 'scramble for Africa' and the legacy of racism which slavery bequeathed to imperialism.

That legacy made the decolonisation process immeasurably harder and longer and, in places, more embittered than it should have been. But, by and large, the process itself has been accomplished. The Commonwealth was made possible because of it and because of the manner of its accomplishment. Yet, in one sense, decolonisation was a notional equalisation; the deeper economic disparities remained – inequalities embedded in the structures of a world economic system that had not yet recognised the convergence of principle and policy, the conjuncture of human solidarity and global interdependence. The moral imperatives for change, the hard-headed compulsions of mutual need which demand it, are unavoidable. As Barbara Ward once memorably declared: "We dare not forget the really poor, who are the great majority, because prosperity, like peace, is indivisible".[2]

Yet, the reality of life within the poverty belts of Africa and Asia, and within the many enclaves of absolute poverty beyond them, is that about one billion of 'the world's huddled masses' are caught in the trap of poverty and are still yearning to be free. How far are they from the margins of slavery? Are they not bound hopelessly in servitude to economic forces they cannot even comprehend, much less resist? In his book, *India – A Wounded Civilisation,* V.S. Naipaul described the reality of grinding poverty as he found it in a village in Bihar:

> In the village I went to, only one family out of four had land; only one child out of four went to school; only one man out of four had work. For a wage calculated to keep him only in food for the day he worked, the employed man, hardly exercising a skill, using the simplest tools and sometimes no tools at all, did the simplest agricultural labour. Child's work; and children, being cheaper than men, were preferred; so that, suicidally, in the midst of an over-population which no one recognised...children were a source of wealth, available for hire after their eighth year for, if times were good, fifteen rupees, a dollar fifty a month. Generation followed generation quickly here, men as easily replaceable as their huts of grass and mud and matting...Cruelty no longer had a meaning: it was life itself.[3]

What Naipul saw in India was but a sample of the hellholes of absolute poverty that exist in all the continents of the South. Even in those countries that we categorise euphemistically as 'low-income' and 'least developed', a year's earnings amount to just about two weeks social security benefit for an unemployed worker in Europe. In the report of the Brandt Commission, which we called, *North-South: A Programme for Survival,* we said this:

> The crisis through which international relations and the world economy is now passing presents great dangers, and they appear to be growing more serious. We believe that the gap which separates rich and poor countries – a gap so wide that at the extremes people seem to live in different worlds – has not been sufficiently recognised as a major factor in this crisis. It is a great contradiction of our age that these disparities exist – and are in some respects widening – just when human society is beginning to have a clearer perception of how it is inter-related and of how North and South depend on each other in a single world economy.
>
> The extent to which the international system will be made more equitable is essentially a matter for political decision. We are looking for a world based less on power and status, more on justice and contract; less discretionary, more governed by fair and open rules.[4]

Power and status again, the old enemies of freedom; justice and contract, the goals towards which Wilberforce reached. But between the idea and the reality still falls the long shadow of slavery. How much has changed, how much remains the same! Servitude within the feudal societies of Europe preceded slavery in the dominions abroad, just as domestic reform preceded abolition; both were essentially inhumanities within national societies. We must now widen our horizons, looking to our global society and the unequal relations of states and people within it. It is a fearful prospect; one that should fill us with resolve to ensure that the malignancy of otherness deepened by the stain of race does not perpetuate such rank divisions in the state of man. In one sense, the difference between the eighteenth and nineteenth centuries on the one hand, and the twentieth on the other, is that we are now confronted not with so many separate feudal societies but with a human society that bears all the attributes of a feudal state: not with one state and two people, but with one earth and two worlds. The latter cannot endure any more than could the former. Challenge is now unavoidable, not least because interdependence of the human condition has acquired a sharper focus in so many areas – in international security, in the preservation of the environment, in conservation of the resources of a small planet that an expanding human race must share, but, most pointedly of all, in the world economy.

For even the strongest economies, it is clear that policies now have to be informed by the fact that the 'global economy' is a reality; that the self-interest of any nation can only be pursued effectively through taking account of the mutual needs and interests of all nations. In the area of international co-operation for development, therefore, not only is it right to do good, it has become necessary as well. It was not lightly that the Brandt Commission urged that if the world fails "to become stronger by becoming a just and human society"[5] it will move towards its destruction. We have lost the option of ignoring our interdependent state – of ignoring the reality that we have become one world. And since we can no longer ignore it, we must respond to it.

Indeed, it is remarkable how true today rings the argument of mutual interest that Wilberforce used in the 1820s in a narrower context. As he girded himself in 1823 for the foundation of the Anti-Slavery Society and the long push towards emancipation, he was not afraid to bolster the claims of humanity and justice by the argument of self-interest. In his *Appeal to the Religion, Justice and Humanity of the Inhabitants of the British Empire on behalf of the Negro Slaves in the West Indies* he asserted that:

> While we are loudly called on by justice and humanity to take measures without delay for improving the condition of our West Indian slaves, self-interest also inculcates the same duty, and with full as clear a voice.[6]

The appeal to self-interest was not the core of a case coated
with humanitarian concern; that concern itself was central;
the call to self-interest was designed to bring along those
whom the moral imperative was not strong enough to move.

The free trade doctrines of Adam Smith had by then taken
deep root; they provided the conjuncture which Wilberforce
needed. It was an age, he declared, in language that is as
apposite to our age as well:

> ...in which it has been incontrovertibly established by the
> soundest of our political economists – that the base and
> selfish, though plausible, views, which formerly prevailed so
> widely among statesmen, and taught them to believe that the
> prosperity and elevation of their country would be best
> promoted by the impoverishment and depression of its
> neighbours, were quite fallacious; and when we have now
> learned the opposite and beneficient lesson – that every
> nation is, in fact, benefited by the growing affluence of
> others and that all are thus interested in the well-being and
> improvement of all.[7]

Accordingly, as with slavery 150 years ago, the demands
of compassion, of morality, of humanitarianism, even of
human solidarity, do not today stand alone; they need not
contend in vain against the claims of national interest. They
are, in fact, being constantly reinforced by the compulsions
of mutual interest. We have reached in our global society
that conjuncture of principle and prudence, of morality and
'sound policy', that made the abolition of slavery possible
150 years ago and makes inevitable now the eradication of
its continuing legacy of servitude and inequality.

There is no higher need than that we should understand
this convergence well, should acknowledge that we have to
find in our minds the way to do what we know in our hearts
to be right; should recognise that poverty is not only a stain
spread across our civilisation, but also an economic blight
that will ultimately destroy the first fruits of that civilisation

and the prosperity of those who would reap them. Humanity must respect, world-wide, the precept that Wilberforce laboured for all his life in the context of slavery and knew at the end had prevailed; namely, that justice and survival are conjoined; that the task is to bring man's mutual interests and his moral impluse together.

Wilberforce was driven forward by a profound conviction that slavery transgressed the limits of immorality within community. We must look now to a wider community and to a new morality, but the limits are the same. Why do we not answer the call of their transgression? Is it because we have lived for so long in a world of separate worlds that we find it hard to recognise the one world we have become? Or are we reluctant to give up our comforting illusions of 'otherness', to acknowledge our inseparable humanity, fearful lest morality prove too fragile a support for oneness, or our self-interest be left unprotected and unserved?

Our political and economic systems must now provide conceptual space for the reality of an interdependent world economy. We talk, all of us, about that 'world economy' and we accept its interdependent character even as we acknowledge its existence. Yet, we continue to act as if the 'world economy' is merely the sum total of national economies, a statistic extrapolated from national economic reality.

While the world has accepted at one level of perception the reality of a world economy, while governments themselves speak of commitments to world economic recovery, most continue to act as though that world economy does not itself need attention and management. Governments, international institutions, the banking community, transnational corporations, all know that it does; yet the skills of management so exalted at home remain withheld at the global level. The collective search for world economic recovery is deferred and we rush like lemmings – separately, but together – towards the abyss of economic disaster, continuing the pretence that our fate is ours alone, that humanity is separable.

Two hundred years after Wilberforce went from Hull to Westminster, are we willing to accept from our human society the kind of world satirically endorsed in Brecht's *Threepenny Opera?*:

> Some in light and some in darkness,
> That's the kind of world we mean.
> Those you see are in the light part.
> Those in darkness don't get seen.[8]

Do we really believe that such a feudal world could now subsist? If we do, we will have learned nothing from the history of the Anti-Slavery Movement. We will be as purblind and myopic as the old plantocracies, unable to recognise that they could not hold back the dawn and that if, instead, they welcomed it, they, too, would share in the light and warmth it shed.

"One day", said Martin Luther King speaking of his dream – not just a dream for America but for all the world: "One day, the sons of former slaves and sons of former slave-owners will be able to sit down together at the table of brotherhood".[9]

We are all bidden to the feast, but until we bridge the differences that still divide mankind, barriers of race and poverty, of ideology and of religion, above all, the barriers in our minds that preserve the prejudice of 'otherness', we cannot hope to reach that table. We must begin to make our way towards it; how better to do so than by following the signpost established by Wilberforce over 150 years ago in his exhortation against slavery:

> Let us act with energy suited to the importance of the interests for which we contend. Justice, humanity and sound policy prescribe our course, and will culminate our efforts.[10]

Notes and References

1. David Brion Davis, "Slavery and 'Progress'," in Christine Bolt and Seymour Drescher (eds), *Anti-Slavery, Religion and Reform: Essays in memory of Roger Anstey,* (Dawson, Folkestone, England, 1980), pp. 363 *et seq;* Christopher Lloyd, *The Navy and the Slave Trade. The Suppression of the African Slave Trade in the Nineteenth Century,* (Cass, London, 1968), pp. 156-620.

2. Barbara Ward cited by Brian Johnson, (1981) I *The Environmentalist,* (Lausanne: Elsevier Sequsia S A), p. 96.

3. V.S. Naipaul, *India: A Wounded Civilisation,* (Knopf, New York, 1977), p.20.

4. *North-South: A Programme for Survival,* The Report of the Independent Commission on International Development Issues under the Chairmanship of Willy Brandt, (Pan Books, London, 1980), pp. 30 and 65.

5. Ibid., p. 33

6. William Wilberforce, *An Appeal to the Religion, Justice and Humanity of the Inhabitants of the British Empire on behalf of the Negro Slaves in the West Indies,* (Hatchards, London, 1823), p. 68.

7. Ibid., pp. 69-70,

8. Bertold Brecht, R. Menheim and J. Willett (eds), *The Threepenny Opera,* (Methuen, London, 1979), p. 84.

9. Martin Luther King, Speech to Civil Rights March on Washington, 28 August 1963, cited in D.L. Lewis, *Martin Luther King, a Critical Biography,* (Allen Lane, The Penguin Press, London, 1970), p. 288.

10. Wilberforce, op. cit., p. 77.

The Other World
in this One

In its January 1976 issue, the London journal 'The Round Table' published an article by Shridath Ramphal drawing on some of his first reflections as Commonwealth Secretary-General.[1] In it he articulated the Third World's call for a new more equitable international economic order and the compulsions of interdependence that were making the need for a less unequal world a matter of importance to all people. They were themes that were to occupy him in his work in the Brandt Commission[2] and throughout his tenure as Secretary-General of the Commonwealth.

For most of the first three-quarters of the twentieth century, international poverty has been as national poverty was throughout most of the eighteenth century – a matter on the periphery of the concern of the rich. It was a cause that touched the hearts of good people everywhere – but it was all too easily put off by the affluent as a subject for Sunday reflection. It did not obtrude into their workaday national life; it did not seem to bear on the quality of that life or to have any relevance to sustained enrichment. For the developed world, international poverty was, indeed, an external issue. It did not affect the price of bread; it did not influence, yet, the price of oil; it did not threaten the value of currencies; it did not hurt.

These are not criticisms, merely; they are reflections on

realities of yesteryear with relevance for decisions we must take in the last quarter of this century – in years that have already begun to witness basic changes in these realities. The simple fact is that in 1976 the issue of international poverty has become a matter of domestic importance to the rich no less than to the poor. It can no longer be relegated by developed countries to the periphery of national concern; it is not a matter for Sundays only.

Why is this so? For an answer, we must go back at least to the beginnings of the post-war era. In 1945, the world emerged from bitter conflict between the dominant powers – a struggle for primacy between the industrialised countries. It was a struggle, of course, that concerned important human values: freedom, democracy, the right to life itself; but, essentially, it was a struggle for dominance among the already powerful. At its end, the world set itself to rebuilding peace and security. But it was the victors, of course, who carried out this task; and the world which they sought to reconstruct was, perhaps inevitably, the model they felt would best preserve the power, the paramountcy, they had fought to secure.

Great vision inspired many of those efforts. The United Nations was the centrepiece of the new international political order. It was to prove to be – although, perhaps, in ways its creators could only barely have foreseen, and which even today many continue to denigrate – a truly vital organ of peace. But basic to the conception of the reconstructed post-war world was the retention and enlargement of power. Even within the headquarters of peace the 'major powers' were more equal than others under the Charter. The political dimension of their power was thus assured; but that power derived essentially from an economic strength founded on and sustained by the patterns of international economic relations that had dominated the pre-war world.

They were the patterns of an international economic system that assigned to states and peoples predetermined economic roles and predictable economic fortunes. They were patterns that took as their starting point the economic ideology of free market forces – an ideology whose focus was the economic growth of the industrialised countries, and whose unspoken premise often was the supportive role of those states and peoples that were primary producers mainly. For those subordinate players, economic hope was supposed to rest in processes by which the wealth of the rich would trickle down to the poor of the earth. It was an ideology, of course, that could not be written into the Charter, for among the architects of the Charter was the Soviet Union, committed not only to a centrally-planned economy of its own but itself intent upon a global crusade for the universality of its ideology. The West, for its part, preserving the economic system despite the countervailing political processes of decolonisation, supplemented the Charter by the Agreement of Bretton Woods and, later, by the GATT. Thus was re-established an international economic system directed to the attainment not of global but of sectoral ends.

It has been urged that the system these agreements affirmed has "served the world well".[3] The old economic order has, it is true, served some nations well; but it is indisputable that it has served many countries ill, and among these are the poor countries whose present circumstances derive in large measure from the working of this system. No global economic system can be judged satisfactory that fails to serve the basic needs of the people of this planet – their needs for food, for shelter, for health, and for the development of the intellect that marks them out as human. But what is the reality of the working of this old economic order? How has the system served the people of the developing world? What will be, for them, the record at the end of the decade of the 1970s?

After a monumental effort by the developing countries themselves; at the end of two decades of international action devoted to development; on the basis of nearly three decades of the working of the Bretton Woods and GATT regimes – the result by 1980 is likely, we now know, to be annual increases of per capita income of $3 to the poorest group, compared with increases of $175 per capita for the richest, who were already at the start of the decade in 1970 thirty-eight times better off. By 1980, the gap in per capita incomes would have widened to forty-two times.

Nearly one billion of the world's poorest subsist on incomes of less that $75 a year (less than fifteen pence per day) in an environment of squalor, hunger and hopelessness.[4] As the President of the World Bank, Mr Robert McNamara, said at the 1975 meeting of the Board of Governors of the Bank:

> They are the absolute poor, living in situations so deprived as to be below any rational definition of poverty. Absolute poverty is a condition of life so limited by illiteracy, malnutrition, disease, high infant mortality and low life expectancy as to deny its victims the very potential of the genes with which they are born. In effect, it is life at the margin of existence.[5]

In an even more vivid contemporary commentary, the enlightened and courageous report, *What Now?* prepared by the Dag Hammarskjold Institute of Sweden on the occasion of the Seventh Special Session of the General Assembly in 1975, recorded, in support of its plea for "another development" geared to the satisfaction of needs and beginning with the eradication of poverty:

> In Africa, one child in seven dies before the age of one year; in Asia, one in ten; in South America, one in fifteen; but in Europe and North America, one in forty. Half of the city dwellers of the Third World do not have direct access to drinking water. Half of the population of the Third World have never been to school, and two-thirds of their children have no school to go to; and the hungry, the sick, the badly-housed and the illiterate are obviously the same.[6]

This is the reality of the Third World. These are the people whom the old economic order is said to have served well. In reality, the old economic order has not served them well.

The old order has not served them at all. It was not designed to serve them well, or to serve them at all. And the fault lies not in its workings, but in the system itself. The system promised order, stability and growth for the industrialised countries, for those who already wielded economic power; but it implied disorder, insecurity and deprivation for those who did not. Upholders of the system take it for granted that some countries are rich and others are poor, and assume that by helping the rich to become more rich we will help the poor to become less poor. They ignore the possibility that some countries may be rich because others are poor, and that the price of sustained growth in the developed world may be sustained poverty in the developing.

The developing world is convinced by hard experience that international poverty is not a mere aberration of international economic relations which minor adjustments can correct – but the unspoken premise of the old economic order. However different may be the prospects from other casements, this is how the old economic order looks from a Third World window. This view is itself one of the realities of the contemporary scene. If it is at least acknowledged as such, it will become easier to understand why the developing world calls for a new international economic order.

Two UN Development Decades have yielded bitter disappointment; three UNCTADs have institutionalised frustration; and nearly thirty years of post-war internationalism has seen the political equality of states guaranteed by the Charter almost totally nullified by pervasive economic inequality between the world's people. What is surprising, perhaps, is that the challenge to the system which preserved these economic inequalities should have come so late. In fact, it could not come before. In the early post-war years, when the old order itself was reinforced by the Bretton Woods and GATT regimes, the Third World Countries, for the greater part, were voiceless captives of the colonial system, powerless to influence the decisions being taken about the kind of world they would inherit. It was only in 1947 that India became independent, marking the start of the process of modern-day decolonisation. It was only in 1956 that the dismantling of the French empire in Africa began, and a year later that the first of Britain's colonies in Africa attained freedom. Over more than a decade and a half since then, the developing countries have been almost excessively patient in their trial of prescriptions for development that, in retrospect, served merely to mask the basic ailment and, indeed, to worsen the prospect for a more equal world society.

Take aid, for example: the World Bank has projected that the United Nations target of 0.7 per cent of GNP of the industrialised countries in official development assistance could be reached were they willing to commit to ODA a minor fraction of no more than 2 per cent of the incremental wealth – 2 per cent of further growth – which they can expect to receive in the second half of the decade. Despite this, ODA relative to GNP for OECD countries is steadily falling: from 0.39 per cent in 1969, to 0.33 per cent in 1974.[7]

In trade, the record is no better. Produce more, sell more, earn more: that was the simple formula. With major effort, developing countries produced and sold more; but their net earnings, their terms of trade, steadily declined. The amount of cotton, or sisal, or tea, or bauxite they had to produce and export in order to buy, say, a tractor, or antibiotics, or an irrigation pump, kept increasing. Despite all their effort, they grew relatively poorer. They were developing on a basis of diminishing returns. And there were other problems when they tried to diversify their economic base – efforts to industrialise, to process their raw materials and produce simple manufactured goods, were frustrated by high tariff walls, differential freight rates and administrative obstructions to trade, all obstructing their entry into the markets of the rich countries.

When the new reserve assets, the SDRs, were created, developing countries asked for a link between SDRs and development finance. What was the result? As one Commonwealth Minister wryly remarked at last year's meeting of the IMF and the World Bank: "We asked for the link and we got a Committee". Aid a mirage, trade a cul de sac: the poor getting poorer and the rich getting richer. For the poor, to use the words of Santayana, life was not a spectacle or a feast, it was a predicament.[8]

It was while they were taking the measure of this predicament that the oil producers acted. Is it any wonder that their success in using their collective strength to win a better price for oil and to turn the terms of trade in their favour acted like a tonic throughout the developing world? For the first time in history, a group of primary producers working together had prevailed over the industrialised nations in a field in which they had traditionally dictated prices under the existing system of international trade. OPEC's success brought many problems for other developing nations, severe problems for some of them; but it pointed a way forward out of the development impasse, the predicament of poverty.

Despite the crippling impact of oil price increases, that glimpse of wider horizons encouraged developing countries to look anew at their collective strengths and to entertain the hope that the old rules, which seemed to condemn them to perpetual penury, were not immutable and could be challenged. It encouraged them to conceive of a new world economic order that would make effective development probable – that would buttress, rather than frustrate, their own efforts to develop. They had long recognised that the essential effort of development must be their own. What they sought was an environment – an international economic system – propitious, not hostile, to their effort.

In making that effort, it is to many Third World countries a maddening contradiction that some developed states refuse to accept as legitimate at the international level mechanisms they have themselves employed, indeed devised, for advancing some of the most noble objectives within their own societies. Built into the ethos of Western democracies are the right of workers to establish trade unions, the legitimacy of collective bargaining and the strike weapon – the collective withholding of labour. Yet when the poor of the world adopt similar methods to redress economic injustice at the international level, some developed states dispute their reasonableness or even their legitimacy.

How else would the societies of Europe or North America have moved away from feudalism and privilege, have moved towards just economic societies, save through the collective effort of the deprived? How shall we ever move towards a just world community unless through organised effort of those now condemned to international poverty? How else, save by collective action, can they effectively challenge a system their experience compels them to reject as unjust?

The analogy with national conditions is valid, also, in relation to many of the equalising mechanisms actually employed at the national level. Within every major industrial country and regional economic community it is now accepted that the unrestricted operation of free market forces can lead to results out of tune with prevailing concepts of a just national or regional society. The operation of the market often fails to achieve an equitable distribution of income among peoples or of activities among regions. And the market is vulnerable to manipulation through the exercise of unequally distributed market power.

Recognition of these failings has led to corrective intervention. Many developed countries have devised mechanisms for transferring income from the relatively rich to the relatively poor within their societies. Some of these mechanisms involve direct transfers. Others involve direct interference in market forces. Thus freight rates and food grains are subsidised, minimum prices for agricultural products guaranteed and marketing controlled.

Such intervention results in some redistribution of activities within regions, and it has often been supplemented by machinery designed to stimulate and assist the development of human and natural resources in regions which lag behind. Even a society as dedicated to *laissez-faire* as the United States has elaborated stiff, anti-trust and anti-monopoly measures in an effort to curb overweening economic power. And across national boundaries, within the European Economic Community, the Regional Development Fund, designed to implement a policy of balanced growth, transfers community resources from rich regions to poor.

Developing countries find it difficult to appreciate why these national mechanisms are not also available at the international level to redress international poverty and global inequalities. In 1974, the UN General Assembly adopted a Programme of Action for the establishment of a New International Economic Order.[9] Its essential features are not so different in kind from measures already accepted within developed states. Their adoption within the international community would not of necessity lead to chaos and disaster. What is needed is not an act of invention but an act of will, to carry these perceptions of economic justice, of balanced growth, beyond the frontiers of developed states.

It may be objected that in the international community, unlike the nation-state, there is no supreme authority capable of enforcing balanced development. But have the equalising mechanisms of all developed states really derived from the exercise of sovereign power? Canada, for example, has created machinery for transferring resources so that each Provincial Government has an acceptable minimum financial capability. This has been achieved within a federal system, not by constitutional litigation or amendment or by an imposed federal will, but by negotiation and consensus using the techniques of international diplomacy. Is this not an object-lesson for the international community? It is for just such an approach to equity that the developing world contends and organises.

To secure more effective negotiation in place of the imposed perceptions of the developed states has become a basic quest of the developing countries. As the Interim Report of the project for reviewing the international order (the RIO Project, co-ordinated by Jan Tinbergen) pertinently observes:

> the basic objective of the emerging trade union of the poor nations is to negotiate a new deal with the rich nations through the instrument of collective bargaining. The essence of this new deal lies in their obtaining greater equality of opportunity and in securing the right to sit as equals around the bargaining tables of the world.[10]

This is why solidarity is so essential an element of Third World action. It needs to be understood. A new order involves change – fundamental change in international economic relations. That change can be achieved by agreement, by a process of consensus, or it can be secured by compulsion, by confrontation and the clash of contending strengths. The solidarity of the Third World is often assailed as a posture of confrontation. If this means that the Third World seeks imposed solutions, the assertion is wide of the mark; for few developing countries would put high the prospect of success thus pursued.

But consensus between contending interests is not achieved through moral suasion alone – it is more often rooted in a balance of strength that itself compels reason and reinforces morality. It is to the creation of such a strength that the solidarity of the Third World is directed – a strength which is real enough to command respect and to encourage genuine dialogue and ultimate consensus. Seen thus, the solidarity of the Third World is not the posture and intent of confrontation, but an essential catalyst of consensus. It is not merely a legitimate tactic of negotiation but a necessary element of global harmony.

What OPEC has done; what other producer associations may, but only may, succeed in doing; what Third World solidarity in the Non-Aligned Movement, or in the Group of 77, or in the ACP Group of States, is seeking to do, is to create conditions for more effective negotiation. Take prices, for example; with rare exceptions, such as the old Commonwealth Sugar Agreement, prices of primary products, whether of minerals or of agricultural products, have not in the past been the subject of effective as distinct from notional negotiations. Prices of manufactures are often not negotiated at all, merely invoiced. In both cases, prices are controlled by the developed states – whether as consumers or as producers. To make real negotiation in this area possible is surely not to seek confrontation – unless the developed world is implacably opposed to any change in the basis of human economic relations.

What is true is that confrontation becomes possible as strengths become more equal – but so, too, does consensus. Confrontation has always been within the armoury of the developed countries. It is perhaps now within the armoury of the oil producing states. It is still a long way from being within the armoury of any others. The option for confrontation is essentially an option for the developed states. It is only the opportunity for consensus that is available to rich and poor alike.

But other strengths are emerging within developing states which can make it possible for them to move marginally toward a new regime of development despite an unpropitious economic order. They are strengths which derive not from producer associations or even from negotiations with the richer countries. They derive, in part, from the fact that a new awareness among poor countries of the fundamental character of their economic situation facilitates a more rational approach to its basic transformation. And they derive also from new concepts of development – concepts which enjoin developing countries not merely to mimic the development patterns of the industrialised states, but to strike out in new directions determined more by internal social and cultural realities than by external forces.

An important element of the new awareness of the

realities of international poverty is the acknowledgement by the developing world that self-reliance, both at the national level and at the collective level among developing countries, must be an essential feature of development. Self-reliance is not autarchy, nor is it isolationism, it is not a vision of detached self-sufficiency. It is a conviction that development must come from within each society – conditioned by its history and its social, cultural and economic strengths, founded on its resources, including its human resources, and committed to the national well-being. Self-reliant development is based not on what the world can do for us, but on what we can do for ourselves. It strives to ensure the provision by national effort of the essentials of national subsistence – of food, of habitat, of health, of education. And it seeks fulfilment by exploring new frontiers of co-operation between developing countries themselves.

It is, above all, development committed to the creation of just societies; for there is no rational basis, there is no morality, in the demand for a more equal world community, unless it implies the facilitation of more equal national societies. It is a model of development, therefore, that condemns privilege within developing countries as rigorously as within the world community of states. The Third World must articulate these perceptions of development and be zealous for their translation into reality. It must demonstrate both by precept and by example a commitment to national and collective self reliance; to the dismantling of feudal structures; to the dispelling of pretences of privilege which are even more grotesque in the midst of poverty than they are in conditions of affluence. And it must prove by these advances that the creation of truly just societies, in which basic human values are respected and man's humanity is allowed to develop its potential, is the true fulfilment of the promise of development.

For some developing countries this process is well advanced. For others, it has yet to begin. But whether we are dealing with the one or the other, it is wrong, and it is unhelpful, for developed societies to yield to the too easy temptation to escape responsibility for creating conditions of growth within the Third World by pointing to imperfections which at one time or another have been features of their own national development. The Third World does not divide, as easily as some would have us believe, into "the deserving and the undeserving". It does not do so any more fairly than did the Victorian poor, castigated by their overlords for their indolence and indiscipline.

By the same token, the developed world is not monolithic. Some developed states have, indeed, shared with the Third World some of the humiliations of economic dominion, and have been neither the architects nor the primary beneficiaries, certainly not the primary operators, of the old economic order. These developed countries, many of the middle states, have a special role to play in man's search for a better economic way for all the world's people. They bring to that search a deeper understanding of the aspirations of developing countries, a lower level of vested interest in resisting fundamental change and, for both these reasons, a greater capability for advancing consensus on the mechanisms of change that would fulfil those aspirations.

In the evolution of a new international economic order a major responsibility rests upon industrialised Western countries. Jan Pronk, the dynamic Dutch Minister for Development Co-operation, has rightly observed:

> The new order required by the poor countries will be within easy reach when the United States and the Common Market agree it.[11]

Together, they dominate world trade, international finance and industrial production. But obligation does not rest on them exclusively. All developed countries, of East no less than West, share in the obligation of ending international poverty. It is not enough for Eastern countries to say, as was said at the Seventh Special Session of the United Nations, that they had no responsibility for the colonial exploitation of the Third World. It is not merely a legal issue of restitution or reparation. It is a moral issue that concerns the quality of life of a large section of humanity; it is fast becoming, for all nations, culpable and blameless alike, an issue of global survival.

If these, then, are the realities, what are the prospects for advance toward the promise of the new order? Developing countries have no option but to seek an end to poverty and deprivation. For them, the analogy of the poor within the nation-state is apposite, and the Marxist dialectic is pertinent. "The workers", said Marx, "have nothing to lose but their chains; they have a world to gain". The Third World, or at least a major part of it, has nothing to lose but its poverty. It could have a world to gain. It is important that the developed world understands this psychological reality of the human condition among the poor of the earth.

The way forward must surely lie in a change of attitude on the part of the developed world. Developed states must frankly acknowledge that the need is pressing for fundamental change in international economic relations; that the choice is not between an old order or a new but between a new order or sustained disorder. They must abandon petulance, and cease to deceive themselves that serious demands stemming from deep resentment of pervasive injustice are mere rhetoric. They must acknowledge that, together with the developing states, there is a mutuality of interest in change, the developed world must be prepared to give a good deal more by way of compromise than the developing can be expected to yield.

The new order will not be installed in its entirety overnight; what is needed if the peoples of the world are to be made equal in their economic destinies is not so much the outvoting of a rich minority or their passive acquiescence in the promise of change but the conversion of that minority to the need for change and to the urgency of its imperative. Such conversion cannot be expected from the processes of United Nations action only; other fora, other forms of diplomacy, other machinery for diaologue that possess a potential for promoting such conversion must render service to the cause of change.

This implies, of course, a particular emphasis on reaching the people of the developed world whose governments, however enlightened, need informed popular support if they are to take the decisions involved. The people can themselves help to ensure that the responses made on their behalf are, indeed, enlightened. It is heartening to see how much is being done within many developed countries by individuals and associations and institutions in this regard. The effort, however, has barely begun and current economic difficulties – some themselves the aftermath of the collapse of the old order – do not create an altogether propitious climate for drawing attention to international poverty, even on a basis of enlightened self-interest. All the more reason, therefore, for a sustained attempt to alert the people of the rich countries to the predicament which international poverty implies for rich and poor alike, and to convert them to the cause of change.

Paul Eluard suggested long ago, with penetrating insight, that there is another world, but it is in this one.[12] The promise of the new international economic order is the promise of that other world here on earth. In our search for it, not only the poor but all people and all states must be sedulously engaged; for all are now involved in its outcome.

Notes and References

1. (1976) No. 261, *The Round Table*, p. 61.

2. *North-South: A Programme for Survival,* the Report of the Independent Commission on International Development Issues under the Chairmanship of Willy Brandt, (Pan Books, London, 1980).

3. Henry Kissinger, cited in Shridath Ramphal, *One World To Share*, (Hutchinson Benham, 1979), p. 5.

4. Estimates are not now made of absolute poverty; but since 1975 the decline in per capita incomes and per capita food production in many low-income countries has meant an increase in the number of the absolute poor.

5. Robert McNamara, President, World Bank Group, Address to the Board of Governors, Washington, D.C., September 1975, p. 13.

6. *Development Dialogue*, the Journal of the Dag Hammarskjold Foundation, Uppsala, No. 1/2 (1975), pp. 28-29.

7. The ratio has remained stagnant at around 0.35 per cent in recent years.

8. Shridath Ramphal, 'Aid a mirage; trade a cul-de-sac', *One World to Share*, op. cit., p. 28.

9. 'Declaration and A Programme of Action for a New International Economic Order' adopted at the Sixth Special Session of the General Assembly of the United Nations, G A Resolutions 3201/ 3202 (S-VI) of 1 May 1974.

10. *Reviewing the International Order*, (Rotterdam, 1975); and in a slightly revised form, *RIO: Reshaping the International Order*, Prof. Jan Tinbergen (ed), (Dutton, New York, 1976), p. 16.

11. At an International Symposium on the New International Economic Order held in The Hague, 1975, see Shridath Ramphal, *One World To Share*, op. cit., p. 113.

12. See, generally, Paul Eluard, *Capitale de la douleur*, edited with an Introduction and Notes by Vera J. Daniel (Blackwell French Texts, 1985).

Shadows in the Cave

On 4 June 1981, Shridath Ramphal spoke to the Royal Society of Arts in London on the Brandt Commission's 'Programme for Survival'. The Report of the Commission had just been published. By then, the North-South dialogue had virtually collapsed; the world was beginning to move to the condition of chronic economic uncertainty that was to characterise the 1980s. Shridath Ramphal began his address with a reference to the early Greek thinkers whose works in 'dialogue' became the hallmark of a civilisation not afraid to ask the question 'why?'. He pressed for a revival of that Athenian readiness for profound debate of fundamental issues.

Let me start with the proposition that the famous image of the cave which Plato used to illustrate the condition of mankind still has force today. He depicted, as you may remember, the greater part of mankind as prisoners in a subterranean cavern, chained with their backs to a fire, looking at the shadows thrown on the rock face opposite and mistaking them for reality. The ability to turn and face the light, and struggle upwards to the mouth of the cave and the undiluted light of the sun, belonged only to the philosophers who thus educated themselves to rule in his ideal world, a utopia which he called The Republic.[1] Education, in Plato's terms was a turning round of the eye of the mind.

I cannot share Plato's views on the social structure of the

state. But I am struck overwhelmingly by his wider vision of mankind and its relevance today to our global condition – a condition of crisis which calls, I suggest, for precisely that turning round of the eye of the mind. Nor can I resist the intimations of pertinence in his half-plea, half-assertion: "There will be no end to the troubles of the states, or of humanity itself, till philosophers become kings in this world, or till those we now call kings and rulers really and truly become philosophers, and political power and philosophy thus come into the same hands".[2]

Those of us who were invited to serve on the Brandt Commission on International Development Issues certainly cannot claim to have been philosopher-kings; we were practitioners of politics, of finance, of labour, of journalism, but most of all of development. Yet we did, I believe, contribute to a renewal of the Athenian spirit of dialogue in this modern age. The Report is about dialogue; it rests upon the foundation that it is by agreement rather than imposition; by negotiation rather than dictation; by innovation rather than conformity; by these ways alone that we can create a future for our planet which meets the needs of all who dwell upon it. And it must surely be so, because the era of dominance has passed; the old ways of compulsion are no longer reliable, however strong the nostalgia for them among the ideologues of power.

And this is true even in the highest reaches of military power. What the nuclear arms race now amounts to, for example, is mutual compulsion to devote more and more human and financial resources to developing and stock-piling the most horrendous but unusable power. The process is no longer the accumulation of effective military power, but the misallocation of economic resources in the senseless determinism of an unending quest for balance and some-times even for superiority. And all the while, the evil cult of urban violence that does not hesitate to turn the gun against the world's leaders, hijackings and hostages, a swollen tide of refugees – grim testimony to man's inhumanity and sometimes a response to violence under the guise of law itself or to unmet human needs, which is the same thing – all serve to underline how powerless societies can stand even in the midst of power.

Constantly widening disparities in the quality of life on a planet that every day gets smaller have unleashed dangerous tensions that undermine global harmony. This is the real confrontation the world faces; the confrontation that such contradictions constitute. How are we to react to it? Direct compulsion of the rich is not a viable option for the South. Nor, I suggest, is it an option for the rich to make a fortress of their castle in the North. The way forward must lie in consensus – a convergence of positions on the essentials of new relationships that install world-wide those standards of social and economic justice towards which Western societies have reached at home and cannot now deny in the larger home which humanity has made of our planet.

But there will be no consensus on change without a measure of conversion to it. To be activist in pursuit of that conversion may produce inconvenience, may even induce petulance – Dr. Kissinger used to describe the Third World as 'spoilers'; but it is not undesirable confrontation; it is, in fact, the necessary pre-condition of transforming world society into one more compatible with its longer-term interests of harmony and progress.

How can we achieve that conversion? The moral imperatives for change, the ethical compulsions of human solidarity, are neither irrelevant nor invalid, as Barbara Ward constantly reminded us;[3] they provide compelling arguments, and I should like to return to them. But they are matters of the heart much more than of the head, and our problem is not really one of not knowing in our hearts what needs to be done, but of finding in our minds the way to do it and summoning the will to pursue that way. I would put before you, instead, three other conditions as being essential to progress in the North-South dialogue and an enlargement of the prospects for a healthy and growing world economy.

First of all, an understanding of the interdependence of issues. In the early years of the development dialogue – in the 1950s and 1960s – development was largely beyond the pale of East-West issues. It was touched here and there by cold war considerations; but, basically, the international effort for development was self-motivated and self-contained. Today, the reality is very different. Failure in each area – North-South or East-West – tends to imperil progress in the other. A decline from detente means a steep drop for development. 'Afghanistan' in this sense, in terms of both action and reaction, represents one of the most damaging blows that development received in the 1980s. It may suprise the Soviets, in particular, to hear this; but these implications for development of the impairment of detente were wholly predictable.

And it would surprise the West to be told, but it is equally true, that the record of consistent failure to advance development through the North-South dialogue presents one of the most damaging blows struck against human rights in recent times. The implications of that failure for the millions whom Fanon called 'the wretched of the earth'[4] are as horrible as the depredations of any despot; and, again, they were wholly predictable.

More pointedly, however, poverty, hopelessness and the social and political instability they create in large sectors of the developing world are a virtual guarantee of the emergence of still further areas of East-West tension. Particularly if we return to the reflexes of a cold war, we could be in a dangerous cycle with East-West tensions impairing North-South progress, and North-South failures threatening world peace and stability.

And there is another aspect of this linkage of North-South and East-West issues which language and images and habits of thinking mask, but which have real implications for the West. In practical terms, for North-South and East-West you can read respectively 'West-South' and 'West-East'. The West surely cannot contemplate with equanimity a deterioration of relations with both the South and East. Quite apart from the difficulty of fighting on many fronts – which I know may not deter the ideologues of power politics – such a dual confrontation may push East and South together with implications which the West does not desire and which the South, anxious to make a reality of non-alignment, certainly does not seek. Yet I am repeatedly struck by the fact that hardliners on East-West issues often are hardliners on North-South issues also, with apparent heedlessness of the alliances they are promoting.

My second condition is an understanding of the interdependence of countries and their peoples. In the Report of the Brandt Commission we put the matter thus:

> The North-South debate is often described as if the rich were being asked to make sacrifices in response to the demands of the poor. We reject this view. The world is now a fragile and interlocking system, whether for its people its ecology or its resources... More and more, local problems can only be solved through international solutions – including the environment, energy, and the co-ordination of economic activity, money and trade. Above all, the achievement of economic growth in one country depends increasingly on the performance of others. The South cannot grow adequately without the North. The North cannot prosper or improve its situation unless there is greater progress in the South.[5]

The South, of course, needs the capital, the technology, the managerial skills, the manufactures, the markets of the North. What the North needs of the South may not be as wide-ranging, but they are real enough. The North needs the markets of the South and it needs its raw materials.

And these are not just needs that economists conceptualise; they have direct relevance to the people of industrial societies. More than anything else, they demonstrate why the Third World, far from being a problem, could in fact be part of the solution to the problems, indeed the crises, in the world economy. In a very direct way, progress in the South implies jobs in the North. Already, 35 per cent of the exports of the United States and of the EEC, taken as a group, and over 45 per cent of the exports of Japan go to the developing countries. Seventy per cent of British aid, now cut in the interest of 'recovery', supported exports from, and therefore jobs in, Britain.

And the importance of trade with the South is steadily increasing. It is the market of the future; but a market assumes purchasing power, a capacity to buy through opportunity to earn. Export jobs in Britain cannot be sustained if Third World countries cannot purchase, if their economies cannot grow. The problems of poverty in the South may still appear to be far-away problems, but, in truth, more and more, they have their mirror effect in every home the world over.

The North-South dialogue is about some of those problems; and they are massive problems. The balance of payments deficits of the non-oil developing countries, for example – amounts that need to be financed if world trade, and jobs in the North, are to be sustained – are expected to reach $82 billion this year, 1981, from the already unprecedented level of $74 billion in 1980[6]. The middle-income developing countries constitute a major part of the Third World market to which developed-country exports go and from which vital raw materials come to feed the industries of the North. These countries, their capacity to produce and to buy, are critical to the economic health of the developed world. In recent years, they have borrowed massively to finance their deficits; indeed, their borrowing was essential to the process, in which the Western commercial banks played so important a part, of recycling OPEC surpluses within the world economy. But the limits of this process are being reached. By 1980, the long-term external debt of developing countries had reached $430 billion from just $67 billion in 1970 and $163 billion in 1975. The middle-income countries were responsible for 70 per cent of this debt.[7]

The problem with this build-up of debt is that much of it

has been provided not to finance increases in productive capacity, but to cover deterioration in terms of trade, the rise in interest rates and reserve accumulation. And because of short maturities and high interest rates, debt and debt-service charges are now growing at a higher rate than foreign exchange earnings. In fact, expanding borrowing by the Third World within the international financial system is no longer producing an increase in net transfers to developing countries.

And the situation gets daily more precarious as protectionism in the North still further stifles growth in export earnings from the South. The commercial banking system is now strained. It has already had to be rescued by Western governments from defaults in Poland – a particular irony, you might well think, given the needs of the developing world. But the danger does not end with Poland; it cannot be staved off with *ad hoc* responses to the threat of default in individual cases. The truth is that North and South are caught in a joint struggle to survive the turbulent crossing from the Bretton Woods era to the interdependent world economy that has succeeded it.

The North in this situation cannot rely in a conventional way on domestic policies alone to respond to the crisis. Such a myopic approach is, in fact, producing an external environment unpropitious for recovery and counter-productive to the domestic effort.[8] At precisely the time when high internal inflation constrains domestic stimulation and points to the need for export-led recovery, world trade has been depressed by the cumulative effect of domestic deflationary policies. I mention all this not as a critique on the policies of individual governments but as a demonstration that those policies now have to be informed by the reality of interdependence between North and South if they are to work for either group.

The North needs a prospering South. It also needs the South – that two-thirds of the world not yet industrialised – not to be a storm centre of instability, not to be a cockpit of tension and great power rivalry, and not to produce a population explosion from whose fall-out no part of the world will be immune. Sustained impoverishment provides the seed-bed for instability, tension and rivalry. World population is now increasing by one million every five days. Just under two billion more persons will inhabit the earth before the year 2000 – nearly 40 per cent more than our present 4.5 billion. On present trends, more than 50 per cent of the 6 billion people in the world by then will be in the poorest countries – those with a per capita income now of less than $500 per annum.[9] And at that time, within twenty years, about 80 per cent of the world's people could be in developing countries. Our global society clearly faces the danger of being overwhelmed by income disparities and endemic poverty. Can the remaining 20 per cent, sitting on surpluses and nuclear silos, face that prospect with equanimity.

If the North-South dialogue fails to keep an appreciation of these mutual needs at the centre of its concerns, if it fails to acknowledge the mutual interest of North and South in changes designed to meet them, its agenda will be a barren one and its results will fail to satisfy the interests of rich and poor alike.

I have referred to the interdependence of issues and of nations. They give rise to my third condition, which concerns group action in the energy market and, particularly, a greater understanding of OPEC: understanding not merely of aspirations but of needs and rights. And this plea for understanding of the Organisation of Petroleum Exporting Countries is not new. I remember how insistent I was with myself in the early 1970s to talk not of the 'energy crisis' but of the 'energy catalyst'.[10]

No solutions to the energy question will be comprehensive or realistic which do not take account of the needs – political as well as economic – of OPEC members. This means that they must take into account, in an appropriate way, the question of Palestine. To ignore it, or pretend that it is not relevant to economic issues, or, worse still, to be inflexible on it, is to be insensitve to the complexity of human motivation and to be inimical ultimately to the interests of the West. I do not enter into the issues here. I do not need to. A deep sense of injustice cannot be held in a separate compartment of the mind; it infuses all thought and action. The Palestinian issue is of that nature. It will continue to colour OPEC's approaches to energy questions.

And the agenda must deal with the need of OPEC countries for security of their assets, both in terms of access and value, and for sustained investment opportunities. It must also deal with the problems of the non-oil developing countries both as to supply and finance. Only when the global agenda acknowledges the importance of finding an accommodation on all these issues will it be propitious to consensus on the legitimate needs of developed countries in relation to energy pricing and supply. In other words, the real dialogue cannot be limited only to what the North wants to talk about.

And it must, of course, be a real dialogue that acknowledges new realities. It is easy to forget, for example, that in 1974 the West turned down OPEC's offer of a price regime for oil based on indexation – rejecting it as rhetoric and condemning it as heresy. The 'Chicago School'[11] actually predicted that the price of oil would be back to $3 per barrel within the year. In effect, it was rejection of an offer of contract in this critical area of energy – a rejection that relied on old-fashioned notions of power, economic, political and military – while ignoring the reality that its dispersal had already occurred. And today, of course, the reality is not the avoidance of indexation – for it is applied unilaterally, if convulsively, by OPEC;[12] what was missed was the chance to apply it in a consensual and well ordered manner. Behind the lost chance was a failure of political perception – failure to allow the glimpse of interdependence that had been offered to influence Northern responses to the events of 1974. We are living with the results – with the North still not blaming itself but others, and other factors.

These are but some of the pre-conditions of an effective North-South dialogue. After eight years of talking, it is obvious that they are not being met. In truth, there has not been effective dialogue – and is it not clear that, with few exceptions, it was never the intention of the North that there would have been? We have had eight years of processes of dialogue, the forms of negotiation. Here and there, under the most concentrated pressure – so concentrated as to produce a distorted emphasis – there has been minimal and grudging concession: as in the case of the Common Fund.[13] Basically, however, the approach of the North has been that the only need in the negotiations was to keep them going; that no Northern interest was being served by the changes under discussion; that poverty was regrettable but essentially a matter for the South; that the major Northern interest was to preserve the *status quo* and, above all, to maintain Northern dominance in the management of the world economy and primacy in the gains from its functioning.

It was, however, seldom put like this, and never in terms of its necessary implication that the North could live with the global contradictions of want and waste, of massive suffering amid the miracles of science, of equity within nations but not between them. The North is not evil; its negotiators are not inhuman. Why then the cruel innocence of its indifference to an ineffectual dialogue? The answer lies, I believe, in the perception of our world as so many separate states, for each of whom the supreme duty is to national prosperity secured through an adversary system of international relations and sanctified at the altar of sovereignty. It is a perception from an era that has passed; but it is a perception that has carried over. When I last addressed this Society, I cited the reminder of Regis Debray that "we are never fully contemporaneous with our present"[14]. At moments of great transition in human history that failure to be in tune with our times can have quite disastrous effects. Who can doubt that we are at just such a moment of transition?

For the first time a decade ago, man in space saw the

planet as we had for half a millenium known it to be, one whole. The world lay revealed as a reality – that glimpse of earth rise seen from the moon; but it lay revealed also in all its starkness as an aspiration, an ideal: because back on earth man remained subject not just to the laws of gravity but to the custom and practice of human society, with all its differences, its disparities and its discords. Man's journey into space has had a profound effect on our perceptions of the world – particularly our appreciation of its smallness. Small the earth undeniably is to the astronaut's eye, to the satellite sending back weather pictures of the planet, and to the miracle machines of modern communications which have brought into focus the 'global village' that our world community is. But I am struck as much by the world's wholeness as by its smallness; and what we need is not just weather pictures of the planet, but weather pictures of man.

Too often we misread the signs of our own humanity, mistaking shadows cast by the past for tomorrow's reality, conjuring belief out of hope, applying to the future the narrow perspectives of the present rather than the larger vision its dynamics demand. In the process, we enter a maze of inverted values and lose our way among its twists and turns.

Both East and West are now obsessed with power. Its principal custodians behave like some elite imperial guard for whom loyalty has become more virtuous than justice. How easily forgottten are all the lessons of history, even when they are still fresh; above all, the principal lesson that physical power is no match for moral strength and can never prevail over it.

The East was always vulnerable to this distortion; the West, in a curious process by which it seeks superior power, now seems inclined to debase its moral strengths. I have already spoken of the contradiction between assertions of concern for human rights and an implacable refusal to negotiate those global economic changes that would advance the cause of social and economic justice world-wide. But now it is worse than contradiction, which there is at least hope of resolving. Human rights are being expunged from political manifestos as the soft issues that no self-respecting ideologue of power should be constrained by – unless, of course, they offer opportunities in a cold war context where compassion is allowable if disguised as weaponry.

And so the way is prepared, the climate conditioned, for alliances with regimes the world over on a scale of friendship that sometimes seems to vary inversely with the norms of social justice and democracy that have been one of the richest gifts of Western civilisation to the world's people. In Iran, in Indo-China, in Central America, in Southern Africa, this is the record. Of course, this abandonment of principle is masked by professions of virtue: "We must stand by our friends"; "We cannot allow instability close to our borders"; "We must firmly oppose 'terrorism' everywhere"; "We must not forget those who were our allies in the War". It seems to matter little that the 'friends' are tyrants; that 'instability' has its roots in authority's violence to the human personality; that the 'terrorists' are not always those who wear the unconventional uniforms; that the 'allies' of yesteryear were supposed to be committed to a struggle to rid the world of the bigotry of racial superiority and to uphold the dignity of men and women everywhere.

Shadows again, but people, ordinary people, live with the realities; they see beyond the mask, and are disturbed by the West's confusion of objectives and ideals, of means and ends, of power-play and leadership. Can we not, even now, restore the balance? When patriotism anywhere begins to disdain the path of enlightenment, it is the hallmark of friendship to recall nationalism to its higher purposes. The West cannot lose its way unless Europe permits it; and Europe must not. In the struggle for men's minds Europe is powerful in its armoury of ideas and traditions. It is a fount of generosity and compassion. It has been the cradle of man's internationalism just as it has witnessed the worst debasement of those ideals; and because it has that knowledge of how man's potential for good can conquer evil, Europe is not the weak partner but the strong. It must not allow a distortion of the realities of true power and influence to depirve it of the chance to save the world and itself from the disasters that are looming. It was not lightly that the Brandt Commission urged that if the world fails to "become stronger by becoming a just and humane society"[15] it will move towards its own destruction.

Conventional wisdom which ignores this reality of an interlocking world economy and the important shifts in economic power that have occurred no longer provides the answers to these problems. It is a time for new wisdom to produce a new climate for co-operation and advance the prospects of global negotiations which remain deadlocked in the United Nations system. The longer-term structural changes to which these negotiations are directed are essential; but they must not delay action now to face the crisis that is already at hand. The essential need is for an immediate political response to the existing emergency in the world economy.

Rising unemployment, persistent monetary instability, staggeringly high interest rates, insupportable payments deficits, a wholly unprecedented level of indebtedness – above all, deepening poverty, hunger and hopelessness – all point to the need for urgent agreement by the international community on outward-looking programmes and policies. Yet, nations are turning inwards, industrial societies, in particular, seeking refuge in short-term national solutions which only tend to make matters worse.

The Brandt Commission's Programme for Survival has clearly become more pointed since it was first offered to the world community and the need to embark on its implementation, especially through an emergency programme, can no longer be deferred. Urgent steps to augment global financial flows to developing countries, to revitalise world trade and to produce solutions to critical problems in the areas of food and energy remain at the heart of such essential action. The world, and the world economy, is a unity; its problems, especially its gravest ones, demand unified solutions internationally agreed.

Can we not, at least, meet this essential need to manage our survival? Can we not, after all, make the dialogue a real one? – more conscious now than when it began that development is not just the concern of the two-thirds of mankind that is the Third World but of all the world; that man's needs are mutual and their satisfaction a joint interest of all people; that the *status quo* now threatens all countries and an ineffectual dialogue that merely preserves it hurts rich and poor alike; that time could be short to shape the future before we are overwhelmed by it. What we need for success is in our keeping: wider vision, grander purposes, nobler pursuits, than those implied by a turning inward of our nationalism and a suspension of our internationalism until 'better times'.

Notes and References

1. Plato, *The Republic*, tr. Desmond Lee, Penguin Classics (Penguin Books, London, 1980), p. 317.

2. Ibid., p. 263.

3. 'The Duty to Hope: A Tribute to Barbara Ward', (1981) I *The Environmentalist*, pp. 95-99.

4. Frantz Fanon, *The Wretched of the Earth* (MacGibbon and Kee, London, 1965).

5. *North-South: A Programme for Survival*, Report of the Independent Commission on International Development Issues under the Chairmanship of Willy Brandt (Pan Books, London, 1980).

6. The actual deficit in 1981 was $112 billion. The annual deficit has been reduced to about $30 billion currently but this is a reflection of the steep decline in resource flows to developing countries rather than an improvement in the situation.

7. The limits were reached soon after when, in 1982, the debt crisis broke with Mexico not being able to meet its debt service obligations.

8. In fact this approach led in 1981-1983 to the deepest recession in the post-war period.

9. Subsequent World Bank estimates confirm that world population would reach 6.1 billion in 2000, of which 3.1 billion would live in low-income countries.

10. See *The Energy Catalyst*, Shridath Ramphal's address to the Sixth Special Session of the UN General Assembly on 15 April 1974, (Ministry of Foreign Affairs, Georgetown, 1974).

11. Professor Milton Friedman, the Doyen of the 'Chicago School', even predicted the break up of OPEC; see, Friedman, *Free to Choose,* (Penguin Books, 1979), p. 77.

12. While OPEC's control of supply has weakened subsequently, the Organisation remains intact and could again take advantage of tighter conditions in world markets which are possible even in the medium term.

13. The Fund is still not yet established, although there was some forward movement in 1987.

14. Regis Debray, *Revolution in the Revolution,* (Penguin Books, London, 1968), p. 19.

15. Op. cit., p. 33.

The Trampling of
the Grass

*The Silver Jubilee of the Economic Commission for Africa
was celebrated through a Lecture Series inaugurated by
Shridath Ramphal in Addis Ababa on 29 April 1985. It was
an address to the Ministers of Economic Planning of Africa at
a time of grave economic malaise throughout the Continent.[1]
In his address, Ramphal called for massive international
assistance and for bold policy changes from African countries
themselves.*

Famine in Africa, death and debilitation from hunger and
malnutrition is today a stark and cruel reality. Twenty-one
countries with a total population of almost 200 million face
exceptional food supply difficulties; 30 million are
threatened by starvation. The United Nations says that a
million people may perish – many more than died in the two
atomic explosions forty years ago, which still retain their
ability to jolt the world's conscience. The international
community responded with generosity to the Ethiopian
famine once it was brought into the living rooms of Europe
and North America by the media. But it has to be said that
that was the spontaneous, deeply genuine, humane response
of ordinary, decent people. Some of their governments, who
knew of the crisis, remained unmoved and did not respond
to it with a comparable sense of compassion.

With colossal effort the World Bank has promoted its

Special Programmes for Africa. Despite long-term implications for the already beleaguered IDA VII replenishment, including those for Africa itself, many of us helped that effort. It fell short in reality of even the $1 billion target to which the Bank scaled down its initial proposal for a $2 billion programme, and there was a $6 billion shortfall in the real level of IDA funds overall.[2] The impressive response to the United Nations' emergency meeting in Geneva to meet food aid needs for 1985 turns out, on closer inspection, to have offered little that is additional to existing programmes. There is little prospect, therefore, of adequate assistance for the 21 countries currently identified by FAO as in a continuing state of risk.[3] More worrying still, the sense of public outrage in the West, as the cameras first showed the world the horror of the Ethiopian famine, is now beginning to ebb. We see less of Africa in the news as the pictures lose their ability to shock. Yet the crisis worsens for many countries with minimal stocks and an acute shortage of seeds and other agricultural inputs aggravated by falls in cereal production in 1984 for the second or third year.

But even if this short-term crisis can now be contained, it is superimposed on a longer-term problem of declining food availability. In Africa as a whole, as you know so directly, per capita output was lower in 1982 – before the drought – than in 1970 for all but seven sub-Saharan African countries. An inevitable – if shocking – consequence is that 20 per cent of the total population in sub-Saharan Africa is estimated to be undernourished – an increase of 20 million since the early 1970s. Child mortality is rising and is twice the average for all developing countries. Even before the famine in Ethiopia, one thousand children died every day in this continent. What is usually forgotten, however, is that – at least until the recent drastic 20 per cent reduction in output since 1981 – the growth in African food production was impressive by the standards of the past and even by those of industrial countries today. Unfortunately, the 2 per cent average annual growth of food production was more than swallowed up by population growth, averaging 2.7 per cent per annum and exceeding 4 per cent in some countries.

Worse, the young able-bodied men are migrating to the cities; so a qualitatively weaker farm labour force is having to support urban growth of 5 to 10 per cent per annum. At the same time, the pressure on marginal land contributes to the depletion of stocks of wood, soil erosion and desertification and the danger of irreversible ecological damage.

Population growth is, clearly, an absolutely critical element in the story. And here we pass beyond the food crisis to the wider issue of poverty. As those of you whose governments have active birth control programmes are painfully aware, it is easier to describe the population problem than it is to solve it. Rising child mortality and deepening poverty have the perverse effect of stimulating higher birth rates, since it may seem rational for the individual family, if not for society as a whole, to ensure against risk by having more children, some of whom may live. Poverty is not only a consequence of the population growth problem but its principal source. Indeed, poverty is where we should really start, since poverty not only explains dangerously high birth rates but also the way in which food shortages become famines – those who are too poor to buy food, and have few assets to sell, of necessity go hungry when their crops fail.

The growth of food production – at least until the recent drought – does, however, point to some positive and reassuring features in an otherwise depressing picture. One is the clear evidence of the adaptability and ingenuity of the African farmer. Where physical security, economic incentives and efficient government services have been available there has been evidence of an impressive response by small-holder farmers producing both cash crops and food. The second is the favourable population to land ratio. Although Africa's soils are recognised to be thin and weak on nutrients, easily damaged by too many cattle and over-cropping, given adequate support for agricultural development there is the promise of considerable improvement in production. Where the ingredients of the 'green revolution' – seeds, fertilisers, water – have been brought together in projects in Africa, yields have shown a spectacular improvement. This leads us to the question of where responsibility now lies for remedial action.

Here there is a great misunderstanding and some obfuscation. The message I get from my African friends is that the crisis is caused by drought. The message I get from Western capitals is that the crisis is man-made – more precisely, by African governments. The latter view is clearly based on ignorance of the severe difficulties of farming in a precarious environment with highly variable rainfall. But it has to be said that the problems do not begin and end with nature. In each year of drought the number of countries seriously affected has kept on growing: 12 in 1974; 27 in 1979, 35 in 1984. Rain alone will not wash away hunger.

A good deal of responsibility rests with African governments. There is a familiar litany of past policy failures which, almost everyone agrees, should be acted upon: pricing policies which give inadequate incentives to peasant production; inefficient state marketing and other agricultural service organisations; excessive reliance on subsidised food imports; above all, an urban bias with wages, salaries and amenities which favour city dwellers.

Here, I think, we reach the nub of the discussion: what can Africa do to reform itself, and to what extent does it rely on international reform to make its own efforts productive? My own reaction to these questions is invariably to stress the wider international influences; to point out that external financing crises have also engulfed those African countries which have long been held up by aid donors and experts as models for others to follow. But we do ourselves no favours if we fudge the issue of domestic policy.

A useful point of reference, I believe, is what the World Bank calls an 'emerging consensus on policy issues which dwarfs any remaining areas of dissent'. This is the basis of the 'policy reforms' now being demanded by the main donors as part of medium and long-term adjustment. I think it is useful to spell out what is meant:

- Programmes to cut the birth rate;
- A more 'relevant' structure of education and training;
- A shift in the internal terms of trade towards agriculture;
- Realistic, market-based, exchange rates;
- Improved financial control, including higher interest rates to encourage saving;
- An emphasis on small-holdings rather than large farms;
- Incentives for the private sector, including direct foreign investment;
- Stimulation of exports;
- Stimulation of 'efficient' import substitution, especially in energy and food;
- Closer economic integration in Africa, again emphasising energy and food.

There is little here which, in itself, is either objectionable or impractical. It is becoming less credible to engage in philosophical exchanges on the merits of using market incentives when, even in China and other Socialist countries, such incentives are recognised pragmatically to have major value. Nor should we try to pretend that there is any alternative to external viability. With or without external assistance, exports have to be made to grow to meet import needs – it is a delusion to pretend that African countries have the option of retreating into autarchy. Surely it is both right and necessary to confront Africa's critics and its donors with a positive message: that African governments are not afraid or unwilling to admit mistakes; nor to make radical policy changes.

And those changes need to go beyond economic policy strictly. World military spending, mainly accounted for by the two super-powers, is now close to $2 million a minute – every minute of the day. But as obscene as the quantum of resources devoted to destructive purpose is the military culture that underpins it. That culture is spreading to the Third World where its implications are simply grotesque in the midst of poverty. In a world without collective security and with predatory instincts among nations far from curbed, some military expenditure by Third World countries is inevitable; and in Africa's case there is the special problem caused by South Africa's policies of destabilisation. But these are not the only reasons for it. In an international climate dominated by militarism, some Third World leaders have turned to militarisation, including modern weapons systems, sometimes as symbols of national progress, more often as props to political power at home. And, of course, major countries of East and West are their suppliers – at high cost – of guns in place of aid; guns that take back the fruits of aid. NATO and Warsaw Pact countries come together to man the 'arms bazaar'.

Developing-country expenditure on military purposes has been rising as a proportion of GNP. Serious research submitted to the United Nations Group of Governmental Experts suggests that the 'average' developing country with a GNP per capita of around $350 (1970) and a population of 8.5 million, the first $200 million spent on arms imports, rather than on human needs, could:

(a) Add 20 additional infant deaths per 1,000 live births;
(b) Decrease average life expectancy by three to four years;
(c) Result in 13 to 14 fewer literate adults out of every hundred.

I have described this absorption of the military culture in terms of the Third World generally, for so it is; but Africa is prominent in providing examples of such diversion from development. At this time of crisis Africa cannot ignore this. It is making the continent not stronger but weaker – in economic as well as in political terms.

In all these fields, radical policy changes will only come if there is a genuine resolve to correct what is wrong at home – what has failed to work – what has worked to produce greater unfairness and alienation – models that have proved unsuitable to Africa's people. This is not a plea to move to the left or to the right; but to move in those directions that the needs of real development dictate. There will be different turnings for different countries to take; none can afford the pretence of having found the perfect path to development or, for that matter, the ideal form of economic, social and political organisation – worst of all in mimic alignment with East or West.

I dwell on this not because I believe that Africa does not have the sovereign right to its own choices – even the right to make wrong choices – but because I fear that its very sovereignty is now threatened by a new colonialism constructed on Africa's weakness. This threat is growing steadily in strength and resolve; the response to it has to begin with Africa reducing its vulnerability, its dependency, its fragility – economic, social and political. Correcting mistakes may be a sovereign choice; for Africa it has become the choice of sovereignty. There is nothing so new in this – all countries have faced the same dangers; but most have had a longer time to experiment with their own forms, to make mistakes, to take corrective action. For Africa – as for other new countries elsewhere – there is no such grace period. In our interdependent world, even sovereign choices can easily tip the balance towards irreversible dependency. To survive within that world, Africa cannot afford to offer hostages to fortune. Strengthened by the will to adjust policy to the proven needs of true development, Africa must then demand of the rich world simultaneous recognition of some other responsibilities and realities. And here Africa has a good case. Let me try to spell out some of its elements.

First, Africa has much to its credit. Many of these 'consensus' reforms have been tried over the years if not decades. There has been a major success story in parts of East Africa where tea and coffee, small-scale dairy farming and maize growing have all taken off on small peasant plots. Some governments have tried to use price incentives for food production, often courageously, and – as in Zimbabwe and Somalia – with spectacular success in the recent past.

Secondly, perfectly sensible policy guidelines can be

ruined by simplistic, generalised solutions. Africa cannot be treated as an undifferentiated whole. As between rich Gabon, middle-income Ivory Coast and poverty-stricken Chad; between populous Nigeria and tiny Swaziland or The Gambia; between the generally improving living standards of Botswana or Cameroon, and the decline in the Sudan; between the underused expanses of Tanzania and Zambia and the land hunger of Mauritius, Rwanda and the Kenya highlands, there are enormous differences of endowments and experiences quite apart from policy orientation. For example, a decision in one country to scrap inefficient parastatal marketing boards may make sense; but, elsewhere, the alternative – in, say, a lightly populated area with poor distribution – could be that the supply of essentials reverts to the monopolistic control of a handful of powerful merchants. Policy has to be made in Africa, not in Washington, London or Tokyo.

Thirdly, timing is as important as substance. Unpopular measures, rushed through at the behest of external agencies, could provoke not only instability but a backlash against reform. One of the most damaging consequences of the current crisis is the way in which horizons have been foreshortened. All decisions are reduced to the short-term. Investment, research and development, long-term planning, all have been sacrificed to meet current needs. External agencies have aggravated this problem. Aid donors usually budget annually – a fact which limits forward planning. The system of multi-year rescheduling for debt which was promised by industrial countries has been extended to some Latin American commercial debtors but not by lending governments to Africa, whose treasuries plod a constant treadmill of annual debt renegotiations.[4] The IMF is another major unhelpful influence. The insistence of tough and inflexible short-term monetary and fiscal performance criteria – of a kind suitable to a resilient industrial economy – not only leads to most IMF programmes breaking down in Africa but is wholly at odds with the need for longer-term structural adjustment assisted by agencies such as the World Bank.

And nowhere is a longer-term time horizon more necessary than in relation to some of the more favoured policy
changes – such as those designed to attract more private
foreign investment. I am personally convinced, and I know
that many of you believe, that private overseas investment
on the right terms can usefully play a major role in
development. But multinationals will not commit large sums
of risk capital in a context of extreme crisis, including falling
standards of services and the political turmoil engendered by
growing poverty. International or, at least, inter-governmental support for infrastructural development is a necessary complement to any real enlargement of the role of
private foreign investment.

Fourthly, the reforms proposed, far from being too
radical, are, if anything, not radical enough. For example,
the greater use of price incentives for food production does
little or nothing for the subsistence farmer. Seventy-five per
cent of African food grains production never leaves the
village. Price incentives can only do so much. To be effective
they need supplementation in terms of rural credit for small-
scale farmers, increased extension work and efficient storage
to reduce harvest losses. But all of this requires resources –
and, therefore, external help on a large scale. Financial
flows are essential if rich countries expect Africa to deliver
reforms on a scale which the crisis demands.

Yet, frankly, the capital flows position for the next three
to four years looks terrible. Sub-Saharan Africa has suffered
from a combination of serious reversals on the external
front. First, the terms of trade have deteriorated: over the
last ten years low-income African countries have lost some
20 per cent in the purchasing power of their exports. An
African coffee exporter has to produce 30 per cent more
coffee to buy a tractor from overseas, and much more coffee
for the oil to keep it going. In the face of adverse price
movements, few sub-Saharan African countries have any
major degree of export diversification and this has become
more pronounced in recent years.

Secondly, capital flows have become harder to attract and have hardened in their terms. The World Bank estimates that even if gross flows of aid and private capital are kept at the levels of 1980-82, annual net flows of capital to sub-Saharan Africa could fall from $11 billion to $5 billion in the next three years, with an even bigger fall in real terms.[5] And, thirdly, the recent experience of drought and declining domestic food availability has forced countries to dig into their reserves, or borrow, in order to finance imports which do not contribute to future development. One-fifth of the African peoples are now being fed by grain imports. And Africa has fallen from being a substantial net exporter of livestock and meat 15 years ago to the status of a net importer.

The combination of these factors has led to stagnation in import capacity and slow growth – leading to a decline in per capita incomes of no less than 15 per cent over the last decade. With falling per capita incomes, it is obviously impossible to sustain domestic capital formation. Hence savings, as a share of GDP, fell in low-income Africa from 13.4 per cent in 1970 to 5.9 per cent in 1981. Attempts by African countries to borrow their way out of stagnation have led to overseas debt service payments rising to over 27 per cent of exports in 1984 from 8.8 per cent in 1973. Sub-Saharan Africa has an eight-fold increase in debt in this period. Its external debt stands at $80 billion, having grown more rapidly even than in Latin America. This year it will be paying out $11 billion in interest and capital, almost cancelling out capital inflows. Sudan's debt service, if it was paid, would amount to 100 per cent of export earnings in a good year. Other countries are not far behind. Yet, to date, it is the middle-income, more heavily indebted countries that have been helped most – not Africa.

As a result of their inabilty to pay, African countries have accounted for half of all debt reschedulings undertaken in recent years. There are arrears on trade transactions of around $8 billion, which has caused the loss of credit lines and the disruption of normal trade, reducing most African states to a hand-to-mouth existence. Projections by the IMF suggest that even on relatively favourable assumptions about world growth and interest rates, the burden of debt service will get worse. And the generally optimistic World Bank has shown that even modest improvements in debt service ratios will be at the price of another decade of falling per capita incomes. Such a prospect is barely sustainable in economic, political or moral terms.

There is little doubt that Africa will be heavily dependent over the next few years on major external capital flows simply for recovery. The problem is partly one of assistance for reconstruction and to keep essential services operating. What will be the response of traditional aid programmes which are heavily biased to capital goods from the donor country and towards new projects? How quickly are the aid agencies reorientating themselves to the urgent need for balance-of-payments assistance to acquire the spare parts and necessary inputs to get existing agricultural and industrial projects moving? How is the proper balance to be struck between emergency aid relief – especially food aid – designed simply to keep people alive, and longer term assistance for reconstruction after the cameras leave?

How can the tremendous upsurge of sympathy and popular involvement felt by people in Western countries be carried through by their governments in terms of long-term programmes working in a genuine partnership with the African governments needing assistance?

In the forthcoming report of the Committee for Development Planning[6] we set out the range of policy prescriptions proposed to us by the Economic Commission for Africa. We are calling for their urgent consideration. The tragedy is that just at the time when, paradoxically, and dangerously, the advance of technology, the growth of travel, communications, trade and international capital movements have made interdependence a living reality, a sense of interconnectedness among governments has declined. We are witnessing a major assault on an already fragile structure of international co-operation. In other words, 1984 may have confirmed an Orwellian style '1984' world-wide for the rest of this decade – with absolute power exercised by a small directorate of rich states and even the pretence of equal status in the international community abandoned.

There is a strong feeling, with sinister ideological overtones within significant circles in major countries, that a handful of strong and rich countries can and should run the world, help and reward friends, destabilise and destroy enemies. There is such a profound ideological conviction in the virtues of the market place and the free enterprise system and in the evil of 'communism' and the inefficiencies of centrally-planned economies that the assumption of such authoritarianism at the global level will actually be believed to be beneficial to all concerned; certainly it will be presented in righteous terms. This has implications far beyond economic issues. It has rather special political ramifications for Southern Africa and Central America. But, of course, its most grim implications are for the power struggle between East and West and the temptations it will bring for a nuclear showdown.

It is part of this retreat from international co-operation, retreat from multilateralism, that on North-South issues, the North seems to have decided that there is really no need to negotiate with the South. This is not just a tactical position; it has more to do with ideology than with a judgement of what the traffic will bear in terms of North-South relations. That is why, from 1979 onwards, after the last oil shock was contained, there has not merely been no progress, there have been no negotiations: none in the General Assembly; none at UNCTAD VI; none at Cancun;[7] none at UNIDO IV; and none, of course, at the specially extended spring meetings of the Interim and Development Committees just ended.

At one level of awareness, everyone knows this is happening; yet the South persisted, for example with the pretence that UNCTAD VI was a success, and persisted also with the strategy of 'global negotiations' long after all hope of success for it was abandoned in Third World capitals. Had the North not been under the sway of ideology of the Heritage Foundation,[8] it might well have adopted the tactic of agreeing to some innocuous form of 'global negotiations' and spun out another decade in fruitless dialogue. Because it was under the sway, it was both more aggressive and more doctrinaire in its rejection of dialogue.

Why this retreat from human solidarity? Not, I believe, because the world is not being perceived as the interdependent community that it is; but because the strong within the community are refusing to accept a duty of care towards fellow citizens. Recognition of mutual interests is not leading to fulfilment of mutual needs but to reliance on self-assertiveness and even compulsion. In some important respects, we are acting out at the global level the feudal mentality that lay at the heart of resistance to the reform movements in Europe in the eighteenth century, or in China earlier this century. I suspect that not enough attention is being paid in the Third World to these deeper realities. The South still seems to believe that what it has to do is negotiate a list of specific reforms within a framework of prevailing general agreement on the virtues of international co-operation.

When the Economic Commission for Africa was first established over twenty years ago, a global consensus on international co-operation for development existed and could be made the unspoken premise of recommendations for action. It is doubtful whether that consensus still holds; certainly, it cannot be taken for granted. The alternative to international co-operation would be a drift towards a more rigid, fragmented and power-dominated international environment, a drift away from order, stability, predictability and rules, towards greater arbitrariness, uncertainty and exercise of power; a drift away from the multilateralist trends of the early post-war era, a return to the anarchy of the 1930s. This is the climate in which Africa and the Third World generally must now develop its strategy for a dialogue with the North.

But the South is still fumbling for a clear strategy; its tactics are uncertain and confused. Worse still, it is in danger of developing sub-strategies responsive to regional needs and perceptions: Latin America moving on the debt front; Africa moving under compulsions of a food crisis and the danger of economic collapse; Asia, better off than most, looking for small gains in trade. There is an urgent need for the South to get its act together; and not just for the strength that is in unity. There is a debt problem, for example, in Africa; different from Latin America's both quantitatively and qualitatively, but massive for the countries concerned. If solutions are pursued by Latin American countries separately, not only will they be weaker than if joined by all Third World debtor countries but the 'solutions' they evolve will be regionally oriented and could well worsen the situation of the others; for example, by drawing away from the neediest (including Africa) resources that the lending countries will contribute to relieving the Latin American debt crisis, or by encouraging distortions in trade (to the detriment of others) as a substitute for debt relief.

Unless we face up to these deficiences, the Third World as a whole, but Africa to perhaps a greater degree than most because of its position of relative weakness, is headed for disaster. Let me draw on an analogy from another continent. The first major document of Simon Bolivar, the liberator of Latin America, was the Memorandum of Cartagena. It was written after his first defeat and before the Congress of Angostura helped him to regroup for eventual success. In it he identified the external causes of his defeat; but he examined himself and his revolutionaries also; and did not lack the courage of self-criticism. He wrote:

> We had philosophers for leaders, philanthropy for legislation, dialectics for tactics, and sophists for soldiers.[9]

Last year, 170 years later, at a South-South consultation in

Cartagena, I called attention to the need for such self-examination. I do so again in this continent. Perhaps we, too, shall find that for the Third World generally there has been too much philosophy, too much dialectics, too much sophistry, perhaps, even, too much philanthropy. Above all, let us not again mistake voting power in the United Nations for decision-making and pay the price of resolutions that flatter only to deceive.

What then is needed? Much more co-ordination by the South – at all levels. The North is in constant touch. Their national economic policy co-ordination is far from perfect; but policy co-ordination on North-South issues is very effective. In the weeks before the recent spring meetings of the Interim and Development Committees of the World Bank and International Monetary Fund, EEC Ministers met, OECD Ministers met, against the backdrop of fully researched option papers. All the Third World had was a meeting of the G24 Ministers[10] the day before. Ironically, the South has even been put on the defensive in relation to its own attempts at co-ordination. Over 'Cartagena' the North screamed about threats of a 'debtor cartel' so loudly and effectively that some countries felt the need to disavow any such intent. Yet all the time the North had been forging one of the most effective 'lender cartels' built around its control of the IMF. So effective is it that a developing country that refuses to agree an IMF programme finds virtually all credit facilities in the North closed to it – the World Bank, commercial banks, national aid agencies, even 'Treaty' agencies like the European Development Fund – closures specifically designed to bring the IMF's victim to heel. Of what other elements is a cartel compounded? Yet Portia, not Shylock, the South with its call for justice not the North with its unmerciful lending policies, is made the 'villain' in our present debt crisis.

For the Third World, it must be a time for stocktaking. A start has to be made somewhere in developing a more coherent, realistic and effective strategy for the South. It has to begin, I believe, with some clear thinking and talking among political leaders. If it is to be such an occasion it cannot be either formal or universal in Third World terms. Neither a non-aligned style summit nor a G77 Ministerial Meeting will do. What is needed is something like a Cancun of the South – with no more than twenty to twenty-five Third World leaders from all the regions meeting informally to share their reflections on current economic and political issues. It should not be projected as a decision-making process; it clearly cannot be that. It should not be projected solely in North-South terms; the South has matters beyond North-South relations it can and should discuss. Above all, it must be managed in such a way that it is a time for informal discussion – not the reading of papers. And it does not have to end with a Declaration.

I once put these ideas to a group of Third World ambassadors. There was substantial welcome for the ideas; but a few were worried about giving the impression that the South was getting together to confront the North. This is an indication of how debilitated the South has become. It seems perfectly natural that the North should meet at the Summit in the Group of 7^{11} or in the specific context of global issues as in the Group of $10;^{12}$ but if Southern leaders met it would need to be explained that their intention was not an assault on the North. Basically, why should there be any need to do more than explain that a few Third World leaders are getting together to examine where they stand on North-South and South-South issues, to reflect on what might be done to improve the situation for development, for recovery and for internationalism?

Third World leaders now have to say to each other what they know privately, namely, that there is no realistic prospect for global negotiations[13] nor, indeed, for a comprehensive International Monetary Conference[14] immediately. They need to devise a new strategy that does not proceed on the false premise that there is a global consensus that the world is a community and should be made more tolerable for all its people; a Third World strategy for mutual aid on debt, on commodities, on progress towards a new Bretton Woods, for example; but a strategy so designed that an unconverted North can be induced to accept it. And they need to co-ordinate all this so that when African leaders talk about debt, for example, they do so in the context of an integrated Third World approach and with the knowledge that they have the support of Latin America.

Bringing all this about is a task for the Third World generally; but Africa, I believe, has so essential a need for it that African leaders owe it to themselves to be prominent in the movement to secure it. It may seem logical for Africa to turn inwards at a time of crisis and emergency. And I have, of course, urged that a major part of the response must be at the level of improvement at home: critical self-examination, a readiness to correct mistakes, a sense of urgency about improving efficiency, an acknowledgement that freedom has not been won if the energies and potential of all the people are not released in both the economic and political fields. But this is only half the story. Since Africa's survival on any tolerable basis requires as well a more favourable international environment, Africa must help to secure that environment.

Africa, for example, must be in the front line in securing a resumed North-South dialogue, in organising the South for it, in securing a Third World Secretariat as an essential element of that organisation. If I am right that out of Africa's weakness arises the danger of a new dependency, a new kind of bondage, then the struggle is not unlike that against colonialism itself. Africa must be as prominent now as it was then in ensuring that the entire Third World is mobilising in support of its cause. If it is not, there is a real danger that Third World unity would at best be ineffectual and at worst a mere facade; that other regions of the developing world will look to their own interests and leave Africa to a darkening fate; Third World unity is not a luxury; political action to secure it is not a diversion from responsibilities at home. It is, I believe, an absolutely essential element of Africa's defences in the face of the crisis that confronts it.

There is an old African proverb which I heard first in Swahili, but which must have its counterpart throughout the continent. It is to the effect that "when elephants fight the grass gets trampled". The grass is inevitably the weak, the fragile, the vulnerable, the helpless. And in our global field the elephants are, of course, the super-powers and their military alliances that trample the grass as they struggle against each other for supremacy; but they include other elements as well – all the major economic and political forces, national and 'multinational', that contend for power in our contemporary world. Africa today faces great danger from their trampling of the grass.

But Africa is not alone. A long, long time ago, the medieval poet Langland, in his 'Vision of Piers Plowman', presented the image of the world in its immense variety as 'a field full of folk'.[15] In our interdependent, interconnected world, that image of a world of people has every day greater validity. People – ordinary, decent people everywhere – in increasing numbers recognise that they are part of that 'field of folk'. And there is a growing awareness that the grass grows in rich countries as well as poor ones; that that fate of being crushed down, trodden under, is common to us all, because we are all the grass; all flesh is grass. The lives that are trampled, therefore, are the lives of people everywhere. Everywhere in the Third World; but everywhere in the world where there are weak and vulnerable people. As the outpouring of generosity from ordinary people has shown in recent months, Africa is not alone. It must not feel alone, or act as if it were. This may be a season for the trampling of the grass; but, provided we take care to win the battle of survival, there will come another season when the grass will flourish.

Notes and References

1. See *ECA and Africa's Development, 1983-2000, A Preliminary*

Perspective Study, Economic Commission for Africa, Addis Ababa, April 1983.

2. Replenishment of the funds of IDA VII was eventually agreed at $9 billion over the three year-period July 1984 to June 1987 as against $15 billion estimated as being necessary to maintain the real value of IDA lending to low-income countries.

3. FAO, *Food Situation in African Countries Affected by Emergencies,* Special Report July 1985. Refers to 21 countries identified by Special FAO/WFP Task Force as having exceptional food supply problems in 1984/85.

4. Refers to the general practice of the Paris Club of official creditors (mainly export credit agencies) of rescheduling one year's maturing principal at a time. Two MYRA's (Multiyear Rescheduling Agreements) have since been negotiated in the Paris Club: The Ivory Coast and Ecuador.

5. The declining trend of net flows has continued. There have been negative net flows from banks in the 1984-86 period to sub-Saharan Africa. Net export credits have largely ceased.

6. *The Challenge to Multilateralism: A Time for Renewal,* (1985, UN Doc. ST/ESA169), Report of the UN Committee for Development Planning (21st Session), pp. 33-37.

7. North-South Summit attended by twenty-two Heads of State and governments of developed and developing countries and held in Cancun, Mexico (22-23 October 1981), to consider the future of international co-operation for development and the reactivation of the world economy.

8. Refers to the conservative US 'think tank' which has been an important source of ideas for the Reagan Administration and right-wing Congressmen.

9. Manuel Perez Vila (ed), *Simon Bolivar: His Basic Thoughts,* (Presidency of the Republic of Venezuela, Caracas, 1981).

10. The Group of 24 was a working group set up by the larger Group of 77 developing countries – eight each drawn from Africa, Asia and the Pacific and the Western Hemisphere.

11. The G7 (the US, Japan, France, Germany, UK, Italy and Canada), was formally constituted as a regular Finance Ministers' forum at the 1986 Tokyo Western Economic Summit, and grew out of the informal G5 (the above less Italy and Canada) that had met regularly since the early 1970s.

12. The G10 comprises the major industrial countries that are signatories to the General Agreement to Borrow (plus Switzerland).

13. The call for 'global negotiations' can be dated from the Eleventh Special Session of the UN General Assembly in 1980. Subsequent sessions of the General Assembly have failed so far to agree on a proposal to launch global negotiations.

14. The need for an International Monetary Conference received much attention in the early 1980s. The Seventh Non-Aligned Summit in New Delhi in 1983 recommended a conference on money and finance for development, and in the same year a Commonwealth Group of Experts in its Report, *Towards a New Bretton Woods: Challenges for the World Financial and Trading System,* also recommended a similar Conference and prescribed a preparatory process that could culminate in it. Discussions in the UN and other international forums have not led to such a Conference.

15. William Langland, *Piers Plowman,* newly rendered into modern English by Henry W. Wells (Sheed and Ward, London, 1959), p.3.

For the South,
A Time to Think

In response to the stalemate in the North-South dialogue and to other international realities facing the South, South-South II – the second in the series of international meetings between representatives of the developing countries convened by the Third World Foundation was held in Kuala Lumpur in May 1986. Its theme was "Charting the Way Forward", and Shridath Ramphal was invited to deliver the keynote address. In it, he dealt extensively with the economic challenges facing the countries of the South and with the brutal realities of a hostile international environment. He ended, however, by calling for Third World responses based on a re-examination by developing countries of their role in North-South economic relations as well as in South-South co-operation. He called specifically for an Independent Commission of the South on Development Issues. As a direct result of the South-South II meeting and the efforts of the Prime Minister of Malaysia who chaired it, the South Commission was established in 1987 under the chairmanship of Julius K. Nyerere. Shridath Ramphal is a member.

The unsatisfactory state of North-South economic relations means that greater efforts must be made by the South to evolve new strategies to bring about improvements, even though much of the responsibility for the present state of affairs lies with the North and, in particular, with its attempts to introduce power elements into these relations. The North, of course, has a similar interest in, and responsibility for, improving North-South relations even if, for the time being, a false complacency and a narrow vision obscure reality.

But our concern here is with the South and its responses. Despite all the frustrations, our perspective must not be clouded by too negative an interpretation of the past. The gap which exists between needs and aspirations on the one hand, and achievements on the other, is vast; but this does not mean that no progress has been made. In the World Bank, the International Monetary Fund and GATT, developing countries are not without some influence on the decisions that are being made and that influence is not always marginal. In the Fund and the Bank their influence has in the past been felt on such basic decisions as the system of SDR allocation, the establishment of the IMF Compensatory Financing Facility and the creation of IDA; while in the GATT, their pressures led to the addition of Part IV of the Agreement, which started the process of recognising the special needs of developing countries in the international trading system. And even directly under UN auspices, the Generalised System of Preferences[1] was created and debt relief was provided to the poorest countries under UNCTAD and, more recently, substantial relief operations were organised to respond to the famine in Africa.

The achievements go beyond these practical measures. At the political level they have also been significant, and an inadequate recognition of this could lead to an over-pessimistic assessment of the North-South Dialogue. Through the G77, the Non-Aligned Movement and the G24, much has been done to articulate the interests and problems facing the developing countries; and through the UNCTAD Sessions and General Assembly discussions and special forums and Groups such as the Cancun Summit, the Brandt Commission and meetings such as this, much has been done to give these interests and problems a high political profile in the international system. Although the political momentum for the dialogue built up in the early 1970s has now faded, that build-up was a significant development.[2] The sad thing is that it was not used to better practical effect and to lead to a more sustained dialogue. Some of the fault for that clearly rests with the South.

The task for the South now is to endeavour to rebuild the dialogue and to ensure that any new political thrust is used to the maximum extent possible to bring about practical results. In this connection, UNCTAD, the General Assembly, the Bank, the Fund, GATT and other forums all have their role. The unpopularity of some forums for economic discussion, such as UNCTAD and the General Assembly, has caused some decline in their importance in North-South economic relations, but this must not deter efforts to secure their revival. At the same time, the developing countries must not be reluctant to use other forums, such as the Interim and Development Committees and the Boards of the Fund and the Bank, as well as the GATT, as fully as possible – but to use them, not to be passive spectators from within.

Full advantage must be taken of the continuing financial discussions in Washington and trade policy discussions in the GATT. In the case of the latter, the main thrust now is to launch a new round of trade negotiations.[3] Developing countries must persist in their attempts to ensure that such a round will deal substantially with their problems, which now stand out because of their neglect in the past and the rise of new protectionism, which has fallen heavily on them. Part of the problem in the past has been that the developing countries have not given adequate attention to acting in concert in trade negotiations. Although not hampered by an unequal voting system, their weak individual bargaining power continues to give them an insubstantial role in the GATT. Since they tend to buy more from the industrial countries than they sell to them, and since this balance is particularly unequal in the area of manufactured goods, which is normally a major concern of the negotiations, the bargaining power potential of the developing countries is much greater than they have been able to mobilise so far.

Current preparations for the new round offer them significant scope to influence its modalities and to develop strategies for co-operation in the negotiations which could greatly enhance the benefits that they secure. Time must not be lost in beginning to develop such strategies.

In the past, GATT has been seen too much by developing countries as an inappropriate forum for their active participation and as being in opposition to UNCTAD. But while there remains an overlap of competence in some areas, the relative roles of the two organisations have become clearer. The developing countries have a great interest in protecting the integrity of UNCTAD; they must not see this, however, as being in contradiction to protecting their interests in the new round under the GATT. A full and more forceful participation by developing countries in the new round is an important requirement in the next stage of the evolution of the North-South dialogue.

Developing countries have as great an interest in negotiations on money and finance as they have in negotiations on trade policy. They must, therefore, continue to insist that a parallel programme of negotiations is required on these issues. In their move to undertake a study on reform of the international monetary system through the G24,[4] as a response to a similar study by the G10,[5] they were able to secure increased attention to these issues recently at the Interim and Development Committees. Such tactical moves indicate that developing countries, in spite of their weak bargaining position, have some scope for influencing the course of discussions. Ingenuity must continue to be used to induce progress.

And these efforts by the South to open up new approaches to dialogue and negotiation must not bypass the socialist countries of Eastern Europe. They are, it is true, a special and, in some respects, separate dimension of the North; but the South must not equate difference with exemption. Development is a process to which all who can must contribute. The contributions expected of Western countries are not by way of reparations for colonialism so much as assistance that responds to human needs and, in the longer term, the interests of the world economy itself. The centrally-planned economies should, therefore, make a response as well; and they can do so. It may be a quantitatively different response; but it should not be qualitatively inferior.

There is a great need for a serious negotiating process on monetary and financial issues. The increased efforts of the industrial countries to secure policy co-ordination and greater surveillance of their policies are steps in the right direction. But they do not go far enough in the direction of reform, and they need to emanate from a wider process of consultation. It is not only the developing countries that need a stronger voice in the international economic system, but the middle powers also. This provides scope for tactical alliances to secure a more democratic international economic system.

The maintenance of the unity of the G77, in spite of the diversity of interests among developing countries, is a remarkable diplomatic achievement. Their community of interest remains stronger than their conflict of interest, and recent developments emphasising the importance of official financial flows, debt relief and market access for middle-income countries confirm the continuing need for middle-income and low-income countries to work together. There was a time, not so long ago, when some middle-income countries were reluctant to include indebtedness in North-South discussions for fear of the effect of such discussions on their creditworthiness. Now the call for a political dialogue on debt is more generally supported.

But increased solidarity through the G77 must not mean increased rigidity in the stance of the developing countries. There is a need for a more flexible use of the Group system.

The G77 must provide a solid framework for negotiations at the global level, but it must also serve as an umbrella organisation supporting groups of developing countries which have a special interest and which may wish to negotiate on their own with a particular set of industrial countries. A further flexibility of approach should allow the G77 itself to negotiate and seek agreements with groups of developed countries if agreement on a universal basis seems unlikely. Greater use must also be made of preliminary negotiations in representative small groups in order to make the negotiating process less unwieldy.

In attempting to secure a revived North-South dialogue, both the issues and the process require renewed attention.[6] The need for a programme of negotiations on money and finance to be undertaken in parallel with a new round of trade negotiations has been mentioned above. In relation to specific issues, developing countries must constantly refine their priorities. These priorities can only be determined by the developing countries themselves and will only be determined efficiently through their own technical support system. Even sympathetic international organisations develop their own institutional interests which need not be fully consistent with those of the developing countries.

In the past, the North-South dialogue was characterised by proposals on issues mainly emanating from the developing countries with responses which were usually negative from the developed countries. What is needed is a better balance in the dialogue, with developed countries more ready to take initiatives and with all groups being more prepared to examine positively initiatives taken by other groups. This approach should endeavour to secure better engagement between the North and South through more attention to issues which offer scope for convergence without each side giving up on those which, though controversial, are passionately held. A basic constraint in the dialogue is, however, the weak power of the South, which it must strive to alleviate through greater leverage and unity.

Great effort should be made to streamline agendas without, at the same time, sacrificing balance in the interests of groups and sub-groups. In the near future, issues which should enjoy priority in the dialogue are the adequacy of resources to finance growth targets which are acceptable, debt relief, the roll-back of protectionist barriers, appropriate adjustment policies for North and South, and the importance of SDR allocations in meeting the liquidity needs of developing countries.

As mentioned, a particular handicap of the South which is emerging with greater clarity is the lack of a technical support system. One consequence is greater reliance on the technical work of international institutions, which increasingly are showing lack of objectivity in their effort to accommodate 'political realities'. Thus, on issues like the replenishment of the resources of institutions, staff studies are increasingly tending to produce targets which are determined more by their interpretation of such 'political realities' than their assessment of real needs. And trends and projections of aid and other resource flows are often assessed in the most optimistic light possible to minimise the extent of retrogression.[7]

Greater flexibility in negotiating style and structure, and the other improvements suggested above, would all be greatly helped if the G77 could receive technical support from a permanent secretariat. To those of us who have been early advocates of a Third World Secretariat,[8] it is heartening to note that the idea has become more widely accepted.[9] Even so, however, what stands in the way of a modest start are not financial requirements – which are themselves modest – but a lack of 'will' on a wide enough front.

A Third World Secretariat is usually conceived as a technical support system for negotiations with the North and for the promotion of South-South co-operation. While these must be priority concerns, especially at the intitial stage, there are wider functions which must be addressed and the

Secretariat might eventually have to aim at serving as a 'think-tank' for developing countries in relation to their longer-term interests. Problems of appropriate adjustment measures, the use of power in economic relations, and the spread of control over developing countries' policies are all issues that would require more sustained and in-depth research than is normally demanded by immediate negotiations.

And the South must not be defensive about this. The North has never been hesitant about organising itself and co-ordinating its positions both for the better management of its economic affairs and for its encounters with the South. Indeed, it is ironic that on the only two issues over the last decade that offered the South real collective leverage with the North – oil and debt – the practical out-turn was greater solidarity, co-ordination and collective action by the North. On the oil price in the 1970s and on debt in the 1980s, the North ultimately neutralised Southern power by more efficient and effective organisation – a result to which the South contributed by its own failure to translate declarations on unity into truly concerted action.

The South-South dimension of the work of the Secretariat would, of course, be very important. Current developments in North-South relations make South-South co-operation more imperative, not necessarily as a separate excercise, but as part of an integrated approach. Progress in the South-South relations would help the North-South dialogue. It would not only lead to better preparations and more united approaches, but its very success would spur a better response from the North, since their interests would be in danger of being undermined.

This is not an exhaustive catalogue of what can be done by the South and needs to be done quickly and well. But it is enough to establish that the South can do better at getting its act together and must do so if, at this time of transition in the world economy, it is to respond with imagination and creativity to the challenges facing developing countries.

Where does all this leave us? What should the South be doing? My contention is that the time has come for some hard thinking by developing countries about their place and prospects in the world economy, about what they need to do for themselves and about what they need to do together with developed countries to promote their mutual interest. It is hard thinking that must take place with the benefit of four decades of experience: experience within the South and with the North. And it must be hard thinking – hard in the sense of dispassionate self-examination and rigorous intellectual enquiry. Some of this is being done, of course, by individual effort. But something more is required; a more collective effort, yet one that is sufficiently detached from the daily governmental round to maximise its independence. That independent character is supremely important in two respects: first, in allowing some of the best minds in the South to work together without the constraint of pre-determined policy; and second, in allowing governments to view the excercise as a helpful process without being committed to endorsement of its out-turn. What is needed, in short, is an Independent Commission of the South on Development Issues.[10] The human resources for such a task unquestionably exist; the financial resources can surely be mobilised.

Notes and References

1. Generalised System of Preferences (GSP): preferential trading arrangements extended by individual industrial countries to developing countries generally following agreement at UNCTAD II in 1968.

2. For a comprehensive review of the North-South dialogue, see *The North-South Dialogue; Making it Work*, Report of a Commonwealth Group of Experts (Commonwealth Secretariat, 1982).

3. A new round (the Uruguay Round) of multilateral trade negotiations was launched at a special Ministerial Session of the GATT Contracting Parties in September 1986 in Punta del Este, Uruguay.

4. *The Functioning and Improvement of the International Monetary System,* Report by the Deputies of the Intergovernmental Group of 24 on International Monetary Affairs, August 1985.

5. *The Functioning of the International Monetary System,* Report by the Deputies of the Group of Ten, June 1985.

6. *The North-South Dialogue: Making it Work,* op. cit.

7. Note, for example, the absence of studies by the World Bank in recent times on capital requirements based on the real needs of developing countries. In the past, such studies formed an important basis for discussion on the capital resources of IBRD and IDA. The gap in the capital needs of sub-Saharan Africa in the recent World Bank report *Financing adjustment with growth in sub-Saharan Africa 1986-90* was calculated largely in relation to restoring imports to a past level rather than to bringing about targeted growth rates at satisfactory levels.

8. Shridath S. Ramphal, 'Not by Unity Alone: the Case for a Third World Organisation', (1979) 1 (3), *Third World Quarterly*.

9. There is now wider acceptance by Third World governments of the need for a technical support system. Under the Caracas Programme of Action of the Group of 77, a modest start was made by agreement to provide some technical support to the Chairman of the Group of 77 in New York.

10. A 28-member South Commission established in 1987 is now functioning with a Secretariat in Geneva. Its first meeting was held in October 1987 and its second in August 1988.

None of us anywhere, in the First World or the Third, can speak of peace but listen only to the drums of war. We cannot yearn for peace but live by an ethos of power. We cannot pray for peace, but nurture hate and prejudice and selfishness in our hearts. The peace of the world comes from within each and every one of the people who inhabit it. For every one of us, in however small a measure, peace is in our keeping.

*Shridath Ramphal**

Chapter 8

Tomorrow's World

Perspective VIII   324

The West Indies in the Year 2000   328
(Port-of-Spain, 1978)

Democracy in the Global State   334
(London, 1985)

The World is One   346
(New Delhi, 1987)

Making Human Society a Civilised State   365
(London, 1987)

* *Life is One and the World is One,* the Indira Gandhi Memorial Lecture, New Delhi, 19 January 1987.

Perspective VIII

Throughout the Chapters of this book so far, Shridath Ramphal has provided informed and troubled commentaries on the evolving problems of humanity; problems which spring from the notion that races and nations are not part of a greater family of mankind, but separate and distinct groups in a world whose benefits are reserved only for the rich and strong even at the expense of the poor and weak. In this final Chapter, Ramphal underlines the need for decision-makers the world over to see human society as a single state. He wants them to begin to apply to that global state concepts and mechanisms that have helped to make nation states more just and equitable than they could ever have been if left simply to the supremacy of power within them. At the heart of his vision lies the conviction that it is the rule of law world-wide which is the necessary corollary to our oneness.

As the twenty-first century approaches, official statistics describe a global crisis of contradictions; worse in economic terms than it has been since the 1930s and grave in the extremes of wealth and poverty now existing between developed and developing countries:

- there are over 13 million refugees in the world today; 'famine, desertification, deforestation and armed conflicts are the "root causes" of mass exoduses';[1]

- there are 700 million people living in poverty in the world today; their numbers are increasing;[2] meanwhile, 'a quarter of the world's population consume around 80 per cent of its commercial energy and metals, 85 per cent of its paper, and over half of the fat intake of foods';[3]

– per capita income in the least developed countries is lower today than it was in the 1960s, and many countries are caught in a vicious circle of economic decline, increasing poverty and environmental degradation;[4]

– the prices paid for commodities produced by developing countries have been forced downwards to unprecedented depths and are at their lowest since the 1930s;[5]

– the debt of the developing countries now stands at $900 million – more than a half is owed to banks in the developed world. The ratio of debt repayment to national export earnings is now a half or two-thirds of total visible exports;[6] in some cases it is actually larger;

– there are 30 million 'street children' in the world; they have no homes, no family, no protection and are 'forced by circumstances beyond their control to live on the margins of the adult world'. They live a life of crime, including prostitution and drug trafficking;[7]

– there is a higher rate of unemployment in the developed, industrialised, world today than at any time since the 1930s;[8]

– there have been 150 wars since the end of World War II, killing some 20 million people, most of whom were civilians not combatants. Polemological institutes have counted a mere 26 days of no conflicts since 1949;[9]

– total global spending on armaments – mostly by the developed countries, but increasingly by developing countries as well – now amounts to some trillion dollars per annum.[10]

The crisis permeates the economic and political relationships of all nations and these bald statistics, worrying as they are, paint only a small part of the wider canvas of global disparities and human suffering that now grip the world for they cannot measure, calculate and quantify human anguish.

They do not speak of the millions of children who could live beyond the age of five if they were innoculated against diseases, nor do they address the large numbers of people who have no access to pure water. They do not tell of the insufficiency of doctors and the even greater shortage of basic medicines, nor of the back-breaking toil of subsistence farmers who must still manually till the soil in the scorching heat of a relentless sun.

What then is the answer to this global crisis? In Ramphal's view its resolution rests not in bilateral arrangements between one powerful nation and another, nor between groups of them, but in a genuinely international dialogue underpinned by an ethic of human survival.[11] The late Barbara Ward understood Shridath Ramphal's concerns – his almost compulsive urge not to see the problems of a country only in nationalist terms but to seek out the international dimension which, in his view, nurtured solutions. In her introduction to Shridath Ramphal's book, *One World to Share,* she wrote:

> ...make no mistake about it, Mr. Ramphal's profoundest concern is not for this bloc or that group or yet another trading association. It is for humanity itself. He knows to the roots of his being that nationalism is not enough. No society can survive half slave, half free, half chucking away 65 per cent of its restaurant food, half on the brink of starvation. We go forward to a world either of increasing responsible planetary institutions or to ultimate catastrophe. The final shape of these institutions may not yet be clear... Mr. Ramphal does not dogmatise but in all his addresses we sense the urgency of his eloquence, the commitment of his heart.[12]

This final Chapter looks at the world through the eyes of Shridath Ramphal – eyes which have seen close up the realities of underdevelopment in the South and witnessed the disinterest of one official or another from the North; eyes whose vistas have been informed by the knowledge that despite the shrug of indifference from some in the North, developed countries cannot maintain their quality of life without the natural resources and the markets of the South;

eyes whose vision of the world is one in which governments commit themselves to the establishment of international mechanisms to govern the world on a basis of democracy, equity and the rule of law, and mankind acknowledges, at last, our inseparable humanity.

R.S.

Notes and References

1. *Refugees: Dynamics of Displacement,* A Report for the Independent Commission on International Humanitarian Issues, (Zed Books, London, 1986), p. xv.

2. Gro Harlem Brundtland, 'We are all Neighbours', *Towards Sustainable Development,* (The Panos Institute, London, 1987), p. 14.

3. Shridath Ramphal, *infra,* p. 370.

4. Gro Harlem Brundtland, op. cit., p. 14.

5. *Global Challenge: From Crisis to Co-operation, Breaking the North-South Stalemate,* Report of the Socialist International Committee on Economic Policy, (Pan Books, London, 1985), p. 86.

6. Ibid., p 36.

7. Susanna Agnelli (ed), *Street Children: A Growing Urban Tragedy,* Report for the Independent Commission on International Humanitarian Issues, (Weidenfeld and Nicolson, London, 1986), p. 15.

8. Shridath Ramphal, *Infra* p. 339.

9. *Modern Wars: The Humanitarian Challenge,* Report for the Independent Commission on Humanitarian Issues, (Zed Books, London, 1986), p.24.

10. *Global Challenge,* op. cit., p. 198.

11. Shridath Ramphal, Infra, p. 383.

12. Barbara Ward, Introduction to Shridath Ramphal, *One World to Share,* (Hutchinson Benham, London, 1979), p. xxvii.

The West Indies in
the Year 2000

On 28 January 1978 the University of the West Indies conferred an Honorary Degree of Doctor of Laws on Shridath Ramphal at its St. Augustine Campus in Trinidad. Returning to his West Indian roots, Ramphal spoke of his sense of belonging to the region and his enduring commitment to West Indian regional unity. This time he argued the case for unity by looking to the year 2000 and envisaging the kind of world which a fragmented West Indian region would greet in the twenty-first century. Choices, he urged, are inescapable. At the centre of those choices, he asserted once again, is the option to remain West Indian.

We cannot, of course, be absolutely certain what kind of world the year 2000 will usher in; but some projections are reasonably clear. It will be a world, no doubt, that has grown more truly interdependent – conscious of the limits of conventional power, military and economic, recognising with circumspection man's capacity for global self-destruction – acknowledging the danger of diminishing resources on a more and more crowded planet. Hopefully, it will be a world less obsessed with sovereignty which, throughout the preceding century, was so often a masquerade for bigotry and self-aggrandisement. And perhaps, therefore, it will be a world released from the grip of the adversary complex that has so often frustrated action towards a mutually reinforcing planetary order in the second half of the twentieth century.

It will be a world, assuredly, of giant states: of a China of 1,150 million people; of an India of 1,060 miillion; of a Brazil of 215 million; of an Indonesia of 240 million; of the former super-powers of the old century still major powers of 265 (USA) and 315 (USSR) million; of a united Western Europe of 390 million. And it will be, also, a world of great regions drawing strength from regimes of co-operation among their peoples: perhaps, of burgeoning regional arrangements in West Africa and in central and Southern Africa; of new economic alignments in West Asia; of integrated economies in South-East Asia and among the Andean states and the Central American states of Latin America; of economic union in Western Europe and in Eastern Europe as well; of new economic linkages within North America itself and perhaps Australasia also.

It will be a world, I believe, in which nations great and small will have acknowledged in a variety of ways the essentiality of their need for each other – their perception that there are no sanctuaries of survival left on earth, save that of which we jointly make the entire planet.

And it could be a world of unthinkable technological sophistication when to be literate as a society may be measurable in levels of scientific excellence unattainable save in a societal framework of many millions of humans.

And what of humanity itself? Will not the twenty-first century see a more universal acknowledgement of the entitlement of all men to the functional enjoyment of a life of dignity and well-being – an entitlement deriving from their humanity that aims at the satisfaction of the basic needs, material and non-material, individual and collective, of all men and women? It will be a world that has begun to usher in a new economic order creating global structures more propitious to the realisation of those rights in the economic, social and cultural no less than in the civil and political fields: an order, who can doubt, that maximises the gains from enlarged co-operation within regions, building on complementarities, including the complementarities of social and cultural affinity. In short, it could be a century of co-operation, not just for survival, but for life at tolerable levels of existence and respect for the human condition everywhere; a time, altogether, for togetherness.

By the year 2000, all the West Indies will be a region of just over six and a half million people: smaller as an entire region than the great majority of the world's states. Yet it will comprise some sixteen sovereign countries – perhaps the highest density of government anywhere on the planet – the world's most intensively bureaucratised, and perhaps politicised, region. We shall greet the new century with something like a parliamentarian for every 11,000 people; with a government minister for every 34,000. On present form, we could have an oil refinery for every 500,000 people. India, with the eighth largest industrial production in the world, could still have one refinery to every 60 million. And the West Indies by 2000 might, on a conservative estimate, have six international airlines: one for every one million people. All of Western Europe, pioneers in aero-technology, will probably have one for every 23 million. And, of course, epitomising the things we meanwhile fail to do, we could continue being exporters of primary products neglectful of the complementarities at hand that await only a regional will to achieve more balanced development for the greater economic gain of each of us and of the region as a whole.

These are some of the matters that our choices concern; there are many others besides. And the choices will concern means, not ends only. The world order of the twenty-first century will not arrive as a natural phenomenon. It will come only as a new planetary bargain struck by man as a basis for co-existence in the face of the irresistible interdependencies of the time. It will be a bargain hammered out laboriously through persistent negotiation. It will derive from human consensus; from consensus itself informed by the realities of confrontation – mutuality of interest in change having become better understood as the perils of the *status quo* for all become more discernible.

What lies ahead in the present century is the process of striking that global bargain. There could be a role for the West Indies – as there was a role for CARICOM in the very much smaller negotiations with an enlarged Europe.[1] What is more, the world, and especially the Third World, which persists in seeing us in the West Indies more unified than we often see ourselves, believes that we have in our collectivity a role to play. The Third World, indeed, looks to us, out of our own recent record of forging regional unity of purpose and sustaining regional unity of action, to give a lead in the wider process of co-operation among developing countries.

And our own history holds lessons for us that complement those expectations. We spent the decade 1948-1958 putting together the Federation of the West Indies as the vehicle for releasing the region from colonialism. In the next decade, we dismantled the Federation and, leaving our smaller brothers in dependency, hit the freedom trail in isolation. Yet, in the decade 1968-1978, we have felt the need to rebuild the structures of co-operation – this time to our own designs; and we have begun to occupy them. They are not perfect, and their imperfections have been all too crudely revealed by the harsh economic winds that have blown against them. But does anyone doubt that if we care enough about being West Indian – and if we believe enough that West Indian men and women deserve a place of dignity in the world of the twenty-first century – we can make those structures proof against all weathers or improve our technique for managing them?[2]

We are all too prone in the region, when difficulties arise, to seek to solve them by pulling down structures and erecting new ones – when the cause of the difficulties may be not with the structures at all, but either with the external environment over which we can exercise little control or with the ways in which we manage the habitation. It is a tendency we shall have to curb.

The alternative is to accept an almost cyclical interpretation of West Indian political behaviour which commits us to
breaking down in each decade all we have built up in the one
preceding it – only to acknowledge in the next the
imperative of co-operation that our condition imposes and
to commence the process all over again. The trouble with
such a regional lifestyle, quite apart from its inherent
wastefulness, is that each experience of dismantling renders
more difficult the succeeding process of reconstruction and,
in the end, leads to a condition of irresistible disintegration
and drift.

Can the West Indies even remotely entertain the notion of
such an alternative? Are we really to prepare for that newer
world of the twenty-first century by retreating each into our
tiny enclave, with greater or lesser assurance of prosperity
and security, accepting with equanimity the need for even
tinier corners for our West Indian micro-states? Do we
believe that, abandoning co-operation among ourselves, we
can yet hope to secure the world's co-operation for our
separate salvation and to influence global development in
conformity with our separate needs? Is it not altogether
more likely that we would be exchanging a degree of
interdependence, however small, for one of complete
dependence and of a type that could easily be more
traumatic and destructive of our creative abilities than the
colonial dependency so recently discarded? I cannot
conceive that the choice for the West Indies brooks of
uncertainty. But neither do I doubt that we can suffer by
default the fate we may deplore but decline actively to
frustrate.

Being West Indian is worth caring about and working for.
The path to regionalism will never be free of difficulty and
hazard. To pursue it will demand always immense patience,
compassion and even sacrifice. For our politicians it will
promise further moments of heartbreak and deep
frustration, and it will demand of them great courage and
steadfastness. But no process of working towards unity is
free of such moments. European politicians face no lesser

challenges as they work at consolidating their Community. The real challenge is to maintain faith in the importance of being West Indian and to sustain the processes of dialogue that alone can preserve its substance and give it enduring worth.

In the end, however, it is the people of the West Indies themselves that must say how much being West Indian means to them. It is they who choose the way forward. Each of you can help to ensure that it is the less travelled regional path that the West Indies takes towards the year 2000.

Notes and References

1. *Supra,* Chapter 3, pp. 116-121.

2. See, generally, *CARIFTA and the New Caribbean,* and *From CARIFTA to Caribbean Community,* (Commonwealth Caribbean Regional Secretariat 1971 and 1972, respectively); and *The Caribbean Community in the 1980s: Report by a Group of Caribbean Experts,* (Caribbean Community Secretariat, Georgetown, 1981).

Democracy in the Global State

Invited by the Committee for a Community of Democracies to deliver an address at the English-Speaking Union, Shridath Ramphal chose as his theme the unfulfilled aspiration for democracy in the society of nations. He issued, in the process, a challenge to those who espouse democracy at the national level to be ready to practice it at the international level.

"A rising sun" was how Benjamin Franklin once described democracy;[1] yet there are many examples each year of countries where that sun has been eclipsed; in a few, by long dark nights. At the frontiers of democracy, where its roots are tender and anchored on the thinnest soils, the casualty rate can be high. Over the last thirty years, more than half the sovereign states in existence today have been subject to the successful 'coup'. As a way of changing governments, it is more widespread and sometimes even more popular than elections. In all too many Third World countries ambitious, impatient or frustrated men have learned the lesson Tacitus long ago ascribed to the Roman Empire: *"Evolgato Imperii Arcano* – the secret of empire was out – an Emperor could be made elsewhere than in Rome".[2] Often, it is true, their leaders must cope with an external environment which, on the one hand, applauds them as success stories for democracy while, on the other, it multiplies the factors of their failure by wholly contradictory economic and political policies. In such circumstances, all too easily, the shadow of 'the man on horseback'[3] falls across society – with the military promising both the restoration of order and the eradication of economic 'inefficiency' or worse.

Vulnerability does not only arise at the periphery. Some societies with long and proud democratic traditions have been subject to pressures and strains which have shaken their democratic foundations and threatened their future survival. Even in the list of 'developed democracies', there are some countries who can all too vividly recall less happy times. But for all the temporary setbacks, Roosevelt was right when he said:

> Democracy alone, of all forms of Government, enlists the full force of men's enlightened will... It is the most humane, the most advanced, and in the end the most unconquerable of all forms of human society. The democratic aspiration is no mere recent phase of human history. It *is* human history.[4]

He might have added: it is an aspiration whose fulfilment will take many forms.

Imagine a Parliament whose upper legislative assembly is part nominated and part hereditary; whose membership is around 1,400, and whose quorum for the conduct of business is three; and which can only operate as a revising chamber, providing most of its membership stay away. As with the aerodynamics of the bumble bee, so with the British House of Lords, there is no clear objective reason why it should work. Yet work it does, because all involved wish it to work. Take away consent, remove the will to make complicated institutions work, and the mockery and the breakdown of democracy can be the result.

The House of Lords has a democratic function that is not immediately apparent beneath its dignified and traditional elitism. Conversely, many political scientists – of whom Bagehot was merely one – have argued convincingly that the popularly elected House of Commons, seemingly an "efficient" democratic component of the British Constitution, has functions which should perhaps more properly be considered "dignified".[5] All is not always what it seems.

If countries with a long democratic tradition sometimes have difficulty explaining their democratic institutions according to the yardstick of pure principle, they should perhaps show greater understanding of more recent arrivals in the family of democracies. Consent and legitimacy are intertwined with tradition and culture. Twentieth-century African democracy, for example, will not reflect, in quite the same way, the democratic forms of Europe or, indeed, of Westminster.

I emphasise this because I see 'democracy' as a broad rock upon which international understanding, and a revitalised community of nations, can be built – rather than a narrow definition which seeks to impose a particular cultural view, drawing limits rather than reaching beyond, and excluding when the need of the age is for organisations capable of transcending the barriers of culture, of creed, of race, and of continent.

I have said something about democracy itself and the challenge it faces. But there is a greater challenge to democracy internationally – to internationalism itself. Those who are for democracy locally and nationally must also be its champions internationally, for its values and principles are indivisible.

The Committee for a Community of Democracies reflected from its beginnings a concern with the state of the world and the divisions and dangers that bedevil it. Your starting point was a determination to resist the tides threatening to sweep us away from international co-operation and order and a belief that the values and principles of democracy formed a bulwark around which the like-minded could rally, and from which the long march back to sanity could begin. What does that actually involve?

I believe that humanity's most basic and most pressing need is to develop ethical responses to the predicament we now face in relation to both the continued evolution of the human species and the quality of human existence – to both peace and development. How will a Community of Democracies respond to these challenges?

Perhaps for the first time in human history, millions of people the world over are not just uncertain about their future or concerned about their children's future, they are deeply anxious about the future of our small planet.

The argument that a nuclear deterrence strategy which, until now, has underpinned the arms race, has succeeded in keeping the peace between East and West for nearly forty years cannot be easily dismissed. But, as nuclear weapons and weapons states proliferate, as military balances become unstable through new systems, as the destructive power of nuclear weapons becomes more apocalyptic, as tensions rise both directly between the super-powers and in regions which they claim as spheres of influence, as the rules of international law on which rest our prospects for an ordered world are made subservient to super-power paranoia, as ordinary people grow suspicious of their own leaders let alone those of others, the proposition that if our children are to inherit the earth we must have the capacity to destroy it several times over has lost all credibility.

The situation becomes only more obscene with the threat of militarisation of outer space. What we are facing, but not facing up to, is a major policy change from securing peace through preparing effectively for war – the classical deterrence theory – to guaranteeing security by a war to end wars. We are being prepared for a collective jump from the frying pan into the fire – the fire of the global holocaust itself. We are not facing up to that danger because the reality is largely hidden from us. The arms race is presented on all sides as a defence capability: 'Star Wars'[6] is presented as a shield not a sword. That is what they said as well about the first atomic bombs that eventually fell from the skies over

Japan. The ethics of human survival compel us to demand the withdrawal of that threat to human civilisation – a fate from which no country or people would be insulated. The 'nuclear winter' will envelop us all.

Will a Community of Democracies be inspired by an ethic of human survival? There are some worrying signs. Is democracy working for internationalism? Are the world's democracies in the forefront of human endeavours to secure a more peaceful and a more just and equitable world? More particularly, are the democracies in the vanguard of a movement for democracy within the global state? If we postulate an interdependent world in which human destiny is interlinked, can democracy within the national state be meaningful if the society of nations resembles not so much a democratic as a feudal state with power in the hands of a few; prosperity, the heritage of a handful; power, the prerogative not of people but of warlords; change, not a matter for human consensus but the dictate of those who hold sway for the time being?

There is a powerful role for a Community of Democracies to play were it to come into being wedded to the reversal of all this. And a reversal it will have to be, for these, unmistakably, are trends now conditioned and fortified by the policies of many of the world's great democracies.

The arms race, for example, is a grave act of immorality not only because it threatens man's physical existence, but also because it impairs his prospects for more balanced and sustainable development. When a thousand billion dollars are devoted every year to military expenditure, when the great majority of the world's scientists and engineers and technicians are engaged in military related research or production, when the military related culture assumes paramountcy in the corridors and council chambers of world power and spreads even to the developing world, real development is not only neglected, it is negated. And so it is for all countries, rich and poor, but with the most devastating consequences for the poorest

For the world economy as a whole, it is close to the worst of times – and not only because of the arms race. It is a time which has produced greater unemployment in the industrialised world than at any time in the living memory of anyone under fifty; which has produced a debt problem of such staggering proportions that it threatens countries whose creditworthiness has never been in question; which has seen commodity prices fall in real terms to their lowest levels since the 1930s; which has produced foreign exchange deficits for the vast majority of developing countries so severe that they are depriving many an economy of even the capacity for survival; in which current distortions have reached a stage of 'mature anarchy'; in which protectionist sentiments have risen to such levels that they are becoming uncontainable even by governments for whom 'free trade' is part of the political credo.

What all this means is that development has declined, that the poor have got poorer; that the prospects for the absolute poor, the world's marginal people, have become more hopeless and not more hopeful. Despite the horrors of the current crisis, the World Bank cannot discount the prospect that per capita incomes in Africa, already some of the lowest in the world, will decline still further over the next ten to fifteen years – that people in Africa will actually be worse off as we reach the year 2000.[7]

There are no self-correcting mechanisms that promise resolution. The path that leads away from crisis is the path towards reform: changes of conduct, of policies, of structures; changes at the domestic, international and institutional levels; changes to which all must contribute, developed and developing countries, free market and centrally planned economies. There are many paths to reform, but the goal of reform must be accepted and the journey towards it begun. Will a Community of Democracies accept that fact and ensure, as it could, that the journey begins? Separately today, Western democracies seem unwilling to do either.

In the first five years of the 1980s there has not merely been no progress on North-South issues, there have been virtually no negotiations. The annual meetings of the Bank and the Fund have been turned into tutorials for developing countries on domestic economic policy – tutorials given by those whose domestic economic policies are turning the world economy upside down. The IMF then follows up as a rod of correction for slow learners: imposition rather than dialogue. But it is worse than that. All this is happening against a backdrop of nationalism that takes us back to the decade before 1939; of anti-internationalism that batters the structures of international co-operation built patiently, and with sacrifice, over the post-war era; of militarism that implies a recrudescence of power and authoritarianism in our global society; of arbitrariness and indifference to principle that erodes the foundations of world order, and of dogmatism that makes a virtue of extremism.

It is this latter trend that is most worrying of all – the trend towards a more authoritarian world; not one governed by world order, but one ordered by the strong. We seem to have forgotten how diminished co-operation brought the world to economic disaster in the 1930s and to near self-destruction in the war that followed. Living together, sharing the world, demands co-operation not compulsion; co-operation between nations on as wide a global scale as possible. That is the only feasible, humane and enlightened way to advance the common and mutual interests of all nations. Such co-operation implies a sense of shared responsibility for human welfare – a perception of human solidarity. It also implies acceptance of the need to seek consensus in the international community on collective responses to that responsibility. At the heart of multilateralism lies the aspiration for an increasingly democratic world.

Forty years ago, the world made itself a promise of co-operation through the United Nations. The quintessence of that promise was progress towards democracy in the global state; towards a world less susceptible to the usurpation of power on a global scale, less vulnerable to the imposition of one nation's will: one more hospitable to world order, more hostile to arbitrariness and compulsion. A world, in short, not permanently skewed: with the few always more than the many, the wronged forever wrong, the righteous never right, poverty in the midst of plenty, a life of crisis for most, a crisis of leisure for some.

The truth is that peace and prosperity are indivisible. Heightened East-West tensions, for example, have both resulted in a decline from detente and impaired progress in the North-South dialogue and, therefore, in development. And they are leading also to a turning-away from the concepts which inspired the establishment of the United Nations. They are leading to a questioning of the very concept of international co-operation which the cataclysm of 1939-45 had stimulated, only to be immediately threatened and undermined by ritually institutionalised super-power confrontation in the succeeding uneasy peace. It is a tribute to the best ideals of the United States, enshrined in its history, that it attempted for so long to overcome the obstacles intruded into the international machinery by the cold war and ensuing confrontation and made an outstanding contribution – not only financial – to post-war internationalism.

But what is now the picture? The Soviets have traditionally made no pretence about helping only their ideological friends – and helping them mainly with arms; of not responding to human needs because they are human needs and, therefore, mutual needs as well. They have never been more than modest in their support of the United Nations system; often they have been openly hostile. They may genuinely sense dangers today in the steep decline of multilateralism, but they have contributed little over the years to strengthening it against erosion. Without a democratic process of whatever kind, there is no natural force to compel a change of direction. Totalitarianism, unlike democracy, has no inbuilt self-correcting mechanism. It must usually self-destruct to change. Only a slender chance exists of a conjuncture of forces which might turn the Soviet Union towards a more genuinely internationalist posture.[8] The United States, to whom human needs really were once important, seems now to have abandoned any higher motivation. It seems weary of attempting to make the machinery of international co-operation work despite the difficulties – and much of this weariness must be attributable to preoccupations with super-power politics and East-West tensions. The trouble is that, in the case of a super-power, particularly at a time of tension and fragility, the implications of thus turning away from multilateralism and world order can be grave for the entire international community.

When it can actually be repeated today, as it was at the 1964 Republican Convention, that "extremism in defence of liberty is no vice",[9] we enter that dark area where democracy turns upon itself, turns against its highest traditions and keeps unworthy company. Extremism always parades in a virtuous garb. For Hitler's Germany it was 'Lebensraum'; for the Soviets, it is 'Proletarian Power'; for the Americans now, it may be 'Liberty'. Behind the slogans, however, lurks always the basic cult of power; the conviction that the world not only can, but should be, run by the most powerful within it; that a thrusting nationalism unbridled by internationalist sentiment or principles or rules, should rule our ends, never mind the ways and means. In the process, the rule of law world-wide yields place to the law of the jungle.

The world's middle-powers of East and West certainly know it to be their duty to champion the cause of internationalism; they even recognise the danger for themselves of super-power politics eclipsing multilateralism. The trouble is that those who can contribute most to drawing the super-powers back to world order, back to sanity, away from the margins of apocalypse, are themselves locked into the military alliances of East or West – in some cases not just functionally but ideologically as well. Western Europe and the East European allies of the Soviet Union should be the most ardent and eloquent interlocutors for international co-operation and for peace – for their peoples, to a greater extent than most others, know the horrors of war, have glimpsed the holocaust. It is a major part of our present predicament that, at the governmental level at any rate, this influence is being withheld as the super-powers head for the ultimate shoot-out.

Will a Community of Democracies make a stand for independence within alliance? Will it acknowledge that solidarity, like patriotism, is not enough;[10] that it is not synonymous with silence and supine support? Will it assert that alliance does allow for – indeed, argues for – recalling one's friends, however powerful or dominant, to the basic values of the alliance of friendship, including the pre-eminence of survival? Will such a community acknowledge and assert that even for the allies of super-powers, there must be some habitable political ground between surrogation and neutralism?

In one sense, of course, it can – if it were to be truly a community of people wedded to the ethics of human survival, inspired by the vision of one world and by the right of all its people to share in it more fairly. For in people there is surely hope. Whether it is in the arms race, or development and recovery, or international co-operation in general, there is a powerful factor for good that is at work: people – ordinary people everywhere are on the move.

To a far greater degree than their governments, people recognise – for the most part intuitively – that the demands of compassion, morality, humanitarianism, even human solidarity, are not today in contention against the claims of national interests or even of self-interest; they understand, particularly the unemployed, that the roads to justice and survival are conjoined; that the task is to bring the mutual interests and the moral impulses of mankind together. People are the world's true hope; they are the custodians of the ethics of human survival which, like lanterns that they carry in their hands, will in Tagore's words "make enemy of the darkness of the farther road".[11] If a Community of Democracies can be truly a people's movement of East and West, North and South, there is no limit to what it can achieve for peace and for development and so for human survival.

Notes and References

1. *The Report of the Constitutional Convention,* 17 September 1787; (Benjamin Franklin was referring to the emblem – a sunburst – on the President's chair, as the last members of the Convention signed the Constitution. He was sure it was a rising sun). Quoted in *The Home Book of American Quotations,* selected and arranged by Bohl, (Dodd, Mead & Company, New York, 1967), p. 14.

2. S.E. Finer, Foreword to Edward Luttwak, *Coup d'Etat* (Penguin Books, London, 1968), p. 9.

3. S.E. Finer, *The Man on Horseback: the Role of the Military in Politics,* (Pall Mall Press, London, 1962).

4. President Roosevelt's Third Inaugural Address on the steps of the Capitol, Washington, 20 January 1941.

5. Walter Bagehot, *The English Constitution* (Fontana Edition 1963), and the adaptation of the idea in such contemporary works as John P. Mackintosh, *The British Cabinet,* 2nd ed., (Methuen, London, 1968).

6. The 'Strategic Defence Initiative': a key element of President Reagan's nuclear defence policy and a stumbling block in disarmament negotiations between the super-powers.

7. World Bank, *World Development Report,* 1984.

8. Delivered in advance of the INF agreement signed between the United States and the USSR in November 1987, which ushered in a more positive climate for internationalism and global security. For a post Reykjavik comment, see Shridath Ramphal, *Time for a Third Try,* address to 'Parliamentarians Global Action' at the United Nations, New York, 3 November 1987 (Commonwealth Secretariat, 1987).

9. Senator Barry Goldwater, speech on accepting the Republican nomination, San Francisco, 17 July 1964.

10. "Standing, as I do, in the view of God and eternity, I realise that
     patriotism is not enough. I must have no hatred or bitterness towards
     anyone". Edith Cavell, spoken to the Chaplain who attended her
     before her execution by a German firing squad, 12 October 1915.
     (Reported in *The Times,* London, 23 October 1915).

11. Rabindranath Tagore, *Collected Poems and Plays* (Macmillan &
     Co., London, 1950), p. 272.

The World is One

On 19 January 1987, Shridath Ramphal delivered the second Indira Gandhi Memorial Lecture at the Vigyan Bhavan in New Delhi. His address was one of personal recollection and tribute to Indira Gandhi in the presence of her son, India's Prime Minister, Rajiv Gandhi. It was also the occasion of a penetrating argument that 'peace' is more than the absence of war. Essentially, he posed the question whether for most of the world's people the post-war era had been truly an era of peace.

To be asked to deliver the Indira Gandhi Memorial Lecture is to experience a swift personal transition from initial pride through a sense of unworthiness to plain intimidation. The transition is only quickened by awareness that Indira Gandhi's son and successor will preside, and that Olof Palme stood here a year ago inaugurating this Memorial Lecture.[1] When he did so, he recalled his personal links to India through the marriage of an Indian doctor, Upandra Dutt, to the daughter of his great-grandparents. But India's sons and daughters went not only to the coldest north but also to the warmest south; and I am here because my own great-grandmother journeyed about that time – just over 100 years ago – to the sugar plantations of Guyana. I have recalled that journey before, and my own roots from whence it began in Bihar. I mention it here in remembering the particular joy of my earliest close encounter with Indira Gandhi – when she, too, made that journey from India to

Guyana a century later in 1968, and I had the honour to attend on her as a stripling Minister of Government.

Those were early days for us on the international scene; but India was always a star from which we could take our bearings with confidence; and we did. "When in doubt, vote with India" was a guideline not only for Guyana's fledgling diplomats, but those of many a new country. It was sound guidance; India was, after all, the spiritual leader of the Non-Aligned world and Non-Alignment was the bedrock of our foreign policies; but more than that: Indira Gandhi – as you have done also in your time, Prime Minister – kept alive the flame of Pandit Nehru's internationalism, and that was a light we could all follow with complete assurance.

Mrs. Gandhi was one of the first Commonwealth Heads of Government whose counsel I sought in my first days as Secretary-General. I came to Delhi from London before all else. Like her father before her, she had an appreciation of the potential of the Commonwealth as an association bringing diverse nations together to pursue the interests they hold in common, despite their diversity. She seemed to sense that, like India, the Commonwealth as a confluence of many cultures, could work for unity within variety; and that it had a distinctive role within the spectrum of international organisations in which Third World countries could advance their interests.

I know how much she valued the opportunity which Commonwealth Summits afforded, not merely for 'across the table' discussion with colleagues from all continents, but for informal contact and consultation with individual colleagues in the friendly atmosphere which is the mark of Commonwealth gatherings. She had many personal friends among those colleagues and was at ease in their company, talking with confident fluency about disarmament, about the super-powers, about the problems of development, the policies of financial institutions, and all those many other issues – not to mention each other's domestic political provocations – that national leaders talk about when they meet. She was equally fascinating when she turned from 'high politics' to the day-to-day problems of the Indian peasant, to the skills of Indian craftsmen, to the traditional dancing of India or, as she sometimes did with special rapture, to the joys of being a grandmother.

On my first visit as Commonwealth Secretary-General to India in 1975, Indira Gandhi gave me a painting by the contemporary artist Sivanesan: a painting of a young farmer, his wife and child returning home after the day's work in the fields. It is a picture of rural India; dignity and hope stand out in the painting of the three figures against the background of poverty. I gave it a title of my own: 'A Will To Face The Future'. It embodies for me the message of the painter, as well as the essential graces of the person whose gift it was[2].

My last memory of Indira Gandhi is of being with her on this very platform facing the press at the end of the Commonwealth Heads of Government Meeting in November 1983. She had guided the proceedings of that week-long meeting – the last major international meeting over which she was to preside – with characteristic charm and unruffled efficiency. She had been a gracious and thoughtful host to Presidents and Prime Ministers from all round the Commonwealth. Nothing escaped her attention – from the largest agenda items to the smallest detail of housekeeping – in New Delhi and in Goa. At the press conference, as we sat here together, she summed up for the several hundred journalists present what the meeting had accomplished.

I recall her, as clearly as if it were yesterday, drawing their attention to a particular sentence in the Goa Declaration on International Security, which was a principal outcome of the Summit and which so clearly bore the stamp of her own passion for peace and global understanding. She commended to the media the sentence: "Meeting here in India, we cannot emphasise too strongly our belief that the ethic of non-violence must be at the heart of all efforts to ensure peace and harmony in the world."[3] Less than a year later, by a malign twist of history, she herself was laid low by a senseless act of violence – as was Olof Palme, so soon after his commemoration of her life's work for peace. Can it be to any other than that same theme of peace that I devote this Lecture?

I was a member of that Commission on International Security Issues[4] that Olof Palme chaired. But, I was also, with him, a member of the Commission on International Development Issues that Willy Brandt chaired;[5] and that joint experience underlined for me the inter-connectedness of the two Commissions' themes. The Brandt Report on Development Issues is also about security; the Palme Report on Security Issues is also about development. The inescapable linkage is peace. In what follows, therefore, I want to suggest some parameters of peace that go beyond the conventional, and to ask whether there can, in fact, be any doubt that our human situation falls well outside them; to answer that the world is not at peace; to warn against the illusion that our challenge is to avoid war rather than to achieve peace. Central to everything I shall say is one simple truth; one which I believe Indira Gandhi understood with special clarity, namely, that while war is the ultimate antithesis of peace, the absence of war is not necessarily peace. Peace is more than freedom from armed conflict; it is ambition that reaches beyond armistice. To ignore this deeper quality of peace, to limit its reach, is to conjure with illusion.

This false image of peace is, of course, the mirror image of our perception of war – a perception formalised in terms of armed conflict. We know, in that sense, what war is; and we so far acknowledge its inevitability, almost its naturalness, that we make rules for it: 'rules of war' made, with supreme irony, in response to high humanitarian instincts. Rules that govern the conduct of war, the treatment of prisoners, of the sick and wounded, of the victims of war at sea and the treatment of civilians. It is as if we have inherited the perceptions of some earlier era when war was accepted as a natural if unpleasant element of human existence, given a place even within a system of world order. It is a touch of humanity amid the horrors of war that these rules and conventions exist, and that organisations like the International Red Cross sustain them. But what about the 'rules of peace'?

As people everywhere recoiled in horror in 1939 from the looming calamities of World War II, that war, like its predecessor, came to be seen and fought as a "war to end wars". As it ended in 1945, the United Nations was devised in a rare moment of collective enlightenment – a creative act to which India contributed, almost as a symbol of the new world that peace would bring. This time we would, through the United Nations, "save succeeding generations from the scourge of war",[6] we would make it the repository of what were agreed to be the 'rules of peace'. The post-war era would be an era of peace. Today, there are some who assert that it has been an era of peace; peace for them being the absence of a major war.

But not everyone is so sure. And the questioning goes beyond 'major' and 'minor' wars. It took the United Nations thirty years to reach agreement on the definition of 'aggression' for the purposes of the Charter.[7] Perhaps those who are so certain about the meaning of 'peace' and 'war' would cite that as the ultimate in international semantics. In truth, it was a groping for a deeper understanding of 'war'; for an acknowledgement that, as between states, there is behaviour other than outright war that our human society must regard as unacceptable and must, therefore, outlaw. Are not 'contra' operations such behaviour? Is not economic aggression another example?

The agreed definition of 'aggression' did not ultimately encompass all these. But that definition has not ended the debate; people will continue the quest for a world order under which, both by definition and intuition, war is understood and acknowledged to be the absence of peace, rather than peace perceived as the absence of war. Over fifty years ago, W.B. Yeats, decrying, in his 'Supernatural Songs', mankind's endless cycles of destruction, wrote with poetic insight that:

> Civilisation is hooped together, brought
> Under a rule, under the semblance of peace
> By manifold illusion.[8]

It is against that illusion that I warn: with all the more insistence since the danger from misjudgement increases ineluctably.

The nineteenth century used to be described by English writers as 'the Great Peace', when Britain was, broadly speaking, 'at peace' between Waterloo and World War I. It is a description which in its own terms invites inquiry about, for example, the Crimean or the Boer Wars. But, those apart, what of the many other wars of empire which kept Britain's forces permanently employed somewhere on the globe – in the Chinese Opium Wars, on the frontiers with Afghanistan, in India during the so-called Mutiny, in the Sudan, in Ethiopia even – what Kipling, aptly for my purpose, called "the savage wars of peace"?[9] The British public were able to celebrate victories, to enjoy their spoils – and to forget. For them, it was a time of peace – *Pax Britannica.*[10]

But those who were conquered or subdued by force of European arms saw things in a different light – and still do. It would be hard to persuade the Ashanti, the Zulus, or the Maoris that Britain had not been at war. They know that they had been. They had no illusion of peace. The dichotomy, of course, has parallels in the history of other imperial powers.

And still, today, illusions persist. Is it not, for example, essentially a major power fallacy that the post-war era has been a time of peace? Were the Hungarians of 1956, or the Czechs of Dubcek's "Prague Spring" of 1968, in their enforced submission, casualties of someone else's peace?

Was military intervention in Suez in 1956, was the 'Bay of Pigs' in 1961, or the mining of Managua's harbour in 1984 not each an act of war?

Is there peace within South Africa? It may be natural to answer 'no' today: the brutal repression of a racist regime and the armed struggle of a people yearning for freedom make that palpable. But was there peace for fifty years before, when many in Europe would have answered 'yes'; years in which the West invested in and helped, almost without demur, in building apartheid South Africa into what it chose to describe as 'a bastion of the free world'? Illusions of peace again! Whose freedom? And, without freedom, what peace?

Such illusions are dangerous for they encourage deliberate obfuscation. Mr. Botha now implies, for example, that a 'whites only' election can settle the destiny of the majority non-white population; and sanctions, he says, will help those opposed to democracy. But it is he and the apartheid system that oppose and defy democracy. Sanctions, he claims, will lead to a totalitarian regime; but that is precisely what now exists in South Africa. This is the 'double-speak' of apartheid. Illusions of peace only help it to become the 'double-think' of even decent people.

Reality, world-wide, is very different. The 1984 report of the United Nations Secretary-General on conventional disarmament[11] revealed that, since 1945, there have been over 150 armed conflicts (defined as having more than one thousand casualties), accounting in all for some 20 million dead – almost all of them in developing countries and a great many of them civilians. There are currently nearly 50 wars or armed conflicts of one kind or another; indeed, it has been calculated that "there has not been a single war-free day since September 1945".[12] Is it possible then to say we are at peace – unless we really are in an Orwellian '1984' situation where 'peace means war' – or the desolation that war brings.

Were the worst nuclear scenario ever to unfold, I wonder

what the first visitors to the planet from other worlds would say as they surveyed the desolation. Would they, perhaps, say, as Byron did about the Roman super-power long ago, updating Tacitus:

> Mark! Where his carnage and his conquests cease –
> He makes a solitude – and calls it – peace![13]

But the aftermath of war is not the only solitude we make or the only one we venture to call peace. Is not that solitude with us in the deepening silence of the world's millions overborne by poverty? People for whom life is survival until tomorrow – and always only tomorrow; millions who simply pass away from want without ever knowing the reason why; over 1,000 million of the world's absolute poor trapped in a vicious cycle of deprivation. Are they at peace – living as they do within the shadow of the solitude of the grave? Do we dare to speak of peace in our time while they endure the ravages of poverty's aggression against basic human values? When we talk of 'preserving' peace, what do we preserve for them?

Like justice and freedom, peace is indivisible. As justice is about the quality of life that the law ordains not only within countries but within our global society, so peace goes beyond relations between states to the environment of every human life. And that environment is enhanced or polluted not just by war and preparations for war but by a whole variety of relationships shaped by human conduct. At the heart of them are the relationships between rich and poor in the world.

We recognise that a national society cannot be at peace if power, privilege and prosperity are the prerogatives of only a few, with deprivation, degradation and despair the lot of the many. Why do we think our world society can be at peace when such disparities prevail within it, such yawning disparities between a few who prosper and the great majority trapped in poverty? For those entrapped, but in truth for all of us, it cannot be a time of peace.

War, in our minds, conjures up a fearful toll of human life: the tragedy of many who die prematurely and others whose lives are blighted by the deprivations and deformities that go hand in hand with conflict. By these same standards, many hundreds of millions pass all their lives in war-time. Only illusions of peace blur the sombre reality. Life expectancy, for example, is less than 40 years in Sierra Leone or Guinea, compared with 75 years in France or Japan; infant mortality rates are in excess of 150 per thousand in Mali or Ethiopia, compared with six in Finland or nine in Canada. If only one child in sixteen were to die in the Third World before the age of one, rather than the one in eight who on the average die at present, two and a half million lives would be saved each year. On present demographic levels, if average life expectancy in the Third World were to be raised to that of the developed countries, some seven million more would live not die every year.

Over a period of five years, the ravages of poverty and under-development take their toll of a minimum of 35 million lives. Ironically, that is also the minimum number of combatants and non-combatants who perished in the five years of World War II. For some, war never ends. Per capita GNP – income per head – is our rough measure of poverty and wealth; it is less than $200 per head in Burma and Bangladesh, compared with $16,000 per head in Switzerland and $15,000 in the United States. It is more than futility, it is downright provocation, to ask Malians or Bangladeshis to hail the end years of the twentieth century as a time of peace. The Horsemen of the Apocalypse were charged to kill with famine as with the sword; today, they acknowledge no frontiers, certainly none that insulate the Third World, which has some disturbing parallels with the biblical "fourth part of the earth" over which they were given dominion.[14]

But the paradox is that poverty diminishes humanity both directly by taking lives and indirectly by making life more unendurable for ever-enlarging numbers. In terms of the prospects of peace in the next century, few factors are likely to be more important than world population growth. The trends should fill us with foreboding, especially their conjuncture with poverty. It took 150 years (from 1750 to 1900) for the world's population to double; but, from 1950 to 1980 it rose from 2.5 billion to 4.8 billion – doubling in about 30 years.[15] The annual increment is now about 100 million people: a new Bangladesh every year; an acceleration of both population and poverty. Twenty-two cities now have a population of more than seven million. Twelve are in the developing world. By the end of the century – just 14 years away – there will be 35 cities of over seven million, and 23 of them will be in the developing world. Mexico City, now 18 million, will have grown to over 26 million – the entire present population of Canada.[16]

None will suffer more from this urban explosion than tomorrow's children, for whom the future is anything but a promise of peace. Already, the phenomenon of street children – at present, some 30 million who know no home but the street – casts a grim shadow of abandonment, illiteracy, unemployment and alienation across a generation yet unborn.[17] How many millions are we condemning to life as primitives at the centre of our cities of the twenty-first century? Is theirs a prospect of peace?

If there is to be hope of improving on these prospects of enlarging the potential for peace, it must lie in real development, in reducing those gross disparities between prosperity and poverty. This is the central challenge of the Papal assertion that "development is the new name for peace".[18] Meeting that challenge requires a world economic environment that offers something more than that the rich will grow richer at no slower a pace, and that the poor will actually not get poorer. It means looking towards a new, more equitable, order of world economic relationships in which the gap, far from enlarging, begins to close. It means managing the world economy for the benefit of all the world's people.

And the agenda of anxiety is a long one. It is a time of vanishing forests and encroaching deserts; a time once more of famine and of refugees; a time of disappearing persons. It is a time when rain sometimes falls with an acidic content the equivalent of lemon juice. It is a time of Bhopal and Chernobyl, and of toxins in the Rhine. It is a time of drug abuse of the most frightening proportions, and of the excesses of national and international terrorism, sometimes even at the level of state action. More and more, we resemble that time in the sixteenth century when Sir Thomas More described the world as "ruffled and fallen in a wildness".[19] Inevitably, it is a time of human hunger for peace in its deepest and most profound sense.

But as people hunger for peace, nations prepare for war. And the plague of global militarisation only aggravates the hunger. Has that disease, with all its contagiousness, passed the threshold of reversibility? Has the Third World now become both a victim and a carrier? The two super-powers, with only 11 per cent of the world's population, control 97 per cent of its inventory of nuclear weapons. They account for more than half of the world's military budget and 80 per cent of the military research budget. But as important as any of these is the fact that, between them, they account for such a vast proportion of the arms moving abroad. The spread of the military culture is virtually a concomitant of the arms race.

During 1980 to 1984 the total value of conventional arms transferred in commercial or official trade was US$69.7 billion. The United States held its lead as the world's major arms exporter with 39.7 per cent of this total, but the Soviet Union was not so far behind at 31.4 per cent, while France, at 9.1 per cent, was sprinting into double figures: high achievers in the export of the militarist culture almost frenetically promoted at the arms bazaars.[20] Attractive credit terms, often unavailable for food or medicine, are never in short supply for arms and, in the case of the United States and the Soviet Union, arms come often as part of aid programmes. In the decade up to 1980 US weapons, on the authority of the Department of Defence, were sold and transferred to 130 different countries.[21] This is to say nothing of the thriving illicit trade in arms. No wonder the world's terrorists have no difficulty in getting hold of Kalishnikovs, Uzis and M-16s! And now arms have even become barter for hostages, with profits re-invested in other militarist adventures.

The reverse side of this coin is also a pernicious development. In the 1970s, military expenditure in developing countries, including China, rose by 6 per cent a year in real terms, compared with only 1 per cent in developed countries. On 1985 figures, Third World military spending has increased five-fold since 1960, and now amounts to about 23 per cent of the staggering annual global expenditure of some US$1,000 billion.[22] The poor are now finding resources for arms; but at what cost to poverty's victims? As much as one quarter of the Third World's crippling debt burden results from arms purchases. While such arms imports have fallen recently, due partly to declining oil revenue and to the debt crisis, Third World arms production has continued to grow, with now over 50 developing countries having indigenous arms industries. At present, the spread is of conventional arms technology; but Third World countries will soon be demanding the next generation of conventional weapons systems now in the hands of the industrialised countries.

The link between technology and the arms race is a part of the new realities. Of all the world's scientists and technologists at work today on research and development, one out of every four is employed on weapons. Numerous companies exist chiefly on what are euphemistically described as 'defence' contracts. What vested interests are being acquired in the preservation of the military culture? How hard will these interests strive to sustain it? Already it is being said that a major cutback in defence expenditure in the United States would severely disrupt its economy and add significantly to unemployment.

This is a sobering reflection. Are we building prosperity for industrialised societies, and perhaps some newly industrialising ones, on the production of increasingly unusable weapons of destruction? And are we doing so to the point where sustaining this production becomes for these countries a desirable, even compulsive, objective in itself? If this is so, what are the implications for disarmament, or even for arms control? Has the military culture spawned an economic structure which now, in turn, generates new incentives, even imperatives, for further militarisation? And all this in the name of peace!

Were we really, then, at Reykjavik, on the threshold of a decade that would have brought us close to the end of nuclear weapons? Certainly, the tentative agreements that President Reagan and Mr. Gorbachev almost reached, then rejected, came close to a promise to release the world from the nuclear thraldom of what some would still call this 'era of peace'. It would have been a monumental promise.[23] All the fire-power expended in World War II amounted to no more than six megatons of TNT. The world's current nuclear arsenal is the equivalent of 18,000 megatons – 3,000 World War IIs. A single US Trident submarine represents 24 megatons of destructive power – four World War IIs. For the two atomic bombs that changed the world in 1945, there exist today some 50,000 nuclear warheads. Has the world fallen, indeed, "into a wildness"?

Is the option of agreement gone? Each side says it remains. But what are the realities? One certainly is that not everyone was disappointed by the retreat at Reykjavik. Some, specially in Europe, are now saying more openly than before: "Thank goodness, they didn't agree". The military/industrial complexes of both alliances may have come close to being routed; they are now regrouping, on both sides; and they will be joined by others. The challenge ahead is whether they will be allowed to resume their ascendancy. For the sake of all humanity, the people of all countries, this must not happen.

Quite recently, at last August's meeting of the Six Nation Peace Initiative, the Colombian novelist Gabriel Garcia

Marquez, evoked a post-nuclear-holocaust world of ever-lasting night, hurricanes and polluted orange rain, a world peopled only by cockroaches.[24] Later, at Madrid, International Physicians for Prevention of Nuclear War reasserted that human life could cease on this planet in the wake of a major nuclear war.[25] No Tacitus would be left to write of the solitude man made of his planet in the name of peace.

But India's Vikram Seth, in his marvellous poetic novel, *The Golden Gate,* says it all already when he writes:

> So tell me, how much will it please us
> That mankind with its crazy ways
> – Bach, Rembrandt, Socrates, and Jesus –
> Will burn to ash and swiveling haze?
> Will it console us to be knowing
> In the swift instant of our going
> That Red Square, like our children's creche,
> Will soon be charred or ulcerous flesh?
> And then, when the soft radiation
> Descends on what's not been destroyed
> – Trees, whales, birds, wolves – the birthless void –
> Think how the crown of earth's creation
> Will murder that which gave him birth,
> Ripping out the slow womb of earth.[26]

Can we really say, can we really believe, that it is a time of peace while we live with this in prospect?

With human survival itself at stake, peace in its truest sense requires international co-operation on a massive scale as never before. Instead, old instincts of unilateral power are reappearing in new garb. The United Nations itself - our repository of the 'rules of peace' – is under siege. Under challenge are all our evolved concepts and structures of world order. Imperfect though they are, these constitute the highest points we have reached as a global society in developing perceptions of the world as a community of people and nations and in creating structures of organisation and management that conform to such perceptions. All people and countries are the potential victims of this retrogression from an environment of world order. Worst of all, if we thus fail to acknowledge our inseparable humanity and to conduct human affairs in that light, we will ensure that peace remains an illusion.

That is why, Prime Minister, the Five Continent – now the Six Nation – Peace Initiative, is so crucially important. It was close to Indira Gandhi's heart; the new vigour and dynamic you have brought to it in your own right is a living memorial to her. In her celebrated address to the 1972 Stockholm Conference on the Environment, Indira Gandhi summed up her vision of human co-operation thus:

> Life is one and the world is one, and all these questions are inter-linked. The population explosion, poverty, ignorance and disease, the pollution of our surroundings the stockpiling of nuclear weapons and biological and chemical agents of destruction, are all parts of a vicious circle. Each is important and urgent but dealing with them one by one would be wasted effort... It is obvious that all countries must unite in an overall endeavour. There is no alternative to a co-operative approach on a global scale to the entire spectrum of our problems.[27]

Margaret Atwood was expressing the same sense of compulsion of global co-operation for peace when she wrote her poem, 'They Are Hostile Nations'. She did not know in those early days of the 70s of the prospect of a nuclear winter. Mindful only of what Jean Paul Sartre had earlier described as the "infinite unity of man's mutual needs",[28] was it her poet's prescience that led her to warn in memorable verse:

> It is cold and getting colder:
> we need each other's
> breathing, warmth, surviving
> is the only war
> we can afford.[29]

Despite the reverses that the spirit of internationalism has suffered within some countries in the last few years, people today to a far greater degree than ever before in human history recognise, acknowledge, understand that they are of one world. It is vested interests of all kinds which cling to a *status quo* that denies this vision. Yet people know it is a true vision; and they are doing something about it. When, in May 1986, 30 million people around the globe participated in the great 'Race Against Time' in over 270 cities and in 78 countries, people were, indeed, taking over, moving aid from the realm of charity into the world of popular politics. Internationalism was being given a new content. Ordinary decent people of innumerable lands were agreeing with Bob Geldof that "to expiate yourself truly of any complicity in this evil meant you had to give something of yourself".

Today, apartheid, famine, poverty, the plight of refugees, the nuclear arms race, environmental degradation are all the basis of popular causes. Sometimes people question whether, by themselves, they can do enough, faced with so much establishment resistance; but, there is no question that they can, and they must persist; for, in the end, people move governments – more quickly and more directly in working democracies than elsewhere, but ultimately everywhere.

Peace, then, is the people of the world working together as brothers and sisters, not as adversaries; men and women and children from all lands understanding their common humanity and that their fate is inseparable on this small planet; people aware that we have only one world and that we have to learn to share its bounty and its fortunes better than we do.

If there is to be peace, real peace, every person, every village, every town, every city, every nation has to live and work for it. There are better ways of feeding the hungry than preserving mountains and lakes of food; better ways of responding to the needs of the poor than making the rich richer; better ways of strengthening the United Nations as a citadel of peace than by quitting its institutions or emptying them of resources. To pursue those better ways is to work for peace.

And, finally, it rests with each of us. None of us anywhere, in the First World or the Third, can speak of peace but listen only to the drums of war. We cannot yearn for peace but live by an ethos of power. We cannot pray for peace, but nurture hate and prejudice and selfishness in our hearts. The peace of the world comes from within each and every one of the people who inhabit it. For every one of us, in however small a measure, peace is in our keeping. Working together in the knowledge Indira Gandhi left with us that 'life is one and the world is one', peace does not have to be an illusion.

Notes and References

1. Olof Palme, *The Inaugural Indira Gandhi Memorial Lecture* delivered on 16 January 1986, in New Delhi (Association of Indian Diplomats, New Delhi, 1986).

2. The painting is reproduced on the dust cover of this book.

3. Goa Declaration on International Security (1983), *The Commonwealth at the Summit: Communiqués of Commonwealth Heads of Government Meetings 1944-1986* (Commonwealth Secretariat, London, 1987), pp. 245-246.

4. *Common Security: A Programme for Disarmament,* Report of the Independent Commission on Disarmament and Security Issues under the Chairmanship of Olof Palme (Pan Books, London, 1982).

5. *North-South: A Programme for Survival,* Report of the Independent Commission on International Development Issues under the Chairmanship of Willy Brandt (Pan books, London, 1980).

6. Preamble to the Charter of the United Nations.

7. Article 1.1. of Chapter 1 of the UN Charter signed at San Francisco on 26 June 1945 states that one of the purposes of the organisation is 'to take effective collective measures for the prevention and removal of threats to the peace, and for the repression of aggression...' Over 20 years later the UN General Assembly, by Resolution 2330 (XXII) of 18 December 1967, set up a Special Committee on the Question of Defining Aggression, stating that 'there is still no generally recognised description of aggression.' The Assembly, having considered the Committee's report, finally adopted a definition by

Resolution 3314 (XXIX) of 14 January 1975.

8. W.B. Yeats, Supernatural Songs: XII, Meru, 'A Full Moon in March' (1935), included in *Collected Poems of W B Yeats* (Macmillan, London; 1955) p. 333.

9. Cited in Byron Farwell, *Queen Victoria's Little Wars* (Allan Lane, London, 1975), p. xvii.

10. See James Morris's historical study, *Pax Britannica; The Climax of an Empire,* (Harcourt Brace, Jovanovitch, London, 1980).

11. *Report of the Secretary-General on Conventional Disarmament,* (United Nations, New York, 1984), para. 55, p. 26.

12. Frank Barnaby, *South* magazine, (London, August 1986) p. 39.

13. Byron, 'Bride of Abydos', st. 20, Lord Byron: *The Complete Poetical Works,* J.J. McGann (ed.) (Clarendon Press, Oxford, 1981).

14. Revelation of St. John the Divine, Chapter 6, verse 7, *The Bible* (King James version).

15. See Ivan Head, 'What Kind of World do we Live In?', *Address to the National Defence College, Kingston, Canada, 5 September 1986* (typescript), p. 14.

16. *Our Common Future,* Report of the World Commission on Environment and Development under the chairmanship of Dr. Gro Brundtland (Oxford University Press, Oxford, 1987), pp. 235-243.

17. Susanna Agnelli (ed.) *Street Children: A Growing Urban Tragedy,* Report for the Independent Commission on International Humanitarian Issues (Weidenfeld and Nicholson, London, 1986).

18. Pope Paul VI, encyclical 'Populorum Progressio', *Fostering the Development of Peoples* (Catholic Truth Society, London, 1967), p. 35; cited by Pope John Paul II, address to UN General Assembly, 2 October 1979, *UN Chronicle* (New York, July-October 1979), p. 89.

19. Sir Thomas More, 'Dyaloge IV', Wks., 274/2, cited in Sir J. Murray (ed.) *A New English Dictionary on Historical Principles Vol. VIII Pt.1,* (Clarendon Press, Oxford, 1910), p. 874, col. 3.

20. Ivan Head, op. cit., p. 45.

21. Ibid., p.47.

22. R.L. Sivard, *World Military and Social Expenditures* (Washington, D.C.: World Priorities, Inc., 1986); and *World Armaments and Disarmament, SIPRI Yearbook 1985* (Taylor and Francis, London, 1985).

23. At the US-Soviet Summit talks on disarmament at Reykjavik, Iceland, in October 1986, tentative agreement was reached between the two superpowers on: roughly 50 per cent reductions over five years on all international strategic weapons; the removal of all European-based intermediate range (INF) weapons and a freeze on shorter-range ballistic missiles in Europe; negotiations and verification to precede a possible ban on nuclear testing. A US proposal to eliminate all ballistic missiles over ten years foundered on Soviet objections to the US insistence on freedom to research, develop and deploy the 'Star Wars' Strategic Defence Initiative after ten years. Although a failure in themselves, these near-agreements paved the way for the US-Soviet INF Agreement of 8 December 1987. On 'Reykjavik', see the London *Economist* of 18 October 1986, p. 28, and the *International Herald Tribune* of 15 October 1986.

24. Reported in *The Times*, London, 8 August 1986. Also *Financial Times,* London, 6 August 1986.

25. *The Nuclear Threat to Europe: Risks and Prescriptions. Proceedings of the 2nd European Symposium of International Physicians for the Prevention of Nuclear War,* (IPPNW, London, 1986). Reported in *El Pais,* Madrid, 22 October 1986.

26. Vikram Seth, *The Golden Gate,* (Vintage, America Publishing Co., Washington, D.C., 1987), verse 4.20, p. 82.

27. Indira Gandhi, Address to the United Nations Conference on Human Environment, Stockholm, 14 June 1972, published as 'Man and His World', *Indira Gandhi on Peoples and Problems* (Hodder and Stoughton, London, New edition, 1983), p. 66.

28. Jean-Paul Sartre, Preface to Frantz Fanon, *The Wretched of the Earth* (MacGibbon and Kee, London, 1965).

29. Margaret Atwood, 'They are hostile nations', *Margaret Atwood – Selected Poems* (Oxford University Press, Toronto, 1976), p. 161.

Making Human Society
A Civilised State

Shridath Ramphal's ideas on a regional identity, on Third World solidarity, on the mutuality of interest of all countries in a more just and equitable world, has led him to a holistic view of human society. His reflections on peace led him to ponder the ethics of human survival and question a global order characterised by power. In the 11th Corbishley Memorial Lecture, delivered at the Royal Society of Arts in London on 22 June 1987, these ideas came together in an argument that human survival itself is now making it imperative that the rule of law be established between nations – that we must give to human society the attributes of a civilised state.

When Professor C.F. von Weizsacker gave the Seventh Thomas Corbishley Memorial Lecture in 1983, he referred to the ideas of Immanuel Kant in that part of his Lecture devoted to peace and ethics. What he said was this:

> Kant says that the civilised state has been achieved within our nations, but that between the nations the natural state still prevails. The civilised state means the rule of law... Kant continues that there will be no end to the sufferings and tragedies of history until the civilised state, the rule of law, is also established between nations.[1]

Two hundred years after Kant, von Weizsacker's conclusion was that a minimal condition for both a functioning world economy and the political preservation of peace had to be the rule of enforceable law. A few years earlier, in 1981, Willy Brandt's Commission on International Development Issues had reached a not dissimilar conclusion – through processes for which none of us would claim the credentials of philosophical reasoning. In a key passage, the Commission underlined its essential thinking:

> One ambition of this Report is to propose steps along the path to what would genuinely be called a society of nations, a new world order based on greater international justice and on rules which participating countries observe.[2]

Earlier in the same Chapter (which dealt with 'Mutual Interests') we had signalled the attributes of that society of nations. We said:

> We are looking for a world based less on power and status, more on justice and contract; less discretionary, more governed by fair and open rules.[3]

One further statement from the Brandt Report is central to my thesis: a statement which may appear to blur Kant's distinction between law and morals but, in reality, complements it:

> All the lessons of reform within national societies confirm the gains for all in a process of change that makes the world a less unequal and a more just and habitable place. The great moral imperatives that underpin such lessons are as valid internationally as they were and are nationally.[4]

In this Lecture, I shall try to pursue these particular ideas within the framework of a general thesis that not just 'sufferings and tragedies' but human survival itself is now making it imperative that the rule of law be established between nations. My propositions are that we simply must give to our human society the attributes of a civilised state – and that this mandate has an essential and inescapable ethical dimension, the dimension of what is the right and just way for the people of this planet to behave towards each other.

But, first, let me try to illustrate Kant's basic proposition that the civilised state means the rule of law. Four years ago, in 1983, we marked the 150th anniversary of the abolition of slavery. That monumental reform was the result of the conjuncture of new economic realities with the passionate crusade of the Anti-Slavery Movement in this country: the conjuncture of material interest and humanitarian impulse. Its consummation, which we were specifically commemorating, was legal reform – the enactment of the Abolition of Slavery Act, 1833. For 100 years before that Act slavery had subsisted, sanctified under British law, Magna Carta notwithstanding. Lord Mansfield could assert, as he did in *Somerset's* case in 1772, that "the black must be discharged":[5] but that was more a commentary on life in England than on life which English law ordained elsewhere. Half a century later, Lord Stowell could assert in the High Court of Admiralty that Mansfield's judgement "looked no further than to the peculiar nature, as it were, of our own soil; the air of our island is too pure for slavery to breathe in".[6] Not so the air of Caribbean islands, polluted by slavery's legitimation under English law.

Mansfield's judgement, of course, was of great moment for Somerset, freed on the return of a writ of habeas corpus. But in another sense, it confirmed, as one commentator put it, that "English law was wonderfully flexible in accepting systems that were fundamentally different inside and outside the metropolis".[7] In the end, the Anti-Slavery Movement recognised that it was the legal framework, both metropolitan and colonial, which sustained slavery. What the Abolition of Slavery Act did was to change the law. It gave Magna Carta a reach beyond the banks of Runnymede – a reach that common lawyers had hitherto not missed as they proudly viewed the legal order within narrow domestic walls.

This matter of the reach of the rule of law, the domain over which enforceable law rules, is central to both the reality of the civilised state and the quality of its civilisation. To underline this, let me remind you of a particular extension of the reach of the common law: both for its relevance to life within nations and its potential for life between them.

It derives from a famous decision of Britain's highest court, delivered in 1932 by Lord Atkin. As a piece of litigation, it had humble beginnings – a snail in an opaque bottle of ginger beer. But what Lord Atkin adumbrated was an extension of the rule of law to relations between individuals that was, indeed, a giant step; confirming, as it did, that we all owe a duty of care to our neighbour, a duty to act in a reasonable way to avoid injury to him, or her. In Lord Atkin's judgement, who is our neighbour is anyone we ought reasonably to have in contemplation as being affected by our actions. What is reasonable, is what ordinary people – "the man on the Clapham omnibus" – understand to be reasonable: like not selling an opaque bottle of ginger beer contaminated by the remains of a snail.[8] In a general sense, that had always been unreasonable. After that decision of the courts, however, it was unlawful – and that has made all the difference.

Today, that duty of care we owe to our neighbour is imposing new imperatives not yet brought under the rule of law – as the definition of neighbour, and the concept of neighbourliness, are themselves being transformed in our interdependent world. Our closely-knit, interlinked human society is a contemporary reality, however much the instincts of yesterday recall us to old nationalisms and summon up the adversary habits of crude sovereignty. What interdependence means in the global context is that we all need each other, in some measure: for prosperity, for subsistence, for survival even. The rich might be able to prosper in a world from which the poor had vanished; the poor might be less poor in a world without the very rich; the West might be able to dwell in harmony if from the East there came neither torment nor threat; the East, the centrally-planned economies, might be able to accept a procrustean bed if capitalism were not there to provoke envy. The simple truth is, however, that these are wholly irrelevant scenarios; for neither rich nor poor, West nor East, have the option to go it alone. For better or worse, all of us must share this planet, acknowledging our mutual needs and that in their fulfilment lies a mutual interest.

Our shrinking world holds no human sanctuaries. There are no shelters that insulate anyone, anywhere, from disease, from poverty, from nuclear holocaust, from environmental collapse. The concept of jurisdiction, increasingly, has meaning mainly for lawyers. Planet earth has become a global village, a human neighbourhood. The duty of care we owe is to all the world's people who are our neighbours now. The nature of that duty, the notion of what is reasonable conduct in relation to others, is known intuitively not only by 'the man on the Clapham omnibus', but by ordinary people the world over. We must, in new and broader jurisprudence, provide conceptual space for these realities; we need to develop new precepts of rights and duties as relevant to our time as any that Lord Atkin formulated in an earlier era. We need the rule of enforceable law between nations if we are to make human society a truly civilised state.

That is why we called in the Brandt Report for "a world based less on power and status, more on justice and contract"[9] – a continuation internationally, within the society of nations, of the struggle for just national societies. In common law systems, we grew up on a jurisprudence which taught us, in the terms of Sir Henry Maine's famous epigram, that "the movement of the progressive societies has hitherto been from status to contract".[10] Maine's proposition was challenged as not necessarily being a universal law of legal history. But many national societies, admittedly not all, have made that progression, or are still making it, through eras of slavery, of feudalism, of the beginnings of social and economic reform, to the flowering of just consensual communities. Societies did move from status to contract – the sophistry that feudalism was founded in agreement notwithstanding. And the law itself helped the progression – indeed, was its very essence. Today, the challenge is basically the same.

That is not, I know, how it looks from the city centres of the industrialised world; but I ask you to believe that that is how it looks to several billion people in the paddy-fields of Asia, in the scorched grasslands of Africa, in the urban slums of Latin America. And it seems that way to them not on the basis of ideology or bias or even envy but out of a living experience of degradation and hopelessness in the midst of plenty. Today, the developed countries of East and West, which account for a quarter of the world's population, consume around 80 per cent of its commerical energy and metals, 85 per cent of its paper, and over half of the fat intake of foods. Is it any wonder that poor and hungry people eat next year's seed corn to stay alive, that they over-exploit thin soils, over-graze fragile grasslands and cut down disappearing forest stocks for fire wood?

We pride ourselves on being the management generation; yet we have little to be proud of in our management of the world economy for the benefit of all the world's people. Ours is a time of world-wide yearning, a hunger almost, to make our human society a civilised state: a time, therefore, which must impose on us moral, no less than functional, obligations.

Such obligations are inescapable for another reason. In the early aeons of existence, human beings on our planet faced a real challenge of survival – challenge from a hostile and untamed environment. But the human race soon overcame that primary challenge and never since then, despite plagues and pestilences, trials and tribulations of many kinds, has the threat of human extinction ever been seriously revived – that is, until now. The all-encompassing nature of the danger which now faces us is widely acknowledged. In 1983, for example, Commonwealth leaders, representing a quarter of all the people of the planet, against the background of their differing approaches and analyses, nevertheless shared a common perception, that "in the context of heightened tensions and the continuing build-up of nuclear arsenals, the future of civilisation as we know it could be threatened".[11]

And here there is a difference from immemorial times. Now, in strange reversal of man's predicament, the threat to human survival comes not from forces ranged against the human race on a hostile planet, but from the power which man's genius has vouchsafed him over the planet itself. The threat of human extinction comes now from man himself. When we speak of human survival today, we no longer mean survival of family, of tribe, of race, of culture, or even of civilisation. We mean, comprehensively, what we say: saving the human race from self-destruction. Yet it must be the primordial duty of every generation to preserve for the next at least the right to life. Beyond the mandate of self-preservation, that duty imposes an immense ethical obligation.

But the ethical dimension is inescapable for another reason, namely, our growing awareness that it is precisely the undeveloped nature of a universal morality that has put human existence at risk. How content can we be to live by the politics of power if at its apogee it condemns us all to death? How proud can we be of our incredible but amoral science if at the pinnacle of its achievement it threatens not to save but to sacrifice us? What value should we place on our genius if, unconstrained by a global morality, it leads the human race to self-destruction? W.H. Auden responded to such questions when he wrote, as if on behalf of that entire 1930s generation yearning for survival: "We must love one another or die".[12] Fifty years later that ultimate challenge remains valid; only more insistent.

It is that very same understanding, rooted in a rejection of the ways of the world, that led Pope John Paul II – in his message to the 40th Commemorative Session of the UN General Assembly in 1985 – to call as a matter of ethical choice for a "reversal of the immemorial tendency of individuals and peoples to settle their conflicts by force and defend their interests by violence".[13] It is that same understanding – more intuitive, it is true, than spiritual – that has led millions of ordinary people the world over to call for the ascendency of 'peace and love'; to demand, in the words of John Lennon's song, that we "give peace a chance".[14] In our threatened world there is in the human spirit an irresistible urge to elevate the moral imperative to a place of primacy in global affairs.

In 1945, with the pain and anguish of war still unhealed, nations acknowledged their moral duty to preserve peace – to save succeeding generations from the scourge of war. In founding the United Nations, they solemnly promised "to beat their swords into ploughshares and their spears into pruning hooks".[15] They understood in that brief period of enlightenment the ethics of human survival. The war, after all, had ended with the first nuclear explosions ever to take place in conflict; and nations knew that these had to be the last.

That understanding, sadly, has faded over time. It was made so subordinate to doctrines of deterrence that global militarisation now has little need for rationality, though it has long passed levels which 'deterrence' could defend. Today, annual global military spending has probably reached US\$1,000 billion; more than US\$2.5 billion a day – nearly US\$2 million a minute; figures so enormous as to make the imagination boggle. The real cost, of course, is how the same resources might otherwise be used. We can choose to ignore, we can never defend, the ethical implications of the choices our generation has made. In the end, depsite all the promises of 'operation ploughshares', we have turned the post-war period into an era of militarisation and spawned a military culture. This virus of militarisation has now assumed epidemic proportions, infecting not only the industrialised countries but also the developing world. We must ask: what are the implications of this global militarisation for the effort of making human society a civilised state?

I mentioned earlier that I was a member of the Brandt Commission. Just over a month ago the Report of another Commission was published, one with which I was also associated, the World Commission on Environment and Development – the Commission that I expect will become known as the Brundtland Commission, chaired as it was by Mrs. Gro Brundtland, the Prime Minister of Norway.

The Brundtland Commission has urged the world to be guided by concepts of sustainable development: by "an approach to human progress which meets the needs of the present without compromising the ability of future generations to meet their own needs".[16] We are talking here not just of the economic development of developing countries but of all development – in short, of human progress. The requirement that such development be 'sustainable' is an injunction to all countries and all people. Sustainability has to be both perceived and measured in global terms. It is not simply a question of the degree to which each nation can sustain or improve upon its national level of development, whether that level is one of existing prosperity or only of ambition for it.

Even as the Commission was working, a series of tragic happenings induced by accident or evolution, provided a graphic demonstration of the dangers all humanity faces: Bhopal, Chernobyl, the Rhine chemical spillage, forest destruction in Northern Europe, the Mexican liquid gas explosion, and the unfolding human and ecological catastrophe in Ethiopia and elsewhere in Africa. Other dangers are less visible. Some scientists believe that a mass extermination of species is taking place mainly as a result of the clearance of tropical forests, eliminating not only a large part of the earth's biological inheritance but also stocks of many species which could be of immense value to us in the long-term. Recent studies estimate that over the next 20 years a fifth of the world's plant and animal species may become extinct.[17]

A serious and immediate threat is the steady build-up in

the atmosphere of carbon dioxide emissions from fossil fuel burning. Acid rain from emissions of sulphur dioxide and nitrogen oxides causes ecological havoc thousands of miles away. Other atmospheric pollution includes damage to the ozone layer by chloroflurocarbons, like those released daily from millions of aerosol cans, and the 'greenhouse' warming of the planet from both carbon dioxide emissions and deforestation. A prevailing scientific consensus serves notice on us that in tampering in these ways with the composition of the atmosphere we are taking unwarranted risks with our common future.

It is surely beyond contention that in specific and important areas collective management of global resources is urgently needed to avoid sustainable limits being surpassed. Yet such management is not evolving. Our most major effort to date has been in the area of the 'global commons'. Yet the principal result of that effort, the Law of the Sea Convention,[18] is being held hostage to the instincts of narrow national interest. The ethic of one world lags too far behind the separatist habits of an earlier era.

If in all this the right to life is really at stake, and who can doubt that it is, could there be any greater ethical compulsion than that we act decisively to secure that right – to take it altogether out of danger? Why, then, are we not doing so? Why are so many governments ready to embrace – or, at least, acquiesce in – a world characterised by disorder, insecurity, massive human suffering and risk of self-destruction? The world's governments are not evil; they are not in conspiracy to enlarge human disparities, to destabilise world society or to destroy us altogether.

At least in part, the answer lies in the drift away from the global morality that once underpinned a growing internationalism. With that erosion of moral values as the foundation of human solidartiy, the vision of our oneness, of an inseparable humanity, of a world community of people, has not sharpened as it should have done; the spirit of global co-operation so carefully nurtured in the early post-war years has withered; an old, narrow, inward-looking nationalism has re-emerged, fortified by an adversary system of international relations, nurtured by concepts of national sovereignty and, in the case of the super-powers, national sufficiency and even primacy. This is bad enough in itself; it becomes more dangerous for the world's political system and more debilitating for the world economy when it is so much at variance with the palpable unity of human needs and the mutual dependence of nations in meeting them. Internationalism has lost its ethical moorings just at the moment when it needed a firm base from which to respond to the expanded dimensions of global interdependence that the 1970s and 1980s have highlighted – including, among them, the challenge to human survival.

This weakening of internationalism is the result of many factors, among them, regrettably, our experience of the inadequacies and frustrations of international co-operation since 1945. But it is also, in some measure, induced by the passage of time: time which has blurred human memory of how diminished international co-operation brought the world to economic disaster in the 1930s and to near self-destruction in the war that followed.

Today, the United Nations itself is under seige and there are several specific assaults on internationalism. There has been hostility from powerful states to the ILO, to UNESCO, to the World Court, to UNCTAD, to the International Fund for Agricultural Development – even to the International Planned Parenthood Federation and the Committee for Development Planning. The arduously-negotiated Law of the Sea Treaty has been stalled, and in place of the North-South dialogue there is a deafening silence. These are ominous developments – associated as they are with a new respectability for doctrines of dominance whose political and economic strands are interwoven. On the political side these doctrines translate into the ascendancy of unilateralism over pluralism, of militarist intervention over peaceful means of conflict resolution, of national will over global goals. On the economic side, there is the same emphasis on compulsion – the preference for bilateralism over multilateralism; the paramountcy of conditionality over dispassionate assistance; the elevation over social needs of what the Pope recently (in Argentina) called "the inhuman laws of the market".[19]

And, as frightening as anything else in this return to the cult of national power, are the indications that democracy itself is being made subservient to it. The bombing of Tripoli just over a year ago had been preceded by American naval manoeuvres in the Black Sea and in the Gulf of Sidra: manoeuvres described by Pentagon officials at the time as "intended in part to buttress President Reagan's request for more military spending next year." "After past incidents", they said, "in which the United States flexed its military muscle, the President's popularity boomed and his policy won renewed support in Congress".[20] And the macho militarist posture is not a secret political weapon new-found by the White House. France, the year before, displayed its own talent for it when, at a time of electoral choice at home, it persisted with nuclear testing in the Pacific. Despite – or, perhaps, because of – the outrage of small nations whose habitat is that ocean, defiant testing was good for votes at home. I do not exempt the Soviet Union and its allies from criticism. But it is precisely my point that we do not expect an 'Afghanistan' style from the traditional defenders of democracy; still less that democracy itself should be manipulated to sustain an anti-internationalist culture or gratify lapses into it.

Small wonder then, when genuine democracies behave in this way, that imposters feel free to follow. Just over a month ago, on the eve of the 'whites only' election, South African forces flagrantly violated Zambian sovereignty and murdered Zambian citizens in Livingstone. The correspondent of a London newspaper reported from Johannesburg that "the weekend military clash involving South African forces inside Zambia was seen yesterday as having strengthened Pretoria's hand in the white election now only ten days away".[21]

The implications of these trends are horrendous. Under challenge are all our evolved concepts and structures of world order. However limited, they are the highest points we have reached as a global society in developing perceptions of the world as a community of people and nations and in creating structures of organisation and management consonant with such perceptions. All people and countries are the potential victims of this retrogression from world order. If we fail to alter course, how can we hope to respond effectively to the need to make our human society a civilised state?

These are not new questions; but they have to be asked with a new urgency if we are to end what Camus once called "this confrontation between the human need and the unreasonable silence of the world".[22] There was another time, 50 years ago, not so different from our own, when a similar confrontation between need and complacency pushed men of vision towards demanding the rule of enforceable law as the basis of human civilisation. They failed then, and the war that followed has erased memory of their efforts. But we do well to remember them again, especially on this occasion which honours the memory of Father Corbishley, who played so active a part in pursuing the objectives of the Wyndham Place Trust in promoting a concern for peace, world order and the rule of law among people of religious faith.

Founded in 1932 as what was described as an "International Society to promote International Law and Order through the creation of an Equity Tribunal and an International Police Force",[23] the New Commonwealth Society was concerned with a global Commonwealth of Nations in the broader sense. Its aim was to reconstitute and revitalise the League of Nations as an international authority 'possessing the power to alter the public law, and to enforce it'.[24] It sought to enable the League, by increasing membership and powers, to undertake any action which, in the words of the League's Covenant, "may be deemed wise and effective to safeguard the peace of nations".[25] There were 17 national sections – the beginnings of a coalition of countries in the making.

Lord Tweedsmuir – Governor-General of Canada, the novelist John Buchan – was one of its Trustees, Harold Macmillan was a member of the International Executive Committee. Clement Attlee was an early member of the 'British' Commonwealth Section, of which Winston Churchill was the President. In 1934, the Society republished an exchange of open letters between Einstein and Freud called *Why War,*[26] in which these great men argued that the one sure way of ending war was 'the establishment, by common consent, of a central control which shall have the last word in every conflict of interest'.[27]

On 25 November 1936, Churchill spoke at a luncheon in London under the auspices of the Society as follows:

> Where we differ from most other peace societies is that we contemplate and advocate the use of force against the aggressor in support of law. We think it utterly futile to have a League of Nations or an International Court unless behind that there is an armed organised force capable of procuring respect for their decisions. We believe that the world will one day proclaim that a structure of this kind is not only right, but necessary, if any elevated form of human civilisation is to be achieved, and even if such civilisation as we have been able to develop is to be preserved and not cast down once again in the barbarism of the dark ages.[28]

As late as 1958, Attlee, in a lecture in memory of Lord David Davies, who founded the New Commonwealth Society, re-stated the Society's complaints with the League of Nations in calling for "collective security under the United Nations":

> What is needed in the world today is the enforcement of the rule of law... Unless mankind succeeds in meeting the challenge of the present day it will not survive...

> We just cannot afford any longer to indulge in the exercise of unfettered individual sovereignty... If we do not accept such a submission to a world authority we shall not get peace.[29]

In the 1930s the Society was clearly in the vanguard of international thinking. It was, sadly, too late a response to the 'unreasonable silence of the world'.

Churchill was a man of empire; but his internationalism, shaped by his long crusade against the weakness of the League of Nations and the conflict he saw looming, overrode imperialist ambition. The lessons of the 1930s never left him. On 6 September 1943, World War II was at its apogee when, receiving an honorary degree from Harvard University, Churchill spoke of his vision of the future beyond the conflict. His theme was Anglo-American unity and the fraternal association of the Commonwealth. As so often, he used words which have since passed into legend. The Atlantic Alliance and the Commonwealth Association he saw as offering

> far better prizes than taking away other people's provinces or land or grinding them down in exploitation. The empires of the future are the empires of the mind.[30]

But his vision was an even wider one. He also said:

> We have learned from hard experience that stronger, more efficient, more rigorous world institutions must be created to preserve peace and to forestall the causes of future wars.[31]

He saw as a central and creative task the working out of the "form a system of world security may take" – a task which included coming to grips with "whatever derogations are made from national sovereignty for the sake of a larger synthesis". Churchill complained that if the League of Nations had failed, it was "largely because it was abandoned, and later on betrayed." And he counselled the youth of America and Britain that...

> there is no halting-place at this port. We have now reached a

stage in the journey where there can be no pause. We must go on. It must be world anarchy or world order.[32]

And that, of course, was the compelling vision that led, two years later, to the United Nations; the vision that Roosevelt did not live to put into words himself but left Truman to convey to the founding conference at San Francisco:

> We still have a choice between the alternatives: the continuation of international chaos...or the establishment of a world organisation for the enforcement of peace.[33]

And, in the words I have cited elsewhere, but make no apology for repeating:

> If we should pay merely lip-service to the inspiring ideals and then later do violence to simple justice, we would draw down upon us the bitter wrath of generations yet unborn.[34]

Notice that same insistence on a choice between 'world anarchy' and 'world order'; the same emphasis on 'enforcement' of peace. But we have paid lip service to the ideals of the Charter and done violence to simple justice.

The United Nations was created at San Francisco for the purpose of maintaining international peace and security. Chapter VII of the Charter contains a blueprint for an international security system with an enforcement capacity to deter aggression and prevent local disputes from erupting in armed conflict. Had it been implemented, it could have gone a long way to establishing the rule of law world-wide and saving the world both from the scourge of war and the waste of resources on the instruments of war. But, the Charter's promise was not kept. The security system it embodies was placed under the exclusive direction of the Security Council, on which the United States and the Soviet Union sit as permanent members with the right to veto its decisions. Their power struggle was carrried into the Council chamber itself, frustrating agreement on implementing the Charter's key security provisions.

A few years ago, the Independent Commission on International Security Issues – the Palme Commission – in its Report, *Common Security*,[35] called specifically for the strengthening of the United Nations security system by a return to the concept of collective security – at least initially in the context of Third World conflicts. It recognised that the world, as it evolves into a more mature community, must somehow ensure that the answer to a threat of aggression, and to aggression itself, must not depend only on the capacity and resolve of the victim to respond. That recognition is timely and relevant in our present situation. States do not permit the law of the jungle to hold sway within their national societies; they should not allow it in the global society. It is time to ensure, as the Charter promised, that the burden of making the world safe for all is shared by all.

In Attlee's lecture in 1958, which I referred to earlier, he talked of the logic of common security and the resistances it has traditionally faced:

> When Sir Robert Peel introduced his Police Force, people in London were horrified; they thought it was a great invasion of the liberty of the subject. Rich people had lots of servants to look after them, but they thought it was a shocking thing to be taxed for a Police Force. I have no doubt that there was the same kind of reaction at the end of the Middle Ages when local forces were substituted by national forces. The local lord or count, used to looking after himself, thought it an appalling invasion of his privileges. If you look at the development of government you will find that the same objection has always been raised whenever an attempt was made to supplant individual effort by the collective activity of a nation, or a state or even a municipality. It was generally only the compulsion of events which produced the desired end.[36]

Do not current events impose such compulsions, requiring us to put in place a global regime of collective security under the rule of enforceable law? Is it not palpable, for example, that such a need now exists in Southern Africa, where South Africa's 'policies of destabilisation' are a euphemism for systematic aggression, directly and by proxy, against African Front-Line States? And, in quite another part of the world, in the Gulf, should we not be talking in terms of international action, United Nations action, rather than national assertiveness, to protect the world's shipping from the excesses of the combatants? Only the rule of law, applied by all nations acting together, can make the world safe for each and every nation.

The Palme Commission's recommendations envisage a structure of preventive peace-keeping, involving fact-finding missions, military observer teams and military collective security forces, all to be deployed in advance of armed conflict. A vital element of the proposal is that such action under the Charter should be under-pinned by a political 'concordat' between the permanent members of the Security Council to exercise restraint in the use of the veto, thus ensuring that the UN has both the will and the means to prevent armed conflict rather than having to face the imponderables of political reaction to a conflict once it has broken out.

The Palme Report was followed by a call by the UN Secretary-General in 1982 "to reconstruct the Charter concept of collective peace and security" and to meet the need of governments for "a workable system of collective security in which they can have real confidence".[37] Over forty nations sponsored a resolution requesting the Security Council to give due consideration to the Secretary-General's Report. Once more, however, after two years of wholly ineffectual consultation, the Security Council failed to respond to the hopes of the world. And apathy has been piled on inertia. To borrow words used by Freud in his letter to Einstein, published by the New Commonwealth Society in 1934, these non-results "conjure up an ugly picture of mills that grind so slowly that, before the flour is ready, men are dead of hunger.[38] The 'common security' of the world's people cannot be left to those whose concept of an ordered world is one ordered by themselves alone. At no time in the post-war era has there been more pointed a need for a return to the internationalism which was the dominant ethic of the men of 1945.

So I return to ethics as I end. The moral dimension of human survival is more than an option we can take or leave; more than material for pious declarations; more than a masquerade of righteous policy. Without an ethic of survival there cannot be certainty that, in the end, collective wisdom will prevail; that we will summon up a common will to preserve and share the future. On the contrary, if we fail to develop and sustain a system of world order that responds to that ethic, we will assuredly, in some ultimate crisis, assess the demands of preservation not on the basis of the human 'self' but in accustomed narrow terms – only to confirm in irreversible ways that our option always was, as Churchill saw it in 1943, 'world anarchy or world order'; an option which, in today's terms, must mean world order or world's end.

Mahatma Gandhi was once asked what he thought of Western civilisation. He reflected for a while and then answered cautiously: "I think it would be a good idea".[39] He was not, I believe, being cynical. Fifty years later, it is becoming clear that a final judgement on our 'civilisation' is, indeed, going to depend on how we respond to the wider challenge of making human society a civilised state.

Notes and References

1. C.F. von Weizsacker, *Strategies for Peace: The Seventh Corbishley Lecture* (Wyndham Place Trust, London, 1983), pp. 9-10.

2. *North-South: A Programme for Survival,* Report of the Independent Commission on International Development Issues under the Chairmanship of Willy Brandt (Pan Books, London, 1980), p. 75.

3. Ibid., p. 65.

4. Ibid., p. 77.

5.   Sommersett's Case, Howell's *State Trials* Vol. 20, p. 1.

6.   *The Slave 'Grace'*, 1927, High Court of Admiralty, 2 Hagg. 94 Vol. II 1825-1832; 166 ER 179.

7.   M. Craton, J Walvin and D Wright, *Slavery: Abolition and Emancipation. Black Slaves and the British Empire: A Thematic Documentary* (Longman, London, 1976), Chapter 3, 'Slavery and the Law', Introduction, pp. 157-158, at p. 157.

8.   *Donoghue v Stephenson* [1932] A.C. 562.

9.   *North-South: A Programme for Survival*, op. cit., p. 65.

10. Jerome Hall, *Foundations of Jurisprudence* (Bobbs Merrill, Indianapolis, 1973), p. 9, quoting Sir Henry Maine.

11. Goa Declaration on International Security, 27 November 1983, *The Commonwealth at the Summit: Communiqués of Commonwealth Heads of Government Meetings 1944-1986* (Commonwealth Secretariat, London, 1987), p. 245.

12. W.H. Auden, 'September 1, 1939', *Selected Poems* Edward Mendelson (ed), (Faber and Faber, London, 1984), p. 88.

13. Cardinal Agostino Casaroli, Secretary of State of the Holy See and Special Envoy of Pope John Paul II, delivering a message on behalf of the Pope to the UN General Assembly's *Commemoration of the Fortieth Anniversary of the United Nations*: statements and messages (United Nations, New York, 1985), p. 145.

14. John Lennon and Paul McCartney, *Give Peace a Chance* (Northern Songs Ltd., London, 1969).

15. A statue inscribed 'Let us Bend Our Swords Into Ploughshares', by Soviet sculptor Eugeniy Vuchetich, is set in the United Nations Garden in New York. The inscription derives from *The Bible*, Isaiah, Chapter 2, v. 4.

16. *Our Common Future*, Report of the World Commission on Environment and Development under the Chairmanship of Gro Harlem Brundtland (Oxford University Press, Oxford, 1987), Chapter 2, 'Towards Sustainable Development', pp. 43-66.

17. See Edward C. Wolfe, 'Avoiding a Mass Extinction of Species', *The State of the World, 1988, World Watch Institute Report,* (W.W. Norton and Co., New York and London, 1988) Ch. I pp. 101-117. Also Wolfe, *On the Brink of Extinction: Conserving the Diversity of Life, World Watch Institute Paper No. 78* (World Watch Institute, United States).

18. *United Nations Convention on the Law of the Sea:* Final Act of the

Third United Nations Conference on the Law of the Sea (United Nations, New York, 1983).

19. Homily during Mass in Bahia, Blanca, printed in full in *L'Observatore Romana* weekly edition in English, No. 19, 11 May 1987, p. 8.

20. *New York Times*, 19 March 1986.

21. *The Independent*, London, 27 April 1987.

22. Albert Camus, 'Absurd Walls' in *The Myth of Sisyphus,* tr. J. O'Brian (Penguin Books, London, 1986), p. 32

23. *The Aims and Objects of the New Commonwealth Society and Institute*, revised edition, (New Commonwealth Society, London, April 1939).

24. Ibid.

25. Ibid.

26. *Why War? 'Open Letters' between Einstein and Freud* (New Commonwealth Society, London, 1934).

27. Ibid., pp. 12-13.

28. Winston S. Churchill, *Speech at a Luncheon at the Dorchester Hotel, London, on 25 November 1936* (New Commonwealth Society, London, 1936), p. 3.

29. Earl Attlee, *Collective Security under the United Nations* (David Davies Memorial Institute of International Studies, London, 1958), *passim.*

30. Winston S. Churchill, *The War speeches of the Rt. Hon. Winston S. Churchill,* compiled by C. Eade in 3 Vols., Vol. II, p. 514.

31. Ibid.

32. Ibid., pp. 514, 511.

33. Address by President Truman to the Opening Session of the Conference on International Organisation, Opera House, San Francisco, 25 April 1945.

34. Ibid

35. *Common Security: A Programme for Disarmament*, Report of the Independent Commission on Disarmament and Security Issues under the Chairmanship of Olof Palme (Pan Books, London, 1982), pp. 162-166.

36. Attlee, op. cit.

37. *Report of the Secretary-General on the Work of the Organisation* (United Nations, New York, 1982), p. 2.

38. *Supra,* n. 26.

39. Mahatma Gandhi to an interviewer (attr.), cited in *Penguin Dictionary of Modern Quotations,* Second Edition, 1986, J.M. and M.J. Cohen (eds.), p. 128.

Appendix A

The Grenada
Declaration, 1971*

*As modified in the light of decisions taken at the Meeting of Signatory
Heads of Government held at Georgetown, Guyana, 8 November 1971.

ACKNOWLEDGING it to be the inescapable destiny of the
peoples of the West Indies to be bound together in
Nationhood;

MINDFUL of the lessons of past efforts in the cause of West
Indian Unity;

CONSCIOUS of the urgent need to end all forms of
colonialism in the Caribbean and to secure the effective
independence of its peoples;

BELIEVING that the aspirations of the peoples of the West
Indies for political freedom and social and economic justice
can best be fulfilled through the creation of a West Indian
Nation;

DESIRING that in the creation of the Nation the peoples of
the West Indies shall be fully involved;

ACCEPTING it to be the responsibility of those who hold
these truths to be fundamental to act now in their fulfilment
and in so doing create a West Indian Nation of which all the
people of the West Indies may one day be a part;

The representatives of the people of Dominica, Grenada,
Guyana, St Kitts-Nevis-Anguilla, St Lucia and St Vincent
assembled at Grenada this 25th day of July, 1971, hereby

declare it to be their intention to seek to establish out of their Territories a new State in the Caribbean and to this end to proceed as follows:

(a) A Preparatory Commission will be set up by 1 February, 1972, to prepare for the establishment of the new State. The Preparatory Commission will, if possible, be established within the Commonwealth Caribbean Regional Secretariat under a budget to be separately provided by the Participating Territories.

(b) The Preparatory Commission will be headed by a Chairman, to be selected by agreement between the Heads of Government of the Participating Territories, who will have responsibility for recruiting all necessary personnel within the ambit of the Commission's Budget.

(c) In addition to the Chairman, the Preparatory Commission will comprise members drawn from the Participating Territories nominated by the respective Governments after consultation with the Chairman.

(d) As far as practicable, Members of the Preparatory Commission will function as technocrats exercising specific responsibilities during the life of the Commission.

(e) Questions of policy affecting the work of the Preparatory Commission will be referred by the Commission for decision by a Council of Ministers of the Participating Territories that will meet periodically for this purpose. The Council will comprise one Minister from each of the Participating Territories designated for this purpose by the Government of that Territory.

(f) When the Preparatory Commission has reached an advanced stage in its work a Constituent Assembly will be established comprising not less than one and not more than three members from each Participating Territory nominated by the Government of that Territory. The Constituent Assembly will have a limited existence and will be responsible for drafting the Constitution of the new State.

(g)   The Constituent Assembly will be serviced by the Preparatory Commission and will rotate its sessions throughout all the Participating Territories holding at least one public session in each Territory. In the organisation of its work the Constituent Assembly will ensure the fullest participation of the people of the Region in the formulation of the National Constitution.

(h)   It will be the aim of the Constituent Assembly to complete the draft Constitution as early as possible. It will be the aim of Participating Territories to secure the necessary Parliamentary approval for the establishment of the new State and to take the necessary constitutional steps (see (i) below) to provide for its establishment.

(i)   The new Constitution will be promulgated and elections will be held throughout the State – assuming this to be the arrangement for assembling the first Government of the State provided for in the Constitution.

(j)   During the life of the Constituent Assembly the Governments of the Participating Territories will endeavour to co-ordinate their policies and programmes over as wide a field as possible, but more especially in relation to their dealings with the outside world; and it will be a particular function of the Preparatory Commission to secure such co-ordination.

(k)   During the life of the Constituent Assembly, Participating Territories will determine the nature of such changes as they wish to make in their territorial Constitutions – taking account of the work of the Constituent Assembly.

(l)   If in the light of the Report of the Constituent Assembly Parliamentary approval is secured for the establishment of the new State, the Participating Associated States will, by legislation enacted pursuant to Section 10 and the Second Schedule to the West Indies Act, 1967, terminate their status of association with the United Kingdom as from the promulgation of the new Constitution and amend their Constitutions to give effect to the arrangements agreed upon by the Constituent Assembly for their association with the other Participating Territories in the new State, and the

Independent States, by constitutional amendment, will likewise provide for their association with the other Participating Territories in the new State.

(m) Both the legislation to be enacted by the Associated States and the constitutional amendments to be made by the Independent States will empower the Constituent Assembly to promulgate the Constitution of the new State.

(n) With a view to enabling other Member States of the Conference of Heads of Government of the Commonwealth Caribbean Countries to participate in this Declaration and in action to be taken under it, this Declaration will be published simultaneously in the Capitals of all Participating Territories on and not before 1 November, 1971. Prior to such publication and at the earliest opportunity the Secretary-General of the Commonwealth Caribbean Regional Secretariat will bring this Declaration to the notice of the Heads of Government of such other Member States and convey to them the sentiment of West Indian fraternity that underlies the Declaration and the invitation which the Declaration extends for their participation in it.

Appendix B

Gleneagles Agreement
Commonwealth Statement on
Apartheid in Sport

The member countries of the Commonwealth, embracing peoples of diverse races, colours, languages and faiths, have long recognised racial prejudice and discrimination as a dangerous sickness and an unmitigated evil and are pledged to use all their efforts to foster human dignity everywhere. At their London Meeting, Heads of Government reaffirmed that apartheid in sports, as in other fields, is an abomination and runs directly counter to the Declaration of Commonwealth Principles which they made at Singapore on 22 January 1971.

They were conscious that sport is an important means of developing and fostering understanding between the people, and especially between the young people, of all countries. But, they were also aware that, quite apart from other factors, sporting contacts between their nationals and the nationals of countries practising apartheid in sport tend to encourage the belief (however unwarranted) that they are prepared to condone this abhorrent policy or are less than totally committed to the Principles embodied in their Singapore Declaration. Regretting past misunderstandings and difficulties and recognising that these were partly the result of inadequate inter-governmental consultations, they agreed that they would seek to remedy this situation in the context of the increased level of understanding now achieved.

They reaffirmed their full support for the international campaign against apartheid and welcomed the efforts of the United Nations to reach universally accepted approaches to the question of sporting contacts within the framework of that campaign.

Mindful of these and other considerations, they accepted it as the urgent duty of each of their Governments vigorously to combat the evil of apartheid by withholding any form of support for, and by taking every practical step to discourage contact or competition by their nationals with sporting organisations, teams or sportsmen from South Africa or from any other country where sports are organised on the basis of race, colour or ethnic origin.

They fully acknowledged that it was for each Government to determine in accordance with its laws the methods by which it might best discharge these commitments. But they recognised that the effective fulfilment of their commitments was essential to the harmonious development of Commonwealth sport hereafter.

They acknowledged also that the full realisation of their objectives involved the understanding, support and active participation of the nationals of their countries and of their national sporting organisations and authorities. As they drew a curtain across the past they issued a collective call for that understanding, support and participation with a view to ensuring that in this matter the peoples and Governments of the Commonwealth might help to give a lead in the world.

Heads of Government specially welcomed the belief, unanimously expressed at their Meeting, that in the light of their consultations and accord there were unlikely to be future sporting contacts of any significance between Commonwealth countries or their nationals and South Africa while that country continues to pursue the detestable policy of apartheid. On that basis, and having regard to their commitments, they looked forward with satisfaction to the holding of the Commonwealth Games in Edmonton and to

the continued strengthening of Commonwealth sport generally.

London, 15 June 1977

This Agreement, recorded in the Communiqué of the
Commonwealth Heads of Government Meeting held in
London in June 1977, was reached during the Retreat
weekend by Heads of Government held at Gleneagles in
Scotland.

Appendix C

Commonwealth Expert Group Reports on
International Economic Issues (1975-1987)

1.   Towards a New International Economic Order
      Mr Alister McIntyre (Chairman) 1977

2.   The Common Fund
      Lord Campbell of Eskan (Chairman) 1977

3.   Co-operation for Accelerating Industrialisation
      Mr L K Jha (Chairman) 1978

4.   The World Economic Crisis:
      A Commonwealth Perspective
      Professor H W Arndt (Chairman) 1980

5.   Protectionism: Threat to International Order
      Sir Alec Cairncross (Chairman) 1982

6.   The North-South Dialogue: Making it Work
      Ambassador B Akporode Clark (Chairman) 1982

7.   Towards A New Bretton Woods:
      Challenges for the World Financial
      and Trading System
      Professor Gerald K Helleiner (Chairman) 1983

8.   The Debt Crisis and the World Economy
      Lord Lever of Manchester (Chairman) 1984

9.   Technological Change: Enhancing the Benefits
      Professor M G K Menon (Chairman) 1985

10.   Vulnerability: Small States in the Global Society
        Mr Justice P T Georges (Chairman) 1985
11.   Jobs for Young People: A Way to a Better Future
        Mr Peter Kirby (Chairman) 1987

Index

Abidjian, Ivory Coast: African
ministerial meeting at,
1973   118
abolition of slavery   15, 207,
210, 224
    apprenticeship period,
    after   44-5
    Bill, second reading of   54
    and colonialism in
    Africa   254
    compensation to planters,
    after   61
    economic excuses for delay
    of   27
    Emancipation Act, 1833   59,
    61
    in the English-speaking
    Caribbean   44
    and Gladstone, William
    E.   60
    interest and principle,
    conjunction of   367
    Ministerial Plan for   57 n.24,
    70, 71 n.3
    opposition to   52-3
    unfinished business on, in South
    Africa   204
Abolition of Slavery Act
1833   44, 48, 367
Accra, ACP Resolution at   136
acid rain   356, 374
Action Programme for Economic
Co-operation between Developing
Countries   154, 155 n.3
Acts of the Assembley of the
Charibee Leeward Islands   91,
n.1
Addis Ababa, OAU summit at,
1973   118
Adams, Grantley   167
Adams, J.M.G.   162-3

Adamson, Alan H.   47, n.4
Afghanistan, and Soviet
Union   184
Africa
    arms spending in   298
    and the Caribbean   131
    and debt   306
    and decolonisation   211
    democracy in   336
    differentiations,
    economic   300
    ecological damage in   294
    economic integration, need
    for   297
    Economic Planning, ministers
    of   293
    export growth, need for   297
    external capital flows, need
    for   303
    famine in   293
    farmers, adaptability of   295
    foreign investment, need
    for   301
    'green revolution projects';
    in   296
    and Latin America   145,
    149, 214
    population increase in   294-5
    poverty in   255, 370
    rural credit for smallholders,
    need for   301
    slave trade in   200
    small farming successes
    in   299
    twenty-first century   329,
    339
    urban migration in   295
    see also Sub-Saharan Africa
African, Caribbean and Pacific
Countries (ACP)
Ambassadors, Brussels meetings

of   119, 120
    Brussels meetings with EEC,
    1973   118-9
    Caribbean involvement
    in   35, 168
    co-ordination of, in Brussels
    statement   119
    'eight principles'   118
    and EEC   23, 35, 36, 112 *et
    seq.,* 116 *et seq.,* 123 *et seq.,* 131,
    150, 175 n.2
    exports to Britain   112
    Georgetown *ad hoc*
    meeting   113-6
    Guyana Accord   114
    Lomé Convention,
    signed   135
    ministerial spokesmen
    of   120
    negotiating conditions, creation
    of   271-2
    Secretariat   120, 168
    single spokesman for, in EEC
    negotiations   114-119, 131
    unification of   116 *et seq.,*
    123
ACP-EEC Conference, Brussels
    1973   113
ACP/EEC ministerial meeting,
    Jamaica, 1974   120
African National Congress
(ANC)   233, 234, 240, 243, 245
Africans of Guyana   20, 21, 22,
44
Agreement of Dickenson
    Bay   168, 175 n.1, 180
aggression, definition of   250-51
*A History of Indians in
Guiana*   29 n.10, 47 n.9, n.10,
72 n.10
*A History of the Guyanese Working
    People 1881-1905*   64
aid
    to Africa   303
    Caribbean-Latin American
    competition for   140
    and development   250
    guns, in place of   298, 356

    value of, decline in   267
    to West Indies, bilateral and
    multilateral   107
*Akin to Slavery; Prison Labour in
    South Africa*   206 n.7
Algiers Non-Aligned summit,
    1973   25 170
A Life in Peace and War   30
    n.32
'Alliance for Progress'   184-5,
    191 n.4
Amerindians of Guyana   16
Amin, Idi   218
'An Act to prevent the importation
    of slaves...'   55-6 n.10
Andrews, Rev. C.F.
    and indenture in Fiji   65
    and Ramphal family   68
Anguilla   97, 101 n.9, 102
Angola, and South Africa   219,
    236, 243
A New System of Slavery   72 n.9
Angelli, Susanna   327 n.7
Anstey, Roger   56 n.10
Anti-Apartheid Movement   217
Antigua   100 n.4, 102
    and CARIFTA   123
    slave insurrection, 1831   54
Anti-Slavery Movement   51,
52, 55 n.5, 61, 204, 367
*Anti-Slavery: Religion and
    Reform*   56 n.10, 72 n.7
Anti-Slavery Society   257
    indentured labour, protest
    over   62
Apartheid   59
    colonialism, worst form
    of   209
    cosmetic changes to
    216-7
    denial of humanity   231
    dialogue for ending, attempt
    at   225 *et. seq.*
    'double-speak' of   352
    indenture, similar to   64
    'moral deformity'   210
    moral outrage against   194
    opposition to, duty of   212

passive support for   213,
219-20, 227, 244
'people action' against   241
purpose of 27
and slavery   194, 201, 202-3,
210, 218, 231
specific issues of   239-40
violence of   234
world order, threat to   198
see also South Africa
apprenticeship system, after
abolition of slavery   44-5, 61
Aristotle, on justice   126, 130
n.3, 147-8, 149 n.2
'arkathis'   66, 67
arms
aid, in place of   356-7
illicit trade in   357
race   338
spending   26, 325
Arusha, CARIFTA-East Africa
meeting, 1972   117
Arusha Convention   125, 130
n.1
Ashanti, and 19 century
Britain   351
Asia
and the Caribbean   155
and decolonisation   211
and Latin America   145, 149
poverty in   370
twenty-first century   329
Assam, indenture in   65
Atkin, Lord: *Donaghue v
Stephenson*   368, 384 n.8
atmosphere, tampering
with   374
atomic explosions, August
1945   337-8
deaths from   293
Attlee, Clement   378
David Davies Memorial
Lecture   378-9, 381, 385
n.29, n.36
Atwood, Margaret   360, 364
n.29
Auchlyne, Berbice   68
Auden, W.H.   371, 384 n.12

Austin, Hudson   163
Australasia, twenty-first
century   329
Australia, and South
Africa   222
Austria   190
authoritarianism, threat of   340
'Avoiding a Mass Extinction of
Species'   384 n.17
Ayacucho, Battle of   207, 214

Bagehot, Walter   344 n.5
Bahamas   94, 100 n.5, 102, 174
bananas, importance of, in
Caribbean economy   127
Barbados   45, 102, 162
CARIFTA   123
and Cuba   141-2,
independence 1966   94
Memorandum of
Understanding 1982   165
slave revolt 1816   54
Barbados Heads of Government
Conference 1967   33
Barnaby, Frank   363 n.12
Barrow, Errol   104, 163, 179
bauxite, and Caribbean
economy   128
'Bay of Pigs' 1961   352
Belize   94, 100 n.5, 102, 105
and CARIFTA   123
Guatemala border
dispute   143 n.2
Belgium   103
Benares
indentured labour from   63
Shridath Ramphal's great-
grandmother at   66, 67
*Benevolent Neutrality: Indian
Government Policy and Labour
Migration to British Guiana 1854-
1884*   47 n.8
Berbice   48-9
Magdaleneburg revolet   50
Berbice Association   51, 52
Berbice Commission   49, 50-51
Bhopal disaster   356, 373

Bierck, H.A. Jr,   215 n.3
Bihar District Gazetteer   74 n.30
Bird, V.C.   100 n.4, 179
Bishop, Maurice   163, 164, 182, 183
Black Skin White Mask   74 n.31, 205 n.3
Boer Wars   351
Bolivar, Simon   214 n.1
    birth, 200th anniversary of   207, 208, 210
    and decolonisation   211
    and Haiti   209
    internationalist ideals   208, 214
    in Jamaica   150, 208
    'Jamaica Letter'   208, 209, 215 n.2
    Selected Writings of Bolivar   215 n.3
    Self criticism   306
    Simon Bolivar: His Basic Thoughts   215 n.3
    slavery, abolition of   210
    Wilberforce, meeting with, 1810   210
Bolivar and the Independence of South Ameica   215 n.6
Bolivia, slavery not allowed in   210
Bolt, Christina   56 n.10, 72 n.7
Botswana   300
    South African aggression against   236
'bound yard'   64
Brandt Commission   251, 256, 257, 278-91 *passim,* 314, 373
    and Shridath Ramphal   262, 276 n.1
Brandt Report   349, 366, 369
Brazil   190
    twenty-first century   329
Brecht, Bertold   260, 261 n.8
Bretton Woods Agreement   264, 266, 284
Brezhnev doctrine   182
    in Western Hemisphere   184-5

Brisbane Code of Conduct   212, 215 n.10
Britain
    and abolition of slavery   44, 210
    and Berbice   48, 51
    and colonialism   16, 267
    Commission to British Cuiana 1938   18
    common law, and 'duty of care'   368
    employment in, and Third World exports   283
    Indian indenture, support for, 1844   62
    and Mozambique   243
    Parliament, components of   335-6
    Pax Britannica   351, 363 n.10
    and Southern Rhodesia   195-6
    and South Africa   27, 197, 239
    Spain, imperial, rivalry with   23
    Suez intervention 1956   352
    sugar interests   18
    Treaty of Rome, signed 1972   112
    and West Indies   151
    West Indian 'brain drain'   179
British Empire
    and trade unions, overseas   17
    and West Indies   86
British Guiana (Guyana)   16, 46
    Anti-Slavery Society visit to, 1838   62
    apprenticeship code in   45
    British Guiana Labour Union   17
    Illiteracy in, in 1917   18
    Immigration Agent General   17
British Guiana: British Empire

Exhibition, Wembley 1924   29
n.8
British Guiana in Wartime   30
n.14, 81 n.1
*British Slave Emancipation: The
Sugar Colonies and the great
experiment*   47 n.6
Brougham, Lord   54, 72 n.11
Browning, Robert   138 n.2
Brundtland, Gro   327 n.2, n.4,
363 n.16, 373, 384 n.16
Brundtland Commission   373,
384 n.16
Buchan, John (Lord
Tweedsmuir)   378
Burnham, Forbes   79, 113, 165,
179
Butt, John   72 n.7
Buxton, Thomas   55 n.5
Byron, George Gordon   353,
363 n.13

Caicos, the, part of West
Indies   102
Calcutta
indentured labour recruited
at   61
Shridath Ramphal's great-
grandmother at   66, 67
Cambodia, and the Non-Aligned
Movement   25
Cameroon   300
Camus, Albert   377, 385 n.22
Canada
Caribbean, trade with   151
federalism of   88
resources, transferring
mechanisms   270
and USA   184
West Indian 'brain
drain'   179
'Western Hemisphere,
Community of', exclusion
from   144, 147
Canadian Presbyterians
schools in British Guiana   19
Shridath Ramphal's grandfather

trained by   67-8
Cancun, North-South summit,
1981   304, 311 n.7, 314
Candide   60, 72 n.7
Capitalism and Slavery   56 n.22,
n.23, 71 n.6, 206 n.9
Caracas, and anti-colonial
struggle   208
carbon dioxide, build-up
of   373-4
Caribbean, the
and Africa   131
and the ACP   35, 113-4, 116-
7, 119, 120
and agriculture   106
and Canada   189
'big four'   181
common external tariff   106
Commonwealth
Caribbean   102
Dutch speaking   122
economy of   126-9, 183-4
economic and political
options   177
in the eighties   182
'English speaking'   102, 103,
105, 122, 140, 143, 145, 156
and Europe in 17th century and
18th century   122, 123
and EEC   23, 169
federalism, in Leeward
Islands   82
foreign exchange, and
agriculture   127
foreign investment
policy   106
fragmentation, danger
of   171, 179, 182
French-speaking   122
geographic factors,
special   97
illiteracy in   18
indentured labour in   20
industries   106
integration   32, 112, 123,
129, 162, 171, 173
Labat, J.B.   85
and Latin America   23, 24,

140 *et seq.*, 150 *et seq.*, 174, 189
MDCs   181
manufacturing, growth
of   128
natural resources, exploitation
of   128
peace-keeping, regional   93
pragmatism, danger of   184
Regional Food Plan   36
regional integration
movement   93, 181
regional security machinery,
need for   99, 165
slavery in   20
and South Africa   212
transnational corporations
in   186
twelve separate states,
1962   79
unemployment   127, 128
and USA   23, 165
'what might have been',
speculations on   179
Caribbean Basin,
character of   157-8
new relationships and
strengths   158
Caribbean Basin Initiative   140,
141, 143 n.1, 156 *et seq.*, 185
Caribbean Community and
Common Market (CARICOM)
care for, a way of life   172
erosion of   162, 163
establishment of   33, 80, 81
n.6, 112, 123, 150, 168
future of   173, 175
Jamaica meeting, 1982   163
LDC/MDC relations in   181
and McIntyre, Alister   22
membership, limitation
of   174
progress of   36-7
survival of   170-71, 172
and unity, Caribbean   132
Caribbean Development
Bank   105, 168, 176 n.5
and Latin America   143
Caribbean Free Trade Association

(CARIFTA)
Agreement   33, 113, 123,
333 n.2
Agricultural Marketing
protocol   105
and CARICOM 132, 179
CARIFTA Council, April
1973   34
Georgetown Accord, April
1973   35
LDC/MDC relations in   181
mission to Commonwealth
Africa   117
*Caribbean Ecumenical
Consultation for
Development*   102
'Caribbean Perspectives'   93
*Caribbean Story, Book Two; The
Inheritors*   29 n.5
Carrington, Lord   195
Carlton Gardens, London   70
Cartagena South-South –
consultation   306-7
Casaroli, Cardinal
Agostino   384 n.13
Cavell, Edith   345 n.10
Cayman Islands   102
*Centenary History and Handbook
of British Guiana*   55 n.1
Central America and Caribbean
Basin Initiative   140
Centre for Inter-American
Relations   139 footnote, 150
Cesaire, Aimé   201, 206 n.5
Chad   300
Chaguaramas, spirit of   185,
191
Charter of Punta del Este,
1961   191 n.4
'Charting the Way Forward', South
summit theme   313 *et. seq.*
Chaudhury, Roy P.C.   74 n.30
Chenobyl disaster   356, 373
child mortality   326, 354
in Africa   294
and birth rates, increase
in   295
and poverty-wealth   265

children
  employment of 18-9
  homeless   325, 355
  in South Africa   229, 238
  n.12, 242
China
  hegemony, renounced   194
  labourers from, on sugar
  estates   46
  military expenditure   357
  twenty-first century   329
Chinese Opium War   351
Christophe, Henri   157
Churchill, Winston   224, 224
  n.9, 378, 383, 385 n.28,
  Harvard, honorary degree
  from   379
  'man of empire'   379
  War Speeches of   385 n.30
Cipriani   103
citrus, in Caribbean
  economy   127
Clarkson, Thomas   55 n.5
Claypole, William   29 n.5
Collins, Canon   216, 221, 224
  n.4, n.5
colonialism
  and apartheid   209
  and British Guiana   16-7
  European, in the
  Caribbean   173
  French   23, 63
  and indentured labour   63
  'new'   299
  and separatism   86, 140, 151
colonial territories, UN Charter
  on   90
Comitas, Lambros   30 n.21
Columbia   143
Columbus to Castro   81 n.5
Commonwealth
  and Amin, Idi   218
  apartheid, action
  against   196, 226, 232, 241
  and black South Africa   221,
  217, 244
  and Southern Rhodesia   195
Commonwealth Accord on South

Africe   230 n.2
Commonwealth Currents   205
  n.1
Commonwealth Secretariat   71,
  116, 250
Commonwealth Society of
  India   59
Commonwealth Sugar
  Agreement   272
Commonwealth summits
  Bahamas 1983   196
  London 1977   164
  Lusaka 1979   164, 195
  Melbourne 1981   164
  New Delhi 1983   164
communications media
  and Ethiopian famine   293
  and South Africa   242
Communism   211, 304
Community of the Western
  Hemisphere, proposed   144,
  185
Comprehensive Anti-Apartheid
  Law, US   239
Congress of Angostura   306
Congress of Panama   214
Conventional Disarmament, UN
  Report on, 1984   352, 363 n.11
Cook, Allen   206 n.7
'coolie yard'   64
Corbishley, Father   377
Councils of the Commonwealth,
  Jamaica, 1975   170
Craton, M.   73 n.16, 384 n.7
Crimean War   351
Crichlow, Hubert Nathaniel   17
Crumpston, I.M.   72 n.10, n.11
Cuba
  Caribbean, part of   173
  and Caribbean-Latin
  America   141
  and Grenada   163, 183
  Marti Monument,
  Havan   159
  recognition of, 1972   180-81
Cuffy, slave leader   50
Curzon, Lord   65

Dabydeen, David   29 n.13
Dageraad, Slave revolt,
  1763   50
Dag Hammarskjold Institute of
  Sweden   265, 277 n.6
dairy farming, in Africa   299
Dakar, ACP meeting at   119
Dar es Salaam, ACP meeting
  at   119, 131
Dar es Salaam, African Trade
  Ministers Conference 1973   131
Davis, David brion   56 n.20, 72
  n.7
Dawson, Sir Edward   17
Debray, Regis   215 n.4, 287,
  292 n.4
debt
  and Africa   302-3
  and arms spending   357
  Paris Club   311 n.4
  rescheduling   300, 302
Declaration of Tlatelolco   152-3
Defence and Aid Fund, South
  African   206 n.7, 216, 217, 224
  Annual Conference,
  25th   216
Demas, William   33
Demerara slave revolt 1823   53,
  60
Demerara, and Gladstone
  family   70
Democracies, Committee for a
  Community of   334, 336
Destructive Engagement: Southern
  Africa at War   198 n.3, 248 n.4
detente
  and ACP/EEC
  negotiations   133
  decline from,
  international   182, 341
  and development   281
  super powers, between 133,
  146, 154
  developed countries
  co-operation   38
  and 'deserving and undeserving
  poor'   274
  and debt, in Third

World   325
  energy and metals, consumption
  of   370
  middle states   274, 283
  and militarism   372
  recession, 1980s   37
  and Third World, economic
  crisis   133
  Third World, mutuality of
  interest with   275
development
  and arms race   338
  diminishing returns   267
  and East-West issues   281-2
  Independent Commission of the
  South   321, 322 n.10
  issue of   250 et seq.
  and justice   273
  'new name for peace'   355,
  363 n.18
  and Palme Report   349
  and self-reliance   273
Development Dialogue   277 n.6
Dhangars   61, 63, 70
Disarmament Commission   28
Discours sur le
  colonialisme   206 n.5
Dominica   102, 123
Donne, John   215, n.5
drug abuse   356
Dresher, Seymour   56 n.10, 172
  n.7
Dutch, Antilles   173

Eaden, John   92 n.6
East Agrica   84, 117
East Caribbean
  Grenada coul d'etat   183
  Grenada Declaration   102,
  172
  states, independence of   181
East Indians, ethnic identity fears
  of   21
East-West
  nuclear arms race   337
  power struggle   304
  and South Africa   204

and UN   380
Ebrahim, Ebrahim Ismail   238
n.13
Economic Commission for
Africa   293
Education Ordinance   18
Einstein-Freud correspondence:
Why War? 378, 382, 385 n.26
Ellora, the   65, 67
El Salvador, US military aid
for   141
Eluard, Paul   276, 277 n.12
Ely, John   54, 57 n.21
Eminent Persons Group, to South
Africa   196, 224 *et seq.*, 231 *et*
seq., 239, 243, 244
   composition of   232-3, 238
   n.2
   'Negotiation Concept'   235,
   236-7
   recommendations of   235
energy question, and
OPEC   285
English Speaking Union   334
Environment commission   28
environment, damage to   356
Essequibo, Guyana   44
Ethics of Aristotle   130 n.3, 149
n.2
Ethiopia, famine in   293, 373
Europe
   and Caribbean   122, 128, 131
   ideals and traditions of   289-
   90, 294
   and Nazism   201
   new economic relations with
   Third World   133
   'scramble for Africa'   122,
   254
   twenty-first century   329
   and US   146
European Development
Fund   129, 307
European Economic Community
(EEC)
   ACP, negotiations with   36,
   112 *et seq.*, 116 *et seq.*, 131, 175
   n.2

Britain enters   112
Brussels meetings with ACP,
1973   118, 119, 120, 131
Caribbean and African talks on
approach to   113
Caribbean access to markets
of   127
Common Agricultural Policy,
and ACP   120
Commonwealth
associables   113, 118, 119,
130 n.4
conflict within, signs of   119
Francophone
associates   113, 118, 124
Lagos discussion of approach
to   117
Lomé Convention   135
'options' in Protocol 22 of
Treaty of Accession   113,
117, 118, 119
'reciprocal preferences'   113,
117, 122
Regional Development
Fund   270
resistence to certain ACP
demands   120
and Third World   148, 274,
283
Treaty of Accession   113,
115 n.3, 130 n.4
European Investment
Bank   129
extremism, and power cult   342

famine
   African governments,
   and   296
   countries at risk   294
   and drought, in Africa   296
   in Third World   352
Fanon, Frantz   70, 74 n.31, 201,
205 n.3, 206 n.5, 281, 291 n.4, 364
n.28
fear, self-fulfilling   183
federalism
   failures of, post mortem

on   83-5, 91 n.3
Canadian   88
and nationhood   88-9, 89-90
obstacles to   107-8
and poverty   89
US Confederation   88
West Indian rejection of   179
Federalism, International
Conference on, Lagos 1976   82
'Federalism, Nationalism, and
Reason'   92, n.11
Federalist Papers   107-8, 110 n.4
feudalism, modern   256-7, 273,
305, 369-70
Fiji
and ACP-EEC
negotiations   124
indentured labour to   65
Finer, S.E.   344 n.2, n.3
finance, external
Caribbean-Latin American
compeititon for   140
for developing countried   37,
128
Finland   184
Flanz, Gisbert H.   91 n.3
*Foundations of
Jurisprudence*   384 n.10
Foreign Slave Trade Act,
1806   50
France
arms exporter   356
colonialism   267
former colonies of 23
nuclear testing   376
and South Africa   187
Franck, Tom   83, 91 n.3
Franklin, Benjamin   334, 334
n.1
Freetown, Sierra Leone,
CARIFTA-East Africa meeting,
1972   117
Freud, Siegmund   382
Friedman, Milton   292 n.11
From Columbus to Castro   29
n.4
Furneaux, Robin   53, 56 n.17

Gabarone, bombing of   233,
243
Gabon   300
Gairy, Eric   163, 178
Gambia, the 300
Gandhi, Indira
Commonwealth Heads of
Government meeting,
1983   348
Commonwealth summits,
valued by   347-8
conversation of   348
global co-operation, urged
by   360
in Guyana, 1968   346-8
murder of   349
non-violence, ethnic of   348-
9
painting, gives to Shridath
Ramphal   348
Shridath Ramphal seks counsel
of   347
at Stockholm Conference on the
Environment   360, 364 n.27
Gandhi, M.K. (the Mahatma)
indenture, opposition to   65
on Western civlisation   383,
386 n.39
Gandhi, Rajiv   346, 360
Gauhar, Altaf   253 n.4
Geldorf, Bob   361
GATT (General Agreement on
Tariffs and Trade)   126, 264,
266, 314, 315
Georgetown, Guyana
CARIFTA Secretariat at   33
Commonwealth ministers-
CARIFTA meeting,
1973   117
J.I. Ramphal's school in   19
Non-Aligned ministerial
meeting, 1972   113, 145, 154,
155 n.3,180
Shridath Ramphal's great-
grandmother at   65
*Guyana: A Composite
Monograph*   30 n.20
Guyana Journal, Non-Aligned

Special Issue   30 n.29
Ghana   66, 117, 119
Gillanders, Francis   69
Gillanders, Arbuthnot &
   Co.   61, 69
Gladstone, Jack, slave
   leader   59
Gladstone, John   46
   at Carlton Gardens,
      London   70
   Demerara plantations of   60
   and indentured labout   61,
      63, 65
   mismanagement at Vreed-en-
      Hoop   60
Gladstone, Thomas   60
Gladstone, William Ewart   46,
   70
   maiden speech, defending sugar
      interests   60, 72 n.8
   member for Newark,
      1932   60
   Midlothian campaign   74-5
      n.34
Gleneagles Agreement,
   1977   212, 215 n.9, 217, 391
global society   32, 146
   democracy in   334 *et. seq.*
   collective security   381-2
   federalism   91
   income disparities in, danger
      from   285
   interdependence   255, 259
   move towards   146
   principle and prudence,
      conjoined   258
   and realpolitik   184
   and rule of law,
      worldwide   324
   super power struggles,
      and   310
   twenty-first century   330-31
   unequal relations in   256
Goa Declaration on International
   Security   348, 362 n.3, 370-71,
   384 n.11
*Global Challenge: From Crisis to
   Co-operation*   327 n.5

Goldwater, Barry   344 n.9
Green, William   47 n.6
Grenada
   and CARIFTA   123
   coup d'etar, 1979   163, 164,
      182
   invasion of, 1983   141, 164
   'what might have been',
      speculations on   178
Grenada Declaration, 1971   80,
   81 n.7, 102, 172, 387-90
Group of 7   308, 311 n.11
Group of 10   308, 311 n.12, 316
   322 n.5
Group of 24   307, 311 n.10, 314,
   316, 322 n.4
Group of 77   145. 149 n.1, 154,
169, 189, 271, 314, 317-8, 322 n.9
   Lima meeting 1970   145
Grunfeld, F.V.   205 n.2
Guadeloupe   173
Guatemala, Belize border
   dispute   143
Gulf of Paria   150
Guyana
   apprenticeship, demonstrations
      against   44
   British non-resident
      proprietors   17
   CARICOM, proposed
      exclusion from   163
   and CARIFTA   123
   and Cuba   141-2, 180-81
   'Guiana Order' 1805   50
   independence, 1966   79, 94
   illiteracy in, 1917   18
   Kissinger proposal, rejected
      by   144
   labour crisis, after 1838   45
   private schools in   19
   population, composition
      of   16, 20
   racial integration, opposition
      to   21
   radical Third World
      Country   27
   'tropical Gorbals'   17
   unemployment, in 1930s   18

Venezuela, border dispute
with   143 n.2
West Indian Federation, opted
out of   102
and West Indian political
unity   80
Guyana Accord   114

Haiti
  and Bolivar   209, 210
  illiteracy in   18
Hall, Jerome   384 n.10
Hamilton, Alexander   92 n.9,
  107, 110 n.3, n.4
Hammarskjold, Dag   27-8
Hardinge, Viceroy   65
Harare, bombing of   233, 243
Head, Ivan   363 n.15, n.20,
  n.21
hemisphere, political concept
  of   146-7, 153, 154
Heritage Foundation 305, 311 n.8
Hesperus, the   46, 61
'hill coolies'   72 n.12
Hill, Thomas   57 n.25
History of British Guiana   55
  n.1, 71 n.2
History of the Pelopponesian
  War   137 n.1
History of the People of Trinidad
  and Tobago   30 n.19
Honduras, US military aid
  to   141
Howe, Sir Geoffrey   244
Howick, Lord   44, 60
Huddleston, Trevor   216
human survival
  dangers to   28, 370-71
  and democracies   338, 343
  ethics of   365, 372
  and integration   121
  and internationalism   146
  and rule of law   366
Humanitarian Issues
  Commission   28
Hungary 1956   351

indentured Indian labour in West
Indies   15, 16, 17-8, 44, 59
  African hostility to   20
  beginning of   46, 61
  conditions of life   63-4
  Royal Commission on,
    1871   64
  'slavery, new system, of'   62
  stopped   65
  and wage-bargaining, after
    abolition of slavery   62
  women, lack of   66
  women, moral degradation
    of   65
Independent Commission of the
  South on Development
Issues   38
India   190
  bubonic plague in, 1870s   66
  indentured labour, opposition
    to   62, 65
  independence   266-7
  leadership, moral   347
  the Mutiny   351
  overseas Indian-descended
    people   22
  twenty-first century   329
  and UN   350
India: A Wounded
  Civilisation   255, 261 n.3
India in the Caribbean   29 n.13
Indian Citizenship Act, 1955   21
Indians of Guyana   18, 19, 20
  ancestors of, first arrival   46,
    61
  federalism, objection to   78
  Indian citizenship, disinterest
    in   21
Indians Overseas   73, 74 n.20
Indira Gandhi Memorial
  Lecture   346 et seq.
Indonesia   329
industralised countries
  incomes, transfer
    mechanisms   269
  market, operation of   269
  and primary producers   264
Interim and Development

Committee   315, 316
International Development
Association (IDA)   314
International Fund for Aricultural
Development   375
International Labour
Organisation   375
International Monetary Fund
(IMF)
    compensatory Financing
    Facility   314
    conditionality   189
    debt service, prediction
    on   303
    *The Functioning and
    Improvement of*   322 n.4, n.5
    policies of, unhelpful   251,
    300
    SDRs criticised   268
    Third World, influence
    of   314
International Monetary
Conference   308, 312 n.14
International Planned Parenthood
Federation   375
International Physicians for
Prevention of Nuclear
War   359, 364 n.25
internationalism
    and Africa   309
    and Bolivar   208, 209
    and Caribbean   169, 188
    Churchill's   379-80
    decline in   303-4
    and democracy   336, 338,
    340
    and development   250, 305
    and environment   374-5
    and hemisphere, concept
    of   147
    India   347
    and interdependence   368-9
    Kant, advocated by   365
    and law, enforceable   365-6
    and multilateralism   186-7
    and peace   361
    post-war ethic   383
    'Race Against Time'   361

super powers, against   188
and survival   146
threats to   189-90
twenty-first century   329
and UN   208
Irving, Brian   30 n.20
'Is Britain indispensable to the
Commonwealth?'   198 n.1
Ivory Coast   300

Jagan, Cheddi   29 n.11
Jamaica
    ACP-EEC 1974
    meeting   120
    apprentices, brutality
    towards   45
    'bastion against
    Communism'   162
    and CARIFTA   123, 180
    and Cuba   141-2, 180
    independence 1962   94, 104
    slave revolt, 1831   54
    slave revolt 1825   54
    Shridath Ramphal in   79
    referendum   104, 178
Jamaica Labour Party   162
Jay, John   87, 92 n.9, 110 n.4
Jews, under Nazis   200
Johnson, Phyllis   198 n.2, n.3,
248 n.4

Kala Pani (Black Water)   63,
73, n.17
    sin of crossing, to a Hindu 67
Kant, Immanuel   365, 367
Kaywana Trilogy   49, 55 n.7
Kennedy, John F., Latin American
policy of   191 n.4
Kenya   300
King, Martin Luther   71, 260,
261 n.9
Kipling, Rudyard   351
Kissinger, Henry   144, 146, 185,
277 n.3, 280

Labat, Jean-Baptiste   85, 91 n.6
Labour and Emigration   30 n.17
Labour in the West Indies 29 n.6, n.7
Lancaster House Conference on Southern Rhodesia   195, 241
Lancaster House Conference on West Indies 1961   93, 178
Lange, Prime Minister   222
Langland, William 310,   312 n.15
language barrier, Caribbean-Latin American   140, 151
Lamming, George   64, 74 n. 24
Latin America   23
  abolition of slavery in 210
  and apartheid   207 *et seq.*
  and Caribbean   23, 24, 140 *et seq.*, 150 *et seq.* 174
  changes within   144-5
  and Cuba   180-81
  debt   300, 302, 306
  international economy, importance to   149
  'new'   150, 158
  new dimensions in 1970s   152
  and Non-Aligned Movement 154
  Portuguese speaking   150
  poverty in   370
  Spanish speaking   150
  and Third World   153, 154-5, 157
  in transition   156 *et seq.*
  twenty-first century   329
  and USA   23, 184
League of Nations   377-8, 379
Law of the Sea Convention   374, 375
Lecuna, V.   215 n.3
Leeward Islands, federalism in 82-3
Leeward and Windward Island   94, 100, n.3, 181
Lennon, John   372, 384 n.14
Le Resouvenir, slave revolt at, 1823   60

Less Developed Countries (LDCs) see OECS
Lewis, Arthur   29 n.6, 81 n.3, 190, 191 n.8
Lewis, D.L.   261 n.9
Lewis, Gordon K.   20, 91 n.6, 95, 100 n.7
Lomé Convention   35, 112, 114, 116, 121, 135, 175 n.2
Lowenthal, David   30 n.21
Lusaka, bombing of   233, 243
Lusaka Accord of Southern Rhodesia   195, 196, 241
Luttwak, Edward   344 n.2
Lutuli, Albert   221
Lutuli Memorial Lecture 1970   221, 224, n.4, n.5

Macaulay, Zachary   55 n.5
MacLeod, Ian   104
Macmillan, Harold   237 n.1, 378
Madariaga, Salvador de   155 n.1
Madeira   45
Magdalenenburg, slave revolt, 1763   50
Madison, James   92 n.9, 110 n.4
Maine, Sir Henry   369
Malaysia   84
Malaya indenture   65
Magna Carta   367
Managua harbour, 1984   352
'Man Who Saved Rhodesia Deal' 198 n.2
Mandela, Nelson
  and EPG   233, 235, 238 n.8, 245
  Simon Bolivar Prize   207, 210, 214, 215 n.11
Manley, Michael   162
Manley, Norman   87, 95, 104, 167
Mannington, George   29 n.3, 47 n.3
Mansfield, Lord   367

Maori, and 19th century Britain
351
Mangru, Basdeo   47 n.8
Mark, Laurence   198 n.2
Marlborough House,
London   71, 195
Marshall, Trevor G.   47 n.1
Marquez, Gabriel Garcia   359
Marryshow, Albert   103, 167,
190, 191 n.11
Martin, David   198 n.2, n.3, 248
n.4
Marti, Jose   159 n.1
Martinique   173
Martin Luther King, a Critical
Biography   261 n.9
Mauritius   61, 65, 300
Maxwell-Smith, Simon   138 n.2
McCartney   384 n.14
McIntyre, Alister   22-3
McNamara, Robert   265, 277
n.5
Memorandum of
Cartagena   306
Mexican liquid gas
explosion   373
Mexico
and Caribbean   143
Tlatelolco
Conference   1974 144,
155 n.2
and US   184
Middle Passage   63, 78 n.18
Militarism
and employment   357-8
and super powers   297
Mission to South Africa   225,
229-30 n.1, 233-6, 245, 248 n.7
Mittleholzer, Edgar   49
Modern Wars; The Humanitarian
Challenge   327 n.9
Montego Bay Conference   95,
100 n.6
Monroe doctrine   184
Montgomery, James   56-7 n.21
Monserrat
apprenticeship,
demonstrations

against   44
and CARIFTA   123
Moore, Lee   34
Mordecai, John   81 n.3, 100
n.2, 191 n.8
moral values, erosion of   374
More, Sir Thomas   356, 363
n.19
Morris, James   363 n.10
Moyne, Lord   18
Mozambique   219, 236, 243
Mugabe, Robert   196, 242

Naipaul V.S.   190, 191, n.9,
255, 261 n.3,
Nairobi   117
Namibia   203
occupation of,
illegal   211, 219, 222
Western Contact
Group   243
Nath, Swarka   29 n.10, n.12, 30
n.15, 47 n.9, 72 n.10
Nazism   200-1, 212, 218
Nehru, Jawaharlal   22, 30 n.26,
347
'Nelson Mandela Gardens',
Kingston upon Hull   199
New Commonwealth Society, 1932
377, 385 n.23, n.25, 382
New Delhi, Commonwealth Heads
of Government meeting,
1983   68
New International Economic
Order   25, 250, 270
New York, Caribbean Basin Heads
of Government meeting,
1974   156
New Zealand   220, 222, 224 n.6
Nicaragua   141, 184
Nigeria   190, 300
Commonwealth, threat of
leaving   195
Lagos, CARIFTA-East
Africa meeting, 1972   117
Lagos, Commonwealth
African ministers' meeting,

1973 117
Third Republic   82
'nigger yard'   64, 74 n.21
Nkomo, Joshua   196
Nkrumah, Kwame   237 n.1
Non-Aligned Movement
    Action Programme for
    Economic Co-
    operation   25
    Algiers meeting 1974   251
    Algiers 1973 summit   25,
    170
    and Caribbean   169
    and Cuba   180
    Guyana, ministers' meeting
    in, 1972   113, 145
    inauguration   24
    India, spiritual leader
    of   347
    Foreign Ministers'
    Conference, Guyana, 1972
    24, 25
    and Latin America   154
    OPEC members   252
    New Delhi summit,
    1983   312 n.14
    Second and third
    summits   24
NATO 'arms bazaar'   298
North Bihar   63
North-South   25-6, 32
    Cancun of the South, need
    for   308
    commercial banking system,
    strains on   284
    consensus, need for   280
    'debtor cartel', North's
    complaint of   307
    dialogue suspended   375
    and development   35
    interdependence   282
    negotiations   252, 287,
    304, 313 et seq., 340
    and Non-Aligned Movement
    314
    Northern solidarity   320
    strategy, South's lack
    of   306

    technical support system,
    South's lack of   319
North-South: A Programme for
    Survival   256, 261 n.4, 276, n.1,
    178 et seq., 362 n.5, 384 n.9
Nouveau Voyage aux Isles de
    l'Amerique   91-2 n.6
nuclear arms race   279
nuclear war   26, 304
nuclearn weapons   356, 358
Nyerere, Julius   38, 133-4, 313

oil
    and Caribbean
    economy   128
    'Chicago School'   286,
    292 n.11
    indexation based
    prices   286
    price increase, 1974   251,
    268, 286, 304
oil-refineries
    Indian and West Indian
    twenty-first century   330
One World to Share   277 n.8,
    326, 327 n.12
OAS   141, 143
OAU   118
Organisation of East Caribbean
    States (OECS)   163, 165 n.2,
    172-3, 181, 184
    and CARICOM   34-5,
    176 n.4, n.5
OPEC
    assets and investment
    opportunities   286
    confrontation, in armoury of
    272
    and developing countries
    251-2, 268
    and energy market   285
    surpluses, recycling
    of   283
Our Common Future   384 n.16
outer space, militarism
    threat   337
    ozone layer,
    damaged   374

Pacific states
  ACP-EEC
  negotiations   124
  and decolonisation   211
  Palestine   285-6
Palme, Olof
  Indian links   346
  Indira Gandhi Memorial Lecture 1986   362 n.1
Palme Commission on International Security
  Issues   349, 362, n.4, 381, 385 n.35
  Report of   382, 386 n.37
Pan-African Congress (PAC)   233, 240
Panama Canal   150
'pandas' (Hindu priestly class)   67, 69
Patriotic Front, Southern Rhodesia   196
'Para nosotros la partia es America Latin'   157, 159 n.1
Pax Britannica: The Climax of an Empire   363 n.10
peace
  and global militarism   356
  illusion of   351
  parameters of   349
  'peace and love'   372
  and poverty   353-4
  world   31, 32
  Syndham Place Trust   377
People's National Party, Jamaica   162
Persaud, Guya   69
Persian Gulf, international action needed in   382
Perez Vila, Manuel   215, n.3, 311 n.9
Pericles   136, 137 n.1
'pilgrim tax' in 18th century India   69
planet earth
  'global village'   369
  quality of life on   280
  smallness of   288
  seen from space   287-8
  twenty-first century   328-30
Plato, cave myth   279-80, 291 n.1
Poland   284
Pollsmoor Prison, South Africa   233, 244
Pollock, John   56 n.20
Pope John Paul II   371, 384 n.13
Pope Paul VI   355, 363, n.18
population, African increase   294
population, world increase   292 n.9, 354-5
Port of Spain
  Heads of Government Conference 1972   33
  capital of West Indies, possible   178
Portuguese labour, on sugar estates   45
post-war recession   292 n.8
poverty   262 *et seq*, 324 *et seq*.
  absolute   255-6, 265, 277 n.4, 353
  and arms spending   357
  and cold war   281
  collective action against   269
  danger of, to all   258-9
  deflatinary policies, effect of   284
  and mortality   354
  and population increase   285
  'one earth and two worlds'   254, 257
  and post-war power struggle   263
  and self-interest, enlightened   257-8
power, obsession with   288-9
'Prague Spring' 1968   351
Preamble to the Treaty of Chaguaramas   173
Preston, Dr. A.Z.   22, 161

footnote
primary commodities, and export
  earnings in the South   37
Pretoria regime
  aggression against
  neighbours   236
  changes in South Africa,
  arguments about   213
  cold war attitude   211
  EPG, reaction to   228,
  233
  labour laws, amended by
  223, 224 n.7
  market forces, influence of
  247
  US policy towards   240
Puerto Rico 173

qualifications, professional,
  recognised in West Indies   151
Quamina, slave leader   59
*Queen Victoria's Little
  Wars*   363 n.9

racialism
  and apartheid   194
  Commonwealth
  against   217
  and economics   20-21
  Nazi   200-201
Ramphal. J.I. (Jimmy)   19, 68
  and Andrews, Rev.
  C.F.   68
  and girls' education   68
  West Indian Federation,
  advocated by   78
Ramphal, Shridath (Sonny)
  ACP spokesman, on Lomé
  Convention Trade Regime
  131
  and ACP unity   113-14
  and Adrews, Rev.
  C.F.   68
  and apartheid   26-7, 32,
  194 *et seq.*, 199 *et seq.*, 207 *et
  seq.*, 216 *et seq.*

Attorney General of Guyana
  79
'A Will to Face the Future'
  (Sivanesan painting)   348
Caribbean nationhood, work
  for   22, 93
  and CARICOM   34-5,
  164
  and CARIFTA   33
  childhood in British Guiana
  17, 18, 19, 44
  Commonwealth Secretary
  General   15, 35, 114, 116,
  162, 167, 167, 194, 250
  Corbishley Memorial
  Lecture   365 *et seq.*
  development 250 *et seq.*
  Doctors of Laws, honorary
  degree   328
  and EPG   196
  EEC-ACP
  negotiations   35, 112 *et
  seq.*
  'Federalism in the West
  Indies'   100 n.8
  great-grandmother of   65-
  8, 346
  Grenada invasion, attempt
  to prevent   164
  Guggenheim Fellowship at
  Harvard   79
  Guyan's Foreign
  Minister   15, 33, 35, 142
  and Guyana Accord   114
  on Independent
  International Commissions
  28, 38, 251, 313
  and Latin America   23
  Lomé Convention, signing of
  135
  'man's inhumanity to man',
  awareness of   19
  as a negotiator   24, 25
  and Non-Aligned movement
  24-5
  paternal grandfather
  of   67-8
  as a radical   26

South Commission   252
unique contribution
of   31-2
and West Indian Federation
78-9, 82
UN Secretary General,
qualities for   27
'The West Indies: the
Constitutional Background
to Federation'   91 n.1
world vision of   326-7
Ramphal/Lee Moore
Accord   35
Rawle   103
'realpolitik'   177 *et seq.*,   183
Reagan, Ronald   140, 156, 190,
191 n.10, 344 n.6, 376
Red Cross, International   350
*Refugees: Dynamics of
Displacement*   327 n.1
'Rekindling the Spirit of Lomé 115,
n.6, n.7
*Report of the Commissioners
appointed for the Management of
the Crown Estates in the Colony of
Berbice*   55 n.2, n.8, 56, n.12,
n.13, n.15, n.16
*Report from the Select Committee
on the West India Colonies, 1942* 73
n.16
*Report upon the State of Her
Majesty's plantation in America,
1721*   83, 91 n.2
Republican Convention
1964   342
Resolution of Lagos   132
Reviewing the International Order
277
Reykjavik, US-Soviet
Disarmament talks   358, 364
n.23
Rhodesia-Nyasaland Federation 84
RIO Project   271, 277 n.10
Rio Treaty   141
Roa, Raoul   180
Robottom, John   29 n.5
Rodney, Walter   64
Rodway, James   30 n.17, 55

n.1, 56 n.11, n.18, 71, n.2
Roman Empire   334
Romania   190
Roosevelt, Franklin
Delano   335, 344 n.4, 380
'Root and Reminders'   59
Royal Commonwealth Society,
London   115 n.2
Rugby, and South Africa   220
Russel, Lord John   62
Rwanda   300

St. Lucia   102, 123
St. Kitts, apprenticeship,
demonstrations against   44
St. Kitts-Nevis   34, 101 n.9,
102, 123
St. Vincent   102, 123
Samaroo, Brinsley   29 n.13
sanctions against South Africa
189, 195, 352
abstention from   246
black attitude to   221, 227
Britain rejects   196, 239
major powers recoil from
213, 222
Nassau, agreed at   226
need for   212, 221
opposition to   241
and peaceful change   228
trade, public and private 221
World Conference on, Paris,
1986   225
Sanders, Ronald   198 n.1
Santayana, George   268
Sartre, Jean Paul   364 n.28
Savimbi   243, 244
Scoble, John   62, 72 n.12
Scoon, Sir Paul   164
Sea, international regime for 189
Seaga, Edward   142, 162
Scarwar, Lloyd   30 n.28
Selvon, Sam   21
*Separate and Unequal: India and
the Indians in the British
Commonwealth*   30 n.23
Seth, Vikram   359, 364 n.26

Seymour, Arthur   63, 73 n.18
Shannon, Richard   60, 71 n. 5,
Simms, Peter   29 n.2
Sivanesan   348
Sivard, R.L.   363 n.22
Six Nation Peace Initiative   358,
  360
slaves
  at Berbice, 1803   48
  Berbice Commission's
  regulations for   50-51
  emancipation, determination
  on   54
  in Guyana   16, 44-5
  punishments of, after
  Demerara revolt   53
  at Vreed-en-Hoop   60
*Slaves, Free Men, Citizens: West
  Indian Perspective*   30 n.21
Slave Trade Abolition Bill   49
slavery   59
  at Berbice   50
  in concentration camps 200
  economic rationale
  of   202
  in modern world   210,
  231
  ologarchy founded on   46
  and 'otherness'   71, 199-
  200
  and poor whites   200
  semi-slavery in South India
  63
  and war   200
  'winery shed and ten
  convicts', South Africa 1971
  203
*Slavery: Abolition and
  Emancipation*   73 n.16
small countries and island
  communities
  in Caribbean, and
  CARICOM   172-3
  in Caribbean, and
  EEC   127
  Commonwealth Expert
  Group on   164, 165-6 n.4
  and federalism   79, 86

and international economic
  system   23
  separatism, problems and
  dangers of   97
  and trade   186
  in UN 105
Smith, Adam   258
Smith, Ian   243
Smith, Rev John   53-4, 56 n.20,
  59, 60
  House of Commons debate
  on   54
'Some in light and some in
  darkness'   48, 55 n.5, 193
  footnote₃,   199, 260
Somerset's Case, 1772   384 n.5
South Africa   202 *et seq.*
  Afrikaanerdom   223
  'aid centres'   203
  anti-American feeling and
  anti-European feeling in 244,
  245-6
  'bastion of the free world
  246, 352
  'black homelands and
  townships   202, 217, 218,
  240
  Black Sash   229 230 n.15
  blacks, militancy of   196-
  7, 244
  and Britain   27, 196
  censorship in   242
  Coloured Parliament   216
  Commonwealth,
  and   194, 317
  'constructive engagement' in
  189, 222, 239, 246
  Department of Co-operation
  and Develpment   203
  destabilisation policy of 198,
  381-2
  farm prisons   203-4
  Front Line States, and 197,
  219
  Gandhi, M.K. (the
  Mahatma)   65
  gold mines, contract labour
  in   203

murder in   204, 218
neighbours, measures
against   197, 219, 222,
228, 233, 243, 376-7
'parole system'   203
'pass laws'   202, 203
post-apartheid   244
'rebel' sports tour to   220
Rivonia trial   221
Sharpeville Massacre, 1960
202
sports boycott   212, 216 *et
seq.*
whites-only
elections   231, 232, 242,
352, 376-7
'youth service'   203
see also Apartheid
SADEC   248 n.3
SWAPO   240
Southern Rhodesia (Zimbabwe)
195, 196, 243
Soviet Union
and aid   341
arms exporter   356
and Caribbean and Latin
America   141
internationalism   341
'spheres of influence'
doctrine   184
and Southern Africa   246
in Un   380
twenty-first century   329
and Zimbabwe   242
Spain, imperial   23
species, threatened   373, 384
n.17
Spiro, Herbert J.   91 n.3
'Star Wars'   189, 337, 344 n.6
*Street Children: A Growing Urban
Tragedy*   327 n.7
Stephen, James   48, 49, 55 n.5
sub-Saharan Africa
capital flows, fall in   302
debt, external   302
export diversification, lack of
301
Financing adjustment with

growth in   322 n.7
grain and livestock imports
302
malnutrition in   294
reversals, economic   301
Sudan, the 300, 302
Success, slave revolt at,
1823   60
sugar
and Britain, employment in
27
children, employed on
estates   18-9
estates, immigrant workers
on   46
estates, leasing proposal 48,
49
indentured labour, on estates
61-4
importance of, to Caribbean
economy   127
labour crisis after
1838   45
'price of', in *Candide*   72
n.7
profits from, in 1871   46
Vreed-en-Hopp
estate   60
wage bargaining, on estates
20
Sugar Without Slaves   47 n.4
Surinam   60, 72 n.7, 173
immigrant labour mortality
66
Shridath Ramphal's great-
grandmother in   66
'suttee'   66
Swaziland   236, 300
Sweden   190

Tacitus   334, 353
Tagore, Rabindranth   343-4 345
n.11
Tambo, Oliver   207, 214, 215
n.11, 245
Tamils   63
Tanzania   300

technological sophistication,
twenty-first century   329
terrorism   356
   government, in South Africa
   212
   and illicit arms trade   357
The Agony of the Eight   191 n.8
*The Atlantic Slave-Trade and
   British Abolition 1760-1810*   56
   n.10
The Bow in the Cloud   57 n.21
The Energy Catalyst   252 n.3,
   292 n.10
The Federalist Papers   92 n.9
The Fraudulent Freedom   47
   n.1, n.2
The Golden Gate   359, 364 n.26
*The Growth of the Modern West
   Indies*   30 n.18, 91 n.6, 100 n.7
The Hitler File   205, n.2
The Lure of Realpolitik   161
   footnote
The Man on Horseback   344 n.3
The Mimic Men   191 n.9
The Navy and the Slave Trade
   261 n.1
*The New Slavery: An Account of
   the Indian and Chinese Immigrants
   in British Guiana*   47 n.11, n.12
*The North-South Dialogue: Making
   It Work*   250, 321 n.2, 322 n.6
*The Prospect for Unity in the
   Caribbean*   115 n.2
'The Round Table', article of
   Shridath Ramphal   262, 276 n.1
The Slave 'Grace'   384 n.6
The Struggle for Zimbabwe   198
   n.2
*The Suppression of the African
   Slave Trade in the Nineteench
   Century*   261 n.1
The Threepenny Opera   261 n.8
The West Indies   29 n.3, 47 n.3
*The West Indies: The Federal
   Negotiations*   81 n.3, 100 n.2,
   191 n.8
The West On Trial   29 n.11
The Wretched of the Earth   291

n.4, 364 n.28
Third World and Developing
States
   arms spending   298, 372
   bargaining power potential
   315-6
   and Bolivar   214 n.1
   Caribbean-Latin American
   unity, importance of   142
   collective strength   268-9
   and colonial system   266-
   7
   democracy in   334-5
   and development   31, 37
   and Eastern Europe   316-
   7
   economic awareness
   in   272-3
   and economic system,
   international   264-6
   and EEC   125, 129, 148,
   150
   influence of, on financial
   decisions   314
   and IMF credit   307
   Latin-America   145, 146,
   153, 154-5, 157
   life expectancy in   354
   and Marxist dialectic   275
   medicines, lack of   326
   and military culture   297-
   8, 325, 372
   and Non-Aligned Movement
   271
   solidarity, essential   271,
   306, 309, 315
   SDRs   267-8, 319
   'spoilers'   280
   strategy for mutual aid, need
   for   308-9
   trade, net earning from 267
   UNCTAD   316
   unity   32, 132, 135-6
Third World Foundation   313
Third World Secretariat, need for
   309, 319-20
Thomas, Timothy N.   73 n.20
Thucydides   137 n.1

Tinbergen, Jan   271, 277 n.10
Tinker, Hugh   30 n.23, 61, 72
 n.9, 73 n.14, n.15
trade
  ACP-EEC
  negotiations   36, 127
  Caribbean-Latin American
  competition for   140
  US power in   147
trade negotiations
  and North-South dialogue
  315
  Uruguay Round   321 n.3
trade unions
  in British Empire, overseas
  17
  in South Africa   223
  and Western democracies
  268-9
Trager, Frank N.   91 n.3
Treaty of Rome
  Article 138   118
  'Associates' under   124
Trend, J.B.   215 n.6, n.7
Trinidad
  St. Augustine Campus,
  Shridath Ramphal at,
  1978   328
  apprenticeship,
  demonstrations
  against   44
  CARICOM meeting, 1982,
  163-4
  and CARIFTA   180
  labour crisis after
  1838   45
  and Venezuela   150
Trinidad Guardian   30 n.27
Trinidad and Tobago
  Africans of   20
  and CARIFTA   123
  and Cuba   141-2, 180
  Indians of   18, 20, 21
  independence, 1962   94
  racial co-operation in   21
  and Venezuela   24
  and West Indian
  Federation   78

tropical forests, clearance
  of   373
Tripoli, bombing of   376
Trouble in Guyana   29 n.2
Trudeau, Pierre   92 n.11
Truman, Harry   187, 380, 385
 n.33
Turks, the (West Indies)   102

unemployment   290
  and abolition of
  slavery   27
  in industrialised
  world   339
  in West Indies in
  1930s   18; in
  1970s   128
United Nations
  aid target of   267
  anti-monopolies
  measures   270
  Caribbean states in   169,
  170
  'citadel of peace'   361,
  372
  and democracy   340-41
  equality of status in   105
  famine prediction of   293
  Founding Conference, San
  Francisco   187
  fouding of   380, 385 n.33
  miniaturing of, attempts
  at   187-8
  'more equal than others',
  in   263
  Report of the Secretary
  General on the Work of the
  Organisation   386 n.37
  security system   381
  and Shridath
  Ramphal   27-8
  voting power, Third
  World   307
United Nations Charter   90, 92
 n.12, n.13, 191n.7, 362 n.7
UN Committee for Development
  Planning

Economic Commission for
Africa, report of   303,
311 n.6
Shridath Ramphal Chairman
of   251
UNCTADs   36, 145, 266, 304,
305, 314, 315, 375
UNESCO 375
UN emergency meeting, Geneva
1985   294
UN General Assembly   105,
270, 304, 312 n.13
Grenada invasion,
condemns   164
and North-South
dialogue   314
Papal message to,
1985   371-2
UN Generalised System of
Preferences   314, 321 n.1
UNIDO   304
UN Security Council   188, 380
UN Secretary General, curbing
of   188
UN Seventh Special
Session   374
UN Special Committee Against
Apartheid   207, 208-9, 213
United States
arms exporter   356
Caribbean, importance
to   190
and Caribbean-Latin
America   141, 144, 147,
156 *et seq.*
and Europe 146
and federalism   82, 87-8,
110
'Founding Fathers'   87
and Grenada
invastion   163, 164
internationalism   145,
146, 341
isolation to involvement,
move from   146, 154
naval manoeuvres in Black
Sea and Gulf of
Sidre   376

as neighbour   23
and OAS   141
and OPEC   252
and South Africa   197,
222, 239, 244, 247, 248 n.2,
n.6
'spheres of influence'
doctrine   184
and Third World   274,
283
trading power   147
twenty-first century   329
and UN   27, 380
West Indian 'brain drain'
to   179
and West Indies   151
and Zimbabwe   242
United World Colleges
Movement   231
University of Hull, Shridath
Ramphal lectures at   48
University of New York, Centre
for International Studies   83
University of the West Indies
Distinguished Lecturer
Series   177
honorary degree, conferred
on Shridath
Ramphal   328
Institute for International
Relations   30 n.25, 93
Institute for Social and
Economic Research   22,
177
Urquhart, Brian   27, 30 n.32

*Vulnerability: Small States in the
Global Society*   k165, n.4
vegetables, names of in Gaya and
Guyana   69
Venezuela
and Bolivar   208, 210
and Caribbean   143
Guyana border
dispute   143
Kissinger Proposal rejected
by   144

slavery, freedom
   from   210
   and Trinidad   150
   and Williams, Eric   150
Vietnam, and Non-Aligned
   Movement   24-5
violence
   Papal condemnation   372
   in South Africa   197, 212,
   234, 247
   urban   279
Virgin Islands   102
Vishnu's footprint at Gaya   69
Vishnupad Temple, Gaya,
   Bihar   67, 69
   bell of, gift of F.
   Gillanders   69
   Shridath Ramphal performs
   'puma' at 69
'Vision of Peirs Plowman'   310,
   312 n.15
Voltaire, F.M.   60, 71-2 n.7
Vreed-en-Hoop
   indentured labour at   61,
   62
   Shridath Ramphal's great-
   grandmother at   65, 67
   slaves at 60
Vuchetich, Eugeniy   384 n.15

Walvin, J.   73 n.16, 384 n.7
Ward, Barbara   255, 261 n.2,
   280, 291 n.3, 326, 327 n.12
war, rules of   349-50
Warner, Rex   137 n.1
Watsaw Pact Countries 'arms
   bazaar'   298
Waterford Kamhlaba
   College   231
Webber, A.R.F.   55 n.1
Weizsaaker, C.F. von   365, 383
   n.1
West, the
   and aid to Africa   303
   and South Africa   211,
   216, 239, 245-6
West Germany, and South

Africa   197
West India lobby   49-50
West Indian Advisory
   Group   164
West Indian Federation   23, 78-
   9, 331
   collapse of   82, 86, 93
   Independence Constitution,
   drafted by S.
   Ramphal   79, 82
   island nationalism   94
   and Manley, Norman   87
   post mortem on   84, 85
West Indian independence, 'what
   might have been'   178
West Indian unity and nationhood
   autonomy, sacrifice of
   necessary   94-5
   and economic
   integration   105, 106
   Free Trade Area,
   enlargement of   99
   and identity, search
   for   102, 103, 104, 109,
   167
   and independence,
   experience of   95-6
   obstacles to, overcoming
   of   109-10
   opponents of   107-8
   progression towards   168
   Republic of the West Indies,
   as goal   99
   and Ramphal,
   Shridath   80, 93, 102, 115
   n.2, 328
   social and economic change,
   need for 106-7
   twenty-first century   330-
   33
West Indies
   Associated States   94, 95,
   97, 100 n.3, 105
   'brain drain' from   179
   and Britain   151
   colonialism, movement
   against   20
   exports   18

'Federation of the
Eight'   104
indenture, last bastion
of   65
Indians in   15, 46, 61, 3
and Latin America   151-2
planters, after abolition of
slavery   44-5, 49
protest movements
in   107
region comprising   102
regionalism   179
resources, ownership and
control of   106-7
unemployment and riots in
1930s   18
Western commercial banks   283
Western Hemisphere, proposed
community of   144 *et seq.*
'When elephants fight the grass
gets trampled' (African
proverb)   310
Whitby, the   46, 61
Why Federations Fail   91 n.3
Wilberforce, William   48, 50, 55
n.5, n.6, 56-7 n.21, 205 n.4, 356,
261 n.6, n.7
apartheid, and memory
of   205
at Berbice   49, 51-2
Bolivar, meeting with,
1810   210
death of 54, 57 n.25, 70
emancipation, pamphlets
on   53
Wilberforce Museum   203
Williams, Eric   21, 29 n.4, 30
n.19, 54, 57 n.22, n.23, 71 n.6, 80,
81 n.5, 100 n.2, 206 n.9
Gladstone, W.E., comment
on   60, 71 n.6
at Port of Spain Conference,
1972   33
Venezuela, speech against,
1975   24
and West Indian
identity   167
Wolfe, E.C.   384 n.17

Wooding Commission on
Anguilla   97, 98, 101 n.9
Wool House, Carlton Gardens,
London   70
world, in twenty-first century,
speculations about   328-30
World Bank   265, 277 n.5, 300,
302
Interim and Development
Communittees   307
IDA VII   294
and North-South
relations   26
ODA   267
policy reforms, and
famine   297-7
Special Programme for
Africa   293-4
and Third World
influence   314
World Court, hostility to   375
*World Military and Social
Expenditure*   363 n.22
World War II   187, 325, 341,
354, 377
'war to end wars'   350
Wray, Rev. John   52, 56 n.15
Wright, D.   73 n.16, 384 n.7

Yaounde Convention   113, 117·
118, 125, 129-130 n.1, 130 n.2
Yeats, W.B.   351, 363 n.8
young people
American and British,
Churchill's advice to   379-
80
North-South   26
South African   244, 245-6
West Indian   179, 190
Yugoslavia   103, 184, 190

Zambia   300
South African aggression
against   236, 376-7
ZANU   196

Zimbabwe   196, 241
    food production, price
    incentives for   299
    South Africa aggression
    against   236
Zulu, and Britain in 19th
  century   351

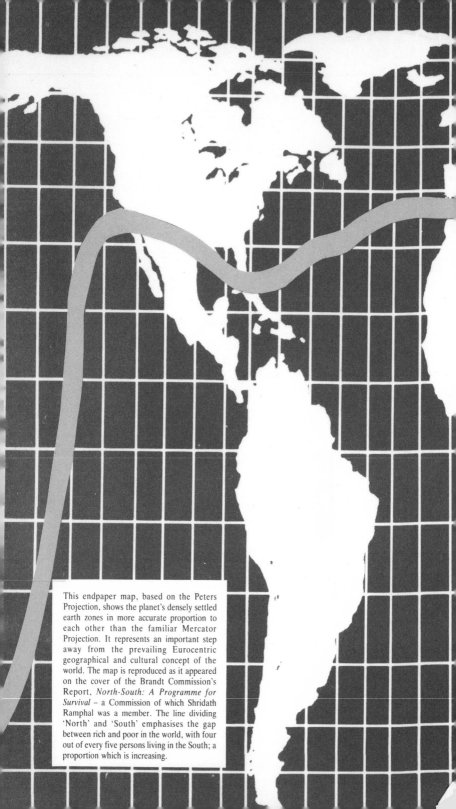

This endpaper map, based on the Peters
Projection, shows the planet's densely settled
earth zones in more accurate proportion to
each other than the familiar Mercator
Projection. It represents an important step
away from the prevailing Eurocentric
geographical and cultural concept of the
world. The map is reproduced as it appeared
on the cover of the Brandt Commission's
Report, *North-South: A Programme for
Survival* – a Commission of which Shridath
Ramphal was a member. The line dividing
'North' and 'South' emphasises the gap
between rich and poor in the world, with four
out of every five persons living in the South; a
proportion which is increasing.